Celtic Paranoia: The Laptop Loyal Diaries 2

Honest Mistakes & Other Stories

My thanks to my good friend Russ, Gaudd from E-Tims, Paul67 at CQN and Che Timvara at Mon the Hoops for articles, information and sources. Also to the Bowling Club CSC (Russell, Jim, Eric and Lennondinho18) for moral support throughout the season.

My Love to Don Don and MBH

Contents

Prologue..4
In the Beginning..5
The Scottish Media Don't Like Celtic..........................7
"It Could Have Been Bad"..17
No O*d F**m Title Decider Rule Repealed, the SFA Review Panel & the Difference Between the Celtic and Rangers Manager......19
The Loch Lomond Booze Brothers and "Whattaboutery"........42
The "Ridiculous" Case of Madjid Bougherra.........................59
Straw Man v Iron Man..70
Celtic Managers and the Scottish Media............................98
The Return of the Man With Nosurname..........................105
David Murray's Laptop Loyal Friends..............................108
Ally Ross Attacks James McCarthy................................115
Keevins Supports the Scottish Team in Europe. Again........117
The Season of the Honest Mistake Begins......................118
Ewen Cameron's "Minority Report".................................122
Scottish Press Suddenly Find a Voice Over Sick Abuse......126
Schizophrenia of the Media: Blindness & 20/20 vision......128
Newspaper Apologises to Artur Boruc.............................129
Media Fury at Mendes Sending Off..................................131
Lapdogs Show Their Pain as Celtic Go Top of the League....133
Violent Conduct By Lee McCulloch Ignored Yet Again.........134
Spin Ratcheted Up to Mach 10 After Gers Sevilla Humiliation 135
First "Honest Apology" of the Season..............................138
Mr. Dignity: Bullet Proof..139
Jim Traynor Questions the Integrity of Honest Pros?.........141
Worst Record of a British team in the Champions League.....142
Union Jack from Battle of Manchester Sold at Christie's......143
Translation of Rangers FC Statement on Shares................146
Lapdogs Still Spinning on Behalf of Sir Minty....................148
Objective Articles on Mowbray, Smith, McCann & Murray.....148
Spot the Difference: Celtic & Rangers Press Conferences...153
The Man With Nosurname Speaks, The Lapdogs Revere......160
Two Sides of the Same Coin?...161
Why Rangers Fans Hate Graham Spiers............................168
Scottish Football "Expert" Craig Paterson..........................173
The BBC on poor attendances at Celtic Park.....................174
The Wisdom of Waldo..176
Time To Get Rid of that O*d F**m Tag..............................178
The Scottish Media: Neither Neutral nor Objective.............184

Catastrophic Decline in the Scottish Football Journalism......190
Ewen Cameron bases a week of anti-Celtic jibes on a call from a Rangers fan..194
Media Using Old Stories to Bum Up Rangers.......................201
Traynor Accuses Mowbray of Having an "Agenda"...............202
Rangers Supporters To Vet Opponent's Team Lines.............204
Graham Spiers Says it's Time for Hacks To Come Clean.......208
Rangers Dressing Room, 12.25, 28th February 2010..............210
The Dougie McDonald Show & Hateley's Neutral Opinion......210
Ewen Cameron: A Police Announcement............................215
Fraser Wishart & The Laptop Loyal's Selective Agenda.........217
How the SFA Appeals Process Works...................................221
More Media Lies Over the Falkirk Pitch...............................221
Scottish Press in Full-On Gloating Mode..............................227
Spiers Acknowledges Historical Bias Against Celtic..............228
Scottish Ref in Danger of Looking Biased to Rangers Shock.232
Daily Record condemns Rasmussen but not Clancy.............233
Co-Op Cup Final Red Card Spin...235
Spiers on RST Buy-out Plan...239
Possible Effect of "Honest Mistakes" on Outcome of season.241
Rangers Paranoia Over Fixture List. Again..........................242
Celtic Get a "Break" According to Walker and Provan..........249
The Importance of Being Humped in the Champion's League.250
Neil Lennon "Quizzed" at First Press Conference.................253
The Expert Knowledge of Mark Hately: World Cup 2010.........254
Gers Through to World Cup Final...256
Jackanory Loving Temporary Return to the Good Old Days...257
Walter Commission Report: The McGregor Assassination.....260
Rangers' "Impressive" European Record...............................263
The Scottish Media: PR Arm of the Football Establishment....265
"Dougie, Dougie" and the Definition of Conspiracy...............276
Jim Traynor's Message to Celtic a Mess of Contradictions....330
The Myth of the Man With Nosurname.................................335
Epilogue: The Near Death of a Salesman.............................338
The Lickspittle Galleries..345

Prologue

*"All truth passes through three stages.
First, it is ridiculed.
Second, it is violently opposed.
Third, it is accepted as being self-evident."*
Arthur Schopenhauer, German Philosopher

"There is not one of you who dares to write your honest opinions, and if you did, you know beforehand that it would never appear in print. I am paid weekly for keeping my honest opinion out of the paper I am connected with. Others of you are paid similar salaries for similar things, and any of you who would be so foolish as to write honest opinions would be out on the streets looking for another job.

The business of the journalist is to destroy the truth, to lie outright, to pervert, to vilify, to fawn at the feet of mammon, and to sell his country and his race for his daily bread. You know it and I know it.

We are the tools and vassals of rich men behind the scenes. We are the jumping jacks, they pull the strings and we dance. Our talents, our possibilities and our lives are all the properties of other men. We are intellectual prostitutes"
John Swinton, Editor of the New York Times, 1880

"Every team gets decisions against them, but it's just honest mistakes. I got a penalty against me in the 1977 Scottish Cup final. The ball hit my thigh, not my arm, and the referee gave a penalty, wrongly, and to be honest, I had forgotten about it 5 days later. I didn't go on about it"
Derek Johnstone, 2010

In the beginning…

Back in December 2008 I gave myself a kick in the backside and resolved that if I didn't start the arduous task of collating and editing my notes I might never get my "Celtic Paranoia" book published. I had heard about print-on-demand technology in the summer of 2007 through a news story about a woman who had self-published her blog as a book, the rather suggestively titled *Girl With a One Track Mind*, and immediately recognised the potential to bring my writing on Celtic's treatment at the hands of the Scottish media to a wider audience. I resolved there and then to have a print-on-demand version of my book published and available by the end of 2007. My romantic vision was a magnum opus along the lines of Nick Hornby's *Fever Pitch* and David Bennie's excellent *Not Playing for Celtic*. Unfortunately though, impetus was lost to procrastination, the domestic joys of being a father and holding down a full-time job.

However by December 2008 and the prospect of two weeks of as much free time as I was likely to get for the next decade, I reached my 'do or die' juncture, or at least my 'do or stop kidding yerself on' juncture. So it was then that I embarked on the journey that would lead to *Celtic Paranoia: The Laptop Loyal Diaries*, aiming to turn it around in a fortnight and in the end taking almost four months. It is doubtful *Laptop Loyal Diaries* reached the heights of the more illustrious aforementioned works but nevertheless I am immensely proud to say it was something that many Celtic fans bought, read and found entertaining; even opening one or two eyes along the way as to the brazenness of the Scottish media's anti-Celtic agenda and the sheer volume of their propaganda devoted to undermining the club. Funnily enough in the summer of 2007, having been writing on the subject on and off since 2002 and having absolutely no experience of writing a book before, I wasn't sure if I had enough material to flesh out a 300 page tome. Needless to say I needn't have worried. In the end 550 pages had to be cut down to 396 to make publication economically viable.

As it turned out, December 2008 was both the best and the worst possible time I could have chosen to start putting *Laptop Loyal Diaries* together. The best because it was only a matter of days before David Murray's infamous "we had to accept the first £3m bid for Boyd" faux pas in January 2009, which meant for the first time the Scottish media were forced to acknowledge that Rangers were facing significant financial difficulties. This led to the print and broadcast of some of the most excruciating and comical excuses for journalism ever witnessed from a Scottish media desperate to assuage their priority audience - Rangers supporters – who of course lapped it all up. After all, everyone likes being told what they want to hear. I recall one Rangers fan citing the building of an office block on Glasgow's Hope Street by one of Murray's companies as irrefutable proof that MIH (and by proxy Rangers) were in rude health.

But it was also the worst in the sense that my original plan was to publish the material I had in place at December 2008 and was keen to devote all of my energies to sifting through and editing my existing text. In the end breaking developments which plumbed new depths of sycophancy could not be ignored, such as Hateley's "*Selling Boyd and Ferguson could be the masterstroke that wins Walter the title*" piece in the Daily Record of 8th January 2009. North Korea or even Fox News couldn't hold a candle to propaganda nonsense like this. So the new material would have to be incorporated pushing back the timescale for publication. In the end I would also have the Scottish media's salivation over the friendly that was more prestigious than the Champions League final (Rangers v AC Milan), and the George Burley/Scott Brown witch hunt to exonerate the Loch Lomond Booze Brothers to cover before *Laptop Loyal Diaries* was finally published on 16th April 2009. Having achieved my goal, I had no further plans than to sit back and bask in the achievement. No matter if only my close friends and family actually went as far as buying the damn thing, I would have my own literary work published, a dusty version of which perhaps some collector in the future might find somewhere on a shelf or in an attic when I am long gone.

However, the season that followed (2009/10) would go down in infamy as one that raised the bar, not only in relation to customary refereeing "honest mistakes", but also the naked bias of the Scottish media in their brazen denial of the obvious and caustic derision and charges of paranoia directed at all connected with Celtic FC. Truly the wagons were circled to protect their own that season more than any other. In terms of providing every possible support to the Establishment club's efforts to win the SPL and secure vital Champions League revenue and to direct the perception and opinions of the wider Scottish football community – i.e. to convince everyone else that Celtic's "paranoia" was spiraling out of control – the Scottish media were stunningly successful. It had taken seven years, from 2002 to 2009, to gather the 500 pages of notes that would become *Laptop Loyal Diaries*. SPL season 2009/10 would provide the same number in a little over 12 months.

The Scottish Media love the Establishment club and they don't like Celtic

The Scottish football media don't like Celtic. This is not a statement based on self-pity or paranoia, but a demonstrable statement of fact. Whether it be over the radio waves, on the television screen or in the written press, Celtic are consistently portrayed as a bumbling, tight-fisted, incompetent, paranoid wreck. If a negative angle can be dug from the most innocuous of stories concerning Celtic, you can be sure the media will have their protractors and set squares out pronto to find it. For example in January 2009 you might reasonably have expected the return of Aiden McGeady to the Celtic starting line-up after being dropped by manager Gordon Strachan following a well publicised "bust-up" to be reported as a positive development. Not a bit of it. Most of the media chose to debate whether this was further evidence that McGeady was on his way out of Celtic Park given that Strachan had selected a few "second choice" players for the Scottish Cup tie against Queens Park, with McGeady now in their eyes, potentially considered by the manager to be in the same bracket. This despite direct statements to the contrary from the Celtic manager himself. You couldn't make it up. Except they did.

Whilst their critical all-seeing eyes are always open and alert when it comes to Celtic, the same is not true in relation to Scotland's Establishment club, Rangers. Referring to Rangers as the Establishment club in Scotland is met with howls of derision both from the media and Rangers fans alike (with little distinction existing between the two) and is enough to have Ewen Cameron playing X-Files music on his radio show before going on to complain of, in his own words, "the media agenda" to victimise fans of the poor downtrodden Ibrox club for their part in "the worst violence witnessed in Manchester since the Blitz" i.e. – all of it. Likewise, fans of other Scottish teams will immediately suggest a visit to a health professional for some prescription medication whilst at the same time holding an unshakeable belief in a "West Coast/Old Firm" conspiracy to ensure a perpetual Celtic/Rangers hegemony. Of course there can be no other rational explanation as to why St Mirren haven't won a trophy since 1987 can there?

The existence of "Establishment" clubs is acknowledged throughout Europe, teams such as Real Madrid, Juventus, Bayern Munich and Dinamo Kiev being widely regarded as such. Real Madrid were funded directly by Franco's regime for decades. But of course favouritism like that couldn't happen in Scotland because its not as if there are any clubs here with strong links to Establishment institutions such as the monarchy and influential secret societies is it?

An Establishment club is simply one that is the most popular and best-supported in any given country. In the case of Scotland this is Rangers. After all this is the club whose supporters regularly proclaim to be "The People" and whose chairman, David Murray, boasted of the club being the second biggest Scottish institution behind the Church of Scotland. It might seem strange to refer to Rangers as the most popular Scottish club given that they are almost universally reviled among genuine supporters of other clubs, however this is a feature shared by other Establishment clubs such as Juventus and Manchester United. The important aspect is they have the biggest fanbase in their respective countries. In this way "best-supported" simply means having the most people identifying themselves as supporters of that club, if not in terms of aspects such as behaviour or actually attending matches. The media will have a natural tendency to be sympathetic to such a club i.e. the most popular and "best-supported". Newspapers, TV and radio stations will not want to put their greatest share of the market at risk by alienating that club's supporters. The easiest way to minimise this risk is to employ a policy of "cheer-leading" i.e. – sycophantic reporting and suppression of negative stories where the Establishment club is concerned. If this club happens to have a chief rival then this editorial stance can be supplemented by employing negative spin and misinformation about the rival to further ingratiate with their priority market.

One might ask why the media would be prepared to alienate one sizeable segment of the market rather than pander to both, thereby giving up the chance to potentially secure an even greater audience share or readership (e.g. an "Old Firm" bias, rather than merely a Rangers bias). The answer is that this simply doesn't work. There is a well-known saying familiar to most people "You can't please everyone". A policy of pandering to both sets of supporters will result in alienating both audiences, as a positive story about one is automatically viewed negatively by fans of the other and vice versa. There is a natural psychological tendency to recall negative experiences more readily than positive ones, so for example, you will vividly remember the time the taxi company kept you waiting for half an hour, but you won't be able to recall specifically any of the dozens of times they picked you up promptly. This explains why we have the incredible experience of being subjected to Rangers supporters talking about the "Daily Rhebel" and the "Evening Tims", with this terminology justified on the basis of these newspapers' "over the top" reporting of the Manchester Riots and other such imagined slights. The fact that the Daily Record and 98% of the rest of the Scottish media did their upmost to blame those unprecedented events on a combination of Chelsea supporters, the failure of the screen, and the old favourite "heavy-handed policing" is beyond their comprehension or they are simply unwilling to acknowledge this.

I put this down to something I call "Spoilt Child Syndrome". Many years ago I read a book on the Old Firm by Bill Murray in which he concluded that newspapers had got the balance of their coverage of Celtic and Rangers "just about right", basing this conclusion on the fact that both sets of supporters perceived an agenda against their club. This, he asserted, proved that the reality of the situation was that newspaper reporting was falling somewhere in the middle. As far as empirical evidence to support such a conclusion goes, this is so flimsy and derisory that it would be rejected if submitted by a first year Modern Studies pupil. To illustrate this point I would draw an analogy between two boys who share the same birthday, one from a very wealthy family and the other from a poor one. The parents of the underprivileged boy forget about his birthday and so when he wakes up in the morning to find they have no gift to present him with he is understandably emotional and upset. At the same time, the other boy awakes to find his parents have bought him a remote control model Ferrari. However the boy is enraged and upset as he was expecting a real Ferrarri. Now, the intensity of the emotional reactions experienced by the two boys might well be the same, however one could hardly argue that the treatment afforded to both was also the same. But Bill Murray would have you believe that petulant piques due to "over-the-top reporting" of appalling violence in Manchester and resentment of a sustained tendency to defame players and fans (e.g."Thugs & Thieves") resulting in numerous cases of newspapers and radio presenters either having to issue apologies or pay damages to Celtic players and managers, is evidence of parity of treatment. I would say to Rangers fans suffering from "Spoilt Child Syndrome", come back when one fan making an aeroplane gesture is reported as a "section" in the Daily Record. As it happens a "section" of Rangers fans made aeroplane gestures at Shunsuke Nakamura in a game at Celtic Park in 2007, ostensibly mocking events that were responsible for the greatest instantaneous loss of life in human history. Not only did the Scottish media fail to exaggerate this in the same way as in the case of the deranged Celtic fan, they didn't even bother to mention it at all. It seems honest mistakes are not solely the purvey of referees.

This explains to a great extent why in Scotland, media coverage of Rangers is unstintingly sympathetic with the media only too keen to promote the image of a dignified, philanthropic club who continue to rise above the paranoiac mindset of certain rivals; this despite claims of victimisation over such issues as fixture scheduling and treatment at the hands of the Scottish national team far outweighing anything emanating from any other Scottish club over the years. In contrast, as sure as night follows day, every single Celtic setback or indiscretion is dissected to the Nth degree in an attempt to present the club in a bad light. Equally, Rangers' follies or problems are only ever brought to the public domain when there is no alternative, and are invariably accompanied by fervent bursts of what Graham Spiers coined "Whattabouttery". For example, dragging Scott Brown into the Loch Lomond Booze Brothers affair, or Keith Jackson spending more time asking UEFA hypothetical questions about action against Celtic than the matter at hand, after they fined and warned Rangers for their fans' umpteenth rabble of racist singing and disorderly behaviour abroad. There are many more.

The latest financial trauma affecting Rangers is the exemplification of this policy in operation. Scottish sports writers and commentators chose to ignore the story and all of its possible repercussions for the best part of a decade. The "we didnae know" excuse simply does not wash for a profession whose basic tenet is built on enquiry and investigation. Think about it. Almost 10 years of looking the other way, as David Murray led the self-proclaimed biggest club in Scotland towards financial and literal oblivion. There was nothing inevitable about Rangers' current plight, certainly if Scottish journalists had done the job we are led to believe they are supposed to do and actually made the most cursory of inquiries into developments. Had they done so and actually reported their findings honestly Rangers supporters might have had the opportunity to rally themselves and find a course of action to the benefit of their club, although it is more than likely that this opportunity would have been passed up, as was the 2004 share issue aiming to wipe £50million of the club's debt, resulting in another Murray paper shuffling exercise between Rangers and his MIH empire. It was with much weeping and gnashing of teeth, that some of Scotland's finest scribblers belatedly put crayon to paper. However, what the public has been presented with can hardly be described as analytical, never mind critical of the crisis facing Rangers. Like so much regarding the Establishment club, we are given very few facts and instead loads of subjective ramblings by journalists through royal blue glasses.

Just a few generations ago, the likes of Hugh McIlvanney and Ian Archer were writing on Scottish football. Now we have lickspittles with word processors doing their job. The likes of Darrell King and Keith Jackson write almost exclusively about Rangers in their newspapers, make appearances on Rangers TV and then are wheeled out on Radio Clyde as supposedly impartial pundits, or if we are really pushing the comedy boat out – experts. The biggest story in Scottish football is the implosion of Rangers football club, the self-proclaimed "Premier Scottish Sporting Institution" (David Edgar, RST) and yet nobody in the media is prepared to take an objective analytical approach to get to the bottom of the situation. Instead, fantastical stories are woven involving shady South African émigrés subject to criminal investigation, shabby barrow boys and dubious London property speculators. We have now entered the hazy twilight world of the deranged hack, whose sole intention is to feed Rangers fans with tales of hope and promise. Joseph Goebbels and Comical Ali could only look on green (or blue) with jealousy at the work of their disciples. Another technique to divert from the unpalatable situation is to magnify the failings of Celtic. They have every right to point out the mammoth failure at Celtic Park in appointing Tony Mowbray and much of what followed, that is their job after all. However it would be nice if they were not so selective about which issues allow them to pretend at being real journalists rather than the plastic ones we see every day.

There is a great book out there waiting to be written about how David Murray ran the great Glasgow Rangers into the ground. The veil is slowly being lifted over the fraudulent years. Rangers bought nine-in-a-row on the back of huge debt which is only now emerging from the murky waters. With the club under investigation of HRMC, it would appear that tax avoiding inducements may have been used to attract Rangers players, effectively undercutting Celtic and other clubs who chose to avoid such a path. Strange transfers took place between Rangers and former employees, which resulted in the Ibrox club being paid way above the odds for quite average talent (Jean-Alain Boumsong, Lorenzo Amoruso, Barry Ferguson etc).

With the honourable exceptions of Glenn Gibbons and Graham Spiers, Scottish football is a journalistic desert wasteland.

Celtic don't need 'Celtic minded' journalists. Fair-minded, objective writers who call it as they see it, would be good enough. It is a scary thought that the anti-Celtic agenda was actually much worse in the past. Jock Stein great man that he was, simply answered Celtic's critics by conquering all before him on the park. It would be good if we could let the football do the talking but it is a big ask and there are a lot of obstacles. There are Celtic supporters who say to me "what these journalists say has no effect on the park, we should concentrate on our own house". Whilst, I agree that Celtic should always strive to have our own house in order, it is naiveté of the highest order to suggest that TV, radio and newspaper journalists have no influence on the mechanics of the Scottish Football Establishment and ultimately what happens on the park. Unpalatable as it may be, these rags have a huge influence over Scottish football opinion and have lobbying power over the SFA and SPL. Stop for a moment and consider:

• Who was responsible for getting Loovens and McDonald up in front of a review panel in May 2009?

• Who was responsible for a massive and successful PR push to get "Seven Fouls" Bougherra's red card for kicking a goalkeeper in the head rescinded in May 2009?

• Who was responsible for putting Sean Maloney on the defensive for the best part of a week with "I'm no diver [nudge wink]" headlines after a penalty was correctly awarded for a foul on him in a 1-0 win over Mothwerwell in August 2010?

• In sharp contrast, who very quickly dropped any mention of the worst example of play-acting witnessed in Scottish football since Kyle Laughable by Alan McGregor in a game against Hibernian the very week before the Maloney "incident" (note that an "incident" has now been manufactured out of a routine penalty decision)?

• Who was responsible for creating hysteria over two perfectly legitimate Celtic goals against Hearts in September 2010?

It doesn't matter that the media were forced, reluctantly through gritted teeth, to admit that the referee's decision in each case were correct (having showed an obvious and curious reluctance to revert to their usual impassioned defence of the "honest mistakes" of the official concerned). 48 hours of radio and newspaper mud had stuck, before TV pictures on Monday evening proved beyond doubt that each and every one of these "dubious /controversial /suspect" (delete as appropriate) decisions was perfectly correct. Great swathes of airtime and column inches were handed over to the ranting and raving of Hearts manager Jim Jeffries with not a word of dissent from our intrepid and fearless broadcasters and newspapermen. Certainly nothing remotely approaching the vitriol heaped upon Tony Mowbray and Aiden McGeady for comments made in the wake of – at best – some of the worst refereeing ever seen in Scottish football, and – at worst – outright refereeing bias having been on the wrong end of a series stretching into double figures of obviously incorrect decisions over the preceding months. By the time TV pictures were available to redress the balance, the seed had already been planted, the horse had bolted and the indelible impression had been left that Celtic had been the beneficiaries of their own "honest mistakes", however far from the truth this has proven to be. The whole thing ceases to become a story and is dropped into the Orwellian black hole along with the McGregor cheating episode.

Not before some nut at the Scotsman by the name of Barry Anderson let loose with an anti-Celtic diatribe in the Monday's edition (13/09/2010). In the febrile mind of this brave Rangers-minded footsoldier, TWO borderline offside goals (which were proven not to be), cancels out DOZENS of glaringly obvious mistakes by referees over the course of the previous season. Here are the detached, analytical and unemotional comments of this so-called "journalist" –

"JUST seven months, ago Celtic were making private submissions to the SFA complaining of refereeing bias against their club. In their own paranoid bubble, they cried discrimination and moaned that a conspiracy was at work amongst officials."

Quite a leap there, from expressing concerns and requesting a meeting to *"complaining of refereeing bias"*. Still, it wouldn't be like a Scottish football writer to twist and distort things to Celtic's detriment.

"Saturday proved conclusively that such a claim was, in fact, pure delusion on the part of the Parkhead hierarchy. By half-time they sat 2-0 ahead against Hearts thanks to one goal which was clearly offside and another which was borderline. They then saw their opponents denied a penalty before scoring a magnificent third in stoppage time to seal a victory thoroughly deserved on the overall balance of play. Curiously, Celtic employees had precious little to say about officials afterwards."

And curiously, the Scottish media had rather a lot to say about the officials and were happy to broadcast, **without contradiction**, the "rather a lot" Jim Jeffries had to say about it all. Even if any of these decisions were proved to be incorrect they still wouldn't have any relevance to the injustices suffered by Celtic the previous season, no matter how much a Rangers supporting journalist would wish to think so. Not only does this clown make a complete laughing stock of himself in the rush to use this as evidence to condemn Celtic, but he also invents a "denied" penalty. Watch out Darrell King, someone is after your cheerleader job. But wait, this Rangers lickspittle is not finished –

"Now, some match officials are incompetent, not only in Scotland but the world over. Others are simply buffoons, but it is a step too far to accuse them of blatant cheating. In February this year Celtic did exactly that with their complaint to the SFA. The Glasgow club have been made to look rather foolish on several occasions since when debatable decisions have gone their way in critical periods of games. Saturday was possibly the most glaring example you will see for some time."

Or the most glaring example of sheer hunnery masquerading as journalism, you'll see for some time. I'd be interested to see the evidence that Celtic accused any referee of *"blatant cheating"*, however close to the mark such an assertion may have been. Perhaps Celtic's lawyers should be too. I'd also be fascinated to see any of the *"several occasions since"* when **debatable** decisions have gone Celtic's way – even one in fact. Anderson must have been watching a different SPL from the rest of us. Something tells me this is not a guy who spends much time at Celtic Park.

The reference to *"debatable"* is interesting, and reveals a mindset that is selectively gathering evidence to meet his pre-determined opinion. "Debatable" decisions, by their very nature, are not really errors, otherwise they wouldn't be "debatable". A "debatable" decision is one which might have been given in favour of either team, and would have been debatable regardless of which team benefited. This is **not** what we saw over the course of the "honest mistake" season 2009/10. What we saw was Rangers benefiting **exclusively** from dozens of **blatant** and **glaring** errors. There was nothing "debatable" about Lee McCulloch not being ordered off for clearly elbowing Michael Paton of Aberdeen in the face. There was nothing "debatable" about David Weir tripping Shaun Maloney in the Rangers penalty box TWICE and no penalty being given. There was nothing "debatable" about yet another Andy Davis-esque Assistant Referee flagging a Ross Forbes goal offside, when the player was at least FIVE YARDS onside. And so it went on and on that season. Notice also, that the all-seeing media eye has suddenly awoken from the slumber which caused it to go to sleep on the Alan McGregor cheating a few weeks ago, and now it is trained and ready to pounce on any perceived error favouring Celtic no matter how slight.

You might recall at the outset of season 2008/09, Celtic were given the benefit of the doubt over a couple of "debatable" decisions. On the opening day against St Mirren, we were awarded a penalty for a tug by Will Haining on Jan Vennegoor of Hesselink with the Celtic striker through on goal. Referee Eddie Smith gave the penalty which was indeed a soft award, although contrary to most media reports the defender did make contact with the Celtic player. As last man, Smith was left with no alternative but to send Haining off. Funnily enough Eddie Smith didn't last too much longer as a grade one referee after this game. The following weekend Charlie Richmond failed to give Dundee United a penalty when Caldwell appeared to foul O'Donovan in the Celtic box. Although, to any fair-minded person, this did look to be a mistake by the referee, what the media totally ignored in their slanted coverage of the incident was that Stephen McManus was blatantly fouled immediately before the incident so play should have been stopped before the foul on O'Donovan. In any case, the unanimous opinion of the Scottish media was that Celtic had benefited from two highly dubious refereeing decisions, and a week later it was time to get out the smelling salts as Rangers had a DaMarcus Beasley goal wrongly disallowed for offside against Aberdeen. This prompted Mr Dignity himself into a wee rant that it was an *"incredible decision for a linesman who is in line with play"*, finished off with a wee touch of comedy about how they don't make a fuss about decisions.

So, what to do about a string of "bad" decisions perceived to be largely favouring one team, and a manager publicly voicing his concerns over the decisions of officials? Did the Scottish football establishment follow the 2009/2010 model of conducting an intensely derisive media campaign to discredit every complainant as paranoid, vigorously defend the honour of referees at every opportunity, dogmatically insist they only ever make "honest mistakes" and demand action be taken against the manager in question for breaching SFA rules on criticism of referees?

Of course not, this is Scotland. What they did was convene a summit at Hampden Park to discuss concerns over the standard of refereeing! You couldn't make it up. Paranoiacs may also recall that this summit in late August 2008 was in part a hangover from a lingering and rather virulent strain of Rangers paranoia from the previous season – the 'Everybody's-against-us-and-willnae-gee-us-another-extention' strain. This summit was reported to be a roaring success and everyone could look forward normal service being resumed i.e. the "honest mistakes" going in the correct direction, however the media had one more example of their brazen hypocrisy in how they treat concerns expressed by the Establishment club over refereeing and everyone else, especially Celtic. A few months later, in November 2008, Rangers had a goal "disallowed" after Kris Boyd petulantly slammed the ball into the net after the referee blew for an offside offence. After the match the Man With Nosurname Who Never Complains About Referees, had another wee rant, this time chiefly against the linesman involved and very helpfully drew attention to the official's Irishy sounding surname "*Mr Murphy was quick to allow a Scott McDonald goal at Celtic Park last season and was quick to disallow that one tonight*". Not only do we have a manager committing the heinous crime of accusing an official of bias and cheating – if we go by the Scottish media's interpretation of similar comments by managers of other SPL sides – but we potentially have a sinister sectarian dimension introduced by drawing attention to the probable ethnicity of the official concerned.

It goes without saying that the media reaction was timid, in fact outright sympathetic to the Rangers manager's view. However BBC's Sportscene results programme the following week really overstepped the mark from the usual level of not so subtle propaganda to laughable hypocrisy when they wheeled out Darryl Broadfoot (now Communications Manager at the SFA) to comment on the Rangers' manager's raving paranoia. Now, if this had been Gordon Strachan, Craig Levein or any other SPL manager, the BBC would have been condemning this slur on the unfairly disparaged official quicker than you could say "get him up in front of the beaks". Not so with the manager of the Establishment team. No, what the BBC did was trawl their archives to pull out footage of the McDonald goal at Celtic Park (which was a nanometre offside), and the Beasley goal at Aberdeen (which prompted a separate Nosurname outburst), to play for their viewers and allow Broadfoot, Murdo McLeod and David Curry to nod sagely and agree that the Rangers manager "*has a point*" (It seems the BBC didn't have another a half an hour to go through all the refereeing mistakes that had favoured Dignity FC by that point of the season). Not only that, but on the matter of Tom Murphy and any alleged leanings he might have, former Herald lickspittle Broadfoot said "*possibly in the instant where a decision is being made a referee or linesman's allegiance might just influence him for a split second*". Incredible.

From the same mouths that berated and continue to berate Celtic fans for our "paranoia" – who defended Dallas, Davis and McCurry to the hilt. Who proclaimed passionately that we can't possibly question the integrity of any official, and that any possible leanings an official might have simply doesn't come into the equation, and that to suggest otherwise is malicious, criminal, not to mention total paranoia; all of this, and now apparently, well, maybe in the heat of the moment an Irishy sounding linesman might make decision to get it up the Rangers. And this from a guy who would end up working at the SFA.

It is nothing less than complete naiveté to think that we can just shut our eyes and ears to this and all of it won't matter. The next referee who comes to Celtic Park will have it in the back of his mind that we got two dodgy goals against Hearts and a dodgy penalty the week before despite the fact that the officials were found to be 100% correct in each case. He might just subconsciously think it much easier to give the other team the benefit of the doubt like Conroy or McDonald in the knowledge that he'll get the full support of the media rather than face a week or more of "under-fire whistler" headlines. I don't buy newspapers or listen to phone-ins, but I make it my business to know what the enemy is putting out there to harm the interests of Celtic FC. Ignoring them is the equivalent of standing in front of them getting slapped in the face over and over again and your dinner money taken out of your pockets. Remember, Loovens suspended, Bougherra off the hook, violent fouls by Lafferty, McCulloch and Weir ignored. Nobody is calling for further action against Alan McGregor for his scandalous act of cheating the other week. Who do you think sets the agenda of what does and doesn't go before a review panel? So I chose to take an interest in what they're saying and hold it up to the ridicule that it deserves. To ignore it, is to bend over in front of them and present your buttocks for entry.

"It could have been bad"

"People are asking how bad is it at Rangers? If we did not take this action, it could have been bad. We need to get the costs down and with the greatest respect, even if we kept Kris Boyd, I do not think there would be any guarantees this season"
David Murray 6th January 2009

Among Celtic supporters, and those with the ability to soberly reflect on the evidence which has presented itself so starkly, season 2009/10 will go down in Scottish football history as the season when the Establishment club became so desperate it did not matter how blatant the cheating became. It was the season that the hackneyed cliché "an honest mistake" was taken to a new level, the last refuge of their media apologists. With Rangers very existence at stake, the £10million available from Champions League participation became the Middle East oil to their US Administration, the taxpayer bailout to their ailing banking corporation, the very oxygenated blood to their living breathing souls, and failure to acquire this vital sustenance could not be tolerated; no matter the cost. The Head of the Family would have to put the word out – the favours were to be called in.

When David Murray made his statement in January 2009 that if Kris Boyd hadn't been sold then things "could have been bad", Rangers appeared to be heading for dire straits. Particularly so, when it emerged later that their chairman – the highly esteemed captain of industry that he is – had been employing a negotiating strategy seemingly devised by the Marx Brothers, revealing his hand before the Boyd deal had been formally completed and at a stroke destroying the club's chances of commanding any sort of significant transfer fees from the hovering English Premiership and Championship vultures, no matter how much cheerleading and hype their media poodles could drum up for their prize assets. There would no Hutton or Cuellar-shaped deliverance in January 2009.

As Celtic opened a seven point lead at the top of the SPL table, the response of the ever publicity hungry Rangers Supporters Trust (RST) was to launch a childish, foot stamping "We Deserve Better" campaign, which predictably had nothing constructive to offer and appeared to amount to nothing more than a plea for someone to swoop in on a white charger and extract the club from their financial morass. On TV and radio, many pundits and "experts" were on the verge of openly weeping, whilst for others total denial was the order of the day. Craig Paterson spoke of the expected fire sale being a positive turn of events "if Walter [Nosurname] is handed the money to find decent replacements". Mark Hateley cringingly wrote of "Walter's masterstroke" in trying to sell his captain and top goalscorer halfway through the season. In the end Boyd and Ferguson stayed, which was the cue for some spectacularly disastrous laurel resting by the Celtic board, signing only Willo Flood for £50,000. With the manager seemingly working his notice, the recipe was complete for a dismal Celtic run-in that allow a technically bankrupt Rangers to win the league with the minimal intervention of "honest mistakes". Despite Celtic's failings playing out in the predictable manner, Celtic fans consoled themselves, with some positively revelling, in Rangers' financial difficulties. In hindsight perhaps all of the difficulties facing Rangers were actually bad news for Celtic too, given that failure to win the league could lead to the unthinkable and threaten the Ibrox club's very existence. Given such circumstances, all the stops would have to be pulled out and favours called in. This called for a two-pronged attack – firstly, escalating the "honest mistakes" and also the selective use of the completely arbitrary SFA Disciplinary Review Panel. Secondly, and in my opinion, more importantly, the clean-up exercise – a compliant media which diverts attention away from topics and incidents that the Establishment bosses deem undesirable, whilst casting their light in a direction more amenable to the agenda at hand.

It was following a poor 1-1 home draw with Hibs in October 2009 that we got a peek behind the curtains into the crumbling house that was the true extent of Ranger's financial turmoil. Did this revelation come courtesy of the Scottish media actually doing their job and following up one of the myriad of sources available to the public for the preceding seven or eight years? No, don't be silly. The greatest story in Scottish football since the Merde signed for the Dark Side was brought to the public arena by none other than Walter Smith who – not for the first or last time – lost his cool completely in a press conference and let the cat out of the bag – the bank was effectively running Rangers. At that point, the Establishment club had already benefited from some customary "honest mistakes" against Hearts, Aberdeen and Celtic, with Celtic on the other hand being denied a match-winning penalty in the final minutes of a game with Dundee United by Celtic-minded referee Steve Conroy (considering a referee to be Celtic-minded not considered to be a symptom of paranoia in Scotland). Despite this, Celtic's win at Hamilton Accies, the day after that now infamous press conference, put us a point clear at the top of the SPL table. This simply would not do; the gloves would have to come off and immediately Celtic would be feeling the full force of *Operation: It Doesn't Matter How Blatant it Gets.* The first signs of this escalation would rear its ugly head in May 2009 with the fiasco that is the SFA Disciplinary Review Panel.

No O*d F**m title decider rule repealed the SFA Review Panel, and the difference between Celtic and Rangers managers

As the SPL reached the split and the season entered the home stretch, Celtic held a slim one-point lead over Rangers. It was at this point that the frequency of those "honest mistakes" that we have all come to know and love started to ramp up well above its already impressive levels. Firstly there was the strange matter of the post-spilt fixtures, a hot-topic from the previous season. As all Scottish football fans are aware, it has been customary since the inception of the SPL split to schedule the remaining Celtic-Rangers match at the first available opportunity. This is ostensibly to avoid the scenario of one of the clubs mathematically clinching the title in a match against their great rivals, a potentially explosive scenario as witnessed unfortunately in May 1999. This has been the great dogma from the SPL, its member clubs and Strathclyde police no less, and was the key argument in 2003, when Celtic were forced to play at Ibrox less than 72 hours after a UEFA Cup semi-final. "We must avoid an Old Firm title decider at all costs" was the mantra from all and sundry, supplemented by "We are only taking orders from Strathclyde police". This was kind of blown out the water when Rangers chairman John McClelland stated "What's all the fuss? This date was agreed between Rangers and the SPL back in August" seemingly without consulting Celtic on the matter. In any case, we were assured that a most laudable concern for public safety was the top priority for all, and would always remain so. Fast forward to May 2009.

According to the mantra of previous years, the Rangers-Celtic match should have been scheduled for the weekend of Saturday 2nd May 2009, the first available date to hold the game. However the SPL curiously decided to defer the fixture to the 9th of May on the following weekend. Holding a one-point lead at this stage it would not be possible for Celtic to build a mathematically unassailable lead from a game played on this later date, however it did open up the possibility of Celtic finding themselves seven-points clear with only nine points left to play for. Although not a mathematical certainty, this to all intents and purposes would be viewed as such, effectively opening up the possibility of all of the worst case crowd violence scenarios much feared by the SPL and Strathclyde Police. Unlikely as such a scenario would be, it was just as unlikely as a deferred Rangers-Celtic fixture in 2003 proving mathematically decisive and in that case conventional wisdom was that any risk was too great a risk.

Of course all of this had nothing to do with the fact that Rangers' key defender, widely acknowledged as their best player, Madjid Bougherra, would be suspended for any fixture played on the weekend of 2nd May. Of course not. But in a happy coincidence, Celtic's Scott Brown would commence a two game suspension on the 9th of May, subsequently ruling him out of the Rangers game. Kill two birds with one stone as they say. Why the game couldn't have taken place on the 2nd of May has never adequately been explained leaving us to discount any nasty talk of conspiracies without any rational explanation to offset such notions.

From this point on things started to get really interesting. Rangers beat Celtic 1-0 to move one point clear at the top of the league. The major talking point of the game arose as eagle-eyed media pundits spotted Glenn Loovens catching Maurice Edu with his studs moments after making a clearance from the edge of the Celtic penalty area. Although this clearly caused Edu a degree of pain and discomfort at the time, typical of any mistimed challenge in a myriad of SPL games, the Rangers player recovered quickly and participated in the remainder of the game with no ill effects. TV footage of the incident was not at all conclusive in determining whether Loovens intended to injure the player deliberately and the player vehemently denied doing so. Loovens was quoted "*I'm a hard player but also fair. I just went in for the ball and at some point my leg had to come down to land on the ground. Edu went off for treatment and I spoke to him as soon as he came back on. I said sorry, asked if he was okay and he told me he was fine. I really don't know what all the fuss is about*". Regardless of this, the media continued to gnaw away at the story like a dog with a gnarled old bone, giving it great prominence in their various TV programmes, newspaper stories and radio phone-in kangaroo courts.

Only three days later Celtic played Dundee United at Celtic Park, winning 2-1. Again, however, the media had their infra-red night vision goggles on and picked up on a mistimed challenge by a Celtic player which became a major talking point and news filler. Scott McDonald caught Lee Wilkie just below the knee with a sliding challenge that was a fraction of a second late. The axe Wilkie and his manager Craig Levein had to grind following the game was with the referee, not the player, for what was clearly an honest attempt to play the ball – an honest mistake if you like. The Dundee Utd manager said "*Stuart Dougal might want to look at the stud mark on Lee's shin instead of showing an amazing amount of arrogance and telling him to get up. And he came over, speaking to me in a manner I thought was disgusting*". Lee Wilkie's take on events was "*McDonald caught me just below the knee, I don't think it was intentional but I still got caught. I said to the referee at half time, 'what were you playing at?' and he said, quite arrogantly, that his kids had had bigger knocks than that, which was a stupid comment to make - his kids must be some size*".

So to summarise – Mc Donald mistimed a challenge on Wilkie, the referee saw the incident, did not award a free-kick and the United player and manager took exception to the referee's manner in dealing with the situation. This is not quite how the Scottish media focused on the story though. Again, we were subjected to trial by radio phone-in with a constant stream of Rangers supporters taking a sudden keen interest in a minor incident within a Celtic-Dundee Utd game, each one calling for the player to be suspended to the agreement of sympathetic panels of ex-Rangers players. STV and

BBC aired multiple replays of the tackle in slow motion to accentuate the apparent lateness of the challenge and acres of newspaper print were devoted to calling for the SFA to review the incident with a view to taking action against McDonald. A question that did not crop up in this typhoon of media hyperbole was – what exactly is the protocol for referring such cases to the SFA video review panel?

This was a question that Celtic FC would officially put to the SFA in writing, leading to the predictable and tiresome accusations of paranoia, without ever receiving a clear reply. To the objective onlooker, the only criteria appears to be that any such incident is subject to a high degree of media hype. This is a disconcerting notion for all those connected with Celtic FC given the Scottish media's track record in where they choose to shine their spotlight, and just as importantly, where they don't. Certainly, the understanding of the average fan and media pundit is that the purpose of these panels is to review incidents that were missed by the referee and which carried a high probability of risking sanction if they had been seen by the officials at the time. So anyone of fair mind would think that Scott McDonald had no case to answer as the referee had witnessed this particular incident and had chosen to take no action. However, any fair minded person would be wrong.

It was later announced that McDonald's tackle would be referred to the SFA review panel along with the case of the monstrous crime that we were led to believe Glenn Loovens had committed. McDonald himself appeared to have a pretty good grasp of the forces at work *"I find it astonishing that the video review panel will be looking at this when the referee was standing only five yards away from it where it happened. I thought these reviews were for incidents that were missed by the referee during the match. Stuart Dougal didn't miss this one. He just didn't think there was anything in it - and Lee's reaction suggests he felt the same way. He even asked me for my shirt at the end of the game. Do you think he would have done that if he thought I had tried to seriously injure him?* **It's only because the tackle has been highlighted on TV and in the papers that the SFA have stepped in**. *It's become a big deal because the ref wouldn't allow Lee to be treated"*.

How does the saying go again? "No journalist or TV presenter ever scored a goal or saved a shot". No they're more powerful than that. Of course in each instance the media were successful in their objective. The McDonald case illustrates aptly the cunning nature of the media's modus operandi, for although the player (Scott McDonald) ultimately received no suspension, ostensibly because he had no case to answer, it made Glenn Loovens his Celtic team-mate's position untenable in the case of his own disciplinary case. It was inconceivable that two Celtic players could have the charges against them dismissed no matter how flimsy the prosecution case. So the media got their pound of flesh from Celtic in the end. No doubt this assertion will be dismissed as paranoia by the sober reflections of neutrals, while they nod in agreement at talk of Celtic's Machiavellian attempts to influence referees this season. Stay tuned for a fantastically barefaced example of hypocrisy on this matter from Radio Shortbread's Jim Traynor and John Robertson later in this book.

Now, any fair minded person might have expected an objective journalist to ask some questions along similar lines to those put to the SFA in writing by Celtic i.e. what is the criteria for referring such incidents to the review panel? The problem with that though, is such a journalist hardly exists in the environs of Scottish football. Instead the following word play which appeared in the Daily Record in a piece containing the self same quotes uttered by Scott McDonald above are typical of the spin put on the story by the Scottish press "*McDonald, 25, faces trial by television after referee Stuart Dougal was unable to get a proper view of the original incident*". At no stage did Stuart Dougal state anything of the sort. This statement could be loosely translated as "the referee was unable to get a proper view as seen through the eyes of a rampant Rangers supporter".

Funnily enough about ten months later, Scott Brown would be sent off on the flimsiest of pretexts in a match against Rangers, and his antagonist in the incident, Kyle Lafferty (who else?) would get off scot-free having started the incident by grabbing Brown around the neck. A hack called Peter Jardine at the Daily Mail reassured his anxious hunnic readership that Lafferty need fear no retrospective censure as – "*SFA rules dictate that, while [Dougie] McDonald may yet decide to reduce Brown's red card to a yellow, the Ibrox star can't be punished retrospectively because the match official witnessed the incident and decided at the time not to take any action against him.*"

Hmmm, obviously SFA rule dictate that match officials can't take restrospective action in relation to incidents they've already seen, unless it's a chance to ban a Celtic player from a close title run-in. In another stunning, yet entirely predictable about-face, 17 months later the Scottish media would suddenly take a keen interest in the mechanics of the Review Panel, with the Evening Times handing over it's back page to a seven point bleating…sorry, clarification request, from the barmy Rangers Supporters Trust. The seven questions therein were broadly the same as those Celtic had been asking for the past two years, with a couple of 'Rangers are the victims' paranoia specials chucked in. So what could possibly have happened to abruptly stir the Laptop Loyal's crusading investigative journalistic spirit out of its slumber on the issue? Simply really – the Review Panel had cited a Rangers player, Allan McGregor.

Returning to 2009, attention would soon switch to Rangers as their 2-1 victory over Aberdeen in their penultimate league game of the season on 16th May produced two notable incidents. Firstly, Aberdeen's Charlie Mulgrew was ordered off after Kyle Lafferty feigned injury from a non-existent headbutt in the most blatant act of cheating witnessed in a Scottish football match in living memory. Later in the game, referee Stuart Dougal was left with no option but to red card Rangers' Madjid Bougherra for kicking Aberdeen goalkeeper Jamie Langfield in the head. There is legitimate debate over whether Bougherra's actions were deliberate, however there can be no doubt that they were reckless and violent which according to the laws of the game is enough to merit a red card. We will take up the curious case of the only country in the world where it's "ridiculous" to send off a player for kicking someone in the head a bit later.

As far as Kyle Lafferty was concerned, an outright defence of the player was a step too far even for the Scottish media, so it would have to be a damage limitation exercise. It wasn't too long before the player was the subject of sympathetic "I've learned from this and am a nice guy really" type articles in newspapers and news websites, coupled with simpering praise for the Manager with Nosurname's tough line in dealing with the player, by doing, well..., not very much. Smith was reported to have fined the player but no figure was ever revealed and in any event, such action would serve merely to save the club some money on wages at a convenient time given their highly indebted position. Ally McCoist was quoted in the press *"It's hopefully something Kyle will learn from. He now knows he has made a mistake, it is not expected from a Rangers player. The only thing he could have done was apologise and he did, so we can move on"*.

'Tut tut, a bad wee boy, come here and get your wrist slapped'. SFA CEO Gordon Smith practically fell over himself to slabber praise all over the Ibrox club for sanctioning the player. *"A great deal of credit should go to Rangers for the manner in which they have acted. I hope this sets a precedent among clubs as how to deal with simulation"*. Here's a revolutionary idea for Mr Smith before we start performing fellatio on officials of Rangers FC– how about not cheating in the first place? I realise this might be considered a bit far out. All of this allowed Rangers to emerge from the whole debacle with their 130 years of unsurpassed dignity still intact, in the eyes of the media and their own deluded supporters anyway, with no-one else able to tell the difference between the two.

Now it isn't difficult for a paranoiac to imagine how the situation may have panned out differently if the same actions were carried out by Aiden McGeady or Artur Boruc. McGeady was subjected to derision and ridicule from all quarters in the media this season for having the temerity to fall whilst evading a tackle with the potential to cause a serious injury. I was listening to this game on Radio Scotland and the reaction of the usually eagle-eyed commentary team and trackside reporter Chick Young was that McGeady had been fouled and the referee has made an error. Five minutes later, Richard Gordon interjected to breathlessly inform the commentary team and the listening public, that the BBC had a TEAM of researchers poring over the footage and could assure everyone that this was a clear dive therefore the referee got it right.

Certainly McGeady received no media plaudits for seeing the error of his ways nor Strachan for a dignified handling of the situation. By way of another contrast, when Kevin Thomson made a pathetic attempt to win a penalty by diving into Georgios Samaras in March 2008, Fraser Wishart leapt to his defence -*"What I would say is that in many instances players lift themselves off the ground when they think the tackle is coming, then the tackle doesn't come"*. In the face of universal criticism from the Scottish media, no comment from Wishart along similar lines in support of McGeady was forthcoming. Similarly Wishart made no comment when newspapers were carrying headlines of "CON MAN" and "CHEAT" directed at Shunsuke Nakamura in relation to a free-kick awarded against St Mirren in February 2008. All of this fury was levelled at Aiden and Naka from the same media who reckon it's "incredible" to red card a player for kicking an opponent in the head. Only in Scotland.

An interesting contrast may also be found between the Man with Nosurname's "decisive" dealing with the situation and the media coverage afforded to the Strachan/McGeady "affair" the previous December. The precise issue with McGeady was never fully confirmed, nevertheless the situation was sufficiently serious for the Celtic manager to drop the player from the first team. Was Gordon Strachan praised to the skies by the media for his "decisive action" and "taking control of the situation"? No, he was subject to constant jibes that he couldn't control the dressing room, he was a difficult personality and couldn't get along with the players. Jim Traynor took great delight in suggesting that Strachan would be sacked if Celtic lost their next league game against Falkirk at a time when Celtic were top of the league. Yes, I'll say that again… when Celtic were top of the league. This wasn't the first or last time the Laptop Loyal would speculate over the potential sacking of a Celtic manager whilst Celtic were top of the table. In 2002, Keith Jackson urged Celtic to sack Martin O'Neill for the heinous offence of failing to sign a new contract a year ahead of the end of his current deal. If only Jacksie, eh? One wonders the vitriol the Record's chief football writer would pour upon a Rangers manager who failed to commit his future to the club unless certain terms and financial guarantees were made to his satisfaction and let the situation drag on over a period of months. It's a pity I can't think of such an example. At a complete random guess, maybe he would pen a series of sycophantic articles, quoting Davie Weir saying that the manager is quite right and perfectly entitled to look after his own interests, and then quote from a series of first team players like Steven Davis and Steven Naismith, queuing up to shower praise on said manager, emphasising how much of a legend he is, how important he is to the club and desperately pleading with him to stay.

It's a pity that no fawning articles such as this appeared anywhere in the Scottish press:

Man Utd boss Sir Alex Ferguson hails Walter Smith

27 Apr Exclusive by Craig Swan (Daily Record)

SIR Alex Ferguson believes the capture of this season's SPL title has confirmed Walter Smith as a Scottish managerial great.

The Manchester United legend took time to break from his own nerve shredding championship chase to hail the stunning achievements of the Ibrox gaffer.

Ferguson, who had Smith as his assistant at Old Trafford, is involved in a frenetic flag fight with Chelsea as his team chase glory.

However, the United supremo and godfather of management has hailed Smith after the Rangers boss extended his remarkable run of success.

Ironically, Smith is at a decision time in his career at the same moment as speculation surrounds Sir Alex's future at United.

Ferguson has yet to commit on how long he will stay in the Old Trafford Job, **while Smith is also undecided as to whether to extend his period at Ibrox as the club gets set for a massive upheaval.**

The Rangers gaffer will take a final decision at the end of the season or in the summer, but Ferguson says Smith has always enjoyed a love of the game which could play a part in swaying the decision.

Or this…

Walter Smith: No decision will be made over my future at Rangers until new owner is in place

16 Apr 2010 Daily Record

WALTER SMITH insists he has not yet reached a decision over his Rangers future despite a growing clamour for him to remain at Ibrox.

Kenny Miller became the latest player to add to calls for the veteran manager to extend his stay beyond the end of the season after David Weir, Steven Davis and Kris Boyd all made similar statements earlier in the week.

However, the 62-year-old believes the ongoing uncertainty, as the Glasgow giants continue their search for a new owner, makes it impossible for him to confirm whether he has a future at Rangers.

"I've said I will wait and see what happens with the club," he said.

"Nothing has changed to make me change my initial decision so we just have to wait and see what happens before we can come to any decision.

Smith's achievements in his second spell have been arguably more impressive than his involvement in the Nine in a Row campaign in the 1990s, considering the lack of resources and financial uncertainty this time around.

Asked whether he believes he is a better manager now, Smith said: "I'm maybe better equipped to handle it now.

"I would hope that when you gain in experience, that you can use that experience well. If you don't, it's hardly been worthwhile gaining it.

"In many ways, it does help you. You still have some awkward decisions to make and I'm probably better equipped to handle the down sides as much as anything.

Or this…

Walter Smith to make decision on Rangers future in next two weeks

10 May 2010 By Keith Jackson

WALTER SMITH left his Rangers bosses sweating yesterday when he celebrated a second successive SPL title.

He admitted he'll spend the next two weeks deciding whether or not to lead the charge for three in a row.

Smith's team let a two-goal lead slip at the death as, for the second time in five days, Motherwell staged an extraordinary late comeback to clinch a 3-3 draw.

But it was a glory day for Smith and his players who lifted the biggest prize in Scottish football in front of a packed home crowd.

Afterwards, however, the Rangers boss revealed he has already held a round of crunch talks with chairman Alastair Johnston as he ponders on the biggest decision of his 18 years in management.

And there was no indication that, during yesterday's meeting, Johnston had managed to convince Smith the club is on the brink of recovering from two years of financial crisis.

Smith said: "The chat with Alastair was a general thing about how I feel about the overall situation the club's in.

"**There was no decision making** other than Alastair trying to gauge exactly where we are coming from football wise. There is not a lot he can do.

"In normal circumstances that would be the kind of chat a manager and chairman would have. But in normal circumstances that chat would have happened months ago."

And Smith says he must play his own part in clearing up the uncertainty surrounding the club by making a quick decision on his own future.

"It is not entirely a decision based on everything going on at the club. If it had been I'd probably have left a year ago.

"The decision will be a partly personal thing. I am not trying to evade the question in any way but there are a whole number of aspects I have to take into consideration.

"I have to make the decision shortly."

Walter Smith will receive the silverware this Sunday, but will he get the answers?

7 May 2010 By Darrell King Evening Times

The weekend ahead promises to be one of the most crucial in Rangers' history, as a behind-the-scenes search for clarity on the future goes on, against the backdrop of the club's first home SPL trophy presentation day in seven years.

Smith is becoming an increasingly frustrated figure, **and justifiably so.** *None of us,* **try and probe as we might** *are likely to find out the full extent of the fires he's been fighting in the past year or so.* [What a laughable notion. The only probing the likes of King has ever done in his puff, is of Smith's rectum with his tongue],

But the clock is now ticking on the most important issue at any football club – just who is the manager going to be?

Unless Smith is given guarantees in the next few days that there will be funding to repair a squad that has been hacked at and systematically downsized over recent transfer windows, **then he is almost certain to walk.**

And who could blame him? *He has been happy to operate without a contract from the end of January until now, just in case a new owner arrived and didn't fancy him, thus removing any compensation bill to bring in a new man.*

But isn't Smith entitled to now put himself first over club politics? After everything he's given to Rangers, *over many years and not just this second spell,* **he has earned the right to be treated in a far better way than this.**

He knows the problems and the issues. In fact, he is the man who has brought many of them into the public domain.

More than that, Smith has continued to drive the message in bold red warning letters to the heart of the supporters [In the absence of "journalists" like you doing your job Darryl] *– many of whom still appear to be in denial – much to the annoyance of faceless men who have barked orders behind the scenes that he should be silenced.*

He was one man they could not control, and they dared not push him too far *given the chaos that would have ensued had Smith departed during Rangers' title defence.*

But his patience is now being tested. *And if he does go as a result of more financial restrictions being imposed – and as of yet budgets have still to be agreed between Rangers and Lloyds – then there could be an almighty backlash from a support which holds him in as high esteem as they have done at any time in his two tenures.*

Smith knows he needs at least six new players. Does he get that money? Does he get hard cash for transfer fees? And how much? What level of player is he pitching at? **These are the issues he must have resolved before any call can be made on what he does next.**

In the midst of all this, Smith also had to cope with the revelations attributed to would-be buyer Andrew Ellis, who was forced to break cover when the

content of his chance meeting and blether with a Sky TV presenter ended up becoming public knowledge.

Smith would be offered a new three-year deal, Ellis said in a hurried public declaration, adding that he would offer a life presidency title to Sir David should he gain control – which he hoped would happen in three to four weeks.

Clearly irked, Smith's response to this was that "maybe the chap concerned should speak to me first before speaking about me". Given the men have never shared a conversation, just what was Ellis thinking about?

As we stated last week, there are many inside Ibrox who simply do not believe Ellis will follow his interest through, unless there is some hidden business going on behind his proposed takeover that has yet to be unearthed. Time will tell on that, but he has no plans to meet Johnston in the immediate future according to his people, which does appear strange. As does his lack of urgency in calling Smith. Ellis, in fact, is close to being bracketed in the "put up or shut up" category that was outlined by Murray in reference to other interested parties last week. But will any of them?

It would have no material effect on his day-to-day running of the team, as long as he has the appropriate financial plan laid out, guaranteed, and is allowed to manage without interference. **Smith simply wants to know what Rangers 2010 will look like – then he can make a decision.**

Undoubtedly, people like Johnston, chief executive Martin Bain and the supporters want to see Smith given the resources to rebuild and strengthen a team that has won six trophies in three years. Unfortunately, they don't hold the key to that. The bank do. And given their actions over the past 18 months, will they sanction what Smith needs?

If they don't, things may be about to get a lot messier – **and the most important man of all could be lost in the fall-out.**

Or...

Novo: It's time Walt was Knighted

By ANDY DEVLIN   The Sun

NACHO NOVO claims Walter Smith should be KNIGHTED.

The Spaniard hailed the remarkable job the veteran boss has done in leading Rangers to the title despite their financial uncertainty. Smith did so without a contract and Novo accused the money men running Gers of showing his gaffer a lack of respect.

He said: "The gaffer deserves a lot more respect than that. He should be knighted after what he has done for this club. I've said before that he should be called Sir Walter given what he has done here."

Novo feels for both Smith and Ibrox chief executive Martin Bain. He said: "You can't blame Martin or the gaffer. They just want the best for the club, but they can't do anything because somebody else is running it."

Novo - who launched his autobiography yesterday - also revealed the secret torment of the Rangers players this term, and his own at leaving. He said: "The off-the-field stuff has always been a problem, the players were worrying about it. Now I can't believe that I'm leaving. I had six years here and they were the best I ever had."

So, lots of plaudits for the fantastic job done by Nosurname and plenty of sympathy for the predicament faced by the manager, not to mention open acknowledgement that he is perfectly entitled to look after his own interests. Furthermore, these articles report on events that are ostensibly a reality which can **no longer** be hidden or denied. There is a complete lack of idle speculation as to possible negative consequences or accusations that the manager's lack of commitment is undermining or destabilising the club. There are no flights of fancy about Nosurname leaving to join an English Premiership club, although that may well be because all Premiership chairman remember that Wattie has been there, failed at that, and spent over £20million on Duncan Ferguson for a return of a handful of goals. It's just a pity none of this actually happened so I could quote it and show up the Scottish media for how hopelessly biased they are.

Anyway, let's remind ourselves of what the Scottish press were saying when Martin O'Neill was in contract talks with Celtic back in January 2003 and throughout the remainder of his tenure. Were the Scottish press magnanimous in acknowledgement that O'Neill was perfectly within his rights to keep his options open? Did they talk up his impressive achievements with Celtic? Did they assure Celtic fans that all the players were right behind their statesmanlike manager? Did they paint glowing pictures of the character of the great man? Did they tout him for a knighthood? Did they daffy duck —

Daily Record 16/01/2003 - "*I'VE FINALLY FOUND MY PARADISE BUT I COULD BE OUT THE DOOR IN A WEEK IF MARTIN CHUCKS IT says John Hartson*"

Daily Record 20/01/2003 - "*FLORIDA NO-SHOW TELLS ME GAFFER WILL GO SAYS CELTS HERO*" By Murdo McLeod

"*Martin O'Neill is going to leave Celtic at the end of this season.*"

"*Martin has brought most of the current players to the club and has led them to more success than any had ever experienced. And when they find out that he won't be around for much longer, **there will be a few whose performances will suffer**. I've seen it happen so many times.*"
Daily Record 21/01/2003

"*Celts legend Gemmell feels the signs do not augur well for O'Neill signing a new deal*".

Actual quote from Tommy Gemmell "*You start to say to yourself that the longer this goes on there may be something untoward – **but then again no news is good news***"

Daily Record 22/01/2003 - "*HAPPY SCOUSE HUNTING*"

EXCLUSIVE by Neil Cameron and Colin Duncan.

"**Snubbed** *Celtic stars are convinced that manager Martin O'Neill is on his way to Liverpool* "

"*Parkhead insiders believe that the Irishman will not sign a new deal and O'Neill **added fuel to the fire** by not holding his normal pre-match press conference for tonight's Lisbon Lion Testimonial against Feyenoord*"

"*Most Celtic fans now **fear the worst** especially with the news that he has sold his house in Glasgow* [Of course the Daily Record always speaks on behalf of most Celtic supporters doesn't it?].*The dressing room is buzzing with rumours that O'Neill has already entered into secret talks with Liverpool and Sports Record was told yesterday that he was looking at property in fashionable Hoylake, 20 minutes from Anfield*".

"*The Celtic players are joking about it* [O'Neill's contract situation], *calling it 'the mushroom' treatment – **kept in the dark and fed a lot of sh*t!!***"

Daily Record 23/01/2003 - "*CELTIC FANS ON A HIGH BUT IT'S ONLY STAY OF EXECUTION* Sports comment by James Traynor"

"*Celtic have secured **nothing more** than a **short breathing space** with this deal which is **firmly weighted to O'Neill's side**. Now he can laugh all the way to the bank with his new contract in his back pocket - but might he also be **laughing at Celtic?**"

Daily Express 23/01/2003

By Davie Provan

"*can we now expect Stan Petrov to be signed up on a new one-year rolling contract? **Absurd isn't it**?*"

[Getting 24 year-old (at the time) Petrov on a contract that would never expire and guarantees the club a transfer fee is a bad idea why exactly Davie?]

Evening Times 22/09/2003

"*SPURS SET TO SWOOP FOR O'NEILL*" By Darrell King and Ronnie Cully

Daily Mirror 24/09/2003

By Alan Nixon and John Cross

"*Tottenham chairman Daniel Levy is refusing to give up on Celtic boss Martin O'Neill after being told Spurs will have to pay £5million to get Alan Curbishley*"

Statement by Martin O'Neill 26/09/2003

"*Four months into the job my future was under scrutiny and it has remained so… I want to be talking about Celtic and I'm really happy to be in the job… If you tell me that the purpose of this is to get another 13 years at Celtic then I would be absolutely delighted… What else can I say? How many times can I say it? How many times do you want to ask me the same thing? How many times do you want to be wrong?*".

Daily Mirror 27/09/2003

By Alan Nixon and John Cross

"*Spurs chairman Daniel Levy returned from honeymoon last night and immediately stepped up the chase for Martin O'Neill.*"

News of the World 28/09/2003

By David Harrison

"*Tottenham Hotspur are poised to make an official approach for Martin O'Neill within 14 days*".

Evening Times 10/10/2003

By Ronnie Cully

"*Robbie Keane is convinced Celtic manager Martin O'Neill is high on the list to replace Glenn Hoddle*"

Daily Mirror 02/01/2004

"*O'NEILL OFF TO LIVERPOOL*"

"*Martin O'Neill is poised to join Liverpool in the summer, **having taken Celtic as far as he can**, and is simply awaiting a call from the Anfield board to set the wheels in motion*"

Statement by Martin O'Neill 02/01/2004

"*It's totally and utterly untrue. How many times have I got to say it? There is no foundation in that at all*"

Scotland on Sunday 22/02/2004

"*Persistent and well sourced rumours suggest Martin O'Neill is set to be appointed the next manager of Tottenham Hotspur*"

The article quotes Martin O'Neill as follows - "*That is completely and utterly untrue. It simply couldn't be more untrue so you can run it if you like*"

"*Yet a source close to Spurs Chairman Daniel Levy insists that ' the deal is as good as done. Hands have been shaken and O'Neill will be at Tottenham in the summer'*".

Daily Record 26/03/2004

"*Celtic's European heroics* [beating Barcelona in the UEFA Cup] *have shortened the odds on Martin O'Neill being appointed as manager of England*"

Evening Times 06/04/2004

By Ronnie Cully

"*Martin O'Neill is being* **frustrated in his attempts to get key men** *tied to new deals. The delay is causing concern among some agents who fear the players may suspect there's* **a problem with the manager's own position**".

The Sun 17/04/2004

By Bill Leckie

"*The question that keeps every Hoops fan awake at night... WILL HE STAY OR WILL HE GO?*"

"*Martin O'Neill has finally admitted it - if Celtic don't shell out to make the great leap forward this summer,* **they'll start going BACKWARDS**

And the stark truth is that unless the Parkhead board does come up with the dosh to let him build a new team, the biggest debate in football this summer will be whether the Irishman will be headed in another direction altogether - SOUTHWARDS

And with the Premiership's managerial merry-go-round sure to start turning again in the close season the rumour mill will also start all over again. Except that this time, it maybe MORE than rumour"

The Sun 23/11/2004

By Bill Leckie

"*Loutish, childish, out of control, not your team Martin, YOU*"

"*The game was ugly but O'Neill's response to it was hideous.*"

For four and a half years he's played the smart arse... Frankly, I've been sick of him for a long time... This was the so called Saint Martin at his twisted, spoiled, uncharitable, one eyed worst... Quite frankly I'm heart sick of him"

"**These days Martin O'Neill deserves the same respect that he shows the rest of Scottish football. Which is less than none**"

What, no knighthood??

The Sun 12/03/2005

"*O'NEILL REFUSES TO RULE OUT CITY - MART CAGEY OVER RETURN SOUTH Celtic boss Martin O'Neill has refused to rule out a Premiership return as Manchester City*

"*But yesterday the Hoops boss would NOT kill the story – despite being given the chance to do so. Instead O'Neill said "Other than the first 36 days of my tenure here you have had me leaving almost every day. Who knows* **at some stage**, *you will be asking me and I might have some different news for you. Celtic had eight managers in nine years, you know, and you got the impression you'd better turn things around quickly".*

Now with the possibility of making loan star Craig Bellamy's deal from permanent for £6million **dismally** *faint, you sense he is questioning* **whether he can take Celtic on again**."

The Sun 12/03/2005

"END OF THE LINE? O'NEILL ADMITS IT WILL BE TOUGH TO TAKE CELTS FURTHER"

By Iain King

"Martin O'Neill is living in fear of waking up one morning soon and knowing he has taken Celtic as far as he can."

A bit of a contrast eh? Here you have two managers who have been highly successful and have led their respective clubs to UEFA Cup finals and yet one is treated like a pariah and the other is lauded as some sort of god-like deity figure. Within a few months of taking over at Celtic Park, Martin O'Neill was subject to speculation linking him with a move to an array of English Premiership clubs. The more these dribbling hacks were proved wrong the more desperate they were to see him leave. Transfer speculation about players and managers is a tabloid's bread and butter, but there was a real sense that these journalists couldn't wait to see the back of the most successful Celtic manager since Jock Stein. There was more to it than simple hype to sell newspapers, this guy really got up their nose.

O'Neill was not someone prone to lengthy statements or rants about perceived injustices, certainly not on the scale of someone like Walter Smith these days, although there were a few notable exceptions when backed into a corner such as the infamous decision to send us to the Death Star two days after a UEFA Cup semi final. No, it was abundantly clear that O'Neill's great crime was simply in making Celtic successful. He was the first manager since Billy McNeill in the early 80s to bring sustained success to Celtic. Other Celtic managers in the intervening period such as Tommy Burns could be patronised by the media as plucky runners up who knew their place, at least in the eyes of the Laptop Loyal. Wim Jansen and Dr Jo Venglos were given the xenophobic ridicule treatment on joining Celtic, but by the time Wim stopped ten in a row it was announced he was leaving providing more ammunition to a grateful media to detract from the achievement. It was not then necessary to put the boot in. Dr Jo and Barnes never seriously threatened to challenge Dignity FC's hold on the title so when Martin O'Neill came in and blew Rangers away 6-2, nearly 15 years of "weearrapeepull" supremacy was threatened and the Scottish media immediately went to Defcon 2. When a treble followed in May, it was up to Defcon 1 and the gloves were off. Of course O'Neill's nationality was another interesting wee dimension to add to the ire of those who would attack the Celtic manager throughout his tenure, just as it would be for one of his best signings, Neil Lennon.

Gordon Strachan arrived and did well enough for there to be serious debate among Celtic fans as to whether he or his predecessor where more successful, and to their relative standing in the pantheon of Celtic managers. Another common link Strachan shared with O'Neill was the derision heaped upon him by the Scottish media. The message from the Laptop Loyal is abundantly clear – if you are a Celtic manager who poses a credible threat to our beloved Rangers we will go after you with everything. When Tony Mowbray came along the threat was there, if for no reason other than the Establishment club's crippling financial problems. In the end Mowbray foundered under their gaitling gun onslaught and I guess over 10 years of the habit dies hard for the Scottish media. Neil Lennon is now the target for their latest military hardware.

In contrast you simply don't get this level of personal abuse heaped on Rangers managers. Little more needs to be said about the media's veneration of the Man with Nosurname. "Big Eck" McLeish, he of the make-believe Indian Sign over MON, was given an easy ride by a sympathetic media. Even when he was leading the club to its worst ever series of results in their history in 2005, this was reported very much as the plucky young Scottish manager battling to turn the club around in the face of many challenges outwith his control, with success just a short moonbeam over the horizon. When the time came for Minty to "mutually agree" him, the press were full of comedic articles about how Big Eck was too embarrassed to step down when the Gers were 5th in the league and now that he'd managed to turn them round and guide them to a fantastic 3rd place he could leave with his dignity intact, completely under his own steam of course [cough]. Dick Advocaat's first two seasons saw adoration approaching Walter Nosurname levels with stories about how "strict disciplinarian, The Little General", turned down Real Madrid to go to Ra Gers. When O'Neill marked his card there followed a 16 month period of "Rangers have turned the corner" from Keith Jackson and co after every magnificent victory over Dunfermline, before it came time for Sir Moonbeam to move him upstairs to play with his toy soldiers. By this point the media were too busy hyping up his young up-and-coming successor to bother with any criticism of the shambles that had preceded the past season and a half.

Only Paul Le Guen experienced anything close to the treatment consistently doled out to Celtic managers, and even this was in a concerned "what are you doing to our great club?" manner. The fact that Le Guen was foreign and said to be of a proscribed religion (or not Rangers-minded you could say if you wanted to portray Rangers fans in an unflattering light) made it easier for the press to be critical; but still he avoided the worst excesses of being branded childish and out of control or a wee smart arse, unlike some other managers we could think of. Like I mentioned, media reflection on the matter, particularly on Radio Snide and Shortbread was very much in the post-mortem, "how does the club turn this around?" vein, rather then the gleeful dancing on the grave, club in crisis parties they have whenever Celtic go through a difficult time.

There was one other significant reason for the media to train their crosshairs on Le Guen however, and that was fact that by the time it was all going pear-shaped under his stewardship, a few Rangers fans were beginning to smell the coffee and question the role of Sir Minty in the club's predicament. After having been promised an £80million moonbeam from the JJB deal (by the Daily Record & co not Minty it has to be said), only to see the arrival of Sebo, Sonko and Svensson, the fans were beginning to see one or two gaps between the smoke and mirrors. Callers to Radio Snide were directed by Darrell King to ask Le Guen why he took the job when questioned on the difference between the promised moonbeam of investment in the team and the reality of an emerging Austria Vienna reserve team. Questioning the stewardship of President Moonbeam was still heresy.

Of course there are those who would explain this disparity away by pointing out that successive Rangers managers have never lowered themselves to engaging in the kind of paranoid tittle-tattle and undignified histrionics that their Celtic counterparts have indulged in over the years. In the case of the Man with Nosurname this leaves our intrepid Scottish media with nothing to go on, even if they wanted to be critical of the man. I mean, it's not as if he has assaulted a fourth official by pushing him after Nacho Novo was sent off against Hibs for nearly breaking an opponents leg. It's not as if he ever used foul and abusive language towards Mixu Paatelainen in the same game. It's not as if he's had to serve a multitude of touchline bans for similar behaviour, culminating in a **four** match ban in September 2009 following another mental rant at Kilmarnock players, the length of the ban reflecting the frequency of such unsavoury spats. It's not as if he's ever been caught on camera flouting such a touchline ban. It's not as if footage exists of him, on two separate occasions, using foul and abusive language to denigrate and humiliate a TV journalist attempting to interview him. It's not as if players such as Kevin Gallacher have given interviews recalling that youth players where intimidated by him for fear of physical assault, this account spun in the Scottish media to merely add to the "Iron Man not to be messed with" image of the ultimate alpha male, rather than something to criticise.

If any of the above were true, I'm sure the Scottish media would be onto it in a flash, with their 20-20 vision and infra-red night vision goggles in the same way they were with the behaviour of O'Neill, Strachan, Mowbray and any other Celtic manager you care to think of. I will say something for Nosurname though – at least he's not paranoid like Celtic managers. You would never catch the manager of Dignity FC questioning refereeing decisions, throwing around accusations of bias or coming away with such paranoid tosh as –

"Mr Murphy was quick to allow a Scott McDonald goal at Celtic Park and was quick to disallow that goal tonight" (13/11/2008) [how can you be quick to allow a goal???]

or

"It was deemed violent conduct but, having had a quick look at television replays, there does not appear to be too much in it. Both players were on the ground and Kenny seems to have been trying to free himself and caught big Dods on the shoulder with his calf."

*"**Will the SFA be closed? That wouldn't be too clever. I'm working this week**."* (31/12/2009)

or (after the appeal failed)

"How can you have an appeals process which is dependent upon the referee admitting that he got it wrong in the first place? It doesn't seem to make a great deal of sense"

or

*"It's an incredible decision for a linesman who is in line with the play. We got a bad one at Tannadice earlier this season, which has been forgotten about, **maybe because we don't make that much of a fuss about it** - same situation here [Pittodrie]"* (23/08/2009)

or

*"According to our lads nothing will happen until next season which is obviously not much good to anybody. But whatever happens **it was an incredible sending off**. I have seen both red cards and first of all I have to say I was disappointed with my own player's reaction. **But the second sending off is incredible.** It meant we lost a player for the majority of the game for a circumstance that was not the case.*** (17/05/2009)

or

"I didn't think Pedro Mendes' first booking was a booking. I felt it was a rather innocuous challenge in the first place. When you do get a yellow card then you're on a bit of thin ice, you've got to watch what you're doing and I wasn't sure about the second one either. I didn't think they were bad fouls." (21/09/2009)

or

*"It's obviously disappointing, although Zenit will be delighted. From our point of view it's disappointing we don't have that kind of leeway. **Everyone in Scotland has made it quite clear they won't do anything for Rangers**. We just have to do the best we can"* (05/05/2008)

or

"***They made it perfectly clear there is no willingness on anybody's part to give us anything. There has been no willingness at all to help Rangers*** *so they're not going to help us now are they? If there was going to be an opportunity to help they could have done it by now. It's been a few days since we reached the final*" (05/05/2008)

or

"*The SFA have started a new trend in criminality - if you leave the scene of a crime early, you are not guilty.*" (16/04/2009)

or

"*Everyone wants people to get ordered off, everybody wants penalties against us,* ***everybody wants everything against us***"

"*We seem to be reaching a ridiculous stage **where refereeing decisions actually become far more important than the game itself**.*" (06/03/2010)

Nobody likes us, and we're really quite upset about it, It's no fair everybody's against us, I'm away tae eat worms. Nosurname not giving any consideration to the thought, that if "*everyone*" seems to feel this way, then perhaps "*everyone*" has a point. As far as refereeing decisions becoming so important goes; I couldn't agree more with him.

Now that we've established that the Man with Nosurname is too dignified to get involved in levelling accusations against referees and the football authorities, another angle for us to consider is his consummate skill in dealing with the media, in contrast to the paranoid, snarling, "heavy-handed" approach invariably taken by successive Celtic managers.

Consider the following account of former Celtic manager Gordon Strachan's "heavy-handed" manner in reacting "disproportionately" to reasonable questions from journalists gathered at a press conference –

Celtic manager Gordon Strachan dodges the Aiden McGeady question

The Telegraph 09 Jan 2009 By Ewing Grahame

After another difficult week for Rangers, Celtic should have been cranking up the feelgood factor for their fans ahead of Saturday's Homecoming Scottish Cup tie against Dundee at Parkhead.

*Instead, the club's **heavy-handed attempts at news management once again needlessly turned a drama into a crisis.***

*A routine inquiry as to whether Aiden McGeady would feature against the First Division strugglers was met by **a disproportionate response** which suggests that all is far from well between the Republic of Ireland winger and his manager, Gordon Strachan.*

*The pair**, who have enjoyed a fractious relationship**, clashed again following last month's 1-1 draw at home to Hearts, when Strachan tore into* the player in the dressing room afterwards and McGeady responded with some personal abuse.

This week he elected not to appeal against the fine **imposed on him for his outburst** but Strachan would not confirm that the player who was voted Scotland's Player of the Year and Young Player of the Year by his peers in 2008 would be involved.

Quizzed about McGeady, Strachan said: **"He'll be there tomorrow, there's absolutely no doubt about it**." Asked whether he would be stripped for action, the manager replied: **"You'll find out tomorrow."**

When the subject of their argument was mentioned, he said: **"It's finished. That's why we move on. To the next question, if you don't mind**."

"You can understand why you're being asked about him, surely?" asked one journalist.

"And you can understand why I want to say nothing about it so if I respect you and you respect me we can move on to something else," answered Strachan.

A pat response along the lines that McGeady, as one of the best players at the club, and could expect to return to competitive action sooner rather than later would have sufficed.

Instead, when club captain Stephen McManus arrived in the media room, he was accompanied by a member of Celtic's PR staff, who announced on their arrival that no questions concerning McGeady were to be asked.

When it was put to her that she could not instruct journalists on which questions are and are not permissible, **she snapped**: "Stephen doesn't want to answer them."

So let's just recap on the Celtic manager's "heavy handed" and "disproportionate" response –

Strachan said: **"He'll be there tomorrow, there's absolutely no doubt about it**." Asked whether he would be stripped for action, the manager replied: **"You'll find out tomorrow."**

When the subject of their argument was mentioned, he said: **"It's finished. That's why we move on. To the next question, if you don't mind**."

"You can understand why you're being asked about him, surely?" asked one journalist.

"And you can understand why I want to say nothing about it so if I respect you and you respect me we can move on to something else," answered Strachan.

Such a delicate wee flower this Ewing Grahame must be to consider Strachan's perfectly reasonable responses "heavy-handed" or "disproportionate". In fact, at the risk of being branded totally paranoid, I would contend that, if anything, it's actually the hack masquerading as a journalist's pile of anti-Celtic shite that is "disproportionate".

Now let's get all this unseemly Celtic paranoia business out of the way and listen to how a press conference should be conducted with dignity by the master himself. The following was transcribed by the author from press conference footage on BBC website under the heading "*Clarity required for Rangers sale*" –

Q: *The club issued a statement last night saying the bank wouldn't oblige the club to sell players in the January transfer window, is that your understanding of the situation?*

WS: "Well they issued the statement and that's it. So I don't need to say anything about that"

Q: *When you said everyone's up for sale, is there a difference between the two statements?*

WS: "As I said, the club issued a statement and as far as I'm concerned that's it finished with"

Q: *Walter, what prompted you to make your comments now?*

WS: "I said the club issued a statement last night. It's me that's hard of hearing, not you lads. [Pause for tumbleweed to pass]. **So they issued the statement last night and that's it finished with now."**

Q: *So that's **good news** for you though that they're saying that?*

WS: "I said the club issued the statement last night and that's fine as far as I'm concerned"

Q: *Walter, there's a lot of negativity around the club. How do you fear it's affecting the players?*

WS: "That's another way of asking the same question [laughter]. **It's a nice female twist on it** [more laughter] **how to do that. There is negativity around the club, obviously comments at Celtic it's the same sort of thing** [eh?]

Press conference continues for a couple of minutes with a bit of chat about injuries and other aspects of the team, until…

Q: *Do you have a message for the fans Walter, who may be worried about the future of the club at this moment in time?*

WS: "Look, I've got nothing to say about that. Ye keep trying. Gonnae just pack it in otherwise I'll just walk away. If ye've got a question about the game then that's it"

In contrast to the "heavy-handed", "disproportionate" grumpiness of the Celtic manager, the Man with Nosurname positively exudes charm and sophistication with his stonewalling and pleas for the media to "gonnae just pack it in" or he'll take his baw hame with him, because it's his baw and nabedy else can play with it if he says so. Gordon Strachan/O'Neill/Mowbray

39

etc are slaughtered for not throwing the lapdogs a bone, yet The Man With Nosurname treats them with total contempt time and again, and **still** they behave like the sun shines out of the man's arse. In all seriousness, if anyone from the "Old Firm conspiracy/bias" crowd can satisfactorily explain this as anything other than bias and mealy mouthed pandering to **Rangers**, then I am all ears.

Of course, press conferences and handling the media are one thing. Dealing with players is another, and this is yet another area where the Man with Nosurname excels beyond the feeble capabilities of successive Celtic managers. It also helps that his superstar players hold him in such high esteem.

Returning to the McGeady/Strachan situation, the player didn't escape the treatment either, the Scottish media seemingly caught in an orgasmic dilemma as to who was more deserving of their contempt. McGeady was painted as an arrogant, difficult, over-rated young upstart who was heading for the exit door. The media were also full of grim scepticism over Celtic's ability to recoup any sort of significant transfer fee for the player now that he was such a bad job-lot.

Artur Boruc was another player who had a few personal issues off the pitch and there were rumours of clashes with the manager and an altercation with Aiden McGeady. In such instances the Scottish media without exception emphasised the negative aspects and possible consequences, such as the player having to leave, Celtic being unable to command a high fee due to the circumstances and Gordon Strachan's authority being eroded or job coming under threat if Celtic failed to win subsequent matches in the absence of the player.

Here, I think, is a typical example of the approach the Scottish media consistently take in relation to such (very rare) stories concerning Rangers, with certain key elements of spin highlighted in bold.

Rangers star Kris Boyd back at training after bust-up with Walter Smith

Daily Record Mar 11th 2009

KRIS BOYD returned to training today after being banned from Murray Park yesterday following a bust-up with furious Rangers manager Walter Smith. Boyd was sent home as soon as he showed up for training but not before Smith had ripped into him over his attitude during Sunday's Homecoming Scottish Cup quarter-final against Hamilton. **No one at Rangers would confirm the confrontation** *but sources inside Murray Park said the striker, who has scored 24 goals this season, looked stunned and was chalk white after having been called to the manager's office.*

It is believed Smith was raging at Boyd's behaviour after the team to face Hamilton had been named. No one needed sophisticated listening devices to realise Boyd was given a verbal working over. He left without a word and although **no time limit has been set on the length of his ban**, [what, no pat response along the lines of 'Boydie' being one of their best players who can expect to return to the team sooner or later?] *he is out of the final unless Rangers suffer a series of injuries between now and the Hampden showdown.*

*Even **if Boyd swallows his pride and makes a grovelling apology** the best he can hope for is a quick return to training. Even **that won't happen until he learns to accept managerial decisions**. Greater respect for his teammates and much more effort are what he will need to demonstrate if he wishes to force his way back into Smith's first team plans.*

*Yesterday, Smith **faced the media** [surely that should be 'Smith was quizzed'?] for a pre-cup final briefing and revealed he would have no problem leaving out either Boyd or **in-form striker** Kyle Lafferty.*

*He said: "**It won't be hard to leave out either player if it has to be done for the good of the team**. Boyd's not an enigma in my eyes. He gets goals but other aspects of his game don't reach the same, **high level as his scoring ability**".*

Summary – The Man with No Surname acts decisively to reprimand his gifted wayward star. The player will be confined to the sidelines for a period of time with no detrimental effect on the first team. The manager acted rationally and effectively and has the running of the club completely under control.

There is no speculation as to a difficult relationship between the manager and player; this is all very much a one-off incident although the player is urged to mend his ways. However his gifted ability and great potential are also emphasised in the article. Note the lack of "*quizzing*" of the Rangers manager.

In contrast to the serenity at Ibrox, representatives of Celtic are engaged in "outbursts", "disproportionate responses", "heavy handedness" and "snapping" in the face of being "quizzed" by the media.

The Celtic manager, and the club in general, is all over the place, being evasive when asked simple questions, all of this leading journalists to quite reasonably read some sort of sinister meaning into this reticence. The journalist also assumes and emphasises a "fractious" relationship between the manager and player. Must be media bias to the O*d F**m again.

The Loch Lomond Booze Brothers and "Whattaboutery"

Of course Celtic managers are not the only ones who compare unfavourably against the Man with Nosurname's utopia of media and man management. George Burley made the mistake of falling out with a few Rangers players during his tenure as Scotland manager although it is far from obvious what Burley could have done differently to avoid the events that subsequently unfolded. Firstly, and this is usually conveniently buried by the Scottish media under an avalanche of hyperbole decrying the ex-Scotland manager, Lee McCulloch suddenly announced his international retirement **on the eve** of Scotland's crucial opening World Cup qualifier in Macedonia the previous August, citing an unwillingness to work under the manager at that time. Obviously someone at Rangers realised the potential PR disaster of this arrogant and petulant stance and the player backtracked desperately within a couple of days, claiming to have been misunderstood and assuring everyone that prioritising time with his family was the real reason for his decision. Fast forward a couple of years and the appeal of quality time with the bairns had mysteriously worn off for McCulloch now that George Burley was no longer the manager of Scotland.

With McCulloch unwilling to divulge the true reasons behind his problem with Burley, speculation abounded, or at least it would have if the Scottish media didn't revert to type and unquestionably accept the official Rangers party line. Well, accept the official party line whilst at the same time the likes of Jim Traynor were sharpening their knives and harping on about Burley "alienating" McCulloch despite no such accusation coming from the player. Did anyone in the media condemn McCulloch for, at the very least, the timing of such a disruptive course of action before an important game which Scotland subsequently lost? Of course not; it was all Burley's fault. It was "poor man-management" we were told. Perhaps the problem is you have to be a man to be man-managed in the first place.

So we turn to events at Loch Lomond in March 2009. Scotland had just been horsed 3-0 by the Netherlands in a Saturday evening World Cup qualifier leaving their qualification hopes hanging by a thread. This result meant that anything less than a win in the next home game against Iceland the following Wednesday would mean certain, if not mathematical, elimination.
Preparation for a match of such importance would be paramount. One would reasonably think that a 31-year old veteran of many Champions League and international campaigns, and an experienced 27 year old international goalkeeper would understand the correct way to prepare without some sort of schoolteacher hand holding exercise. Unfortunately we all know what followed – a crazy booze binge that lasted from the small hours of the morning right up till the following midday when Burley and Steven Pressley were forced to confront the pair and "persuade" them to retire to their rooms;

only doing so after making a scene in the shape of a heated verbal exchange with the Scotland coach and manager in front of stunned onlookers.

Because two key players from their beloved Establishment club were involved, the Scottish media didn't quite see things the same way as outlined above. The revelation that Burley had given the players permission to go to the bar for "a drink" was interpreted by Rangers puppets such as Mark Hateley and Keith Jackson, as the Scotland manager handing them an open invitation to drink themselves into a state of utter inebriation. After all, what more could we expect of a couple of poor wee daft laddies without their mammies to look after them? The story eventually broke on the Monday morning. The first reports in the Daily Record actually condemned the two players in a tone not seen in relation to an employee of Rangers since Paul Le Guen was running them into the ground, or rather banging his head off a brick wall trying to wean professional athletes off Monster Munch, deep fried pizza and lager.

And herein lies the rub, the most stunning events of the so-called Boozegate saga are not the actions of the two half-witted players but the back-straining twisting and turning of Walter Smith, the SFA and the media, who must all have been dizzy from the sheer effort of trying to keep up with the backtracking and the amount of stretching necessary to keep pace with it. From the minute the story broke, the media, Rangers and the SFA were scrambling to condemn even as they sought to make excuses. Initially pockets of the press and media were critical of the pair as the first report by Neil Cameron in the Daily Record was on the Monday morning. However it didn't take long for the customary Rangers-pandering agenda to surface, led by Rangers PR man Mark Hateley, with the rest follow following with gusto as they pursued the Anti-George Burley line with vigour. They wanted the Scotland manager hung out to dry for the crime of allowing grown men to have a drink, for essentially trusting experienced highly-paid professional athletes to be responsible. The Scottish national coach was supposed to have ordered everyone up to bed with no supper. Burley found himself under pressure because he had opted to retire to his own bed rather than act like a kindergarten teacher, and the previous McCulloch episode was also dredged up by the media as further "evidence" to condemn the man, the "family reasons" part of that particular decision conveniently dropped to suit the media's agenda.

In the aftermath it was widely reported that Ferguson and McGregor had been dropped from the squad, however this was wrong; neither player was being omitted from the squad; they were being dropped to the bench. At that stage their international futures were **not** in doubt. Mark this one down for future reference – as far as George Burley was concerned, both players were still in his plans.

Then Gordon Smith waded in with a gammon joint on the end of each arm to make his first public statement on events and incredibly **refused** to back Burley, announcing to the world, on the eve of a **must-win game** with the entire team and management under enormous pressure; that the manager would be called to a meeting at the SFA to explain his decision. Smith's statement went about as far as it was possible to go without openly disagreeing with Burley as outlined in the following excerpt from the Guardian of 1st April 2009 –

"Asked if he backed Burley's decision, Smith would only say: "He's made a decision; I know exactly why he's done it – he's told me his reasons. I'm going along with that just now. After the game's passed, George and I will have an opportunity to sit down and discuss what's happened in the last few days and review the situation and how it's been dealt with."

Speaking at Hampden ahead of tonight's game, Smith revealed Burley did not consult him or the SFA board over the matter.

"We weren't involved in the decision at all. ***It's George's decision*** *how he was going to deal with the situation that's arisen. He has to deal with behaviour and any sanctions that are taken. He also picks the team 100%.* ***It's his decision*** *whether the players are away from the squad. We have to give him autonomy in that respect. But we'll be reviewing the situation – I've told George that."*

There are numerous ways to undermine a manager, but for Burley's superior to do so in the press and on TV and radio just before a game of such importance was an extraordinary thing for Smith to have done and doesn't reflect well on his character or senior management credentials. Note that Smith states that such matters are entirely the manager's domain.

Following the SFA chief executive's Pontius Pilate act and public pronouncement demonstrating his lack of confidence in the manager, Scotland went out and managed to win the match, beating Iceland 2-1 without the help of the 'Booze Brothers'. It was a vindication not only of Burley but also of those who claim that, Ferguson in particular, is not all he is cracked up to be, and perhaps should be making way for someone younger who could bring a more attacking dimension to the Scottish midfield. Many in the press indeed, made such noises, their hands being forced by the incredible sight of the two half-wits appearing hell-bent on shedding any last remaining semblance of respect or credibility by making V-signs to the fans/and or the media during the national anthems. Apologists for these morons would go on to suggest that the V-signs were not in fact directed at the Scotland fans (who had booed the announcement of their names over the tannoy), but at the media. OK, so I guess that's alright then. The next time Scott Brown or Shaun Maloney flick the V sign to the TV cameras that won't be a problem then eh? Glad we've established that.

Rangers then added their twist to the whole saga by taking their own action, and on the surface at least that action was unprecedented and quite extraordinary; but not for the reasons the press breathlessly claimed when they reported it. Rangers announced they would fine both players, suspend them for two games and that effectively the career of both players at the club was over. This was exactly what the press said it was – incredible. Their reasons, for avid media watchers like me, were even more unbelievable. Walter Smith's comments on it make interesting reading, particularly with the hindsight of how everything panned out. "*Obviously what happened last Sunday with the Scotland players is regrettable*" he said, "*Then we had an incident on Wednesday with two players from our own club and that's what we have had to act on.*"

So, Smith's (and the club's) actions were directly related to the **match on Wednesday**, as he said at the time. No ambiguity about that at all. He further went on to say, "*The most disappointing aspect for me was the subsequent reaction on the bench and from the club's point of view I don't think that was a good image to portray.*" Mark that one down for future reference too.

The press reaction was adulatory. Walter Smith was hailed, once more, as the hardest and most astute manager in Scottish football. A man not to be messed with. A combination of wily old fox and the ultimate alpha male. Rangers were hailed as heroes, protecting the virtue of the nation by standing up to the plague of the over-paid ned footballer culture, along with sorting out the banking collapse, global warming and nuclear proliferation. A rather excited Hugh Keevins called it "*the most principled act in Rangers recent history*", without explaining whether "recent" meant longer ago than the previous week. This "*most principled act*" in recent history would soon be outdone in less than two months time with the fining of Kyle Lafferty for his defining work "A Guide to cheating that would embarrass the 1967 Racing Club side", followed by more of the same simpering praise and plaudits; no-one in the media stopping to consider that each of these acts of unprecedented dignity were the direct result of acts of unsurpassed cheating and loutishness. However, Bonkers was not alone in hailing Nosurname's action as a massive statement on behalf of fair play and decency.

And the ridiculous thing is many within the Scottish media looked at what Rangers had done and genuinely *believed* their outpouring of undiluted bullshit. Many years of unthinking obedience to the party line creates a mindset where such behaviour becomes ingrained, automatic and renders the journalist incapable of stepping back and engaging objective thought processes. So they printed Martin Bain's words as though there was no contradiction in them, and I put them here in front of you, so that you may view them for yourselves.

"The overall conduct of the players during the last week while on Scotland duty has, regrettably, fallen considerably short of the standards expected by Rangers Football Club and our supporters, and has brought the club into disrepute. The management of the club has taken the view that this has damaged both Rangers and Scotland, and is unacceptable."

Who knew it was so easy to bring down the Wrath of the Gods for the crime of disgracing the name of Rangers? Gascoigne beat his wife, Goram honoured dead terrorists, all the drunk drivers, bar-room scrappers, Malcolm's FTP autograph, the rioting amongst their support –
all you had to do was act like big kids and give the vicky to some journalists and the club would have hammered them into oblivion. Probably.

The ironic thing is that Keevins was right – taking action to ban these two clowns **was** the most principled action taken at Ibrox in recent years, but the same could have been said had David Murray insisted on giving the green straw remover a different job, or insisted on keeping Eggs Benedict on the Argyle Restaurant menu, or requesting the kit makers use a colour other than "tangerine" for the club's away strip. The *"most principled action"* in their recent history turns out to be a classic case of damned by faint praise. Not only that, but this *"most principled action"* turned out to be hollow words yet again. The question is, why were we surprised?

A matter of hours after Rangers had announced this action in defence of their "reputation", the SFA acted in defence of their own, and in the "national interest" when they announced both players would henceforth be banned from representing the Scottish national team. The statement was unequivocal.

"In light of the events of the past 48 hours, and following further discussions between the national team manager and the Chief Executive, it has been decided that Barry Ferguson and Allan McGregor will no longer be considered for international selection by Scotland."

So much for it all being George Burley's decision then. In any case, this appeared to put the whole thing to bed, something Ferguson and McGregor could have done before lunchtime at Cameron House and prevented the whole affair. Except, that wasn't the end of it at all.

The twisting and U-Turning was now reaching dizzying proportions. You see, its perfectly acceptable for Rangers and the Man with Nosurname to take any draconian action they see fit, quoting whatever absurd justification such as high *"standards"*; but it is quite another for an outside party to have the temerity to attempt to censure employees of the Establishment club, even if such a censure amounts to the same action taken by Spoilt Child FC themselves. A clear case of "I can have a go at my own family but no-one else can".

This Rangers and media U-turn was accompanied by howls of "Whattaboutery" as it was alleged that four other players were also guilty of an extended drinking session, although they at least had the sense to retire to bed before lunchtime without the benefit of a blazing argument with the management team, if the story is to be believed. The other players named were Scott Brown, Steven Whittaker, Alan Hutton and Gary Teale, although most accounts of this in the Scottish press (in a clear case of "Old Firm" bias) mysteriously dropped the names of the latter three and mentioned only Brown. The Rangers fans within the media began to bleat that their boys had been "*singled out*", and practically begged the SFA to take action against the Celtic player. Even the Man with Nosurname (who you will recall is far too dignified to get involved in any unsavoury sniping) was moved to state "*The SFA seem to have identified a new trend in criminality – if you leave the scene of the crime early you're not guilty*". Perry Mason speaks right enough. Even in the hallucinogenic world of Laptop Loyal doublethink this was a beauty – the poor wee Rangers boys were being "singled out", by the failure to punish, em, another Rangers player (Whittaker) and an ex-Rangers player (Hutton). Yes damning evidence of the Timmy unseen Fenian hand conspiracy.

But it was only Scott Brown who was the victim of a barrage of lies from a Sunday tabloid whose only fit purpose is the wiping of backsides. The media interest in, and knowledge of, the player extended as far down south as Newcastle where they were able to report in some detail as to a minor matter of a **group** he was in the company of, being spoken to on the train by police for what amounted to singing on a train. Two of the company were removed from the train, although reports in the Scottish media gave the impression, not unintentionally no doubt, that the player was addressed individually, when in fact the police spoke to the group as a whole. I can't be alone in my surprise that the Scottish press is so well briefed about goings on, on trains to Newcastle, as they appear not to be so well briefed when it comes to disturbances involving large numbers of Rangers fans in English cities such as Bradford and Portsmouth. I cannot be alone in looking forward to Rangers' efforts to weed out those fans who were responsible for little skirmishes down south at pre-season friendlies. After all, we wouldn't want anyone to fall below their "*high standards*" or do anything to harm either the name of the club or of Scotland would we?

On the day the lie-filled Brown story broke, Rangers played Falkirk at Brockville and their supporters demonstrated clearly who they blamed for the whole sorry mess when they loudly sang their new anthem, this time directed against elements of their own fan base and a significant part of the population, when they sung "You Can Stick Your Tartan Army Up Your Arse" before breaking into a typically rousing rendition of Rule Britannia. Their disdain for Scotland and the national side is all the more ironic when one considers that the SFA Chief Executive Gordon Smith became the first holder of that office to appear as a guest at the Rangers Supporters Trust Annual Dinner. No-one in the Scottish press commented on this, the man who once said his school team tried harder against the Catholic schools, claimed there was an "agenda" against Rangers in terms of censures for sectarian singing and who offered to postpone his association's own showpiece Cup Final to help Rangers. This we are led to believe by Rangers fans and lickspittles in the media, is a man responsible for vindictively "singling out" the poor wee hard-done-by Rangers players. And they call us paranoid.

This series of about-turns should not have surprised us, neither the wearily predictable 'Whatabouttery" witch-hunt of Scott Brown. Yet the sheer speed and glaring contradictions involved, take Laptop Loyal doublethink to new highs, or lows, depending on how you want to express it. Over weeks one might forget the context in which certain statements were made; over months the comments themselves become fuzzy; until finally people don't remember the detail of what happened in the first place, just a vague sense that the media made a lot of fuss about some Celtic guy who was chucked off a train and he got away with it unlike those poor wee Rangers boys. But you don't need to be an avid reader of Orwell to be left scratching your head in bewilderment at how all of Rangers' "integrity", "honour" and "principled actions" can be cast aside inside a week, and how the almost identical action of the SFA can be seen as "harsh" and "singling out", with the Scottish media sailing along as if all this was perfectly logical. Like I said before, after a period of time, servile adherence to the word of the master simply becomes ingrained in the psyche of the Scottish football journalist, and is self-evidently the truth, in the same way as for some Christians, everything in the Bible is the truth, even the bit about the talking snake and that wacky revelations ending, because it's the Bible, ergo it's the truth. Logic and reason are inconvenient undesirables to be cast out of the nearest window when it gets in the way of the word of the master.

But the pantomime still had a way to play out yet. With a crucial game against Celtic just a week away, there were those of us, cynical devils that we are, who sensed that, with the media's criticism of Burley and the SFA's "mis-handling of the situation", the climate was ripe for the U-turn to complete its full 180 degree revolution. The signs had been present as early as the Sunday, when some of Murray's toadies in the press reported that McGregor could still save his Ibrox career if he changed his attitude, no doubt with the coming Celtic game in mind. Ferguson was still said to be finished; his career at Rangers was done. Of course as we know now that was far from the truth.

A few days later word leaked out of Moonbeams Park that the two Rangers boys had, **not**, in fact, been disciplined for embarrassing the nation and their club, for disrespecting the fans and the press, for sticking two fingers up to the rest of the world and for behaving like neds after a night on the Buckfast. All of Rangers' piety and defence of the nation's honour had been weasel words; they were in fact, being disciplined for antagonising Uncle Walter. Incredibly, the Iron Man of Scottish football had reacted, as Mark Guidi put it, like a husband or wife in a marital tiff, and lost the rag in the heat of the moment, only to calm down a few days later during a "*mellowing of his mood*". As impossible it had seemed only days before, as he rode the crest of a wave of support which Barack Obama himself would have been blushing at, 'Walter' was "*prepared to listen*" to an apology from both players, after a weekend of reflection.

The media who had buried both players the second Rangers had decided to condemn them, were immediately possessed of this forgiving spirit, and they rushed to embrace the new decision, now lauding "Walter" as a decent man willing to forgive and forget. This is particularly galling in the strange case of our 'friend' Darryl Broadfoot, who had scandalously written of the shameless way Celtic had "forgiven" the many "offences" of Artur Boruc whilst Walter Smith had done what was just, true, right and wholesome in defence of Rangers, their dignity and the integrity of the Scottish game. His take on the U-turn by the Rangers manager is that Smith is an "honourable man" and Allan McGregor is more a "victim of naiveté" than he is "malicious". Only in the Orwellian world of Scottish football hacks could two such laughably contradictory positions be greeted with such lavish praise by the media. Surely, if Nosurname's initial decisive action was so laudable, then his subsequent about turn must be an error, or vice-versa? Surely **both** courses of action can't be the correct way to deal with the **same** situation? Well, when it comes to appeasing Uncle Walt and the Gers then no stretch of the imagination is too far. Remember, this is the word of the master, ergo it is the truth.

Now that the Great One had decided that after a period of "reflection" Ferguson and McGregor should not, after all, be punished, the media were directed – armed with official Rangers Football Club statements – to go after the **true** culprits in the whole tawdry affair – why, the SFA and George Burley of course. The Rangers players were mere victims. And they did so with a venom we only see when they are pursuing enemies of their beloved Establishment club:

Evening Times

Exclusive by Thomas Jordan 08/04/2010

RANGERS are furious with the SFA over their handling of the Scotland Booze-gate affair.

The Ibrox club are awaiting the findings of a top-level enquiry with great interest as SFA president George Peat, chief executive Gordon Smith and manager George Burley meet tomorrow at Hampden along with the international board to discuss what went on at Cameron House 10 days ago.

Barry Ferguson and Allan McGregor have been told they will never represent their country again after taking part in a drinking session that lasted until noon - **but none of the other four players involved have been brought to task**.*"*

And the cry was "Whattaboutery!"

Remember the decision from the SFA to ban both players came only after their idiotic display of petulance on the **Wednesday** at Hampden. The Man with Nosurname himself was very clear that he was taking action against them for their behaviour on the **Wednesday**. Yet now the focus of attention had shifted back to events at Cameron House with the media all falling into line like little ducks in a row, screeching and wailing about the "victimisation" of these two poor boys who were so unfairly punished for their "mistakes" on the early hours of the **Sunday**, whilst big bad Scott Brown kicked them, stole their lunch money and ran away. The Scottish media are very much the Establishment club's bitches.

Rangers believe the situation was completely mishandled in the first instance, when the players stayed up late drinking in the hotel bar after their 4am return from Holland.

Had George Burley **dealt with things properly***, it would not have sparked the chain of events which cost the two players their international careers and* **saw them disciplined by Rangers***.*

Burley, according to this source, challenged the squad to a drinking competition and when Barry and Greegs refused to take part because they fancied going to their bed and reading each other some poetry to help them off to the land of Nod, the Scotland manager called them a pair of poofs and put £1000 behind the bar. This was clearly a challenge to the the pair's manhood, an offer that no self-respecting young man could refuse, so effectively they were left with no option but to get tore into the bevvy. Burley only left the scene at ten to midday himself, just before Pressley arrived to collar the other two.

Now consider the following question. If **you** turned up for work severely hungover and/or single fished and had a public blazing row with the boss, would he or she :

a) Discipline you with immediate effect

b) Flutter their eyelashes at you and ask you back to their place to listen to some Scissor Sisters albums

c) Sellotape an ostrich egg to your forehead then dance a fandango with an orangutan

I would suspect a), but then again I'm paranoid.

Of course, most of this "disciplining" had by that point been revoked with reports of a fine being the only action taken, sorry, that should be the only "*most principled action in recent history*" taken.

*A senior Ibrox source told SportTimes: "If it had been nipped in the bud right away on the Sunday, when things started to emerge, **none of this would have happened**.*

How so? I know Cameron House is a five-star luxury hotel used by Hollywood starts and International Statesman and all that, but I seriously doubt they have the exclusive use of a time machine for guests wishing to go back and erase their drunken antics from the current space-time continuum.

"*What our players did in terms of the drinking and **V-gestures** was wrong and totally unacceptable. No-one here is hiding from that. They embarrassed Rangers publicly. But we appear to be the only club that had people there, despite the fact it is common knowledge there were six of them.*"

And the cry was "Whattaboutery!"...

Maybe my eyesight is deteriorating badly with age, but correct me if I'm wrong, I only saw **two** players giving the nation the vicky on Sky TV. Perhaps Brown and the rest were sneaky enough only to do it off camera?

"*The SFA appear intent on sweeping it all under the carpet - apart from what they've done to the Rangers players - and that is just not right when it comes to dealing with discipline on an international trip when others were clearly there.*

And the cry was "Whattaboutery!"...

"*If that is the case, and nothing comes out of tomorrow, which we don't expect it to, then our players have been made scapegoats.*"

And the cry was "Whattaboutery!"...

"*It is fair to say the relationship between Ibrox and Hampden has now crashed to an all-time low **over this affair**.*"

And whose fault is that?

"*Rangers duo Kris Boyd and Lee McCulloch **have already walked out on the Scotland set-up** under Burley, and now Ferguson and McGregor have been sine-died.*"

Note that Boydie and Elbows have previously "*walked out*" on the National Team but it is only "*this affair*" that is responsible for the poor relationship between Dignity FC and the SFA, the behaviour of Spoilt Child FC having been exemplary throughout presumably.

"*There was also serious unhappiness last Friday at the way the SFA handled their decision to axe the players, which appeared to show them piggy-backing on the action Rangers were taking.*

"*If they had wanted to ban the players why did they say the matter was closed?" added the source."*

"*As soon as it became clear what Rangers were doing last Friday, the SFA began to act. They then waited until Rangers had released a statement on the players' futures, before sending out their own minutes later."*

I'm still scratching my head to work out why Rangers announcing the pair would never play for Rangers again is perfectly OK, but the SFA doing the same thing in relation to Scotland is utterly scandalous. The "there were six of them" smoke and mirrors pish is not relevant here. To borrow Rangers' own terminology "If they had wanted to raise the matter of other players being involved why did they take action against their own players first then wait a couple of days before bringing it up?".

Anyway, as per Laptop Loyal protocol, the Evening Times hack finishes with some more fawning praise of the Man with Nosurname

"*Walter Smith has shown calmness in handling Barry Ferguson and Allan McGregor*"

What?? By flying off the handle like an angry spouse and announcing to the world their Rangers careers are over in a furious strop?? Before "reflecting" and "mellowing" on things and then performing a complete U-turn? Doublespeak is upon us right enough. A little Rangers Paranoia to finish…

"*Walter Smith is not on the Professional Footballers' Association Scotland shortlist for manager of the year – a surprising omission, you might think, considering that Rangers could yet win the Scottish league and cup double.*"

Over at the Telegraph, top Rangers lickspittle Roddy Forsyth (who also gets a gig reporting on Scottish football for Radio 5), leaves the Whattaboutery to his capable colleagues and simply goes for some good old-fashioned "We love you Sir Walter" crawly bum-licking –

By Roddy Forsyth
18 Apr 2009

"*One aspect of Smith's management skill that cannot be in doubt, though, is his **finely honed ability to handle a crisis**.*"

Like, for example, when his team only needed 14 points from their last 8 games of the season to win the league, and rather than constantly whine and harp on about the heavy schedule of fixtures facing them, he rallied the troops with positivity and words of inspiration, securing the title on the last day of the season at Pittodrie? No?

Nosurname also demonstrated this finely honed ability when, with the club mired in deep financial crisis, but with the media doing their upmost to pull the wool over everyone's eyes, he blabbed in a press conference about the bank effectively running Rangers, in a selfless move, in no way intended to deflect the heat from himself for the team's poor form at the time.

"*His command of the fallout from the so-called Boozegate affair – which saw the Rangers and Scotland captain, Barry Ferguson, and his team-mate, Allan McGregor, fall from grace after a marathon drinking spree and the public display of derogatory gestures –* **has been immaculate, as befits a manager of such experience**. *The public perception of Smith's disciplinary measures against the pair is that he intended they should never play for Rangers again but that, given the Scottish Football Association's varying attitudes, he felt obliged to soften his stance."*

"**Not so, say sources close to Smith**, *Telegraph Sport can reveal. Their version is that he coolly made his calculations on how the matter would pan out even before Rangers suspended the two from training for a fortnight and fined them the equivalent wages – hence Smith's off-the-record briefings to press contacts that the pair were finished at Ibrox."*

Ah, what a cunning, wily, old, fox, owl-type character rolled into one! And here was the rest of us thinking Waldo had simply lost the plot in a mental rage. No, this was all part of an intricate plan that would have baffled the Enigma code breakers in World War 2.

"**Smith was entirely aware that employment law would not permit Rangers to declare that Ferguson and McGregor could never play for the club again, a course that would have been equivalent to sacking them**, *with the likely consequence of actions for breach of contract by the players' legal representatives."*

Another Perry Mason moment. In the Orwellian world of Scottish media doublespeak, not sacking someone is the legal equivalent of, em… sacking them.

"*However, as unattributed reports of the end of their Rangers careers appeared in print and on air, the players had to come to terms with the prospect that it was true."*

These "unattributed reports" came from nowhere did they? They didn't happen to come from an elderly chap in a cardigan foaming at the mouth looking for a small mammal to kick? No, they just crystallised out of thin air then? OK, now we've straightened that out…

"This week, handed the opportunity to hang a public change of stance on the SFA's vacillations, Smith blithely acknowledged his part in the press briefings, then left everyone involved – Ferguson, McGregor and the media – waiting to discover what happens next. He kept the players twisting in the wind by stressing that although they would be available for selection again – as their contracts insist they must be – he would not necessarily field them."

"**It was a consumate demonstration of who is in charge at the club** and Smith enjoyed the added advantage that, although his squad was short of nine players because of injury and the suspension of his captain and goalkeeper, Rangers won three games in a week to close to within a single point of Celtic, prior to this weekend's fixtures."

"Those who have stepped into the breach – such as Steven Smith, in his first start since 2006 and Christian Dailly – have been **buoyed by his invigorating praise**. Should he choose to restore McGregor and Ferguson, Smith will be selecting two chastened players with **powerful motives to prove their worth all over again during the final decisive games of the campaign.**"

Pockets of the press even spoke of the motivation Ferguson and McGregor would have to earn themselves a transfer to another club, as if this was yet another fabulous positive to come out of Sir Waldo's skillful handling of the situation.

Now, let's recap:

Scotland drop Unbookable and Mythgregor - Scotland say that both will never play for Scotland again - Scotland say there's a chance they might play for Scotland again

Media: *Burley is a joke, the SFA are incompetent buffoons, Unbookable and Shagger have been treated disgracefully*

Rangers drop Unbookable and Mythgregor - Rangers say that both will never play for Rangers again - Rangers say there's a chance they might play for Rangers again

Media: *NoSurname has demonstrated his **finely honed ability to handle a crisis** by his handling of the situation which has been **immaculate, as befits a manager of such experience. It was a consumate demonstration of who is in charge at the club.** The players will now be **buoyed by his invigorating praise** and have **powerful motives to prove their worth all over again during the final decisive games of the campaign.***

With Rangers arming a grateful and salivating media with the ammo to ravage Burley and the SFA, the response from the authorities was to crumble in a heap of nonsensical conflicting statements. Following the SFA meeting to review the events of Boozegate, Gordon Smith refused to re-iterate the SFA's earlier statement that Ferguson and McGregor would never play for the Scotland again. Instead Smith wriggled like a worm on a hook and attempted to weasel his way out of his association's unequivocal statement by laying it at George Burley's door again. This reduced Gordon Smith – as if the man's credibility could sink any lower – to the excruciating level of arguing the toss with Tom English on Radio Scotland, stating, incredibly, that the SFA had not in fact banned Ferguson and McGregor for life, they had merely banned them for the rest of their careers. We look forward to the duo returning to duty for the national team just as soon as they've retired from playing. God, even Craig Brown was criticising the guy. Nurse, we need some medication here!

Of course, Smith went on to fire another very public nail in George Burley's managerial coffin by stating that a new manager would be free to select either player if he so wished. When asked why this would be the case when it was the **SFA** who released the statement that the players had been given a "career ban", Smith attempted to backtrack furiously and laid responsibility for it squarely at the door of the Scotland manager. This was frankly incredible given that it was the SFA CEO himself who spoke out, barely disguising his distaste at the manager's initial decision not to jettison Ferguson and McGregor from the squad and allow them a place on the subs bench, before stating ominously that he would have to meet with Burley to discuss the situation. Now the media was putting the squeeze on over their "harsh" treatment and the man who is supposed to provide leadership to the rest of Scottish football, squirms like an eel and shifts responsibility onto a subordinate. Somehow I couldn't see a Jock Stein, Bill Shankly or Alex Ferguson dealing with the situation in the same way.

The wave of attacks on George Burley's position as manager of Scotland had been launched, and all of the key people had a particularly bluish hue to them. Kris Boyd later declared himself ready to play for Scotland anytime, provided Burley was not in charge (which didn't stop Darryl Broadfoot's astonishing clamour for Boyd to be Scotland's Player of the Year – Broadfoot would eventually find himself a job at the SFA as Chief Press Officer). Boyd may well have been emboldened by Gordon Smith's statement that a change of manager could bring McGregor and Ferguson back into the fold. Nice one Gordon.

Rangers' behaviour throughout was an exercise in desperate self-interest, with no integrity, respect for the nation or selflessness attached to it whatsoever, contrary to the image portrayed by 99% of the Scottish media. The severity of the initial punishment was designed to convince both players they had no future at the club, to make it easier to sell them both in the summer. When the SFA followed suit, Nosurname realised any prospective buyer would have the leverage of dealing with two ostracised players, then there was the poor performance against Falkirk and suddenly he had cause to think again. The bottom line was, just as in the 'Fixture congestion' farce of 2008, Rangers were acting in naked self interest supported by a pack of hungry media wolves to be set upon anyone who got in their way.

George Burley would lose his job by the end of the year and Gordon Smith would step down not long after citing resistance within the echelons of the game and frustration at lack of progress, rather than his own incompetence. Unlike the former Chief Executive, Burley's track record at Ipswich and Hearts suggests he is a capable football manager with no small measure of ability. No-one can deny that he was ultimately a failure as Scotland manager but you wonder just how much he was hampered by immature petulant players who simply didn't fancy his methods and either stormed off in a huff or went through the motions on the park. Paul Le Guen, another manager with a strong record elsewhere, ran into similar problems in dealing with certain "characters" at Rangers, Barry Ferguson featuring prominently in the downfall of both.

Make no mistake, the Rangers pandering media were after George Burley from the moment Lee McCulloch walked out on his country **before a ball had even been kicked in Scotland's World Cup qualifying campaign**. Rangers PR man Mark Hateley wrote the most poisonous bile about the Scotland manager in his shitey Daily Record column back in November 2008, a full four months before his alleged "mis-management" of tweedle dum and tweedle dee at Cameron House. This came out of a George Burley interview for the Scotland on Sunday on 30/11/2008 –

"Mark Hateley wrote a thing (in the Record) after the Argentina match and made some of the most stupid comments I've ever heard in all my life. He said I was a puppet of the SFA for agreeing to the game. That's just ridiculous. Ridiculous. It's crazy stuff. Very annoying.

"Look, I'm here to be shot down, okay? That's fair enough. The job comes with criticism. That's fine. But when it gets personal – and it has got personal – then I have a problem with it. When my mother and father are reading it, a man who is 84 years old, it's not nice, not nice at all. You've asked me about it and there you have it. But that's life, isn't it? If anything, that stuff just makes me stronger."

What Hateley said was this...

"Who the hell does he (Burley) think he is kidding? It seems to me as if, rather than work on the shape and formation he'll need to employ in Holland, Burley attempted to appease the fans (against Argentina) by going on the attack. That is another major sign of weakness."

And this...

"Honestly, this was a ludicrous fixture to take on and it worries me that Burley wasn't strong enough to stand up for himself and tell Gordon Smith and George Peat where to shove it. In fact, it makes me question why this pair appointed such a soft touch in the first place."

And not forgetting this…

"It strikes me now they (the SFA) shirked confrontation when they turned (Graeme) Souness down for the job. And they went for a man who could be manipulated instead. That is a dereliction of duty."

The column was illustrated by an image of Burley as a puppet being dangled on the end of his chief executive's strings. It was barmy stuff, utterly ludicrous, completely lacking in any logic. More than any other title in this country the Record has gone for Burley's jugular and it's been nasty at times.

"The Record's sports editor left me a message the day after (the Hateley piece) to apologise. What can you do? People write things. A guy (working on the same newspaper) had a go before the Macedonia game. Before we had even started the campaign he was criticising me for the way I speak. Totally personal, totally uncalled for. And before we'd even kicked a ball? What he thought he was doing, I don't know, but it was unfair. I think everybody could see that. There's been other things as well but you move on, you forget about it."

This speaks volumes for the type of person Hateley and his ilk are. Who made Englishman Hateley the authority on the welfare of the Scottish national team anyway?

In the end, hampered by a maelstrom of media negativity, sniping and petulant Rangers players acting unprofessionally or withdrawing altogether, results dictated that Burley had to go. Almost as soon as he was gone we were treated to the sickening sight of the Scottish media following Barry Ferguson around like a group lost little puppies begging him to come back to the international fold. This went on for months with the SFA going for their usual weak-minded limp-wristed approach in the face of being told what to do by the Laptop Loyal. Sadly so to did Craig Levein, who gave the player an open invitation to return, perhaps observing the fate of his predecessor and deciding it would be better to go along with this embarrassing circus than run the gauntlet of media knives before his team had even played a competitive game. Many within the Scottish football establishment obviously feel that the national team doesn't have enough thirty-something defensive, sideways passing midfielders. After Scotland embarrassingly struggled to beat tiny Liechtenstein 2-1 at Hampden Park in September 2010, I took leave of my senses and caught a bit of the Radio Clyde Scoreboard phone-in that night.

Darrell King had the answer to Scotland's problems... "*We should bring back Barry, now that we've got people like Weir, McCulloch and McGregor back*"

Can you spot a theme?

In the course of the all too long 10 minutes I listened to that programme for, the only players who were criticised, by name were... Brown and McManus. Can you spot a theme?

Well, its not as if one of them got Scotland out the shit by scoring a last minute winner was it? And I'm sure King & co were just as critical of Granpaw Weir and Alan Hutton who were at fault for the decisive goal in Scotland's 0-1 loss to Netherlands that eliminated us from World Cup qualifying. Absolutely convinced.

Having had to gulp back the powerful compulsion to vomit, I quickly changed to Radio Scotland only to turn the radio off altogether after being subjected to a panel of Derek Ferguson, Tam Cowan, Craig Paterson and Chick Young, followed by an interview with David Weir. Big Granpaw is one of the few who could give Uncle Walter a run for his money in the fawning stakes, as Chick salivated over his every word and agreed enthusiastically that we should be grateful as a win is a win. Then Dickie Gordon in the studio asked whether Barry should be invited back, to unanimous agreement. Quite how a square passing defensive 32 year old midfielder would have had us banging in the goals past the Alpine minnows was not explained.

But this was typical of what had been going on for months in newspapers and media websites, as we were treated to the incredible sight of a man who has shown a complete and utter lack of professionalism and respect for the Scotland team; a man who insulted the supporters and the media with obscene gestures, lording it over the media and coming out with statements like, he would give it some thought even after the lack of respect **he** was shown by the SFA, but we will all have to wait to see how he feels. Spoilt child syndrome right enough. Ferguson should have been hunted out of the Scotland set-up at the first opportunity after the drinking debacle with his equally half-witted pal following him. End of story.

The "Ridiculous" Case of Madjid Bougherra

I touched on the "ridiculous" case of Madjid Bougherra earlier when I talked about Scott McDonald and Glenn Looven's treatment at the hands of the debacle that is the SFA Disciplinary Panel. You will recall that in May 2009, in Rangers' penultimate game of the season at home to Aberdeen, Bougherra slid in dangerously on goalkeeper Jamie Langfield, kicking him in the head and in the process earning a straight red card from referee Stuart Dougal. Although it was unclear whether there was malice involved it was an open and shut case of violent conduct leading to an automatic sending off, and initial reports on TV and radio reported it as such, with more priority given by the media to damage limitation of the Kyle Lafferty cheating show. However, as is so often the case, a post match interview with the Man with Nosurname changed that line almost immediately. After his interview on BBC Radio Scotland, talk quickly turned to the question of whether Rangers would appeal, more as a stalling tactic to allow Bougherra to play in the last decisive game of the season at Tannadice than anything else. Nosurname's words are very revealing with the hindsight of subsequent events:

*"According to our lads **nothing will happen until next season which is obviously not much good to anybody**.*

*"But whatever happens **it was an incredible sending off**. I have seen both red cards and first of all I have to say I was disappointed with my own player's reaction.*

*"I didn't think there was any great contact at all and I will need to have words with Kyle. **But the second sending off is incredible.** The linesman told me it was for deliberately kicking the goalkeeper in the head **which I find incredible**. It meant we lost a player for the majority of the **game for a circumstance that was not the case.**"*

There are several telling things that arise from this statement. First off, is the obvious conclusion that among his many other super powers of dignity and wisdom, Nosurname has the ability to read people's minds and therefore ascertain whether specific acts were committed deliberately or not.

Of course, the Laptop Loyal sprang into action immediately and that evening's radio shows began to – incredibly – talk of Stuart Dougal's decision as being a bit harsh. They began to make a big deal over the question of intent and claimed to be endowed with the same psychic powers as the Man with Nosurname, discounting the possibility that this was in any way a deliberate act. Less than an hour after the incident and already the Radio Snide/Radio Scotland arm of the Laptop Loyal were meticulously putting together a case for the defence a Philadelphia lawyer would have been proud of. Well, I say meticulously, but that was kind of undermined by the fact that these "experts" were either blissfully or willfully, ignorant of the laws of the game. Let's see what the FIFA Laws of the Game have to say about violent conduct and the question of intent:

Page 35 of **FIFA's Laws of the Game** list "Serious foul play" as a sending off offence in its own right.

Page 118 goes on to give FIFA's definition of serious foul play –

"A player is guilty of serious foul play if he uses **excessive force** *or brutality against an opponent* **when challenging for the ball** *when it is in play. A tackle that* **endangers the safety of an opponent must be sanctioned as serious foul play**.

Any player who **lunges at an opponent in challenging for the ball** *from the front, from the side or from behind using* **one** *or both legs,* **with excessive force and endangering the safety of an opponent** *is* **guilty of serious foul play**.

A player who is guilty of serious foul play **should be sent off** *and play restarted with a direct free-kick from the position where the offence occurred or a penalty kick.*

The laws are very clear then – a player who **lunges** at an opponent with **excessive force** therefore **endangering his safety** is guilty of serious foul play, and as such should be ordered from the field. Nothing, nada, zilch and zero about the question of whether such excessive force was intentional.

However, the media had settled on the "intent" defence and they were sticking to it regardless of what petty details like the laws of the game had to say about it. Not only that, but the written press immediately latched onto Nosurname's use of the word "incredible" and quoted it almost without exception when referring to the incident. Darrell King wrote a piece describing Dougal's decision as "incredible" in a tone that would have made you think this was the greatest refereeing injustice since the McCurry show the year before. If this had the effect of giving the impression to some naive souls that all these honest mistakes were "evening themselves out" then so much the better. Over the space of two days the media line ramped up from "Rangers might appeal to allow him to play next week" to "Well it was a bit harsh because he didnae really mean it" to describing the whole thing as "incredible" and confidently stating that the decision would be rescinded.

As previously mentioned, a key plank of Rangers' and the media's erroneous argument (as the two were barely distinguishable), was the question of intent, as illustrated in the works of propaganda over the page, which appeared in the Scottish press over the two or three days following the incident. Note that the press were at great pains to avoid the use of terms such as "kicked" instead *"catching* or *" clashed"* and *"collided"* were used, which imply an accidental coming together of two bodies with neither party more at fault than the other. They also paint a vivid picture of *"stunned"* team-mates and impassioned pleas for justice. They even dragged out Jamie Langfield to repeat the flawed "no intent" defence and triumphantly announced to the world that even the Aberdeen goalkeeper agreed that Bougherra shouldn't have been sent off. This was based on the quote *"I'm not sure if it was a sending-off"*. Hmmmmmm, not quite the same as *"he still* believes the Rangers defender should not have been sent off" as up and coming Laptop Loyalist Scott McDermott enthusiastically trumpeted in the Daily Record. In fact Langfield's full comment could suggest exactly the opposite if the Aberdeen goalkeeper was employing a touch of sarcasm which seems likely – *"I'm not sure if it was a sending-off or if it was deliberate. **I was too busy lying on the deck with stud marks on my neck**"*. Of course I'm paranoid, but I'll go with the sarcasm interpretation.

Evening Times

By MATTHEW LINDSAY

"*STEVEN WHITTAKER today appealed to assistant referee Graham Chambers to hand Rangers centre-half Madjid Bougherra the chance to play against Dundee United.*

*The Gers right-back **was stunned** when Chambers advised referee Stuart Dougal to send Bougherra off against Aberdeen at Ibrox on Saturday. The Algerian defender **collided** with Dons keeper Jamie Langfield as he challenged for his team-mate's through ball.*

However, Whittaker reckons it was a "fair" challenge and is hoping Chambers tells the SFA he got it wrong and gives Bougherra the go-ahead to be involved at Tannadice on Sunday. Walter Smith's side can win their first title in four years if they beat Craig Levein's men.

*Whittaker said: "I passed the ball to Madjid. I just tried to slip it through the defence and he made a good run through the back and tried to go for the ball. I don't know what the linesman saw, but he obviously saw Madjid following through. **It looked pretty honest to me**, but they have obviously seen it differently.*

*"Hopefully, we can get the decision overturned because Madjid is a big player for us and **it will help our cause if he is available to play against United.**" "*

So Steven Whittaker was "stunned" to see a team-mate sent off for kicking an opponent in the head was he? Not as stunned as Jamie Langfield I'll wager. Quite how Lindsay works out that Whittaker was stunned anyway is not decipherable from the quotes attributed to the player, which are pretty much what you'd expect from any player backing up a team-mate in that situation.

Not only was Whittaker "*stunned*", but Kenny Miller was "*astonished*" at the sending off, according to this priceless piece of pish on the Rangers website which was widely copied and pasted into the pages of our esteemed red tops. So much for investigative journalism. Note that the door is always open throughout the Scottish media for Rangers players to queue up and express their "stunned" astonishment at ostensibly routine refereeing decisions; free from accusations of paranoia, sinister attempts to influence referees, or of making explosive statements that "pour fuel" on the fire. Of course, as we will see later, when Celtic players or officials take issue with refereeing decisions the Scottish media don't quite see it the same way.

Madjid 'Not Guilty'

by Lindsay Herron

KENNY MILLER has called on Scotland's football authorities to rescind the red card handed out to Madjid Bougherra in today's explosive 2-1 win over Aberdeen.

The Rangers striker was **astonished** when Stuart Dougal, on the advice of assistant Graham Chambers, sent off Bougherra for **catching** Aberdeen goalkeeper Jamie Langfield on the head.

Now he hopes that the Light Blues appeal the decision and the Algerian defender is free to play in next Sunday's final SPL game of the season against Dundee United at Tannadice.

Miller was involved in a similar incident with Langfield earlier this season **which left the Dons keeper in a far worse situation and no action was taken**. So he is hoping that the authorities will look at the incident for what it was and exonerate Bougherra.

Miller told rangers.co.uk: **"I remember I nearly took big Jamie's head off at Pittodrie earlier in the season when I was going for a ball. I think I burst his lip and nose but I didn't even get booked for it.**

"I was talking to Scott Severin after the game and he said it wasn't even worth a booking."

"It was a coming together of two bodies. We know Madjid and he is not the type of player who would go in to deliberately hurt someone."

"Hopefully we will put in an appeal and succeed with that appeal. **The linesman was further away from the situation than the referee was so I don't know how he could get a better view than the referee or any of the players who were in there.**"

To borrow a phrase from the Man with Nosurname – this is incredible. The party line from the Establishment club is that since they are allowed to run about booting the opposition with impunity, why should this instance be any different?

Of course with the press handing over practically all column inches to Rangers players pleading for their buddy to be let off, and the remainder to lickspittles echoing these sentiments and confidently announcing that the suspension would be rescinded several days in advance of the appeal actually being heard, it was hardly a surprise when the inevitable was announced.

Daily Record

By KEITH JACKSON

"MADJID BOUGHERRA last night thanked ref Stuart Dougal for sparing him from a second successive helping of big-game heartache.

The Rangers defender, who missed the Co-op Cup Final through injury, **has been cleared** to take his place in Sunday's thrilling climax to the SPL title race.

Dougal confirmed yesterday he shouldn't have been red-carded following a clash with Aberdeen keeper Jamie Langfield on Saturday.

Rangers hope they will have Bougherra for their crucial match against Dundee United.

He was sent off for **sliding into** Jamie Langfield. It had been thought Dougal sent him off for the challenge but, according to Chambers, his crime was kicking out at the keeper's head as they lay on the turf.

Rangers hope Chambers will review the incident after they appeal to the SFA today. **If he changes his mind or believes there could be some doubt over intent** the incident will go to the SFA's review panel. They will sit before Sunday and **there is a good chance** they will cut the punishment to a yellow and let Bougherra play at Tannadice.

Dougal said in a statement last night: "Upon returning home I reviewed the Mulgrew and Lafferty incident.

"My views on it have since been emailed to the SFA, the contents of which must remain private until they've had time to consider them.

"Like most people in the ground I was convinced Lafferty had been the victim of violent conduct. I have now seen what others have seen and this will form the basis of my report to the SFA.

"With regard to the Bougherra incident, the assistant referee will review his decision if requested." "

Keith "Jangle" Jackson is all over the place with this piece. Clearly Jacksie is privy to information the rest of us are not, which does not exactly inspire confidence in the probity of the whole appeals process. Jacksie begins by adamantly stating that Bougherra has been "*cleared*", then about halfway through this morphs into a "*good chance*" that he'll be cleared, before eventually revealing that all of this depends upon the assistant referee Graham Chambers agreeing to rescind the original decision. No doubt Jacksie was operating on the same assumption as all us paranoid chaps, namely that the good wee assistant referee would do what he was expected of him.

Daily Record

By SCOTT MCDERMOTT

"*ABERDEEN keeper Jamie Langfield has the stud marks to prove Madjid Bougherra caught him with a flying boot - but still believes the Rangers defender should not have been sent off.*

Langfield was at the centre of controversy yesterday as he went down under a late challenge from Bougherra during his side's 2-1 defeat.

*The Ibrox stopper was **harshly** ordered off by referee Stuart Dougal on the advice of linesman Graham Chambers and will now miss next week's crunch clash against Dundee United at Tannadice.*

*Although Langfield bears the scars from the challenge **he does not believe there was any malice** in Bougherra's slide tackle.*

He said: "I've clearly been caught by Bougherra but I only had eyes on the ball which was there to be won. I think he was going for the ball as well.

"I'm not sure if it was a sending-off or if it was deliberate. I was too busy lying on the deck with stud marks on my neck." "

All three articles refer to intent in some shape or form as a justification for overturning the original decision. This is completely fallacious and it seems to confirm that no-one in our esteemed Scottish media, choc to the brim as it is with ex(mostly Rangers)-players and other assorted "experts", actually know the rules of the game they make a living reporting on.

On the evening of Tuesday 19 May 2009 it was reported (very briefly funnily enough) on BBC Scotland News that Bougherra would be available for selection for Rangers' last game of the season the following Sunday. Begs the question – if a decision is not being made on the matter until Friday – why is it common knowledge on the Tuesday that Bougherra's red card will be rescinded? If the assistant referee and subsequently the SFA Review Panel's decision is a formality, why bother with the charade? We're left with the impression that the Scottish media simply don't care how dubious this all looks to objective onlookers.

There is one final point of note which requires us to return to the Man with Nosurname's initial statement on the matter – "*According to our lads nothing will happen until next season which is obviously not much good to anybody*". Certainly not much good to the Establishment club anyway.

Now, most of you won't need reminded that it took several **months** for Glenn Loovens' appeal of a suspension handed down by the same Review panel for "catching" Maurice Edu with his studs to be heard. This incident happened the week **before** Bougherra's red card, yet the Review Panel was miraculously able to convene with indecent haste in order to exonerate… sorry… give due consideration to… the Rangers player's appeal. In another interesting twist, Loovens' appeal failed, presumably in the absence of anyone from Celtic FC or the media possessing the psychic powers necessary to testify on oath that the player's actions were unintentional, unlike the Bougherra case. I guess Celtic will just need to try harder with those MI5 and CIA contacts.

So again, it's a case of the Man with Nosurname sending out the word that this needs to happen ASAP and his media lickspittles bursting into action to exert pressure on the SFA; effectively the equivalent of pushing on the proverbial open door, but a bit of propaganda and a charade of an appeals "process" looks good for the public and maintains the club's "dignity".

Remember the context to this – Rangers needed a win in their last game of the season to guarantee the SPL title; an SPL title the importance of which to the very existence of the financially stricken Establishment club could not be underestimated. This was high stakes stuff.

In a final poetic twist to the story it was revealed that Stuart Dougal had planned to see out the season, and his refereeing career, with a wee after-dinner speaking slot in a Larkhall Masonic Lodge on the very evening that the SPL title race would be concluded – another one of these little gems that you need to be totally paranoid to read anything into. With the ensuing publicity around this and the Bougherra appeal, Dougal decided to hang up his whistle and apron early, parting with an indignant statement for the benefit of the media and all of us paranoid nuts – "*I wish the organisers every success for the night and have a simple message to the people who feel the need to always look for bias and conspiracy. It is 2009 and I thought that we had moved away from this type of thing*". The sheer irony of that last sentence is surely lost on Mr Dougal.

To finish off, let's have a look at how all SPL teams got on with red card appeals over season 2008/09. Once again reference to FIFA's laws regarding serious foul play seem particularly relevant to the Bougherra case:

(From SFA website):

St Mirren Sending Off Appeal Dismissed
Tuesday, 12 August 2008

St Mirren's appeal against the sending off of their player Will Haining in this weekend's match against Celtic has been dismissed. In accordance with the appeals process, the match referee Eddie Smith reviewed the incident and is content with his original decision to award a penalty and send the player off. Consequently the player will be subject to a one match ban.

Aberdeen Claim Dismissed
Thursday, 09 October 2008

Aberdeen FC's Claim of Wrongful Dismissal in respect of the sending off of its player Charles Mulgrew in the match against Hibernian FC on 4th October has been dismissed, following a review by referee Michael McCurry. The player had been sent off for denying the opposing team or an opponent a goal or obvious goal scoring opportunity as defined by Law 12.

Heart of Midlothian's Claim Dismissed
Tuesday, 30 December 2008

Heart of Midlothian's claim of wrongful dismissal in respect of the sending off of their player Marius Zaliukas in the match against Aberdeen has been dismissed, following a review by referee Iain Brines. Zaliukas is therefore suspended for Heart of Midlothian's next match against Hibernian on 3 January.

Falkirk Appeal Dismissed
Wednesday, 21 January 2009

Falkirk FC's Claim of Wrongful Dismissal in respect of the sending off of its player Patrick Cregg in the match against Rangers FC on 17th January has been dismissed, following a review by referee William Collum.

In explanation of the referee's decision, the following definition of serious foul play as detailed in the FIFA Laws of the Game is provided:

"Any player who lunges at an opponent in challenging for the ball from the front, from the side or from behind using one or both legs, with excessive force and endangering the safety of an opponent is guilty of serious foul play."

Hibernian FC's Claim Dismissed
Wednesday, 06 May 2009

Hibernian FC's Claim of Wrongful Dismissal in respect of the sending off of its player Chris Hogg in the match against Dundee United FC on 2nd May has been dismissed, following a review by referee Stevie O'Reilly.

In explanation of the referee's decision, the following definition of serious foul play as detailed in the FIFA Laws of the Game is provided:

"Any player who lunges at an opponent in challenging for the ball from the front, from the side or from behind using one or both legs, with excessive force and endangering the safety of an opponent is guilty of serious foul play."

Accies fail with McArthur Appeal
12 May 2009

Hamilton Accies have failed in their appeal against the red card shown to James McArthur during Sunday's 1-1 league draw with Inverness. The midfielder was sent off by referee Charlie Richmond following a 66th-minute challenge on Filipe Morais. Richmond said he was happy with his decision *after reviewing footage of the incident.*

McArthur will now sit out Wednesday's Scottish Premier League clash against Falkirk at New Douglas Park. Hamilton manager Billy Reid claimed the dismissal was "really, really harsh".

Pressley loses appeal
17 May 2009

Falkirk have lost their appeal against the red card shown to Steven Pressley during the weekend defeat by St Mirren. It means that the veteran defender will be suspended for Saturday's final game of the season away to Inverness Caledonian Thistle. Referee Chris Boyle reviewed the decision but decided that he was content with the sending off.

Falkirk had insisted that Pressley had clashed heads with Billy Mahomet and had not used an elbow. But, with their claim of wrongful dismissal being rejected, it means that Pressley will miss a game Falkirk must win to avoid relegation from the Scottish Premier League.

Rangers FC Appeal Referred to Review Panel
Wednesday, 21 January 2009

Rangers FC's Claim of Wrongful Dismissal in respect of the sending off of its player Sasa Papac in the match against Falkirk FC on 17th January is being referred to the Review Panel for consideration, following a review by referee William Collum.

Having reviewed the circumstances of the player's sending off, the referee accepted that an error had been made and that the player had not been guilty of serious foul play.

The suspensions incurred by the player as a result of the sending off have therefore been revoked and the player is free to play in the club's next match against Aberdeen FC this Saturday. *It was decided that the claim be upheld to the extent that the offence be reduced to a caution.*

SFA Reviews Ibrox Red Cards
18 May 2009

Rangers' Madjid Bougherra and Aberdeen's Charlie Mulgrew have won the first stage of their appeals against red cards they received on Saturday. Stuart Dougal viewed footage of the match, which Rangers won 2-1 at Ibrox and he decided that Bougherra did not deserve to be sent off for violent conduct against keeper Jamie Langfield. It will now be up to the review panel, which will meet on Friday morning, to decide what action, if any, should be taken against the players.

*But both Bougherra and Mulgrew **appear likely to be cleared to play in Sunday's climax to the Scottish Premier League season**.*

At the end of season 2008/09, the SFA withdrew their Whistleblower website which sought to explain decisions on match incidents and disciplinary matters for some reason that, for the life of me, I can't work out. Anyway, the Loovens case was not heard until well into the following season with the predictable outcome:

Celtic Defender Loses Red Card Appeal

16 October 2009

Celtic defender Glenn Loovens has lost his appeal against a one-match ban for his clash with Rangers midfielder Maurice Edu during the final Old Firm derby of last season.

Loovens, 25, was suspended by the Scottish Football Association's disciplinary committee after they reviewed footage of the May 9 incident at Ibrox - which appeared to show the Holland international flicking a boot at Edu.

He was punished with a one-match ban and had 12 points added to his 2008-09 disciplinary points total for "misconduct of a significantly serious nature". He appealed against the decision but has lost that verdict and will now miss Saturday's Premier League game against Motherwell.

Loovens' case has exposed serious flaws in the SFA's disciplinary process. Despite his clash with Edu taking place more than five months ago, he was not found guilty until the disciplinary committee met on August 7.

*His appeal freed him to play in injury-hit Celtic's opening SPL game of the season at Aberdeen and **it has taken the SFA more than two months to reconvene on the matter**.*

Yet the SFA were able to convene this panel in a matter of **days** to exonerate Madjid Bougherra and allow him to play in Rangers' last day title-deciding game of season 2008/09.

A summary of those red card stats for season 2008/09:

Aberdeen	50% (1/2)
Celtic	0% (0/1)
Falkirk	0% (0/2)
Hamilton	0% (0/1)
Hearts	0% (0/1)
Hibernian	0% (0/1)
Rangers	**100% (2/2)**

So the only appeal throughout the whole of 2008/09 season that was successful – other than those made by the Establishment club of course – was the Charlie Mulgrew appeal in the case of the outrageous Lafferty cheating, over which the Review Panel really had no alternative than to admonish the player. This can therefore be considered a statistical anomaly. Effectively no SPL club other than Rangers were granted a reprieve, yet Rangers themselves were successful in **100%** of their submissions to the Review Panel.

In addition Scott McDonald and Glenn Loovens were the **only** players over the whole season to be referred to the Review Panel after a match **for the purpose of imposing a retrospective sanction**. Are they saying that those two incidents were **the only two in the entire season** that were worthy of punishment but missed by the referee?

SPL referees are very good if that is the case. Another happy coincidence is that the only two players referred to the panel just happened to be Celtic players. Not only that, but these two incidents just happened to occur in the month of May, slap bang in the middle of a very close title run-in. But of course you'd have to be paranoid to read anything into these statistics. Now if anyone from the "Old Firm conspiracy/bias" crowd can explain this to me as anything other than Rangers bias I'm all ears.

Straw Man v Iron Man

A common, centuries old tactic, employed by propagandists across all professions and walks of life, is to create a caricature of an opposing viewpoint or person which can easily be dismantled or discredited, allowing the propagandist to triumphantly boast that his or her argument has prevailed as the only true and logical way of understanding things. This caricature is known as the "Straw Man". The definition of the "Straw Man" technique is:

A straw man argument is an informal fallacy based on misrepresentation of an opponent's position. To "attack a straw man" is to create the illusion of having refuted a proposition by substituting a superficially similar yet unequivalent proposition (the "straw man"), and refuting it, without ever having actually refuted the original position.

The straw man fallacy occurs in the following pattern of argument:

Person A holds position X.

Person B disregards certain key points of X and instead presents the superficially-similar position Y. Thus, **Y** is a resulting distorted version of **X** and can be set up in several ways, including:

1. Presenting a misrepresentation of the opponent's position and then refuting it, thus giving the appearance that the opponent's actual position has been refuted.

2. Quoting an opponent's words out of context – i.e. choosing quotations that misrepresent the opponent's actual intentions

3. Presenting someone who defends a position poorly as the defender, then refuting that person's arguments – thus giving the appearance that every upholder of that position (and thus the position itself) has been defeated.

4. Inventing a fictitious persona with actions or beliefs which are then criticised, implying that the person represents a group of whom the speaker is critical.

5. Oversimplifying an opponent's argument, then attacking this oversimplified version.

Person B attacks position Y, concluding that X is false/incorrect/flawed.

This sort of "reasoning" is **fallacious**, because attacking a **distorted** version of a position **fails** to constitute an attack on the **actual position**.

This is all a bit abstract, so I will attempt to introduce a tangible dimension for the reader by providing more familiar examples of each of the above that I have concocted from my fevered imagination. I must emphasise that these examples are completely hypothetical and in no way based on reality:

1. *Celtic fans think the SFA, Rangers and referees are having secret meetings in darkened smoky rooms in Masonic Lodges all over Scotland as part of a giant conspiracy to formulate a plan to cheat Celtic and ensure Rangers win the SPL title.* [This is plainly nonsense. I mean Celtic got a penalty against St Mirren four months ago, and they also got two goals against Hearts that weren't disallowed for offside. OK, they weren't offside but they were a bit borderline so really should have been disallowed. Celtic should shut up and be grateful that we didn't disallow their two legitimate goals against Hearts, and by the way, Pat McCourt was in an offside position by the time he'd gone past three opponents and put that 3rd goal into the net.]

2. *A player questions how a referee can be "impartial" when reviewing his own decision as part of an appeals process. The media leap on this and portray it as the player launching a paranoid attack against the impartiality of the referee towards his club in general and call for the player to be punished, when in fact the player is actually questioning the process not the referee.*

3. *Filtering out callers with coherent and lucid arguments on your tabloid radio phone-in show in favour of semi-literate drunks. Playing X-Files theme music once the rambling caller has hung up/been cut off is a nice added touch.*

4. *Closely related to 3. above, Celtic manager jeered by a handful of fans following a catastrophic defeat in his first competitive match in a Champions League qualifier. The media leap to his defence in the face of "over the top" criticism and start kite flying about "large sections" of Celtic fans refusing to accept the new manager as he is not "Celtic-minded", whilst at the very same time lauding the "dream team" of the Man with Nosurname and Super Sally for being "steeped in the traditions of the club". All Celtic fans portrayed as "bead-rattling" bigots who won't accept a manager who's not "Celtic-minded".* [It's a little known fact that Wim Jansen and Dr Jo Venglos were avid Celtic fans as they grew up on the streets of Rotterdam and Bratislava respectively].

5. *Closely related to 1. above, Celtic fans think the SFA and referees are all masons who are out to get them. This is utter garbage. Thomas Murphy isn't a mason.*

Although this is a widely recognised and documented propaganda technique, it's likely that few among the Laptop Loyal actually realise this is what they are doing; it's simply a natural product of years of editorial hostility to Celtic having become ingrained in the Scottish media psyche. No need for any conspiratorial meetings in darkened, smoky rooms, it just comes naturally. After all, if I was suddenly asked to referee a Celtic-Rangers match I wouldn't need any instruction from a third party as some sort of co-ordinated conspiracy to give Celtic the benefit of all the 50-50 decisions and an outrageous penalty, it would just come naturally.

The hypothetical [cough] examples I outlined are the more glaring ones. However Celtic "Straw Men" are constructed in the media every day, through the use of subtle and not so subtle use of language that portrays the club as a group of irrational madmen who can't, or won't, accept their just desserts. Consider the press reports that emerged following the Dougie McDonald show of 28th February 2010 where Celtic were defeated 1-0 by Rangers in, shall we say, "controversial" circumstances.

You will recall that in this game, Celtic were denied a clear penalty for a foul on Diomansy Kamara in the penalty area, Marc Antoine Fortune was booked for an innocuous handball early in the game, and after receiving a yellow card in the opening minutes, Madjid Bougherra was permitted to commit a further seven fouls without censure. However the most controversial moment of the match occurred midway through the second half when referee Dougie McDonald incredibly sent off Celtic's Scott Brown for a "handbags" clash with Rangers' Kyle Lafferty. Lafferty was the initial aggressor, grabbing Brown by the neck and then performing some sort of WWE wrestling hold on him. Brown responded by trying to free himself by pushing Lafferty and his momentum carried him forward into his opponent. There was a slight forward motion of Brown's head that appeared to make the merest of contact with Lafferty's **chest** causing the Rangers player to collapse spectacularly to the ground clutching his **face**. On this occasion Lafferty stopped short of checking his nose for imaginary blood.

After the game Celtic released an official statement through the club's website:

"Celtic will appeal the red card given to Scott Brown during the derby clash with Rangers at Ibrox. Referee Dougie McDonald sent off the Celtic captain following a tangle with Kyle Lafferty, with the Rangers player unpunished for his part in the incident.

"It immediately seemed to be a controversial decision to everyone in the ground and certainly any fair-minded person looking at the incident at the time or subsequent TV replays could see it wasn't a red card.

"It was a decision which had a major impact on the game and Celtic will now appeal against the red card, which saw Tony Mowbray's side down to 10 men for the last half-hour of the game.

"Certainly, the Celtic support in the Broomloan Road Stand and beyond were left mystified and angry at yet another refereeing decision in a derby game this season which has gone against the club.

"In the first derby match of this season at Ibrox in October, Celtic were denied a blatant penalty by referee Craig Thomson, who admitted after the game that he had made a mistake.

"And in the game against Rangers at Celtic Park, referee Steve Conroy disallowed a Marc-Antoine Fortune goal, though replays showed that there was nothing wrong

"Now, Dougie McDonald's decision is added to that list and will be the major talking point from the game."

This was a fairly restrained and carefully worded statement, certainly far more reserved than the words most Celtic fans would have chosen. The statement merely points out that for the third time in games against Rangers that season, Celtic had been disadvantaged by an undeniable refereeing mistake. The statement also points out that the Rangers player involved in the most recent incident was unpunished for his part in proceedings and that this incident will be the major talking point from the game. All points made in the statement are factually correct and made without recourse to emotive language. The club could also have mentioned the remarkable leeway the referee McDonald extended to Madjid Bougherra, but no doubt the club wanted to maintain a tone of understatement to avoid accusations of paranoia. They needn't have bothered. The media set to work creating the latest in a long line of hysterical and mentally unbalanced Straw Men for them to go to town on. Again, key elements of spin have been highlighted in bold:

Daily Record

By NEIL CAMERON

SEETHING Celtic last night **accused** the SFA of blundering four times over Scott Brown's Old Firm red card after his appeal was thrown out. The club were "amazed" they will now lose their captain for three matches as they at least attempt to close the gap on Rangers. And **Parkhead bosses refuse to accept that justice has been done**.

But Record Sport understands **the only regret** McDonald has about last weekend's Ibrox game, which Rangers won 1-0, was that Kyle Lafferty was not booked for his part in the game's most controversial incident.

The **experienced official** was satisfied with his overall handling of the game after watching it again and happy with the other decisions he made.

We understand Brown's appeal was doomed because he moved his head towards the Rangers player, deemed **excessive force** and a red card, despite "only" hitting Lafferty in the chest.

The 24-year-old midfielder will now miss three SPL games for his club **who are furious** about an **affair** that was never going to go away even after the final decision yesterday.

Daily Record

By CRAIG SWAN

FURIOUS Celtic last night **slapped in** an appeal to clear Scott Brown of his Old Firm red card. Referee Dougie McDonald red-carded Brown midway through the second period after a clash with Rangers midfielder Kyle Lafferty.

So after two short Daily Record articles we are presented with a picture of a "*furious*", "*seething*" club, clearly not in a rational frame of mind to be presenting reasoned opinion, "*refusing to accept justice has been done*", "*slapping in*" a – by implication – spurious appeal against an "*experienced*" official who was merely following the letter of the law by sending of Brown for use of "*excessive force*", and whose only regret is that he didn't book Lafferty. Note also the sarcastic use of quotation marks around the word 'only' in reference to Brown's head movement.

Note also that the journalist emphasises that McDonald is an "*experienced official*", in contrast to ranting raving irrational Celtic. Certainly McDonald is extremely experienced at making honest mistakes that hamper Celtic. This is an impressive piece of propaganda, and there was a veritable tsunami of derisive hyperbole yet to come from the media, and the Daily Record in particular. Keith "Union" Jackson was on top form:

Daily Record

By KEITH JACKSON

SFA set to throw the book at Celtic over Scott Brown red card web claims

CELTIC'S **bitter feud** with the SFA took a fresh twist last night when it emerged the Parkhead club could be **dragged into the Hampden dock** for **their latest attack** on a referee.

An official club statement which **appeared to call into question the impartiality** of big-match whistler Dougie McDonald was released on the internet hours after Tony Mowbray's side went down to a 1-0 defeat in the Old Firm derby at Ibrox.

The **explosive** wording of the statement - which revealed Celtic's intention to appeal against Scott Brown's red card - has angered the game's hierarchy and the matter was yesterday referred to the General Purposes Committee who will now convene to decide whether or not to take action.

But already it has **poured fresh fuel** on what was a combustible situation between the game's hierarchy and the powers that be at Celtic Park.

Now we have the "*furious*" and "*seething*" club, pouring "*fresh fuel*" onto the already combustible situation, by using "*explosive*" wording to "*attack*" (the latest of many according to Union Jackson) the "*impartiality*" of the referee. Jackson goes on to quote the statement from Celtic's website in full which reveals that no reference to the referee's impartiality is used at any stage, far less questioning it; and if there is any word within it that could accurately be termed "explosive", I will have to update my thesaurus. But this is merely the opening salvo from a Rangers lickspittle furiously defending his own kind:

Daily Record

By KEITH JACKSON

WHAT we needed yesterday at Ibrox was an Old Firm game that would be remembered forever for the football.

*What we got was 90 minutes that would have been instantly forgettable were it not for the decisions made by a referee **whose job was made almost impossible even before a ball had been kicked**.*

Already we have Jackson bemoaning the farce of refereeing that unfolded that February afternoon and placing the blame firmly on **Celtic's** shoulders. Here we have another example of the psychedelic world of Murray lickspittle doublethink – McDonald's mistakes were purely a result of the intolerable pressure placed on the man by the sinister machinations of Celtic before the game. If this is genuinely the case, then it defies logic that without exception, **every** mistake McDonald made in the game went **against** Celtic. Surely logic dictates that if these errors were a result of pressure exerted by Celtic, leaving the poor man cowering with fear at the prospect of displeasing us, at the very least, **some** of his "honest mistakes" would have gone in Celtic's **favour**?

No, in the hallucinogenic mind of the Scottish media, Celtic managed to pressurise an experienced referee into giving a string of incorrect decisions **against** them. Jackson and the rest of the Laptop Loyal also ride roughshod over the fact that Celtic's concerns were entirely justified, having been on the wrong end of a series of glaring refereeing errors over the season, including – but not limited to – two obvious mistakes in fixtures against Rangers, in one instance, prompting a public apology from the official concerned (Craig Thomson). No, Jackson would rather miss that bit out and paint it as a cross between raving paranoia and cynical manipulation.

*And Mowbray must be man enough to shoulder the responsibility for that instead of following the party line and pandering to those who wish to point to other more **sinister reasons** for the failings of his side – **like big match ref McDonald**, for example.*

Where Jackson uses the term "*sinister*" to evoke images of unseen forces gathering in murky, dimly lit rooms, I, and many others, would simply use the term "obvious". But this is the Orwellian world of the febrile Rangers apologist so "*sinister*" it is. Of course, Dougie McDonald's glaring errors had absolutely no bearing on the match result at all did they? It would be sheer mental paranoia to suggest otherwise.

*The man in the middle was on a hiding to nothing from the minute **Celtic chose to plant a story** about their **"concern"** over the current standard of Scotland's **men in black**.*

I'm terribly sorry, but I would have to take issue with the assertion that McDonald was on a "*hiding to nothing*". This may be a far-out, revolutionary concept for such a big Rangers man as Jacko, especially considering the way these "honest mistakes" usually pan out, but there *is* the option of the referee getting all of the key decisions correct is there not? Surely then there would be no need for any "hidings" to be dispensed, or furious defences of your brethren in black to be penned. Sorry, I know I'm being totally ridiculous now. Carry on…

*At the other end Madjid Bougherra went into the book soon after for chopping into Keane from behind but although there were still 85 minutes on the clock the Algerian – to the **disgust** of Celtic's supporters – managed to avoid picking up a second yellow.*

How many fouls was it Boughie committed Jacksie? Did I hear you say "seven"? No? Does that wee detail not fit in with the tone of your piece or your biased agenda?

*Bougherra and Davie Weir formed a rock-solid foundation for this latest smash-and-grab win and – just to stick a flame under Celtic's **simmering resentment** – it was the defender who came loping forward in the dying seconds to play a huge part in Edu's decisive goal.*

*But first the American would feel some **injustice of his own** just moments after replacing Lee McCulloch who had hobbled off midway through a fairly lethargic and limp-wristed first half. Edu thought he had hit a stunning opener with his first kick when, after Celtic's defence had failed to deal with a Steve Davis free-kick, he smashed his foot through the ball from 20 yards out and sent it crashing in off of Boruc's left-hand post. But that man McDonald stepped in to chalk it off after spotting Kenny Miller **handle the ball***

Ah, the old "evening itself out" insinuation. Of course correctly disallowing a goal for handball is just as bad as wrongly sending a player off isn't it? Another detail to note is that Celtic's Marc Antoine Fortune was booked for handball but presumably there's something in the rulebook stating that the bookable offence criteria for players in blue jerseys is different.

*Celtic **hollered** for a penalty when Diomansy Kamara – another earner who failed to perform – **went under** a Bougherra challenge.*

*They [Rangers] were **denied** their penalty in the opening minutes of the second half when Edu **was brought down** by Andreas Hinkel.*

Celtic "*holler*" desperately for a penalty when Kamara "*goes under*" a Bougherra challenge, an ambiguous term that suggests it could possibly be under his own steam. In contrast, Rangers are "*denied*" a penalty when Edu is "*brought down*" leaving no room for doubt or vague terms such as "*went under*". Yet more bias to the "O*d F**m".

Effective as it is in its own right, the Straw Man can often be complemented by building an "Iron Man" antagonist to which he can be unfavourably compared. Already we have a *seething, simmering, hollering,* Machiavellian club, *explosively attacking* an *experienced official*. As part of the propaganda offensive the Laptop Loyal then go on to further augment Dougie McDonald's credentials and character:

Evening Times By ALLISON MCDONALD

Stuart Dougal: Don't blame the referee

*Former referee Stuart Dougal says Dougie McDonald **got all the big decisions right** at Ibrox yesterday.*

*The match referee found himself at the eye of a storm in the build-up to the game, and **was under intense scrutiny throughout the 90 minutes.***

McDonald sent off Scott Brown midway through the second period, a decision Celtic will appeal against. Brown and Kyle Lafferty appeared guilty of a bit of handbags, but Dougal says Brown should have seen red for his part in the act.

One of the biggest grievances Celtic had was why Madjid Bougherra was allowed to stay in the pitch, despite being booked early doors and then continuing to foul throughout the game.

*"**What Dougie would have felt, as I did, was those subsequent fouls were, if you like, small ones.**"*

Hold the presses! Ex-referee in backing up fellow referee shock stunner!! So let's get that FIFA rulebook re-written... "A player shall be cautioned for persistent fouling... only if they're big, bad, nasty fouls". Dougal's mealy mouthed words carry as much credibility as Whittaker and Miller's apparent disbelief at their team-mate Bougherra's plight at the hands of Dougal (funnily enough) the season before. What is the Laptop Loyal's aversion to getting *neutrals* to comment on matters relating to the Establishment club? Stuart Dougal is hardly going to criticise a fellow referee in public. This only happens when a foreign official makes a mistake that leads indirectly to Scotland conceding a last minute goal to Italy, in which case it's perfectly acceptable to throw all sorts of insults at him, including calling him an outright cheat:

"*If it was a player making a terrible decision in a match, he may not play in the next match. UEFA have to ask if he should be in a game like this. He made a horrendous mistake and doesn't deserve to be officiating at a high level*" Alex McLeish (The Sun, 19 November 2007)

"*I hope action is taken against the referee. We've been punished so why should he not be punished?*" Lee McCulloch (Daily Express, 19 November 2007)

"*You would not have seen a decision like that late free-kick on a public park*" George Cumming (The Sun, 19 November 2007)

"*Ethically, what happened at Dumbarton was just not right* [alleged spying on Scotland's training session]. *I'm not sure if there is something In UEFA's rule book which states that this kind of thing is not allowed. But I would be very interested to hear UEFA's views on the matter. I would like to know if there are rules which have been broken and if UEFA believe what the Italians did was a moral or ethical way to behave.*" Gordon Smith (Daily Record, 19 November 2007) "*the foul on Alan Hutton by Giorgio Chiellini was an appalling mistake that could have been described as robbery and cheating. The assistant referee is only yards away from the incident and for the referee not to over-rule him was incredible*" Craig Brown (Daily Record, 19 November 2007)

"*We all accept that officials make honest mistakes. They have to decide instantly on 'is it?' or 'isn't it?' 'Did he or didn't he?'. Jimenez did have these things to consider when he raised his flag. He had to decide whether Alan Hutton had been fouled or not. There was nothing else to consider - but he chose to invent one for himself. In my 30 years of refereeing I've never witnessed such a blatant deliberate error. It was no mistake. The big team were going to get a little help.*" David Syme (The Sun, 19 November 2007)

Yes the – "referees are a bunch of buffoons but accusing them of cheating is a step too far" – principle goes completely out of the window under those circumstances, and quite right too.

Whilst current and former Rangers players, as well as ex-referees, are skilled in calling referees cheats with dignity, Celtic fall well short of the required moral standard. After having the temerity to appeal the referee's error, the club compounded this impertinence by making rational comments on the matter when asked by the press:

Evening Times

By Ronnie Cully 5 March

Celtic fume at appeal failure

*Celtic's **spat** with the game's ruling body looks set to escalate after SFA chief executive Gordon Smith denied there was anything 'political' about the decision not to rescind Scott Brown's red card.*

Aiden McGeady is sure to be called before the General Purposes Committee to explain his comments that referee Dougie McDonald was not impartial in his handling of the game at Ibrox last weekend, during which Brown was sent off after clashing with Kyle Lafferty.

*The club is also **under investigation** for claims on their official website that "any fair-minded person looking at the incident at the time or subsequent TV replays could see it wasn't a red card".*

The Celtic boss said: "Maybe another decision in a massive Old Firm game not to go Celtic's way would be just a little bit too much. If it (the appeal) had been upheld, it would have been proven to be a wrong decision, I think. So maybe the political decision was taken that maybe the right decision had been made."

However, Smith said of Mowbray's assertion that previous refereeing errors had a bearing on the outcome of the appeal: "A political decision? I don't know where that has come from. I have no idea what he means by that. The referee was asked to review his decision and decided he got it right, and that's where we leave it."

Perhaps any "fair-minded" person could have a look at Mowbray's comments and explain where this hack got the world "fume" from? If not, I'll just have to stick with the obvious conclusion that it's merely a continuation of the ongoing character assassination of all connected with Celtic and smoke and mirrors to distract from the logic of any statement made by the club. What's that you say – logic? Why, yes, for although Mowbray and the club were predictably castigated by the media for yet more irrational paranoia, very interestingly, a couple of "pundits" on Radio Scotland were not only able to see the merit in an almost identical assertion in the context of another club, it was one of them that came up with it in the first place!

This breathtaking example of hypocrisy (even by Laptop Loyal standards), began with Jim Traynor talking up the Ellis bid for Rangers to curry favour with the Billy Boy listeners. This got me thinking that moving into the final quarter of the season, the Death Star season books must be due for renewal very soon. Was it a coincidence that No-neck should be bumming up the prospect of a new owner riding in on a moonbeam and a white charger to save the Rangers from financial purgatory? "Nah, tis a ploy, watch this space" I thought.

Traynor then went on to discuss Celtic's comments regarding refereeing, and lo an behold – as well as it all being total paranoia – he says he thinks it's a ruse by the Celtic board because the season books are coming up for renewal. Now this reveals a suspicious mindset, no bad thing for a journalist. However it raises the question why this critical eye is closed when speaking about Rangers' new suitor, but is wide open to see a possible alternative/novel explanation for Celtic's comments about referees?

Then the real fun starts. The subject of Scott Brown's appeal is raised, and, as expected, Traynor and the rest agree that it's not ideal to have the referee reviewing his own decision with no further right of appeal. What was *unexpected* however, was John Robertson's (ex-Hearts) contention that Hearts midfielder Laryea Kingston's appeal against a red card received against Aberdeen the same week, was thrown out simply because Celtic's was denied, the logic being that to rescind the red card for the Hearts player but not Scott Brown would have left the SFA open to attack, therefore the expedient decision was taken to deny both. Traynor agreed there was merit in Robertson's point.

Now if that is true, surely that points to a conspiracy?

Two separate games, two separate incidents, two separate referees, but the outcome decided because the implication of finding Kingston innocent and Brown guilty would fuel the paranoid flame – a "political" decision if you like. It seems that you can put forward speculative but logical hypotheses without being slaughtered by the media, as long as you're not connected to Celtic, otherwise such statements are derided as the height of paranoid nonsense.

Later in the same programme after another afternoon of "honest mistakes" saw Davie Weir go unpunished (not even a yellow card) for a last man foul on Michael Higdon, St Mirren manager Gus McPherson is interviewed by Chick Young. McPherson states the obvious, that Weir should have been red-carded, and goes on to make the loaded statement *"we see a different set of rules getting applied, none more so than when we come here* [Mordor]". This is quite an extraordinary and revealing statement. Note that McPherson didn't say "...and Parkhead" allowing the Laptop Loyal to waffle on about "the O*d F**m"; no he was referring specifically to a different set of rules being applied to Rangers and Rangers only, just as when Craig Levein insisted he was talking only about the game with Rangers when desperate interviewers tried to spin the legendary Mike McCurry show as a case of "the O*d F**m" getting all the breaks. So what's Traynors take on all this? Well the *"different set of rules"* comment is ignored completely in the absence of an "O*d F**m" angle, and his conclusion is that the day's honest mistakes *"just goes to show that other teams and not just Celtic are on the end of wrong decisions too"*. Wait a minute No-neck! You seem to be missing the point here, who are the beneficiaries yet again of another "honest mistake"?? The truth that dare not speak its name, or at least no media apologist for Rangers dare speak of.

Over on Radio Snide, the topics of discussion are - the sending off of Brown, the appeals process, the state of pitches in Scotland and the performance of referees (or more accurately staunchly defending them).

For the Rangers perspective the panel includes three former players -

Gough
Johnstone
Wishart

And to ensure balance, the Celtic perspective on these important matters is provided by...erm...no-one.

No Celtic, or even remotely objective, perspective in the Sunday Mail either as the Laptop Loyal ramp up the campaign to have Aiden McGeady hung drawn and quartered for hinting that a referee who wrongly sent off a Celtic player, let the Rangers player involved in the same incident off scot-free, allowed another Rangers player on a yellow card to commit another seven fouls without censure and denied Celtic a clear penalty, may not have been entirely impartial. Who knows where he managed to get that crazy notion?

SUNDAY MAIL

By Mark Guidi 7th March

Dougie McDonald was biased against Celtic in Old Firm clash, insists Aiden McGeady

AIDEN McGEADY last night **accused** ref Dougie McDonald of showing bias against Celtic in last Sunday's Old Firm defeat.

McGeady wasn't happy with the ref but also felt his club's anonymous **blast** about officials before the game backfired.

Their leaked document questioned the handling of Craig Thomson and Steve Conroy in the first two derbies. **That was designed to put pressure on McDonald**

Mark Guidi obviously shares the same psychic powers that allow fellow Lapdog lackies to prove definitively that no Rangers player has ever intentionally committed a foul, to be certain that this was all a cynical attempt to manipulate the referee. Incidentally the *"handling"* of the games referred to in the *"leaked document"*, as proven by TV footage, involved **two** blatant penalties not given for fouls on Maloney, Weir not even booked for stamping on McDonald, Lafferty not even booked for karate kicking Zhi in the groin, a perfectly good Fortune goal disallowed and Lafferty not sent off for an appalling two footed stamp on Hinkel. Referee Thomson later apologised for his "honest mistakes".

In light of this evidence, clearly Celtic's concerns were groundless and were purely a ploy to influence the referee in true Machiavellian fashion. The notions sounds a bit paranoid to me actually, but it takes one to know one after all.

McGeady said: "The comments before the game might have played on his mind. Of course it didn't look like a red card for Scott Brown." "When asked if he thought McDonald should have given Bougherra a second yellow card for persistent fouling, McGeady replied: "Yeah, of course." **Quizzed** further on his views about the official's overall performance, the Celtic winger said: "If I told you I would get into trouble."

Daily Record
By NEIL CAMERON 9th March

Celtic star Aiden McGeady faces SFA rap over Old Firm referee comments

AIDEN McGeady is set to be **carpeted** by SFA bosses over comments that referee Dougie McDonald "wasn't impartial" in last week's Old Firm clash at Ibrox.

Record Sport understands the Hampden beaks are to contact the Parkhead club soon regarding McGeady's interview.

The SFA have already told Celtic they could be in trouble for comments on their website, in the official club magazine and over the leaking of the club's views on referees.

Even before the game the paranoia talk was really getting ramped up, and the Laptop Loyal were using one their favourite weapons – the Uncle Tim:

Evening Times 25th Feb

By PETER MARTIN

Jock Stein used to say, "Make sure you're good enough on the day, regardless of refereeing decisions that may go against you".

Celtic's legendary manager was far more interested in the performance of his team than any match official's failings on the day. I have never known a time like this at the Parkhead club, when pandering to a section of the support that thrives on paranoia and the notion that 'the establishment has got it in for us', is considered acceptable.

Wake up, smell the coffee, open your eyes and look at the bigger picture.

Given each side's financial state of affairs, Celtic should be comfortably clear in the league, but instead find themselves complaining about all the breaks that have gone against them.

Martin picks up the party line that originated straight from the mouth of Nosurname himself who told the Sunday Mail "*Your team has to be good enough to overcome decisions*" after Davie Weir fouled Michael Higdon when the St Mirren striker was clear in on goal but wasn't even booked. That's all very easy to say when your team is doing quite nicely from "honest mistakes" thank you very much. Now I know I'm paranoid, but can someone explain to me why Celtic should have to be "*good enough to overcome decisions*" or good enough "*regardless of refereeing decisions*"? Could we not just have a level playing field, or is that just too mental a notion? Note that Martin tacitly admits to "*all the breaks that have gone against them* [Celtic]", yet to be a Celtic fan and point this out is unhinged paranoia.

The Evening Times gives Davie Hay a few bob to pitch in with the "Jock Stein told us to score two more than them" patter, as if the Scottish league became some sort of honest mistake handicap chase in the 60s and no-one told us.

EVENING TIMES
By DAVIE HAY 26th Feb
Complaining about match officials has been with us for as long as the game has been played, just like there have always been people prepared to believe Celtic don't get a fair crack of the whip. But if there ever really was a case to be made for certain officials having it in for the club, there is much less chance of this happening these days. The scrutiny they are under from the multitude of cameras covering games would make it impossible to pull off.

Yes, this would be impossible to pull off, unless of course this "*multitude of cameras*" were owned by a media servile to the Establishment club, selectively setting the agenda of which incidents are deemed "controversial" and therefore worthy of scrutiny. As Aldous Huxley said, "*the greatest triumphs of propaganda have been accomplished, not by doing something, but by refraining from doing"*, therefore when Steve Conroy "missed" Darren Dods diving and making a Lev Yashin-esque save inside his own box at Celtic Park, or when Alan Muir penalised Artur Boruc on advice from his linesman for kicking the ball from hand five yards inside his penalty area or Lee McCulloch hits Michael Paton of Aberdeen in the face with a flying elbow, the "multitude of cameras" suddenly go blind, and all those TV "experts" and outspoken "tell it like it is" radio pundits lose the power of speech. Who are you going to believe – what the media tells you, or your own lying eyes? If you're lucky, you might see a replay, but the incident is unlikely to crop up in after match "analysis" and certainly won't be included in STV or BBC's highlights package. Blatant errors such as these are consigned to the furnace at the bottom the Orwellian black hole where they will be erased from history forever.

By way of a slight contrast, when Celtic are awarded a penalty for a clear-cut foul on Sean Maloney at Motherwell, the incident is dissected by TV, radio and the press to the nth degree, and even when replay after replay shows the referee's decision to be correct, the media attempt to goad the manager of the opposition (Craig Brown) into some sort of statement they can use to attack the decision. Eventually they succeeded, when after initially stating the referee was correct, under repeated questioning (no agenda from the Laptop Loyal there obviously) Brown said Maloney *"went down very easily"*. Although this statement is evidently a lot of shite, the question as to whether Maloney *"went down very easily"* is totally irrelevant. The only criterion that matters is whether a foul was committed and TV pictures clearly show there was. This left the only avenue of attack for the media one of the "going down too easily" variety, as if the Daily Record et al honestly believe the game is full of professionals whose priority is to try and retain their balance at all costs when fouled in the opposition penalty box. The notion is utterly laughable, but suffices for some good anti-Celtic spin.

Keep an eye out for the media reaction the next time Rangers are awarded a penalty. It takes a lot for the media to actually admit that a Rangers penalty award is "controversial" but invariably in such cases this is swiftly followed by a steady stream of ex-referees and players keen to shower slabbering praise on the referee concerned and journalists and pundits offering tortured explanations as to why it really was a penalty. In the case of a "controversial" decision going against Celtic, a similar modus operandi is effected with the addition of the customary "the ref was brave to make the decision" pish; as if we are supposed to congratulate Nick Leeson for being brave enough to run Barings Bank into the ground or Sir David Murray for taking Rangers to the brink of bankruptcy. Well actually...

Sure, there are mistakes and poor decisions, and some big ones have gone against Celtic in their two games against Rangers this season. But they happen in most games, not just Old Firm matches.

Right, so it seems everyone in their dog agrees that *"some big ones [decisions]"* and *"breaks"* have gone against Celtic, but once again, anyone with a Celtic affiliation stating what everyone else readily agrees, is paranoia or cynical attempt at manipulation. If anything it's a cynical attempt to highlight the issues that the "*multitude of cameras*" and outspoken pundits fail to do so miserably.

And of course Davie Hay is correct, mistakes are made in games other than Celtic-Rangers games. As we have seen they happen all too often in matches involving Celtic-Dundee Utd, Celtic-Falkirk, Rangers-Aberdeen, Rangers-St Mirren etc. But it takes a true paranoiac to find any sort of pattern to these ostensibly "honest" mistakes.

Now, once more for the "they should be good enough to overcome it" line

"*In private, he* [Jock Stein] *simply told us the best way to overcome any perceived injustice was to go up the park and score two more goals to make sure we won.*"

Och, why didn't we think of that before! Someone remember to remind Wattie of this, next time one of his players is flagged offside or the victim of an "incredible" sending off. Maybe under those circumstances the Evening Times might care to wheel out Tam Forsyth to wax lyrical about how Jock Wallace used to tell them to break two more legs than their opponents to make sure they won, or even that these things happen to Hamilton Accies too. Or maybe they would prefer to plaster the Man with Nosurname's comments all over their pages with blaring headlines about an "incredible red card" and launch a vociferous PR campaign to redress the terrible injustice of it all by having the decision rescinded as soon as possible to allow the player concerned to play in the critical last game of the season. It's certainly a tough call to predict what editorial stance the Evening Times or any other Laptop Loyal rag might take under those purely hypothetical circumstances.

Now we have to return to Peter Martin's anti-Celtic offensive of the previous day (25th Feb 2010) as this was a two-pronged attack. Having started with the "you should be good enough to deal with it" line before going on to the "this is mental paranoia" Straw Man building, the whole thing is rounded of nicely with the creation of the Straw Man's Iron Man nemesis, Dougie McDonald.

Dougie's top man

Dougie McDonald was, for me, one of the worst referees in Scotland. Now I think he's one of the best and a sensible choice for Sunday's Old Firm encounter.

Whatever could possibly have made this consummate Laptop Loyalist change his mind?!!

I hope for his sake Dougie avoids a contentious moment on Sunday that awards or denies either a goal, penalty or a sending-off.

Yeah, it would be much better for everyone concerned if the Gers could beat these Tarriers without the help of the brethren.

I make no bones about telling you a third consecutive game with decisions going against Celtic will have the wagons surrounding Hampden to ask Hugh Dallas to explain the 'agenda' to the conspiracy theorists.

Again we have the paranoid notion that decisions have gone against Celtic actually confirmed by the hack in the usual doublethink fashion. Note that Martin has already decided before the event that any mistakes the referee may make in the future will be of the honest variety. Talk about having an open mind - an open mind being a pre-requisite if Martin was actually a journalist and not merely a propaganda peddler. He is absolutely right about one thing though, the wagons would indeed be circled, but he's wrong about the direction in which they would be facing, full square behind McDonald and Hugh Dallas and facing the *'conspiracy theorists'*. In reality, McDonald can sleep easily knowing he will be fully supported by his brethren whatever transpires.

All this paranoia eh? But does anyone know what the word actually means?

Here's a simple example. An SPL club contacts the SFA to ask for a meeting regarding some issues they have with some decisions made by officials over the course of the season so far. No allegations of any untoward behaviour are levelled, no accusations of cheating or favouritism by the officials are made, simply a request for some dialogue about these matters so that everyone may better understand what is happening and how the situation can be improved.

Five days before a crucial game, the details of the request are made public by persons **unknown**. This leads to furious allegations of rampant paranoia and cynical attempts at manipulation directed at the club concerned. The media again have a field day, ignoring completely the facts.

See how the train just got diverted there? People completely forget what was actually reported to have been said and immediately go on the offensive, slating the club in question for paranoia, where there is no evidence of paranoia, no accusations, no claims of "cheating" or "impartiality", simply a reasonable request to speak to the SFA by way of clarification. This leads to a multiplier effect whereby everything the club has ever said or complained about is now regarded - without question - as total paranoia. Every statement or argument made by the club is now bundled into one giant conspiracy theory.

Brown's dismissed appeal is one example – Celtic appealed after having released an official statement on a number of issues, only one of which was the Brown sending off. The press selectively pick out the line "any fair-minded person could see that was not a red card offence", and go to town, slaughtering the club for accusing the referee of bias and impartiality. The press, and everyone else, saw this as an attempt to accuse the referee of not being "fair-minded". Essentially, they saw what they wanted to see according to their pre-determined view of Celtic as a paranoid wreck or more likely their agenda to paint the club as such.

But could it simply be that Celtic thought that if the referee looked at it again he may change his mind? In the same way – using a totally hypothetical example – if a referee gave a penalty at Tannadice and after being harangued by almost the whole Dundee Utd team and consulting with his assistant he then decided to change his mind and rescind the award. No, it's much more convenient just to boldly proclaim that Celtic are leveling all sorts of accusations at the referee and continue building the image of that Straw Man. Did Celtic say **after** the appeal "*any fair-minded person could see that was not a red card offence*"? No, they simply put forward their case that it wasn't a red card offence, the exact same point made by every club who appeals a sending off. As it happens, Celtic are not the only club to display traits of paranoia when such appeals are heard and then fail. Unbelievable as it may seem, the great and dignified Man with Nosurname usually has a lot to say when the authorities make decisions not to his liking.

The Man with Nosurname on Kenny Miller's sending off against Dundee United on 30th December 2009:

'*It was deemed violent conduct but, having had a quick look at television replays, there does not appear to be too much in it. That's about it so, if there is an avenue whereby we can appeal, then we will do that. If we can appeal, then we will look at it.*

'*Will the SFA be closed? That wouldn't be too clever. I'm working this week.*'

After the appeal failed:

"*How can you have an appeals process which is dependent upon the referee admitting that he got it wrong in the first place? It doesn't seem to make a great deal of sense.*"

Are those comments by Sir Walter "paranoid"? Of course not, he's entitled to his view the same as anyone else, apart from Tony Mowbray or Aiden McGeady apparently. But I would have loved to have seen the media outcry if Mowbray had said "*Will the SFA be closed? That wouldn't be too clever. I'm working this week*". You can bet your last thin dime that would have been leapt upon by the press as a scandalous, flippant attack on the SFA. I'm sure Gordon Strachan would agree wholeheartedly.

The Daily Record gave another superlative example of their desperation to accuse Celtic of paranoia. An interview they printed with Kevin Thomson was accompanied by the statement:

"*McDonald was placed in an **almost impossible position** in the build up to the latest Old Firm clash when **Celtic** leaked grievances about the number of decisions that had gone against them this season. However, Thomson, **who*** *rubbished any conspiracy talk...".*

Wait a cotton picking minute, where did any **conspiracy talk** take place exactly? And if it did, is Thomson the man to be asking for opinions on the matter? Is Kevin Thomson going to say "Yeah, I think Celtic have a right to feel aggrieved at all those decision that went against them and in our favour"? Of course not! The Record have set up Celtic's paranoid Straw Man to be torn down by Kevin Thomson's voice of reason Iron Man in the customary manner.

You see, that's the problem with paranoia. The more you accuse people of it, the more you become paranoid yourself, looking for hidden meanings in every little thing people do and say. The frantic scramble to condemn every comment or grievance expressed by Celtic players, fans and officials is both utterly predictable and pathetic.

What's also pathetic is the petted lip from SFA president George Peat who also joined the queue to get laid into Celtic. Yes this is the chap that practically begged his association to do whatever it would take to appease Rangers in the great fixture furore of 2008, and supported unilaterally moving the date of the Scottish Cup final without getting round to the minor detail of actually asking the other team involved (Queen of the South).

This is what Peat had to say:
"*We find it disappointing and somewhat bizarre that, in the build-up to an Old Firm derby, an unnamed Celtic 'source' would seek to exert additional pressure on match officials by issuing ill-timed and **fundamentally inaccurate** comments*"

Fundamentally inaccurate eh? Makes you wonder if Peat actually read Celtic's statement. Maybe our esteemed SFA president could explain which comments are "fundamentally inaccurate"?

"*Referee Dougie McDonald sent off the Celtic captain following a tangle with Kyle Lafferty, with the Rangers player unpunished for his part in the incident.*"

"It immediately seemed to be a controversial decision to everyone in the ground "

"*Any fair-minded person looking at the incident at the time or subsequent TV replays could see it wasn't a red card*"

"It was a decision which had a major impact on the game which saw Tony Mowbray's side down to 10 men for the last half-hour of the game."

"In the first derby match of this season at Ibrox in October, Celtic were denied a blatant penalty by referee Craig Thomson, who admitted after the game that he had made a mistake."

"And in the game against Rangers at Celtic Park, referee Steve Conroy disallowed a Marc-Antoine Fortune goal, though replays showed that there was nothing wrong

"Now, Dougie McDonald's decision is added to that list and will be the major talking point from the game."

The press made much of the "*fair-minded*" comment, however most TV pundits and many in the press themselves admitted it was obvious the offence did not merit a red card. However, in the hallucinogenic world of Orwellian Laptop Loyal spin, Celtic stating the reality of what is abundantly obvious to everyone else has to be attacked furiously as unhinged paranoia with malicious intent. It appears to the onlooker as a classic case of touching a raw nerve situated dangerously close to the truth, resulting in desperate knee-jerk protestations from the deniers. It seems plausible that Peat hasn't actually read the Celtic statement, just the twisted Straw Man caricature version presented by the press, in which case you could understand why he would accuse the club of making "*fundamentally inaccurate*" statements. If he was led to believe that "*seething*" Celtic have "*blasted*" McDonald and accused him of being "*biased*" and "*impartial*" then Peat's comments would become more understandable. But then again, maybe he's just protecting the Establishment club again.

As it happens Peat has – more than most – a cheek to criticise the timing of statements made just prior to important matches. You may recall his remarks about Chris Iwulemo and the state of the Scotland squad following their 0-4 drubbing away to Norway in the World Cup qualifying campaign in back in September 2009. If the SFA had any backbone, Peat would have been out of a job for that incident alone. Let's just remind everyone of what Peat said **twenty four hours** before Scotland took on Macedonia in what was literally a must-win game at Hampden (remember Burley, to his credit, had the squad "really fuckin up for it"):

"We know there was a terrible display in Oslo but if a certain individual scored when he had an open goal at Hampden against Norway, we would have been three points ahead of them now. "

What was that about issuing ill-timed comments before an important game?

Can we say "fundamentally inaccurate"? Well Iwelumo did miss an open goal so that's factual, but it's a bit of a leap to say Scotland would **definitely** have gone on to win the match and the three points. But, to hell with it, if Celtic's statements can be twisted and branded "fundamentally inaccurate" then we can do the same for George "it wisnae me whit bankrupted Airdrie" Peat.

Of course Iwelumo wasn't the only Scottish striker to miss a sitter or two in the campaign. One in particular lived down to his nickname of 'Misser' consistently. Another veteran defender made a complete hash of a long ball to lay the winning goal on a plate for the Netherlands which ultimately knocked Scotland out, aided and abetted by the £9million Premiership full-back who failed to track back in support until it was too late. Then of course there were the players who went in the huff and wouldn't play at all, and the ones that got boozed up as part of their pre-match preparation causing a massive scandal and totally undermining the manager. For some reason I can't work out, Peat chose not criticise any of those players. The reason Iwelumo was "singled out"(© Rangers FC) ahead of these others, remains truly a mystery wrapped in an enigma inside a riddle.

But there's more…

Back in 2008, the SFA announced that they would be entering into tentative discussions with Wales and Northern Ireland on the feasibility of bidding to co-host the 2016 European Championships.

At the same time, Peat was bumping his gums to the Daily Record (something he does quite often):

"We haven't really got down to discussing it yet but given the increased number of stadia that could be required, I don't think we could cope."

Yes, to use football parlance, it would indeed have been a big ask to come up with a viable bid, but when you are at the preliminary stage of negotiations, you don't expect one of your top blazer wearers to come out and make remarks that rubbish any hopes of putting a deal together. Not if the governance of your organisation has any competence or credibility. So George, do us a favour, be consistent in your rants or don't make any at all. Or better yet, resign and let someone who can take Scottish football forward have a go at the job.

Moving on from the laughing stock that is the SFA, perhaps the reason Celtic get such a hard time from the media for our "paranoia", is because we are the only club who criticise referees and make such bold innuendos against their character? Let's examine that a wee bit further.

The first example that springs to mind is when Sir Walter made a comment about linesman Tom Murphy following a game against Motherwell at Fir Park in November 2008. Rangers technically had a goal disallowed by an **extremely borderline** offside decision, although the player (Kris Boyd) put the ball into the net long after the referee had blown to stop play. Nosurname complained about this in an after-match interview and was quite specific in referring to an, **extremely borderline**, decision Murphy gave in favour of Celtic, fully **seven months** prior, not to mention the suspiciously Irish surname of the official concerned.

"Mr Murphy was quick to allow a McDonald goal at Celtic Park last season and he was quick to disallow that one tonight" (13/11/2008)

Of course, try as they might with all their keen journalistic expertise and insightfulness, it would be utterly impossible for anyone in the Scottish media to read anything sinister or paranoid into any of this, wouldn't it? In fact, it was quite the opposite with Derek Johnstone joining Nosurname in the sectarian innuendo gutter with a piece entitled *"Murphy's Not Bitter"* in the Evening Times.

Added to the fact, this was clearly a one-off aberration by the dignified Rangers manager, who has no further track record in criticising referees…

"It's an incredible decision for a linesman who is in line with the play. We got a bad one at Tannadice earlier this season, which has been forgotten about, maybe because we don't make that much of a fuss about it - same situation here" (23/08/2008) v Aberdeen

God help us if Nosurname ever decided to make a fuss about something. As the season unfolded, the Rangers manager continued in the same vein, not making a fuss about refereeing decisions :

"But the second sending off is incredible. It meant we lost a player for the majority of the game for a circumstance that was not the case." (17/05/2009) v Aberdeen

As it turns out, The Man with Nosurname has had rather a lot to say about referees over the past few seasons –

"But we bring out the best in the Aberdeen support and sometimes the referees get carried away with that aspect, or should I say the linesman. It wasn't a dirty game but then we had the situation with Lee getting sent off. It's not very often you see a linesman running 70 yards to get a player sent off. They won't run for a ball and that is the one circumstance which is a little disappointing….

So it's the Aberdeen fan's fault that Lee McCulloch acted like a thug eh? No "Walter blasts Aberdeen fans" type headlines in the rags following this for some reason. If Strachan, Mowbray or Lennon had said the same thing, essentially accusing a linesman of vindictively getting involved to have one his players sent off, the reaction from the press would be akin to the outbreak of World War 3.

…I haven't seen it on TV and I was standing next to the linesman, so he must be sharper than me and the referee won't speak to me so I don't know the reason why he was sent off. You get a situation where the two lots of players are together and that always happens here. That's not unusual. What is unusual is the linesman running 60-70 yards. If he wants to be a referee, he should be and not a linesman. If the referee, one is in a good position, deems it as okay, doesn't see anything and wants to play on, then ... I'll be interested to see it." (23/12/2007) v Aberdeen

"No it wasn't a sending off. It was an opportunity for the referee to send him off [Kevin Thomson]. *There wasn't any great contact made. If there had been, the player wouldn't have been able to continue like he did for the rest of the game."* (23/09/2009) v Hearts

"I felt Kevin Thomson's one wasn't really a bad tackle; he got the ball, he's played it away… the first one I would say was quite a soft one" (21/03/2010) v St Mirren, Co-op Cup final

Just as with referees and linesman, Mr Dignity doesn't make a fuss over decisions made by the SFA –

"The SFA have started a new trend in criminality - if you leave the scene of a crime early, you are not guilty." (16/04/2009)

"Will the SFA be closed? That wouldn't be too clever. I'm working this week" (30/12/2009)

*"McGregor's was an innocuous foul. In fact it wasn't even a foul, but that is how they see it and we can't do anything about it. Last season, they (the SFA) quickly organised a disciplinary hearing for Kenny Miller's appeal, **so that he would miss the Celtic game**."* (15/10/2010)

Touch of paranoia there perhaps!

"Steven actually hurt his knee twice. At first he thought he was going to be OK but when he went back on he caught his foot in the ground. I've said publicly our own pitch is not a good one this season but for the National Stadium that one is in a shocking condition. By all accounts they can't water the pitch here before games for some reason. I don't fully understand why. Our own pitch is suffering this year but for the National Stadium this pitch is poor" (19/04/2008)

Or the SPL –

"From our point of view it's disappointing we don't have that kind of leeway. Everyone in Scotland has made it quite clear they won't do anything for Rangers. We just have to do the best we can"

"They made it perfectly clear there is no willingness on anybody's part to give us anything. There has been no willingness at all to help Rangers so they're not going to help us now are they" (04/05/2008)

"I felt it was unfair of them to ask us to play two games within two days when it was not necessary, especially after what happened to us last season. I have to say that aspect of the split is an unfair one from our point of view. We have expressed our concern about it." (08/05/2008)

Walter Smith last night promised an official complaint to the SPL after insisting Rangers have been unfairly disadvantaged by fixture anomalies since the controversial league split was introduced 10 years ago. Vowing to query the imbalance, Smith said: He said: "We've not had an answer yet, no. I would hope we would get one. There's a hell of an imbalance when you see it. The fact that we have to go to Tannadice three times and we are having to do that nearly every time. (18/04/2009)

Note the newspaper's (Daily Mail) unquestioning acceptance that there is an "imbalance". More on that later.

"The whole thing about the split is impossible to do. When the human element comes in, there has to be a question as to why Rangers have to do

it so many times and Celtic haven't. Other clubs are having to do it so many times and Celtic haven't and they are the ones who were doing the complaining. The thing that annoyed me about the three games away from home this year is, the season we had the UEFA Cup final, we were told that nobody would be asked to play three games at home or away. Now they have given us three when it suits them. I can't understand that point of view. **Somebody, somewhere, is actually making the conscious decision to do that**, forgetting that they had told us the opposite." (18/04/2010)

Is that not an accusation of "impartiality" or "bias"?

Or other clubs –

"Everyone wants people to get ordered off, everybody wants penalties against us, everybody wants everything against us" (06/03/2010)

You've got to ask why Celtic have never had to do that at all and we've had to do it. Especially last year when they were kicking up a fuss about being treated unfairly when it's patently obvious that it's Rangers who are being treated unfairly and not Celtic." (18/04/2010)

"If he's happy with the way Scottish football is at the moment, then he's in the wrong job. Was the Kilmarnock chairman one of the people who agreed to the Setanta deal? So if he's wanting to turn round and say there's hypocrisy from the statements I've made, he should maybe look at his own self more than anything" (17/09/2010)

Or the media –

"I said the club issued a statement last night. It's me that's hard of hearing, not you lads. Look, I've got nothing to say about that. Ye keep trying. Gonnae just pack it in otherwise I'll just walk away" (27/10/2009)

As mentioned previously, foreign referees are fair game for any accusations you want to throw at them:

"The ref had two decisions to make. One - was it a penalty? And clearly it was. But the second part of the decision is he then has to send the player off. That makes it awkward for the ref. **Tonight he opted out of making what was a very clear-cut decision.**

At Champions League level you would want a better decision from such a clear-cut circumstance. You'd expect better at this level. They have to make strong decisions. That is why they are the best referees. He was perfectly positioned. They have to make strong decisions. When they are chosen as the best referees you say at times anyone can make an error. But he was up with play, he did see it - **and he has opted out of making the decision.** You have to be disappointed with that." (29/09/2010) v Sevilla

Nosurname comes perilously close to questioning the impartiality, and by implication the integrity of the referee in the Rangers-Sevilla Champions League tie (Jonas Eriksson). The inference Mr Dignity is unambiguously making is that the referee **consciously refused to give the decision which he knew to be correct** due to its implications. If that's not paranoia and an accusation of bias then I would like to see what is. Maybe the Laptop Loyal would care to suggest UEFA take a look at these comments with a view to a disciplinary hearing? Perhaps the intrepid Scottish media would care to "*quiz*" the Man With Nosurname on the matter to force him to come up with a justification for this sour grapes shite?

But perhaps the Rangers manager is succumbing to the paranoia bug in his dotage and hence does not represent the official stance of the club on these issues, having become somewhat of a loose cannon? Let's consider some statements from Rangers CEO Martin Bain over the past few seasons:

Rangers and SFA to hold talks over Allan McGregor ban

bbc.co.uk   18th October 2010

Angry Rangers chief executive Martin Bain will hold talks with his Scottish Football Association counterpart over Allan McGregor's suspension.

*"**I fired off a strongly-worded letter to the SFA.** I've since had a reply and I'm due to meet the chief executive later this week," said Bain.*

*Rangers had been **angered** by the way the investigation into the incident had been handled by the governing body.*

"We are angry about it, the procedures are wrong and hopefully the new chief executive will address those

*"Allan McGregor receiving a retrospective ban in the fashion that he did is something that **has angered the club greatly**," said the Rangers chief.*

"As a football club, we weren't going to say anything publicly about our actions because we have no intention whatsoever of being accused of undermining Scotland and their performance with two matches imminent," he added.

"But we are angry about it, the procedures are wrong and hopefully the new chief executive will address those in the coming week."

I particularly love the part where he says they weren't going to say anything in case they were accused of undermining the Scottish national team, then he goes ahead and says it anyway. And is it undermining the Scotland team he's worried about, or just the accusation of doing so? Given Rangers' track record of undermining the national team over recent seasons, including tapping up the national team manager no less, I'd imagine the latter is much nearer the mark.

'Sporting integrity' argument over SPL fixtures revisited by Rangers
STV 13 Apr 2010

*Martin Bain has taken a **cheeky pop** at comments made by Celtic chief executive Peter Lawwell in 2008.*

Although Rangers sit a mere six points away from clinching this season's SPL crown, the Ibrox club have been dealt an unusual set of games, which will see them play three consecutive away matches against Hibernian, Dundee United and Celtic.

*Celtic meanwhile **will benefit** from the changes made to the fixture list in order to try and give each team an equal number of home and away matches. The potential Champions League participants will welcome Motherwell to their home ground for a third time this campaign, instead of having to travel through to Lanarkshire.*

That has riled Bain, who has seen his team play on a "difficult" pitch at Fir Park twice as scheduled. "Celtic are not being asked to go and play on the difficult surface at Fir Park when they have only played there once this season," he said. "Does that equate to 'sporting integrity'?"

Every single comment, no matter how small, from Celtic players and officials which is in any way perceived to be questioning authority or critical of another party is reported by the media as *"seething/raging/fuming"* Celtic/Lennon *"claimed/insisted"* etc etc. In contrast, Establishment club officials are *"frustrated"* and have *"cheeky pops"*, *"demand answers"* or *"remonstrate"* with referees and the authorities. If only Celtic could learn to lower the tone of their protests like the Man with Nosurname being the doyen that he is:

Telegraph
By Ewing Grahame
21 Sep 2009

Frustrated *Rangers manager Walter Smith **remonstrated** with Kilmarnock's Connor Sammon before being sent to the stand at RugbyPark. Smith was ordered from the technical area by referee Steve Conroy following Pedro Mendes' dismissal in the 43rd minute of Saturday's 0-0 draw with Kilmarnock at Rugby Park. The 61 year-old, **the doyen of Scottish managers**, was guilty of **encroachment** when he entered the field of play to **remonstrate** with Kilmarnock players, with striker Connor Sammon a particular target for his **ire**, because he believed that they had attempted to persuade the official to produce a second yellow card for the Portuguese midfielder.*

Note that the offence committed by Nosurname is *"encroachment"*, nothing to do with f-ing and blinding at Kilmarnock players and the referee. No, that's what we call *"remonstrating"* when it comes to Spoilt Child FC. There are a multitude of examples, but a particularly interesting comparison can be drawn with Neil Lennon's spat with MIB Stuart Dougal in 2005, where a few verbals was twisted by the Laptop Loyal into an attack on the poor referee that Jean Claude Van Damme would've been proud of, followed by demands for Lennon to be hit with at least a **ten** match ban.

But back to Mr Dignity and his favourite subject – fixture scheduling, from May 2009:

Walter Smith blasts SPL for treating club unfairly over fixture list for second year running

May 8 2009 Keith Jackson

WALTER Smith last night waded into the latest fixture row to engulf the SPL and insisted Rangers have been unfairly treated for a second successive season.

*Record Sport exclusively revealed on Wednesday that the Ibrox club are furious with the rescheduling of next week's top-flight card - and the fact title rivals Celtic **will benefit** from an extra two days' rest between games.*

*We told how chief executive Martin Bain had **demanded an explanation** from the SPL over the decision to force Smith's side to play Hibs at Easter Road on Wednesday night and then have them back in action at lunchtime the following Saturday against Aberdeen.*

*And yesterday, as Smith braced himself for tomorrow's Judgment Day derby, he insisted his side has been let down once again by the same people **he blamed for wrecking his chances of winning last season's title**.*

Smith said: "I felt it was unfair of them to ask us to play two games within two days when it was not necessary, especially after what happened to us last season.

"I have to say that aspect of the split is an unfair one from our point of view. We have expressed our concern about it."

Smith is also understood to be astonished at the decision to appoint linesman Tom Murphy for tomorrow's lunchtime crunch - *just five months* after he slaughtered him for denying Rangers a late winner in a 0-0 draw at Motherwell.

Just the five months eh? Back in 2005, only a few weeks after the debacle at Tynecastle that ultimately won Spoilt Child FC the league that season, Andy Davis was selected to run the line at the Celtic-Dundee United Scottish Cup final. When it was suggested by a Celtic source that perhaps this wasn't the wisest decision in the world, the media predictably went on the offensive slaughtering Celtic for their paranoia, for casting aspersions at the poor unjustifiably maligned official and of course the old "making his job impossible" chestnut. Makes you wonder how Tom Murphy has managed to struggle on in the face of adversity doesn't it? Well somebody's got to wonder about it, as the media sure aint going to.

In contrast, the Scottish media are practically canvassing for the Man with Nosurname to be allowed to vet the officials allocated to Rangers games. If five months is considered too brief a time lapse between having the temerity to displease the Master and officiating another Spoilt Child FC game, what would be an acceptable length of time? A year? Two years? Five years? Or Gordon Smith's suggestion – after he's retired?

As we have seen, lapdog heads were exploding left, right and centre in aneurysms of sheer rage and hatred when Celtic had the temerity to release a statement on the club's website stating that "any fair-minded person" could see Scott Brown should not have been sent off. Funnily enough, outpourings of indignant fury and derision were completely absent ten months prior when Rangers questioned two refereeing decisions via the official club website:

Bougherra Decision 'Incredible'

WALTER SMITH is fuming after finding out why Madjid Bougherra was sent off after today's 2-1 victory over Aberdeen at Ibrox.

Linesman Graham Chambers informed the Gers gaffer that he felt the Algerian deliberately kicked Dons' keeper Jamie Langfield in the head after the pair collided going for a 50/50 challenge.

Smith insists the explanation was 'incredible' and was unsure if the club could appeal the decision.

Bougherra's sending off is the second controversial decision against Rangers in the space of four days after Nacho Novo's goal against Hibs was disallowed when it appeared to cross the line.

So we have Spoilt Child FC wailing about a player being sent off according to the laws of the game and a goal not being given because the whole of the ball hadn't crossed the line. So, were the Scottish press incandescent at these sinister aspersions cast by the Establishment club on our great and honourable referees? Of course not. On the contrary, what they did, was to lift the club's statement and print it verbatim in the pages of their various rags as incontrovertible fact.

Money saving tip for Rangers fans in these hard economic times – cancel your Rangers News subscription and buy the Daily Record instead to get Rangers news, written by Rangers supporters, for Rangers supporters.

As we have seen, mentioning certain facts that the Scottish football establishment would rather were left hidden, without even actually levelling any accusations of bias, is enough to bring forth a paranoiac reaction of utter derision along with the predictable parrot cry of "paranoia". In the wonderful Orwellian world that is Scottish football, making simple statements of fact that don't suit the party line, are enough to instigate frenzied, hysterical accusations of paranoia and malicious intent, far outweighing anything that has emanated from Celtic fans over the years.

These furious knee-jerk reactions are a clear indication that the claims of the "paranoid" indeed have much foundation otherwise it would not be necessary to attack them so ferociously. Outside the petty insular world of Scottish football, branding opponents "paranoid" or "conspiracy nut" is a widely deployed tactic by those in positions of power who seek to avoid unpalatable debates for the fear of having their duplicity exposed. Whether it be US Administrations, UK Governments or the Soviet Politburo, any opponent branded "radical", "dissident" or "extremist" may as well be arguing that the earth is flat for all the weight that his argument can carry in the face of so-called sober, informed political commentators. Constrained in this way, the Celtic paranoiac can provide massive quantities of empirical evidence to support his argument, yet the Establishment can rest in the knowledge that as far as everyone else is concerned – the "sober informed commentators" – he is simply howling at the moon.

Celtic Managers and the Scottish Media

"If one morning I walked on top of the water across the Potomac River, the headline that afternoon would read 'President Can't Swim'"
Lyndon B Johnson

"We would win 4-0 and the first question would be, 'Do you think you were a bit lucky because they could have had a goal?' or 'Do you think you were a bit lucky because they hit the post?' It was all negative even when we were doing OK"
John Barnes

Months before the European Championships kicked off in 2000, Martin O'Neill signed up to be a pundit at the tournament for the BBC. O'Neill had a good relationship with the broadcaster having carried out the role with some aplomb at France 1998, proving to be a well-informed, insightful and humorous commentator and excellent foil for the other panel members, particularly Alan Hansen. The average viewer warmed to O'Neill, as did the rest of the UK media. The feeling was reciprocated – O'Neill liked the media, he enjoyed debating football with like-minded people and was clearly knowledgeable and enthusiastic about the game.

However by the time he took his seat for the opening match on 10th June 2000, the attitude of the press – or more accurately, the *Scottish* press – had shifted subtly but perceptively, and he now found himself criticised for keeping the engagement. What had happened in the intervening time to turn O'Neill from something of a darling of the media, into someone certain elements north of the border were now taking shots at it?

The answer is obvious, if not liable to get you branded paranoid for stating it – he had just become the manager of Celtic FC. Within weeks indignant headlines were blaring out from the pages of Scottish newspapers, attacking O'Neill for neglecting his managerial duties at Celtic by honouring those he was contractually obliged to do so with the BBC. It didn't matter that he brought back Belgian centre back Joos Valgaeren, a rock of the Celtic defence over the next three seasons, the Scottish media were unanimous in their criticism of O'Neill for this "jolly". His first couple of pre-season friendlies were shaky and after a 2-4 home reverse to French side Bordeaux, he became the first Celtic coach – but not the last – to be greeted by broken crest headlines in the papers before he had even taken on a competitive game.

His time at Celtic was to be haunted by stories that he was on the verge of leaving almost from the word go, about his bad away record in the Champions League, by tales that he led a dressing room of "ageing players" who were out of control and, occasionally, the ridiculous idea he enjoyed stirring the sectarian soup. When O'Neill had the temerity to respond to such attacks, it only strengthened the hostility of the Scottish media who moved to portray him as some sort of cantankerous dishonest character. All in all, his treatment by the media in Scotland was shameful, reflected by the fact that on several occasions they were obliged to pay, not insubstantial, sums of compensation to him, either as the result of court action or under the threat of it.

Gordon Strachan was another who enjoyed his time in the pundit's chair and who had a natural aptitude for discussing the game in an informed and entertaining manner. Here was another guy who was loved by the press, principally because many of his comments, both as a manager and pundit, where sprinkled with liberal doses of humour that made for great footage and copy. Strachan was unanimously thought to be a knowledgable and witty observer of the game. When the Scottish national team manager job became vacant following the departure of Berti Vogts in 2005, the Scottish media considered Strachan to be a strong candidate for the job, along with Graeme Souness and Walter Smith. Among the 'Tartan Army' Strachan was the top choice. Instead the SFA threw a bone to an out of work Walter Smith with many in the press, whilst keen to laud the return of the Man with Nosurname, offering kind words and suggesting that Strachan was a touch unlucky to have come up against a candidate with so much experience.

A mere matter of months later, Gordon Strachan was back in Scotland, but something had happened to sour the relationship of this witty and knowledgeable character of the game with the local press and media. Over this short period of time, the man who had been much loved by the media as a true character, with such strong credentials as a manager that he was considered a serious contender for the job of Scotland manager; had become an arrogant smart arse, who's flippant responses to their questions was an affront to the Celtic fans who's best interests these selfless champions of public interest were merely endeavouring to serve. It didn't take long before every word was being twisted out of context and his credentials called in to question. Didn't you know he's never managed a big club? Didn't you know he's never managed in Europe? Didn't you know he's never won a trophy? Didn't you know this was the guy who got Coventry relegated from the English top flight after 30-odd years (ignore that fact he saved them from relegation for the previous four seasons)? In the Scottish media's time honoured fashion, the temporary blindness that masked all of these questions when Strachan was linked with the Scotland job, were now glaringly illuminated by the sudden compulsion to put on the night vision goggles. This compulsion arose because, of course, he had just taken the Celtic manager job, instantly becoming a target for the same media who had loved his quirky sense of humour and his way of deftly dealing with criticism. All of a sudden he was arrogant, unfunny and, most laughable of all, disrespectful to the gossip-peddling lackies for Murray propaganda who call themselves football journalists in this country.

When he lost his first competitive game – the Nightmare in Bratislava – the knives were already sharpened and waiting to be plunged into his back. However in a stunning juxtaposition of hypocrisy even by Laptop Loyal standards, we were treated to the sight of Gordon Smith and Craig Paterson on TV and radio, defending the Celtic manager from entirely fictional calls for him to be sacked by Celtic fans. As with Strachan's disciplinary issues with Aiden McGeady a few years down the line, the media were confronted with a situation where they would be forced to offer a superficial defence of one party so that they could mount a Straw Man attack on the other – in this case, "defending" the Celtic manager's position (as if it could be seriously threatened after **one** game anyway) so that they could attack the Celtic fans. Yes, along with the ludicrous notion that there were great swathes of Celtic fans demanding Gordon Strachan's sacking after one game, the media had dreamt up the charge that the majority of Celtic fans would not accept him as he wasn't "Celtic-minded" (i.e. the majority of Celtic fans are small-minded bigots). Aside from the fact that there was no evidence whatsoever for such an assertion, other than Gordon Smith and James Traynor wittering on about it on the BBC, this ignored the fact that Strachan was Celtic's **fourth** manager to have had no prior connection with the club (the figure is actually six but I have allowed for Martin O'Neill's self-confessed affection for the club and Liam Brady's Irish nationality).

This also becomes all the more transparently hypocritical when one recalls the simpering praise showered by the media on the management dream team of the Man with Nosurname and Ally McCoist, not to mention their esteemed captain Barry Ferguson, for being "steeped in the traditions of the club". I myself have a pretty good idea what these "traditions" are and am not sure they're anything to be boasting about. Add to this, the self same "he's not Celtic-minded" Celtic–fan-bashing media's criticism of Paul Le Guen for failing to grasp "what the club is all about" and his failure to "empathise with the fans"; coded language for not being "Rangers-minded" if you ask me, but then again I'm..etc etc

When Celtic followed the Bratislava debacle with a 4-4 draw at Motherwell, many in the Scottish media excitedly predicted that the newly resurgent Hearts would "split the Old Firm", sending Celtic crashing into third place in the Scottish Premier League. Well, they were almost right, I suppose.

Martin O'Neill and Gordon Strachan learned quickly not to feed the hand that bit them. Press conferences became cagey affairs with O'Neill becoming adept at using two hundred words to say nothing and Strachan the more confrontational approach of simply pointing out the absurdity and/or inaccuracy in the media's line of questioning. Some said these things were merely part of the personalities of both men, but they were not the only Celtic managers in recent years not to have good relationships with the hacks. Kenny Dalglish saw his own deteriorate so much that he took the press on a whirlwind tour of the Gallowgate, to vent his frustration, and in famous incident, Hugh Keevins was removed from the Celtic Supporter's Club before he'd even taken his seat, by a gentleman named Finbar O'Brannigan.

It was May 2000 and Dalglish had taken over from Barnes as manager, ostensibly in a temporary measure, at a time when the whole club was in disarray. In our club's darkest hour since the receivers were preparing to visit in 1994, there was no sympathetic "how do you turn this around?" or "have you got any message for the fans who might be worried?" stuff from the press. Hugh Keevins howled about the *"ultimate denial of free speech!"* after the Celtic Supporter's Club episode and was therefore granted the opportunity to fax Dalglish with the questions he would have asked had he been present at the press conference. The Celtic manager/Director of Football responded to them and this exchange was subsequently published in the Sunday Mail shortly thereafter:

SM: Have you ever at any time regretted the decision to leave England and return home?

KD: Naw

SM: Have you sought consultation with your chief executive in light of Guus Hiddink's appointment as manager?

KD: He hasn't been appointed yet.

SM: To what extent do you blame the players and not the management for what's happened this season?

KD: We all have equal responsibility

SM: If you had the opportunity over again, would you still go for John Barnes as your first managerial appointment in your role as director of football?

KD: I've answered this one before. I believe John Barnes will go on to be a good manager

You don't have to be Noam Chomsky to understand the agenda being pursued by Keevins and his newspaper. In the course of these questions Keevins invites Dalglish to criticise his players, disavow himself of the appointment of John Barnes, declare his return to Celtic a mistake and, comically, tries to discomfit Dalglish by speculating on his future in light of Guus Hiddink's appointment as manager. Another revealing detail is that it is highly unlikely that Dalglish would have used the slang term *"Naw"* in written correspondence such as this, therefore the assumption must be that Keevins or someone else at the Sunday Mail altered the response in this fashion. This speaks volumes for the editorial stance of that rag. Remember, this is the joint top-scorer and most capped player in the history of the Scottish national team, and we are presented with the spectacle of grubby hacks doing their utmost to denigrate his character. Utterly pathetic, but par for the course unfortunately.

So, King Kenny got sick of it all and decided to take his case to the people, stating that since the media could not be trusted to report his comments truthfully, he had no choice but to conduct press briefings where ordinary fans could observe them and listen first-hand to comments the press might otherwise have taken out of context.

And how they wailed, and how they howled, and how they complained; at first saying that Dalglish was putting their safety at risk, and then going on to complain about the poor facilities available, as though they were some sort of high powered UN delegation. When Dalglish pointed out that the fans' behaviour throughout was impeccable, when he observed that there were adequate facilities to plug in their microphones and tape recorders, the complaints shifted to the spectacle of a club like Celtic conducting its business in such a way. Dalglish hit back by reminding them that their own behaviour had led to him having no other choice in the matter.

It has always been thus. The Scottish media has never given Celtic, or its managers, a fair press. At a time when he was one of the most respected coaches in Europe, at a time when his expertise was being sought in every area of the game by UEFA and FIFA, Dr Jozef Venglos was lampooned by a media which knew the sum total of nil about any of his accomplishments on his appointment at Celtic. "DR WHO" and "BLANK CZECH" headlines greeted his appointment throughout the Scottish press, penned by vindictive little hacks whose combined knowledge of football would hardly amount to 1% of that of the new Celtic manager. Too add insult to..em.. insult, these hopeless ignoramuses couldn't even get his nationality right, Venglos being Slovakian, not Czech. When he signed 33 year old Lubomir Moravcik the howls of derision from every supposedly "informed" media quarter could be heard back in Bratislava. Hugh Keevins infamously lambasted Celtic for this "*old pal's act*" and for not "*prising enough from the biscuit tin to shell out the £500,000 it would have taken to get a proven talent like John Spencer*". Lubomir Moravcik.... John Spencer.... Lubomir Moravcik.... John Spencer – it's almost an insult to one of the most skillful players to ever pull on the Hoops to see those two names on the same page. No, instead of signing an over-paid ex-Rangers and Chelsea reserve, Celtic went out and bought – for a bargain of the century £300,000 – a veteran of the Czechoslovakia team which reached the quarter-finals of the 1990 World Cup and with eight years of experience in the top flight of the French league under his belt. It was abundantly clear a matter of minutes into Lubo's debut for Celtic that the manager knew far more about the player than any of the "experts" in this petty little insular country who very vocally touted the signing as a joke.

Proving that fools never learn, it was the same scenario with Wim Jansen the year before, another highly respected coach in Europe and the Far East, the man who stopped the seemingly unassailable Rangers charge towards ten-in-a-row. Jansen might have been forgiven for turning and leaving the moment he arrived, as he was greeted by an avalanche of negative headlines, one in particular bad taste in the Sun saying he was "*The Worst Thing To Hit Hiroshima Since The Atom Bomb.*" As it turned out, he was the worst thing to hit Rangers since Billy McNeil had returned in our centenary year, and the magnificent legacy he left behind – Henrik Larsson – was to give us more memories than we ever dared dream.

We know the "sporting" media in this country is shameless in its pursuit of Celtic managers. History teaches us this. We know too that the flip side of the coin is their hero-worship of the Man With No Surname, a man who can do no wrong, a man who, no matter how bad the result, no matter the terrible event, no matter the set-back or reversal, is protected and nurtured by the very people who ruthlessly gun for every incumbent of the job at Celtic Park. In the wake of two devastating home reverses in the Champions League by an aggregate score of 8-2, radio and TV reports excitedly babbled about the Man with No Surname *"planning for the future"* at Ibrox, when by his own admission just days before, in the absence of a contract or new club owner, doesn't know if he even has one! Did it ever dawn on the "journalists" concerned that this was a contradiction? Probably not.

Every Celtic manager in the past fifteen years, and possibly more, has had to deal with an openly hostile media. Only one Rangers manager in the same period was ever put under any semblance of the same pressure, and it wasn't the one who led Rangers to the worst sequence of results in their entire history, surpassing even the pre-Souness wilderness years of the early to mid-80s. Is it a coincidence that this man was about as far from being a traditional "Rangers man" as you could ever get? The press at the time railed against him over the way he treated a "true Rangers legend" like Barry Ferguson and only those among them with a handful of scruples – a very small minority – are now willing to acknowledge Paul Le Guen was correct in his assessment of what was wrong at the club. It was the press who led the howls for a return to "Rangers values", and they did so at the same time they were accusing a section of Celtic fans of hating Gordon Strachan because he was not "Celtic minded", spinning that into some kind of sectarian code.

The hypocrisy of the Scottish media is everywhere you look and Paul Le Guen provides fertile ground for a myriad of examples. As we've seen, Gordon Strachan, Martin O'Neill, Kenny Dalglish, Dr Jozef Venglos and Wim Jansen were all exposed to negativity and downright hostility almost the second they walked in the door at Celtic Park. Tony Mowbray was not long in feeling the media's ire for daring to speak out about the media "agenda" and Neil Lennon's first act as Celtic manager was to field questions on who might have been offered the job ahead of him and whether he felt insecure about being given only a one year contract in the press conference to unveil his appointment.

In contrast, Paul Le Guen's appointment as Rangers manager was greeted by an orgy of euphoria throughout the Scottish media, with every journeyman signing from Austria Vienna or relegation threatened French clubs greeted as the signing of the new Lubo or Henrik Larsson. The press eagerly printed headlines trumpeting *"Le Guen's £80million War Chest"* as they danced along in their Walter Mitty world of signing Ronaldo and building £700million stadium, casino, hotels in earth's orbit, even as Sir Moonbeams was beginning to run out of the paper needed to shuffle the ever increasing debt mountain onto.

The Scottish national team is also a subject that just keeps on giving when it comes to the hypocrisy of the media's shameless pro-Rangers agenda. They chose to view Sir Walter walking out on the national side in a slightly different light than the respective choices made by Aiden McGeady and James McCarthy. Whereas these boys were "traitors" and "sell-outs", Wattie was merely showing loyalty to his first love, and so that was all perfectly OK, regardless of minor issues such as tapping up, an offence for which Celtic were fined several hundred pounds in 1994, when Tommy Burns returned to his "first love".

The press relationship with The Man with No Surname has ceased utterly to be anything approaching objective. The press coverage he gets has crossed the line into outright hero-worship. The same media who grills our manager with an intensity which is missing when you watch coverage of the inquiry into the Iraq War, has come to a point where The Man with No Surname is the source of all wisdom in the land. When his side lost heavily at home to Unirea Urziceni in their cataclysmic Champions League group, the hacks gathered as if in a state of subjugated fear of the after-match press conference. With the object of their love and adulation in no mood for tough queries they abrogated the most basic responsibilities of their profession and asked him a few token questions along the lines of "where do we… sorry…you, go from here?", before letting him retreat back to the sanctuary of the blue room. Every single person who failed to speak up that night is a disgrace to journalism, and what makes it worse is the utter impossibility of even imagining Tony Mowbray or Neil Lennon being offered a similar route of escape. If Celtic had suffered such a defeat they would have had the manager's head on a pike dancing around it likes savages quicker than you could say "Artmedia".

Indeed, so beloved by the media is The Man with No Surname that it was he, and not the mountain of available evidence – evidence so readily available that many well sourced and researched articles had been appearing on Celtic fan websites and forums over many years, continuously dismissed as biased "paranoia" – who got the press writing about the state of Rangers finances. Who knew, as some Celtic fans scooped the subservient, silent press by over **five years** on the full repercussions of the Rangers and MIH debt, that all it would take was one statement from The Man With No Surname before all the dominos would start to fall? Forget that every single thing he said merely confirmed what a number of us "paranoid" Celtic fans have been saying for a long, long time – he was the one who set the media machine in motion, or more accurately, the frantic damage limitation machine in motion.

Last season, Tony Mowbray slammed down the gauntlet and said 'enough is enough', and joined the ranks of the "paranoid". Mowbray was very precise in the words he chose. He spoke not of a press which simply thrives on bad news, but of a clique with "*an agenda*". We know what he means, and we know what the agenda is. Tony Mowbray's inadequacies which were cruelly exposed over his time in the Celtic job should not disguise the fact that with each new Celtic manager, the media hostility is cranked up another notch, with all-too tangible consequences on and off the pitch.

The Return of the Man With Nosurname

Sports journalists are supposed to be neutral, their views impartial. They aren't supposed to wear their colours, except the national ones. They are meant to give an honest, objective and unemotional assessment of what they see and hear, ever mindful of the fact that, far more than political journalists, their readership is varied and widespread. Any newspaper can survive by turning on one group of political elites or another; in fact, this is how most of them thrive. But when a sports department at a national news agency leans in one direction, or for one team, the end product becomes nothing more than an extension of the club's own publications.

Today, the vast majority of the sports media in this country have, by their recent conduct, confirmed what most of us knew anyway; they are four-square in the corner of Rangers, and this makes them incapable of doing either a professional job or an honest one. Make no mistake about it; the sports media in this country are one hundred and ten percent biased, just like our political commentators. The return of the Man with Nosurname at Rangers is one event, that showed our Scottish journalistic class in all it's partisan glory.

The "resignation" [cough!] of Paul Le Guen and the exhilaration over the incoming Great White Saviour, Walter Smith, saw history re-written, precedents ignored and patriotic loyalties and SFA regulations conveniently forgotten. Even in North Korea, where every single media outlet is controlled by the state, there is more diversity of opinion than the Scottish sports media provided on this issue.

"You never go back to a club you've left," said Derek Johnstone earlier in the season, when Walter Smith's name was first suggested. Most of the press agreed. *"Le Guen will be given until the end of the season,"* they all said. *"David Murray has said so."* And Murray never lies, not even when he promised moonbeams from JJB and then wouldn't cough up for better than Filip Sebo. *"David Murray doesn't sack managers"* was another myth peddled by the media unquestioningly, at the very time the Rangers chairman paws preparing to appoint a manager he sacked ten years before. Nosurname's return was announced to a reception among the media that made the reaction to his predecessor's appointment seem as enthusiastic Jim White's the day Celtic stopped the ten. *"Rangers will sign the best of Scotland's young players,"* blasted most of the media circus. Alan Gow, yes, well he's young – younger than Davie Weir anyway.

On the subject of the Saviour's return – that's the Saviour to save them from Le Saviour – Radio Clyde, our most partisan radio station as it is literally filled to the brim with ex-Rangers players and fans posing as journalists; the aforementioned Pie Man Johnstone said, to the widespread agreement of his colleagues, that Rangers had done everything above board in their approach for Walter Smith, that no initial approach had been made until the SFA were contacted over the weekend.

The common perception about football fans is that we have short memories, that we can't focus on events for longer than two minutes at a time and that we forgive everything except failure. I think most of us would agree with the third, to a certain extent, but only an idiot, or someone wrapped tight in a Union Jack, would accept Derek Johnstone's blatant nonsense as fact.

Every newspaper in the country, every media outlet in fact, had Smith as manager the moment Le Guen had gone. Since the vast majority of the Scottish sporting press couldn't predict rain in November let alone something of this magnitude we can only conclude that they were either all extraordinarily lucky in their predictions, or they had some inside information, and this degree of uniformity can only mean that someone was briefing all of them, in a co-ordinated manner. That someone, was either an SFA or Rangers insider. No prizes for guessing which is the more likely.

Chick Young, live on TV outside Ibrox, was positively overwhelmed by the emotion of the event – the return of the man who famously turned him over and spanked him in the Ibrox tunnel (watch the video on YouTube when you finish reading this) – the bulge in his trousers suggesting either great excitement or the theft of a small banana from the Ibrox canteen. There, live on TV, for the nation to see, he almost wet his pants as he told us that Moonbeams had once again acted with the decisiveness and precision for which he's renowned and got the man who would lead Rangers back to the top of Scottish football. Chick Young, who wouldn't know Love Street from a hole in the road, actually knew before the SFA who the next manager of Rangers would be.

That isn't proof, of course. Chick and the rest might actually have been acting on instinct, or guessing. If we were looking for proof, Andy Webster provided the 'smoking gun' for any aspiring investigative journalist, if such a person actually existed within the Scottish sports press. Webster, we were told, is part of Smith's new-look Rangers side, but he was signed on Friday night, before the SFA were approached about their manager. At first the media, to a man and woman, reported that Webster was a Smith signing, and the first of many with the boys from Hibs to follow follow. Then, with the SFA talking about pursuing legal avenues, the press claimed that he was actually a Le Guen signing, difficult to believe as he was sacked the day before Webster signed.

If not a Smith signing, and not a Le Guen signing, then Webster must have been a Murray signing, and if the deal was negotiated during Le Guen's spell in charge, when Le Guen didn't fancy him, then we need to ask if the chairman was making moves behind the manager's back, something Romanov would have been slated for. Furthermore, if you believe the other media theory, that Murray himself conducted these negotiations without a manager in place, then things at Rangers really are every bit as bad as at Hearts – he's even been in the dressing room to rally the troops. The boy on Big Ron Manager quit when that happened, knowing that he'd just lost any respect the players had for him - not that the media were interested in making any such comparison in relation to their beloved Rangers. The dressing room meeting in fact, was touted as a "turning point." There were so many "turning points" during the Le Guen season, the Indy500 must have been missing a few of them.

The Webster saga is a mess of contradictions, and we will never get to the bottom of it. The Scottish media certainly won't. With no manager officially in place, Rangers were out and about hiring staff and, if the media are to be believed, talking to players too. And still the Scottish press claim that no tapping up had taken place. Either Smith was running Rangers, in breach of his Scotland contract, giving the nod over such things as hiring and firing, and making a mockery of all the claims that he and Rangers have done everything "above board", or Murray was making club policy on the hoof, hoping that the appearance of forward motion would distract anyone from looking at the whole picture, which reveals a shambolic state of affairs from top to bottom.

Walter Smith brought a lot of experience to the job, of course, as he is the famous Nine-In-A-Row manager. They just love telling you that don't they, 'nine-in-a-row long since having lost any association with Celtic's original and best achievement among the denizens of the Scottish press. And of course, it was built at a time when Celtic couldn't find two bob for the electric meter. But it all ended in tears eventually, with Smith being sacked – which is another piece of history that was re-written, only for the Cardigan to inadvertently spill the beans in an interview whilst at Everton, something he was to make somewhat of a habit of.

It's odd that he should be touted as a guru coach on the basis of a few good results with Scotland, offset against a draw and a home defeat to Belarus. Nosurname's messianic skills were not in evidence at the last club daft enough to buy into the Nine-In-A-Row legend, Everton, where his fifty-odd wins, fifty-odd draws and sixty-odd defeats ended with him being sacked again. In fact, after a lengthy period in the wilderness he was on a three month old pals act with Sir Govan prior to the SFA offering him the Scotland job.

The Scottish press conveniently ignores this too, of course, and is now acting like Smith did **us** a favour only to be held against his will when he asked for a little back. The same Scottish journalists who, foaming at the mouth, demanded that Shaun Maloney and Stephen McManus who pulled out of a meaningless Japanese tour never play for their nation again, as punishment for their "treachery" and "stabbing the country in the back" (phrases some of the tabloids used, I kid you not) are now falling over themselves in their joy as Smith leaves the national side to return to "the club he loves."

"But its Rangers," they all say, "Walter simply wouldn't have done this had any other club came calling." Which is something we'll never know, since no other club wanted him. There is no News in the Record, and no Truth on Clyde, just a raft of Rangers propaganda, leading the Billy Boys down the path of the new Ten-In-A-Row Reich.

David Murray's Laptop Loyal Friends help take Rangers to the edge of oblivion

When Celtic signed Andreas Hinkel in January 2008 it was the opening salvo in the usual transfer window war between Celtic and Rangers. Except for the first time since the transfer window system was introduced, it wasn't. What none of us could have predicted was that Rangers response would be a three-fold embarrassment of the highest order, starting with their fanciful Moonbeams Park redevelopment plan.

At that time the business press, alone within Scotland's media, had published the facts as they stood in January of 2008. The overall debt of MIH stood at £643 million. The value of the company's assets stood at £788 million. Interestingly, net debt rose substantially during the 2006-2007 financial year, from somewhere in the region of £430 million to the ghastly £643 million figure. Whether or not this was down to exceptional outgoings, perhaps in land purchasing or something else, it had a huge effect on the debt figure and put serious strain on the company. A similarly bad year could wipe the company out. Of the £643 million debt, £527 million was due over the course of the next four years.

These were the hidden facts behind the leaking of the plans to redevelop Ibrox and the surrounding area. In times of such dire need it's important that as many sectors of MIH operate as well as possible. One of those, of course, is Rangers, what the accounts refer to as "Football Operations". In 2007 the figures were inflated by the JJB deal. In 2008, 'Football Operations' were able to post a nice extra chunk of cash on the final day of trading – the final day of trading, friends. In light of all this, the motivation behind the Sunday Mail fairy story about plans to redevelop Ibrox quoting figures which would outdo both the Wembley Stadium and Arsenal's Emirates stadium developments, has been made abundantly clear by this peek behind the veil of the MIH accounts. As a result, the full context of selling Hutton, a move which did not square with Rangers' apparent footballing priorities, is revealed. In selling Hutton, Rangers allow the Murray Empire to pretend all in the garden is rosy. If it costs them the title that is small potatoes compared to the cataclysm facing MIH if they'd don't start plugging the ever increasing number of holes in the dam.

During that January 2008 transfer window we were been given a small glimpse of the chaos going on within Murray's business empire, for nothing which happens to one arm of the business can be separated from the malaise any longer. Each part of that empire connects to the rest, and to sever one part is to kill the whole thing stone dead. The fate of Rangers is inexorably bound to Murray. The press, which was orgasmic with delight when he shifted £50 million of debt from the shoulders of Rangers FC and simply put it elsewhere within MIH, portraying this as a philanthropic gesture straight from his own personal fortune rather than the paper shuffling exercise it was, has never given consideration to the prospect that on the day the rent comes due on Murray Holdings, it will put the existence of Rangers FC at great peril. That day inches ever closer, and Rangers, like every other part of the empire, are feeling the squeeze ever more tightly, as we now know from yet another inadvertent spilling of the beans courtesy of Mr Dignity himself.

The Scottish press has aided Murray in his quest to keep things looking neat and rosy. Certainly, they assisted in pushing the redevelopment plans into the public domain, fulfilling Murray's double purpose – first in keeping the price of his land holdings in that area as high as possible, and secondly in trying to provide a utopian vision to Rangers supporters who have become increasingly skeptical in recent years.

They have good reason to be. The redevelopment plans also had the net effect of covering the initial moves to sell Alan Hutton. This deal, one of the biggest to take place in Britain during that transfer window, is the gap in the curtains we were never supposed to peer behind. This came in the midst of a title race as close any other in Scottish football history. Rangers were without a trophy for the previous two seasons, and although a League Cup Final win was on the horizon, this would hardly placate fans who hoped for a league flag. It seemed a very curious time to be selling any players, never mind their most highly rated players. There was also the pantomime around Rangers' attempts to shove Daniel Cousin out of the door with minor details such as FIFA rules to be cast aside. 2007/08 was a vintage season for Rangers in that respect, the one that would see the club christened, Rearrangers, as they succeeded in getting the SPL to postpone a league fixture, to extend the season (although not sufficiently long for their liking) and begged FIFA to change their rules on player transfers.

The Alan Hutton transfer saga was a drawn out affair, and any sensible person could see as events unfolded that the player himself was never going to be allowed to turn down the move. The role of the Scottish press this sale should not be underestimated. They were fully behind Rangers right from the first, and gave birth to the £9 million figure before any club had made an enquiry about the player. The Scottish press built the legend of Alan Hutton, and then helped Rangers sell it. Spurs bit, and then bought, whilst other clubs stood scratching their heads. Who can look, seriously, at the player and place that value on him after what amounts to a half a season of promise? When Juande Ramos was asked initially, about Hutton his response was that he had never heard of the player. This was after the initial bid had been made, and accepted by Rangers. It is entirely possible that this was a case of a manager denying an approach so as not to pique the interest of other clubs, or to avoid embarrassment if the proposed deal fell through, but if so, it would seem unnecessarily brazen for Mr Ramos to deny all knowledge of the player, a simple 'we have no interest in the player' type response would have sufficed. In any case, Hutton himself gave the move the thumbs down almost at once.

Then began, the most bizarre transfer saga in recent Scottish football history. Murray invited the player in for talks, and apparently sent Martin Bain down to England to resurrect the deal after Spurs called it off. Hutton was told to consider his future, which he did, concluding again, that he wanted to stay at Rangers, much to the distress of Murray and Bain, who'd manage to talk Spurs into making another bid. So they tried a new tack – they did something almost unprecedented in Scottish football – they offered the player a cut of the transfer fee in order to go.

Consider that for a minute. Since the first bid, Rangers never changed their stance in that they were reluctant to let the player leave. Nosurname himself said that everyone at Rangers wanted the player to stay. Yet, they offered him a reputed one million pounds to lay aside his own professed loyalty to the club and pack his bags. The evidence suggests that this too failed to sway the player, but he was dispatched down to Spurs for talks anyway, and whilst down there was persuaded to make the move. There was no prospect of a red carpet return once he'd gone down to London. Even as talks were ongoing, Walter Smith and Kris Boyd were telling the press the player had changed his mind about staying in Scotland and was chasing the money on offer in the EPL.

Equally bizarre were some of the pronouncements made during the on/off transfer saga of Daniel Cousin. Early in the season, as the player was being touted as the next big superstar, someone at Ibrox leaked details of a £3 million clause in his contract. At the time we were told it could only be triggered in the summer, but as we drew closer to the transfer window things altered ever so slightly. We started to hear whispers that it might just apply during the January sales. This prompted a statement from Martin Bain, on the 30th of November, which is worth examining in full.

He said; ""*I am disappointed that someone has chosen to bring into the public domain details of a contractual agreement with a player. There is an exit clause in Daniel's contract, but it cannot take effect until the end of the season. And the fee required under the terms of the deal is £3m.*"

Firstly, the "*someone*" in question was clearly in possession of a copy of the contract, because the press had every detail of it. This means the leak came either from the player's camp or from Rangers'. This statement was followed by a typically fawning piece of what passes for journalism from the pen of Mark Hateley, where he said:

"*I think that would be a blow because he is an important part of the Rangers squad ... It's a period of rebuilding for Walter and he would like to hold on to key players and I think Daniel comes in to that category. He is a top-class striker with loads of experience who can score goals.*"

A bare two months later, the clause Bain had denied existed was triggered, and Mark Hateley, writing again in the Daily Record, had likewise changed his tune when he wrote "*Yesterday was a good day for Walter Smith at the January sales. To quadruple the money you paid Lens for a player who is no spring chicken at the age of 30, and who only came to this country last August, is a superb piece of business.*"

I will not labour the point, which is that although Hateley's crayon drawings appear in the Record, he is very much David Murray's bitch, and without the Record's willingness to let him publish propaganda-disguised-as-fact would doubtless, instead, be a breathless contributor to the Rangers News. Then there was the transfer of Georgios Samaras to Celtic. The player was originally linked with Rangers in the usual breathless and hyperbolic fashion by the Scottish press. However, the minute Celtic registered interest the prospects for Rangers changed dramatically and realising this they dropped out of the race rather than face the prospect of being snubbed, or as their media puppets would have reported, "held to ransom". Rather than just acknowledge that Celtic got the better of Rangers in this instance and move on, the Samaras deal prompted one of the most unintentionally comical moments ever heard on Radio Clyde.

In response to a Rangers fan incensed by Celtic beating his team to Samaras's signature, Darrell "I only write about Rangers" King told him that the reason Rangers were unable to close the Samaras deal was that they were "*busy trying to complete the sale of Alan Hutton*". Consider that for a second. For close to 30 years I've listened to talk of big spending Ibrox money men and the Parkhead biscuit tin, the beggars and the tarriers. Now, in 2008, we have the amazing about-face of not only the media failing completely to question the lack of resources invested in the Rangers squad, we actually have journalists promoting the idea of Rangers not having the time to sign players because they are too busy trying to **sell** the ones they have! This is presented as a perfectly logical and sensible policy, and of course it is, in the full context of Rangers' predicament. But of course King is trying to present the absurd juxtaposition that, without any financial restraints coming into the equation, Sir Moonbeams & co simply decided that their top priority would be – ahead of strengthening their first team squad for a neck and neck title run-in – to concentrate on selling one of their best players. The irony is, King's assertion was no doubt entirely true, just not motivated by the

111

laughable contention that this was purely designed to bring in funds which would be reinvested on players.

I thought this comedy act would be the highlight of our transfer window amusement, but I was wrong. Just as the Hutton deal was being confirmed, on the very last day of the January transfer window, Rangers' entire senior management team traveled to Italy, as if on some sort of Keystone Cops convention, in what appeared to be an effort to sign a hitherto unheralded Italian striker. Of course this would end in tears (of laughter for the rest of us), and would throw up some interesting questions, not for the Scottish media of course, but for the rest of us non-Rangers supporters, or the small number of Rangers supporters who were intelligent and balanced enough to want to look beyond the lickspittle spin to find out what was actually going on with their club.

Andrea Carriocola is a name most of us were unfamiliar with, but we were told by the media that Rangers had been tracking the player "for months." Assuming this is true, it appears odd they would leave it up until the last few hours of the transfer window to make their move. Not so odd if the whole deal depended on cash coming in via the Hutton deal, but remember Rangers and the media assured us there was no pressing need to sell the young full-back.

Particularly strange, as the player was formally offered for sale at the start of the month. Indeed, reports in Italy in the last week stated interest from both Brescia and Torino, and declared that despite interest from clubs "outside Italy" his preference was to stay in the country. These reports are available online and elsewhere, and I daresay the club should have been aware of them before sending over Martin Bain, Walter Smith and the Ibrox medical team; in short, everyone required for the completion of a transfer deal of that type. They held talks all day, and the Scottish press was kept fully updated except in respect of the final fee, but were given just enough information to encourage jumping to conclusions and so they began to spin it ever higher – four million, five million, six million, seven million, and the player's mediocre track record was elevated to the level of the next big young superstar waiting to burst onto the scene, although skeptics like myself pondered why a player of such ability and huge potential would wait till he reached 27 years old before suddenly flowering into the next Roberto Baggio. Of course, entirely predictably, no deal was concluded with Rangers, the player joined Brescia of Serie B and the entire Rangers management team was "stranded" in Italy due to bad weather preventing them from springing any plan B into action, other than the loan signing of goalkeeper Neil Alexander.

Carriocola, in the meantime, was the subject of a sustained media assault on both Radio Clyde and Radio Scotland, as his – previously much hyped – CV was rubbished and his decision not to opt for the SPL was laughably judged to be a lack of ambition. In the Daily Record, Lorenzo Amoruso was wheeled out under the terms of his retainer, to give his opinion on the matter. This amounted to not much more than a crawly bum lick homily to what such a massive influential club Ra Gers really are accompanied by the opinion that the player had shown a lack of mettle and ambition by staying in Italy. *"He'll not attract much attention from the Italian national coach playing in Serie B"*, was Amoruso's withering assessment, in contrast of course, to the abundance of players to have been selected for the Italian national side whilst plying their trade in the SPL. It should also be noted that Carriocola's scoring record which was suddenly given in evidence to condemn the player, was available from numerous sources, and hadn't dissuaded Rangers from their attempts to sign him in the first place, or the Scottish media from bumming him up to the high heavens.

Chick Young offered us his own explanation as to why the deal was not done to Rangers satisfaction, which was right up their with Darrell King's hilarious "they were too busy trying to sell Hutton" effort – it was very complicated. I would imagine this remark was not sanctioned by Rangers PR people, as Brescia closed it without any apparent difficulty, but you can never be too sure. Being gazumped by a Serie B club is bad enough, but to have it ascribed to unprofessionalism, however unintentionally, when the entire Rangers management team has flown to a foreign country to get the deal done is the stuff of farce.

An obvious question arises from this botch-job – why in the hell did Rangers take all their heavy hitters to Italy in the first place, to negotiate a transfer the Italian press was widely reporting as without hope of success from the outset? During the Daniel Cousin saga, the Man with Nosurname was asked if he was happy to let the player go, his reply was: *"Managers have decisions to make in terms of identifying players and then they pass that on to other people to deal with. It's the same when someone comes in for a player. Martin Bain will ask me if I am happy to let that player go. So you still have the decision-making part of it. The bit that has been taken away is the bit that you would want taken away - dealing with the financial matters and contracts."*

Nosurname was clearly stating for the record his lack of involvement in Rangers transfer negotiations, stating all these matters were the purview of Martin Bain. Yet, there he was, in Milan, involving himself in precisely those matters. I cannot help but wonder if the entire Carriacola deal wasn't a smoke and mirrors exercise, with the entire Rangers delegation being sent to Italy to give merely the appearance of deeds, rather than because there was a realistic chance the deal would go through. The Scottish press, which never examined the goal scoring records of Filip Sebo, Federico Nieto or Francis Jeffers, had Carriacola's records to hand, as though they'd been given them in advance, and set about rubbishing the player the moment the deal fell through. All this childish "we didnae want him anyway" stuff is all very well, but the more discerning Rangers fan might wonder why if the player's credentials were so poor, the club were keen enough to send over their manager and CEO in an attempt to sign him? Surely this suggests a severe lack of judgement at the very least. That's the problem with the smoke and mirrors game, you can't always control the direction of the smoke.

Were Bain and Smith sent to Italy to waste the final day before the window closed? Were they sent to squander the last hours of the window on an impossible errand, because had they been here in Scotland the Rangers fans would have expected real money to be spent? Certainly the theory remains plausible given the mounting financial distress facing the club. Daniel Cousin and Alan Hutton were sold to plug holes, not to raise capital for transfer fees. They were sold in an effort to keep the whole Murray ship from sinking without a trace, regardless of what that meant to Rangers and their 2007/08 title challenge.

Ally Ross panders to the bigots with attack on James McCarthy

Over the past ten years, Scottish journalists have queued up to launch bitter personal attacks on Celtic players and managers. Martin O'Neill, Neil Lennon, Aiden McGeady and Artur Boruc have all been on the end of a media onslaught at one time or another, and on more than once occasion. A common theme that seems to have irked bigot fans and journalists alike is their allegiance to a proscribed nation across the water, whether the North or the South, certainly in the case of the first three on that list. In the autumn of 2008, the international eligibility fascists turned to a new target who for once wasn't a Celtic player. This time their derision was aimed at James McCarthy, a 17 year old Hamilton Accies midfielder, who under questioning from grubby hacks, had the temerity to confirm that he would continue to represent the Republic of Ireland, as he had been doing at youth level for the previous two years. This led to the predictable jibes and innuendo from our esteemed Scottish press, including one particularly scathing piece from Sun "TV-critic" Ally Ross, which sounds like his job is to sits in a room firing insults at a TV set all day. Apparently his actual job is less demanding than that. Ross is so fiercely patriotic, by the way, that he's lived in London for the best part of a decade, in the process surely contravening some arbitrary code of nationalism that he and is ilk would have applied to McCarthy and Aiden McGeady.

In the interests of balance one would have thought that the "patriotism" displayed by Lee McCulloch and Kris Boyd would have afforded Ross and his peers ample opportunity to "even the scores" in the interests of balance, or as non-paranoid fans of the nice wee polite teams would put it "Old Firm bias". Aiden McGeady and James McCarthy may play for Ireland but they have never given the Scottish national team or fans the vicky. And just ask Stephen McManus and Shaun Maloney about the treatment Celtic players get from the Scottish media for pulling out of a Scotland squad for a meaningless friendly, far less announcing they won't play again until there is a change of manager.

Anyway, back to Ally Ross who had some pronouncements to make back in October 2008 about the grave consequences of McCarthy's "treachery", having departed from his usual "TV-critic" role to poison-pen a "personal view" ahead of Scotland taking on Norway at Hampden. Getting a bit ahead of himself by referring to the player's options when his playing career ends, the London-based hack said "*Commercially, he's a bad lot. No newspaper executive with a brain will ever offer him a contract*". As if - like Ross - selling your soul to pen bigot-pandering venom along with the rest of the Scottish Laptop Loyal is the height of a young man's ambition.

Perhaps "fierce patriot" Ross has been down south sipping cocktails with the London Mayfair set for too long as he seems unfamiliar with Neil Lennon's trials, tribulations and assaults at the hands of the bigots in Scotland (not just Rangers fans either), as he states that McCarthy "*deserves a clip round the ear*". Ross then reveals his rosy eyed Brigadoon-esque view of the country he left behind to pursue the London shilling with the farcical statement "*He can at least though, thank his lucky stars the Scots are such a polite people. In England there's every chance a few maniacs would have run him out of town at the sharp end of a pole*". With Ally Ross leading the baying mob no doubt.

It wasn't the English who invented "The Famine Song" Ally. No that charming racist ditty was lovingly composed by the "polite" Scots. Scots who are not representative of the majority of non-Rangers supporting Scottish people perhaps, but who the media are more than willing to defend with their usual 'make the victim the culprit' style reporting.
I also struggle to think of any Premiership players being assaulted by "maniac" English fans. In contrast, Neil Lennon alone has been assaulted several times by "polite" Scots (not just Rangers fans). Of course when bigots make it impossible for Celtic players to have a night out without being attacked (McGeady, Brown, O'Dea) this is reported in the Scottish media as being their own fault.

Ross manages the impressive feat of coming out with a diatribe so jaundiced that even the Sun has to emphasise that this is his own "personal view". Perhaps this is because the article includes the usual completely dreamt up pish presented as fact, like - "*Instead his only advice seems to have come from fellow turncoat Aiden McGeady who - through no desire to have the heat taken off him, I'm sure - encouraged the move*".

We're still waiting on any journalist calling a Rangers player a "turncoat", or using such a pejorative term to denigrate a Rangers player or manager in any way. Perhaps one of our venerated Scottish journalists would like to start with Falkirk's Scottish born defender Brian McLean who elected to play for Northern Ireland instead of Scotland?

What's that you say - Scotland never asked McLean to play for them? Well neither did they ask McGeady and that explanation hasn't washed for him. So I'll take that as a "no" then? After all it's a bit much to be getting on McLean's case when you've been ignoring it for four years now. Personally, I don't think McLean has done anything wrong but fail to understand then, how McGeady and McCarthy are turncoats who deserve all the bile you can toss on them and to be assaulted in public, whereas McLean is perfectly OK for doing the exact same thing.

Ross also indulges in some sort of BNP-esque rant about taxes and the NHS services that McCarthy has benefited from as if McCarthy doesn't pay taxes in this country. This is the kind of stuff you'd expect to hear from the Red Hand salute brigade. In one of many cheap digs, Ross suggests that McCarthy should go to live in Ireland when his playing career is over (or the Famine, I'm not sure I'll need to check that again). Well I would suggest that Ally Ross should forget his tartan-tammy Jock act, slink back to London and stick to ranting about immigrants and eulogising reality TV shows.

Remember the subject of this hate-filled rant is a 17 year-old **boy**. Ally Ross must consider himself very brave to be taking on such a formidable opponent.

Ned Keevins supports the Scottish team in Europe. Again

Following the disappointment of Celtic failing to beat Rangers' record for the lowest Champions League points total of any British club the previous season, Ned Keevins gives himself a stiffy over the dizzy prospect of Arsenal pumping Celtic out of the Champions League with this shitey article in the Daily Ranger following the first leg 2-0 victory for the English side, I've taken a leaf out of Ned's penchant for using slang terminology to denigrate people he doesn't like:

Keevins - "*ARSENAL skipper Cesc Fabregas last night insisted Celtic tried to **boot him off the park** in the first leg of their Champions League qualifier*".

Naw he didnae

Keevins - "*But while Fabregas sweats over Wednesday he's **taken a swipe** at what he thought were Celtic's **strong-arm tactics** against him in Glasgow*"

Naw he hasnae

Keevins - "*Fabregas **slaughtered** Celtic's physical approach*"

Naw he didnae

What Fabregas did say:

"*It was a strange game. **Celtic didn't go for the long ball and tried to play good football**, which I didn't think they would*".

He makes a comment "*When asked about Celtic's physical approach*", (i.e. when begged by the Daily Record to say something negative about Celtic) about not expecting to be kicked on the same ankle several times but states "*it happens*". Not quite "*slaughtering Celtic's physical approach*" I'm sure you will agree. Hugh Keevins is a clown and should be put out to grass.

The Season of the Honest Mistake begins

Late August 2009 and Rangers travel to Tynecastle to take on Hearts in the second game of a season, where failure to win the SPL title and therefore the security of the resultant pot of Champions League revenue could have the gravest of consequences for them.

Things weren't looking too clever after only thirteen minutes when Kevin Thomson was ordered off for a wild two-footed lunge at Iain Black, which, luckily for the Hearts player, made minimal contact. According to FIFA's laws of the game – (*Any player who lunges at an opponent in challenging for the ball from the front, from the side or from behind using one or both legs, with excessive force and endangering the safety of an opponent is guilty of serious foul play*) – referee Craig Thomson correctly sent his namesake Kevin off, much to the chagrin of the Man with Nosurname and the Scottish media, including curiously, one particularly high-profile "Hearts" supporting radio shock-jock.

Twenty minutes later, Hearts opened the scoring courtesy of a blunder by their superstar "available at a knock-down price" goalkeeper who let David Witteveen's shot squirm through his grasp and over the line. Rangers were now in a real spot of bother. In the second half, Hearts seemed to rest on their laurels or simply lose all belief in themselves and Rangers with their 10 men looked the more likely to score, eventually doing so through Lee McCulloch on the hour. Not before the same player unleashed a flying hitch kick that made contact with Hearts goalkeeper Barogh's midriff, which went unpunished by the referee and, needless to say, unmentioned by the media. Rangers pushed on for the rest of the game without success, and the game was petering out towards a draw, when surprise, surprise, Rangers were offered a route out of their spot of bother via another spot for a foul by Bouzid on Naismith at least **a yard** outside the penalty area. Of course the media simply reported this as a bog-standard penalty award. Craig Paterson's summary of the incident for the BBC's highlights is revealing as he describes the incident starting from the point where Naismith and Bouzid chase a long through ball –

"...*and here's the winning the goal, I mean its a certain...*[pause – as TV pictures shows it was nothing of the sort despite Paterson's desperation]...*you know you can see...* [second pause - that it's outside the box Craig??]...*the right leg comes across and catches him.*"

Yes, the leg caught him Craig, **outside the box**. Paterson then goes on to totally excel himself with a statement of top-notch Rangers toadery

"...*at the game you think - was it in? was it not? Didn't matter*"

Oh I see, it didn't matter did it?? So it didn't matter when Celtic got a penalty at Hamilton Accies the season before for a foul on Cillian Sheridan that the media deemed to be outside the box did it? Let's have a look at a few choice headlines from the press from November 2008 –

"Referee cost us chance of beating Celtic, rages Hamilton boss Billy Reid - RAGING Billy Reid last night savaged <u>controversial</u> referee Steve Conroy. The Hamilton boss insisted the whistler's <u>blunder</u> cost his team the chance of a famous victory over Celtic." Daily Record 17/11/2008

"Celtic get out of jail after poor show against Hamilton - Celtic were awarded a penalty seven minutes from the break for a foul that happened <u>a yard outside the box</u>. Steve Conroy then <u>compounded his error</u> by sending off defender Martin Canning for the foul on Cillian Sheridan and Hamilton faced 50 minutes playing a man short." Daily Record 17/11/2008

I'm sick of getting red cards against Celtic, says Hamilton stopper Martin Canning - MARTIN CANNING admits he is sick of the sight of Celtic after being red-carded for the second time in only three appearances against them. The 26-year-old defender was sent off only 37 minutes into Hamilton's dramatic 2-1 defeat by the champions on Sunday after pulling down Cillian Sheridan. Television proved the offence occurred outside the area but referee Steve Conroy enraged the home side by pointing to the spot." Daily Record 19/11/2008

Wow, three articles devoted to a Hamilton Accies-Celtic game, with one fully **two days** after the event; you'd think this was a cup final. Note that Steve Conroy has suddenly become a *"controversial"* referee. Can't think why the media would brand Conroy "controversial", and then launch a vigorous defence of Dougie McDonald as one of the best referees Scotland has ever had, after his comedy of errors throughout the "Honest Mistake" season. Well, I suppose that's because he **is** one of the best referees Scotland have ever had, if you happen to support a certain team who play in blue.

Proving again, that the Scottish press either have an expedient interpretation of the laws of the game according to their agenda, or are simply ignorant of them; consider the Daily Record's contention that *"Steve Conroy then <u>compounded his error</u> by sending off defender Martin Canning for the foul on Cillian Sheridan"*. In fact the sending off is independent of the penalty decision. Canning was sent off for fouling Sheridan when he had a clear goalscoring opportunity, whether this happened inside or outside the box; therefore the decision is entirely correct. Obviously the Daily Record's David McCarthy got a little carried away with himself there. Maybe he should have undone a button, loosened his Rangers tie, and had a wee cup of tea before pounding out those words in a blind rage.

But as far as such incidents involving Rangers are concerned, the official media line is –

"Was it in? Was it out? Doesn't matter" just give Rangers the penalty anyway.

Getting back to the Hearts-Rangers game, media coverage was very much of the usual carpet sweeping standard. Whilst they refrained from coming out and saying directly that Kevin Thomson should not have been sent off, they did give great prominence to the Man with Nosurname's claim that it wasn't a red card. Having misrepresented FIFA's rules on the question of intent in relation to violent conduct in the Bougherra case, they now put a sympathetic slant on the new interpretation as espoused by the Divine Cardigan i.e it shouldn't have been a red card because there was "*no great contact*". I'll have to note that down for later – violent conduct is a sending off offence, only when there is "great contact". OK, got that.

They were, however, very quiet on the penalty and McGregor's blunder at the first goal (Artur Boruc makes a mistake that results in a goal... anyone?) and completely silent on Elbows McCulloch's assault on Barogh. The latter incident is met with rolling of eyebrows if you mention it to fans of the nice wee teams, as if you just made it all up yourself.

Andy Walker had the benefit of video replay on Radio Clyde which the referee did not have. So when Andy Walker said that "*it **could** have been a yellow*". He **should** be saying "*Thank goodness Thomson never broke that guy's leg, either with the initial challenge, or with the trailing leg that tried to finish the job*". When he said that it **might** not have been in the box, he should be saying "*it **was** outside the box and **definitely** was **not** a penalty, and why did both well placed officials **not** see this*?" Anyone not saying this with the benefit of replays is simply not being honest. Added to this, at the very time Glenn Loovens was still waiting for the outcome of his appeal, having been dragged up in front of the SFA panel on the say of eagle-eyed persons unknown, **not one** journalist, commentator or pundit raised the question of Lee McCulloch's karate kick after the game.

In any other country, or with any other Scottish team involved, the award of a penalty on 90 minutes would merit comment and debate of some description as to whether such a dubious decision was correct or not. But no, the media complicity kicks in the minute the whistle is sounded, and otherwise eagle-eyed journos who are willing to lobby the SFA to get Scott McDonald or Glenn Loovens up before a disciplinary panel, suddenly lose their specs and can see nothing amiss with the penalty or anything untoward with a friendly boot to the stomach which doesn't even result in a yellow card.

Now you needn't try too hard to imagine what sort of media coverage Celtic would have received if this had been us at Swinecastle:

Dodgy pen = " *Controversial* Craig Thomson`s a Tim... We must start a campaign to stop this diving, the SFA must act"

Dodgy goalkeeping = "Boruc is a headcase ...Tony Mowbray must drop him and get him out the door ASAP"

Assault on keeper = "SFA video panel must act"

Which leads to another item that was swept under the carpet by the poodles - Walter Smith came closer than anyone from Celtic ever has of calling a referee a cheat in his post-match interview. When asked by Chick Young (from inside his own rectum) whether he agreed with the sending off, Walt Disnae Criticise referees said "*No it wasn't a sending off.* ***It was an opportunity for the referee to send him off***".

The implication appears to be that Waldo thinks the referee was just chomping at the bit to send off one of his players. But he had even more to say about Thomson's shoddy refereeing "*I don't think there was any great contact made and obviously if there had been, the player would never have been able to continue in the manner he did do for the rest of the game.*"

Em... so if Thomson had made contact there was no way the Hearts player would have been able to continue? I think you'll find that your statement inadvertently proves the referee was correct Inspector Clouseau.

If this had been an interview with Mr G Strachan, T Mowbray or N Lennon, you can be sure Chico would have leapt on this statement like a dog with two dicks on soggy rag, demanding an explanation for such rampant paranoia. Of course faced with Sir Dignity himself it was quickly on to the next question faster than you could say "Disciplinary hearing at Hampden for questioning the integrity of an official". Then it was back to the impeccably neutral BBC team of Billy Dodds and Derek Ferguson (spot the connection) who had been forced to inform listeners through gritted teeth that the referee had made absolutely the right call with the red card.

Faced with the words of his master, 'Doddsy' swept the Dignity FC manager's raving paranoia under the carpet with a meek "*Ach well you'd expect the Rangers manager to say that*". Well actually I totally agree with you there Doddsy, but I anxiously await my next lecture from a Rangers fan on how they never complaining about referees or officialdom.

HONEST MISTAKE NO.1 – Lee McCulloch not sent off (or even booked) for kicking Hearts goalkeeper

HONEST MISTAKE NO.2 – Rangers given penalty for foul outside the box

POSSIBLE EFFECT – Rangers not reduced to 9 men and score winner from penalty (Rangers -2 points [possibly 3], Celtic 0 points)

Ewen Cameron's Minority Report

Now I did say there was one exception to the media view that the Thomson red card was "soft" but correct. That exception was "Jambo" Ewen Cameron, who from his demeanour on his pishy radio phone-in show after the game, appeared to be rather chirpy and feeling absolutely no pain at all about the result for some inexplicable reason.

Cameron makes a big show of claiming to be a Hearts fan and constantly showers himself with praise for being "outspoken" and "calling it as he sees it". Well he demonstrated a curious lack of concern at the treatment meted out to his own team, Hearts [stifled laughter], at the hands of the referee in this game. Instead he used his precious air-time to bemoan the Kevin Thomson sending off as harsh, confirm that a penalty awarded for a foul outside the box against the team he purports to support was indeed the correct decision, added that Obua of Hearts should have been sent off and went on to wax lyrical and at length about the *"fantastic"* Rangers supporters who were *"a joy to speak to"* and how fortunate he was to have had the *"absolute privilege"* to share a recent train journey with. Listening patrons of the Glasgow Underground immediately began to check their radios for a technical fault.

Of course, Cameron is a typical case – Scottish football journalists consisting of a strange cohort of Celtic, Hearts, St Mirren, Dundee United, Motherwell, St Johnstone, Aberdeen, Clyde, Airdrie United and Shettleston Juniors supporters with not a Rangers fan in sight. No Scottish football journalist – that group who take great pride in describing themselves in self-aggrandising pieces as "fans with laptops", is a supporter of Glasgow Rangers – the most widely supported team in the country. It is almost inconceivable to the paranoiac that this could genuinely be the case given that it effectively turns the demographic of the wider Scottish football fan completely on its head. However, that is only the view of the paranoiac, and instead we are assured by those of sound mind that the implausible reality presented to us, is indeed the truth, and that our next dose of soma is now due.

As far as Ewen Cameron is concerned, this extravagant praise of Rangers fans is not an isolated case. Cameron seems to have a strange pre-occupation with all things Rangers for someone who proclaims himself to be a Hearts fan. In September 2010, Cameron was moved to write a passionate defence of the Rangers support which contained a healthy dose of the "paranoia" he regularly lambasts the Celtic support for. Although ridiculing Celtic fans by playing X-files music on his radio show the minute someone mentions "the Establishment", this joker would have us believe the Scottish media, along with their English counterparts, UEFA and multiple European police forces, have an agenda against Rangers in some sort of pan-European conspiracy to sully their *"good name"*. Even the notion of Rangers' *"good name"* is enough to trigger fits of uncontrollable laughter. Cameron might care to add the name of Judge Andrew Blake to the list for his part in the conspiracy, which was to brand events in Manchester on 14th May 2008 *"the worst night of violence and destruction suffered by Manchester city centre since the blitz"*. Damn these anti-Rangers High Court judges, now where did I leave my copy of the Ripley's Believe it Or Not theme tune...

Cameron's piece was entitled *"Minority Report"* and made a big play of using the word "MINORITY" in capital letters throughout, in the manner of someone who really doth protest too much. The basic tenet of the whole thing is that all the trouble over the years that has besmirched the *"good name"* of the Establishment club, has been caused merely by a minority of fans and therefore it's just not fair to mention it more than once. Now, the very fact such a defence even needs to be made is informative in itself to the objective reader, but stay tuned because Cameron has his paranoiac theories about why Rangers are constantly in the limelight on the issue.

Before we go into that, it should be stated that it is not actually necessary to go through Cameron's ramblings and take them apart in a methodical fashion, because blaming all the club's hooligan woes on a MINORITY is a meaningless statement in itself, because **all** hooliganism is perpetrated by a MINORITY. Those responsible for the trouble that led to the senseless and tragic deaths in the 1985 Heysel Stadium disaster were a MINORITY. The Millwall thugs who ripped the Kenilworth Road seats up at Luton and threw them onto the pitch in that iconic footage from the 80s were a MINORITY. The Serbian neo-nazis who caused the abandonment of the recent Italy-Serbia Euro qualification tie were a MINORITY. Stating that everything is hunky dory and poor wee Rangers are the innocent victims of media "hype" is nothing more than Cameron's stock-in-trade – smoke and mirrors. The **real** question is this, why is the problem so much worse at Rangers than any other club in Britain? Yes that includes even your big bad Chelseas and Millwalls, who incidentally are on really quite friendly terms with much of the Rangers support as it happens. Here's an excerpt of Cameron's Rangers paranoia:

"Certain media were quick to write about the 'rioting Rangers support' as soon as Rangers drew Man Utd; scaremongering at its worst. Some of the things that have been said and written about the Rangers travelling fans have been unfair. **Is there a media agenda against the club? In my opinion the answer to that question is an <u>overwhelming YES</u>**. *I won't name names, but there are a few who are obsessed with all things Rangers and are just waiting for an excuse to put the boot in;* **<u>is that fair? NO</u>**. *Does the club do enough to defend itself and its real fans; I don't think so. Much of the time the Rangers support find themselves spitting into a gale force wind in their battle against* **unfair treatment**, *as the club sits back and says or does very little.*

When you look back at the highly publicised incidents involving Rangers over the past four years, you really do have to worry about some of the reporting. I think you have to feel deep sympathy for the supporters who are being dragged down by a **MINORITY**.

So let me get this straight – this guy, who has made a career out of winding up fans and slating Celtic fans for being paranoid, is coming out and announcing to the world that the Scottish media is biased against... Rangers? I always suspected a neck of zinc and copper alloy was required to work in the Scottish sports media, but this stream of paranoid pish should really win some sort of award.

The repeated use of the word 'MINORITY' almost had me wondering if I had picked up the meaning of that word wrongly. I am sure that it means less than half, although Cameron's use of the word suggests an attempt to apply some other meaning, more akin to an infinitesimally small number. Less than half of 100,000/150,000/200,000 supporters (depending on what rabid Rangers fan you want to believe) rioting is a lot of trouble however much you use the word MINORITY.

From the material that is spouted on his show – including an alleged "dossier" of every penalty and red card given for and against Celtic and Rangers in their entire history claiming to "*prove*" that Rangers have suffered more at the hands of referees – it must be assumed that Cameron is either a very dedicated researcher or has been spoon-fed quotes and "facts" from Rangers supporting friends. His radio show often doubles up as the broadcasting arm of the Rangers Supporters Trust, given the amount of air-time handed over to the ranting of David Edgar and company. It seems plausible that at least some of the material within "*Minority Report*" has been embellished by such sources.

The very fact that Cameron listed four separate occasions (Villareal/ Osasuna/ Manchester/ Bucharest) where a MINORITY of Rangers fans caused trouble leading to fines from UEFA, or in the case of the 2008 UEFA Cup Final, worldwide condemnation, should perhaps hint at a common denominator in the trail of wreckage which culminated in **jail sentences** for a MINORITY of Rangers fans. As referred to earlier, the anti-Rangers Judge hearing the case compared the destruction of Manchester to that experienced during the blitz. The damage inflicted during World War 2 was inflicted by a MINORITY of German bombers, but this was little comfort to those on the receiving end.

By the way, something that Cameron coincidentally failed to mention is that a MINORITY of supporters turned up at Ibrox to watch a live beam-back of the UEFA cup final at Ibrox. This beam-back, although devoid of any provocative away supporters, was apparently more troublesome than any SPL match that season with over 20 arrests made for violence outside the ground. Again, only a MINORITY of supporters were involved.

Cameron claims there is a media agenda against the club. The English media who covered the trouble in Manchester, just like the Spanish media coverage in Villareal and in Pamplona (Osasuna) is highly unlikely to motivated by bias against Rangers, it's just another story (although in the case of Manchester quite a spectacular one), they point their cameras, record the footage and move on to something else the next day. Like every club Rangers have a MINORITY of supporters that they would rather keep away from the glare and attention of the media. Celtic are not whiter than white, but we are far removed from the seething mass of rabid threshing hatred that was seen at Manchester and on a smaller scale in other European cities.

Burying heads in the sand and blaming the authorities/heavy handed policing/inadequate stewarding/not enough turnstiles/a lack of toilets etc etc etc for widespread scenes of violence simply lacks any credibility whatsoever. Motherwell and Liverpool supporters both made peaceful visits to the Steaua Stadium in Bucharest the same season, yet when Rangers came to town, a MINORITY of supporters broke seats and hurled them at the police. There are a significant number of people who attach themselves to Rangers, especially for European games, who feel that they are above the laws of the land and are entitled to special treatment. With each passing incident the attraction of traveling with Rangers increases for supporters more interested in trouble than team tactics. Although Cameron is regarded as little more than a wind up merchant, his platform can be dangerous with the message of "you've done nothing wrong lads" coming across loud and clear and galvanising the MINORITY.

MINORITIES can be big numbers, and dangerous. A MINORITY of people voted for a Conservative government, a minority of Scots voted the SNP into Holyrood. The MAJORITY of Rangers fans who don't get into bother may cringe at the actions of the MINORITY, but that doesn't mean to say their existence should be brushed under the carpet and the whole thing blamed on the crazy notion of a media witch-hunt against the Establishment club. That will only give them a provocative green light to wreak more carnage next time.

30th August 2009 Hibernian 0-1 Celtic

HONEST MISTAKE NO.3 Ian Murray handles ball twice in box. Richmond denies penalty.

The Evening Times said *"Charlie Richmond's performance was inconsistent and, at one point, left Lennon leaping like a truculent teenager in his technical area. Had Richmond focused more on getting decisions right – like Ian Murray's double handball in the box when pressurised by Keane after just 16 minutes – and less on posturing dramatically when blowing his whistle, it would have made for a much more efficient performance. As it was, Celtic managed to overcome his shortcomings and their own sluggish start to grind out a win. "*

Daily Record *"Ian Murray – Lucky not to concede a penalty in the first half but showed plenty of effort. Charlie Richmond – Got too many things wrong. Missed Murray's handball in the box although he got the actual spot-kick right."*

POSSIBLE EFFECT McGeady sent off debatably for "diving". Celtic win 1-0 so no effect in terms of points (Rangers -2 pts   Celtic 0 pts)

Scottish press suddenly find a voice over sick abuse

Fans of "family club" Motherwell had themselves a great time with a few copies of the Rangers karaoke book up at Pittodrie for the fixture on 29th August 2009, exposing yet another chapter in the hypocrisy-ridden annals of Scottish media history, as the Scottish press fell over themselves to furiously condemn the sick chants of "paedophile" directed at the Aberdeen manager.

Strangely enough, the very same journos flaunting their high moral standards in the Daily Record, Sun, Daily Express etc. have remained completely silent on the Big Jock Knew slur which has been on the go for at least three or four years now, propagated by Rangers fans with notable support from their maroon cousins from the capital. Well, completely silent, except for the Daily Record making a hilariously witty pun on it within their Winner section then implausibly claiming that this similarity was completely coincidental.

The usual predictable double standards from the media in Scotland – protect their own, go for everyone else.

An objective account of the matter appeared in the Scotsman on 30th August 2009:

NO OFFENCE FROM PLAYERS, JUST FANS
By Andrew Smith at Pittodrie

THERE is no way round it. It was nasty, petty and distasteful... and that was just the conduct of a small clump of Motherwell fans.

With both sets of players failing to produce anything to command interest or rouse the home fans in as abject a manner as you could ever have the misfortune to witness, attention inevitably turned towards the lustily rendered sing-a-longs by a clump of young Motherwell supporters.

These followed McGhee's comments on Friday that it was "ludicrous and unfair" he had become a target for the Fir Park faithful's ire for leaving the club to join Aberdeen in the summer.

Maybe we aren't on the ball, but few of us were aware of the depth of the ill-feeling that McGhee seemed to anticipate. It became a self-fulfilling prophesy because he so openly, though not without justification, insisted he deserved appreciation for what he did at the Lanarkshire club, a period that included his admirable leadership after the death of Phil O'Donnell.

It doesn't do to delve into the psyche of the football supporter who has been spurned; it is too bilious for most reasonable people. The fact then that McGhee was indeed baited throughout by a section of visiting fans wasn't what shocked during the opening period. It was the sheer unrelenting venom of the enmity displayed in charming ditties.

Two minutes in it was "if you hate Mark McGhee clap your hands". Fair enough. A couple of minutes later they told him he was "a w****r". Then he was "a fat Celtic reject and "a poor Tony Mowbray".

All acceptable if, by that stage, somewhat wearing. But is it OK for supporters of any club to call a manager a "sad Fenian bastard". Or is that only an issue when the club is Rangers? And what about their jeer that he was a "paedophile"?

"Some of it was pretty disgusting, and totally out of order," McGhee said. "I would like to think it's not the majority. I don't know what this is all about. I didn't do anything to deserve that. I'm quite proud of what I achieved at Motherwell and still have a great feeling for the club. I had two great years there. I thought it would be more humorous. I don't mind being called fat but some of the other stuff was out of order."

The Schizophrenia of the Scottish Media: 20/20 vision and temporary blindness

12th September 2009 Celtic 1-1 Dundee United

Celtic were held to a draw at home after continuing the bad habit of losing an early goal – on this occasion after just six minutes. Georgios Samaras equalised ten minutes later but Celtic were unable to find a winner in the remaining 74 minutes play, or more accurately, Celtic were unable to find a winner that the officials couldn't find a reason to disallow. Samaras scored a second with a header in the 59th minute, but despite remaining in line with the last defender, referee Conroy (the "controversial" tag mysteriously dropped by the media for some reason) chalked the goal off after his assistant flagged for offside. Added to that, in the closing minutes of the game Darren Dods dived full length across the United penalty area to perform, what could accurately be described as a Lev Yashin-esque "save", with his right arm to cut out an Andreas Hinkel cross, prompting Craig Levein to joke in his after match interview that he was disappointed Dods hadn't caught the ball. Penalty? Ha ha, I'll crack the jokes.

Scotland on Sunday – "*Levein left the field quietly at the end and there was probably a reason for that. His side appeared to come out the right side of two highly contentious calls in the second half; a Georgios Samaras "goal" chalked and a Celtic **penalty claim** waved away by referee Steve Conroy*"

If the Honest Mistakes had started on the pitch; off it, the Scottish media carpet sweeping had also started in earnest. STV coverage on the Monday evening news subjected us to a **slow motion close-up** of the handball resulting in the free-kick that led to **Celtic's** goal and insinuated that there was some dubiety about the award. Then onto Samaras's wrongly disallowed goal which Raman informed us "*was ruled out for offside*". Not "*wrongly*" ruled out, or "*controversially*" ruled out, or even "*ruled out after a debatable offside decision*", just "*ruled out*". Obviously Raman and his STV colleagues felt that decision was correct, unlike everyone else with functioning eyesight. Needless to say, the reincarnation of Lev Yashin **failed to even get a mention**. Sweep, sweep.

But on this occasion STV were out-hunned by the BBC, which is quite an achievement. Not only did the free-kick that led to Celtic's goal get the slo-mo treatment, the commentator described it as "*disputed*". Watch footage of the most obvious handball it is possible to see in a football match and send your answers on a postcard to, *Rewrite History competition, Black Hole, Room 101, Ministry of Truth*. For extra effect the commentator referred to a "*raging Craig Levein*" but just manages to stop himself from saying "*and quite rightly so*". Celtic fans are then reported to be "*dismayed*" at the official's decision to disallow Samaras's "goal", with no indication given of why Celtic fans should be "*dismayed*", or perhaps even "*raging*" if we were really pushing the boat out. Lev Yashin did make an appearance in the

BBC's five minutes of highlights on their website but no slow motion replay was shown (shockeroonie) and all the BBC had to say about it was Celtic had a "*claim*" for a penalty. Yes Celtic had a "*claim*" for a penalty in the same way someone might "*claim*" that grass is green. In contrast to "*raging*" Craig Levein, the BBC took great delight in Big Tony Mowbray taking it on the chin and declaring that it was "*a fair result*". Despite having previously been a player here, BTM clearly had a lot to learn about the Laptop Loyal if he thought he could leave it to them to report fairly on our treatment at the hands of referees. Nice guy; but too nice for the media jackals in Scotland.

By the way, I can't emphasise this enough. Going back to the Dods/Yashin incident – we are talking about an **outfield player** diving across his penalty area to cut out a cross with a save that an international class goalkeeper would have been proud of with **no penalty being given**; an incident that, for sheer surreality, almost rivals the footage of that Zaire defender charging out the wall to boot the ball upfield when facing a Brazil free-kick in the 1974 World Cup but the BBC didn't think it was worthy of even one replay, and STV **don't deem it worth a mention at all** in their reports. If the tables has been turned and it was Gary Caldwell playing the Safest Hands in Soccer with impunity we all know the media would have been all over it like a rash, calling for video evidence to be introduced immediately, and who knows, the SFA might even have called another emergency summit at Hampden to address sub-standard refereeing.

Instead, what we are subjected to is tales of Celtic scoring from a "*disputed*" free-kick, a hard-done-by "*raging*" Dundee Utd manager and a meek Celtic manager agreeing it was "*a fair result*". And we are expected to believe this is incompetence over bias. Well considering mad Raman went on to refer to the Scotland manager as "*George Bertie*" in the next item of that particular report, I would have to conclude – incompetence **and** bias.

HONEST MISTAKE NO.4 Samaras goal wrongly disallowed for offside

HONEST MISTAKE NO.5 Penalty not give for blatant handball.

POSSIBLE EFFECT Two goals for Celtic denied (Rangers -2 pts, Celtic +2 pts)

Newspaper apologises to Artur Boruc

In contrast to its "see-no-evil, let's drag Celtic into it then drop the story as soon as possible approach" to the Allan McGregor allegations, the Scottish Sun plastered this photo of Artur Boruc straightening a girl's hair over its front page, minus a Rangers club crest, alongside lurid allegations that Artur had taken two girls home for sex behind his wife's back. Of course straightening a girl's hair is an obvious post coital activity isn't it? Except, that the story was a pile of made up shite and the girl in question is Artur's sister and was in fact taken in Poland years before. Another "honest mistake" that managed to just slip out of the hack's laptop, then past sub-editor and then editor and into print. The Sun were forced to print the following apology -

In a report on May 5, 2009, headlined "Riddle of Boruc, the brunette and his hair straighteners", we claimed that Artur Boruc had brought two girls to the house he shares with partner Sara Mannei and had sex with one of them. We published a picture which we said showed him straightening one of the girls' hair. We now accept the picture was in fact of Mr Boruc and his younger sister Paulina in Poland some years earlier, and that neither did Mr Boruc invite back nor have sex with either of the girls in our story."

We apologise to Mr Boruc and Ms Mannei for any embarrassment caused."

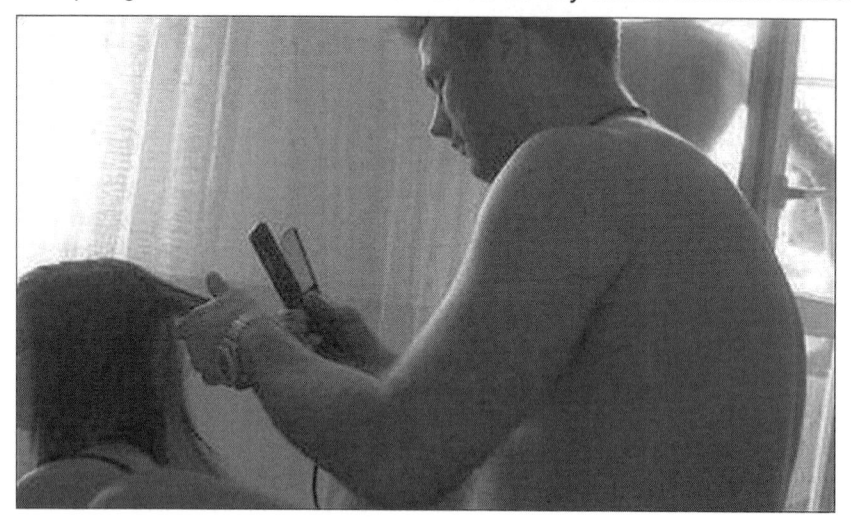

20th September 2009 Celtic 2-1 Hearts

HONEST MISTAKE NO.6 Niall McGinn tripped in the penalty area with five minutes to go and the score at 1-1. Dougie McDonald does not award the penalty.

Daily Record – *"The Northern Irish international was brought down inside the box by Lee Wallace with five minutes to go of Sunday's SPL clash at Parkhead, only for referee Dougie McDonald to award a corner to the bemusement of everyone inside the stadium."*

The Herald – *"Celtic should have been given a golden opportunity to clinch all three points when substitute Niall McGinn nicked the ball ahead of Lee Wallace inside the box five minutes from the end of regulation time, only to be brought down by the left-back. Referee Dougie McDonald had a long look - then awarded a corner."*

POSSIBLE EFFECT Celtic win 2-1 so no effect in the end, however the score was 1-1 with only five minutes to go this was a big call with potential to deny Celtic 2 points. (Rangers -2 pts, Celtic +2 pts)

Media fury at Mendes sending off

21st September 2009   Kilmarnock 0-0 Rangers

The season before we had the "incredible" sending off of Madjid Bougherra for the petty infringement of kicking an opponent in the head. On the same scale of the Laptop Loyal interpretation of FIFA's Laws of the Game through blue glasses, a second yellow card for kicking an opponent the stomach is "harsh". Much was made in the Scottish press and media following Rangers' 1-1 draw at Kilmarnock. Its true what they say, an animal is at its most dangerous when wounded and backed into a corner, hence much anger and indignation among the Laptop Loyal about the "*unprecedented / staggering/ excessive*" (choose suitably exaggerated adjective to suit your agenda) number of bookings in the match (eleven).

The Scottish media held this up as evidence of poor Rangers being hard-done by at the hands of officials again (stop laughing at the back). Even the most fleeting of glances at the facts surrounding that particular game show you just how distorted reporting of games involving Rangers has become – remember Rangers were the victims of Irishy sounding referee Steve Conroy here. Stats:

Kilmarnock 5 bookings
Rangers 4 bookings

Kilmarnock 1 sending off
Rangers 1 sending off

Yes, you would be hard pushed to notice that Kilmarnock had a player sent off (Manuel Pascali), as it was lost under a deluge of hyperbole in the media on Pedro Mendes "*harsh*" sending off.

Let's compare Pascali's uncontroversial sending off with Mendes's "controversial" sending off:

Pascali sent off for two innocuous fouls – the 2nd a standard "tug" of the jersey on the halfway line with no imminent prospect of a goalscoring opportunity

Mendes booked for kicking an opponent in the stomach, and then booked again for a violent lunge at an opponent running at speed, which could easily have caused serious injury.

OK, I suppose kicking someone in the stomach isn't quite as bad as kicking someone in the head which is an automatic red card... oh no wait...

It's no coincidence that Conroy and Tom Murphy (spot the connection) are the only two officials which the Scottish media have countenanced criticism of, and were prepared to put on the defensive. After the Mendes sending off, the Scottish media took a sudden unaccustomed interest in the following week's Motherwell-Hibs game which Conroy just happened to be officiating. Of course the same media showed not an iota of concern for the much more compelling case of Kilmarnock's Manuel Pascali who also ordered off after a second yellow card for an innocuous pull an opponent's jersey on the halfway line. In any case, headlines of "*I Back Whistler Conroy - Hughes*" started appearing in the red tops as hacks suddenly developed an unprecedented preoccupation with the Hibs manager's opinion of Steve Conroy. The top story on STV's Friday evening sports bulletin concerned the Hibs managers' support for the "*under-fire*" referee as John Hughes was reported to have "*no concerns over Conroy handling the match*". This followed the type of interview with Raman Barwaj usually reserved for the eve of a Cup Final.

Why Steve Conroy was "*under-fire*" and why Hughes should have any "*concerns*" was clearly understood by everyone. It's been a long time since a Motherwell-Hibs match was the top Scottish sports story and it'll be a long, long time until that is the case again. Of course it's no coincidence that Steve Conroy did not come "*under fire*" after the ridiculous decision not to award a penalty to Celtic against Dundee United on 12th September. The message to Conroy is clear - "*We're watching you. If you're going to make a mistake, you damn well better make sure that mistake benefits the Establishment team or there will be repercussions.*"

"Hearts fan" Ewen Cameron was typically representative of the collective media fury as the Rangers fans with laptops expressed their disappointment at the loss of another two points. Cameron pontificated at length about the referee's sub-standard performance and stated that "*surely 11 bookings in one game is an SPL record?*"

Cue a clued-in Celtic supporting caller who is known to me and who will only be identified here as Dev Advocate.

Dev Advocate: "*Do you remember a certain Old Firm game at Ibrox that finished 3-0 to Rangers?*"

E Cameron: "*Yes I remember it well*"

Dev Advocate: "*Do you remember how many bookings there were in that game?*"

E Cameron: "*No, not off the top of my head no*"

Dev Advocate: "*There were 11 bookings in that game, so there goes your record Ewen, and do you remember how many Celtic players were booked?*"

E Cameron: *"I don't know 4, 5..."*

Dev Advocate: *"No, Ewen NINE and I don't remember you or anyone in the media complaining then"*

E Cameron: *"Ah but of course you and the rest of the Celtic fans complained non-stop about it at the time and now you're criticising Walter Smith..."*

Dev Advocate: *"Yes, Ewen correct. We did complain at the time and what did you say about it Ewen? You said we were all PARANOID and that it was simply SOUR GRAPES. So how is it, Celtic fans were all paranoid for complaining about getting NINE players booked in one game and Walter Smith is perfectly correct to complain about the number of bookings in a game where the OPPOSITION had more players booked?"*

E Cameron: *"Em...err...em.... maybe you've got a point there....[oh shit, there goes my Winalot]"*

Dev Advocate did a great job, however he didn't quite manage to slip in the fact that whilst NINE Celtic players were booked in that game, Daniel Cousin managed to knock Stephen McManus unconscious with a headed "challenge" that was so late it was practically an off the ball incident and yet wasn't getting booked in a game where the referee dished out yellow cards like confetti.

Oh, and the referee in that game – Mike McCurry. You would have to be paranoid to read anything into that though.

Lapdogs show their pain as Celtic go top of the league

The Herald and Evening Times come up with a vintage display of Laptop Loyal Dom with their match reports on Celtic 2-1 Hearts (20 Sep) and Kilmarnock 0-0 Rangers games (21 Sep). The two Dowell's are clearly in much pain as Celtic overtakes Rangers at the top of the SPL.

Darrell King in the Evening Times doesn't mention Walter Smith being sent to the stands. A neutral might have thought that a red card would have been worthy of some sort of comment but not in the weird and wonderful world of the lapdogs and lackies that constitute the Scottish football press. Graeme MacPherson at the Herald finds Wattle's latest dignified spit the dummy equally un-newsworthy. Must be "Old Firm" bias.

Chief Ranger with Laptop, Darryl Bentfoot's match report of Celtic's 2-1 win over Hearts in the Herald fails to mention Maloney's free kick hitting the bar, describes the Celtic players with the exception of Fox, McGeady and McGinn as "*mediocrity*", and later in the article states McGeady was "*exasperated by the dross around him*". He then goes on to give N'Guemo a 3 in his player ratings.

Bentfoot must be upset by this "mediocrity" and "dross" leap-frogging his own team to the top of the SPL. God knows what adjectives he'd use to describe Rangers at the moment. Actually, I've got a pretty good idea.

Violent conduct by Lee McCulloch ignored yet again

26th September 2009 Rangers 0-0 Aberdeen

Following his kung fu kick on Barogh of Hearts at Swinecastle, Lee "Elbows" McCulloch was it at it again a few weeks later as he floored Paton of Aberdeen with a forearm smash. TV pictures show McCulloch looking at Paton then waiting for the Dons player to play the ball past him before slamming his forearm into his face. No yellow card, never mind a red.

This incident was completely ignored by the STV and BBC Scotland TV news broadcasts as well as the Monday evening BBC highlights package. Footage of the incident is available at the time of writing on the webpage if you think I've just made this all up -
http://tinypic.com/view.php?pic=13ztvf9&s=4

The BBC quaintly described the incident thus - "*Lee McCulloch was booked for **catching** Michael Paton in the face before Peter Pawlett's header drifted wide of McGregor's goal*". Blink and you'd miss it.

The Herald took a similar light touch "*Paton was fortunate not to be hurt, too, when Lee McCulloch **caught** him with an arm across the face*"

Is the word "elbow" or "violent" alien to the BBC and Herald vocabulary? Do you think they would have been playing it down if Glenn Loovens or Scott McDonald had been involved in such an incident?

Amazingly it was left to the Daily Record to describe the incident with some semblance of accuracy "*Rangers midfielder Lee McCulloch, however, was fortunate not to pick up a red card from Iain Brines for an elbow on McGuire*[sic]." *Rangers would have been playing 45 mins with 10 men if Brines had done his job*" Lo and behold, the next match up for Rangers was…Celtic. So Elbows McCulloch escapes a three match ban for violent conduct and gets to join in the thuggery the week after against Celtic.

HONEST MISTAKE NO.7 – Lee McCulloch not sent off for elbowing Michael Paton in the face.

POSSIBLE EFFECT – Rangers not reduced to ten men. Effect on outcome of the game uncertain. (Rangers -2 pts, Celtic +2 pts)

Spin ratcheted up to Mach 10 after Rangers' Sevilla humiliation

29th September 2009 Rangers 1-4 Sevilla

Rangers actually played quite well in the first half of this game and possibly had marginally the better of it before going in at half-time with the score goalless. In the second half though, the gulf between the sides became glaringly apparent and Sevilla ran out comfortable winners, taking a 4-0 lead before Neddy Novo scored a spectacular consolation goal. This was the kind of performance that would have had Keith Jackson waffling on about Celtic's *"glaring deficiencies at this level"* (see *Celtic Paranoia: The Laptop Loyal Diaries 4 Dec 2007 Daily Record gutted at Celtic's qualification for the 2nd round of the Champion's League*), but this Rangers so the Laptop Loyal paint a picture of a plucky team denied by a referee's error. TV pictures showed that Rangers should have been awarded a penalty for a foul on Naismith in the 36th minute with the scores at 0-0, and boy did the media let us know about it.

The terminology used by Clive Lindsay and presumably approved by some sub-editor of the Beeb website was akin to listening to a rabid Louden Tavern punter and was as (follow) follows:

"the result will be overshadowed by the decision to deny the Glasgow side a clear early penalty."

Yes UEFA will have to add some sort of addendum to the match result to record the injustice of it all for posterity. Punters from Lisbon to Kiev will be suitably outraged. Anyway, back in the world of the Louden Tavern regular...

*"Rangers were **further angered** when the referee denied them **a clear corner** as they applied some early second-half pressure and then awarded Sevilla **a soft free-kick** against McCulloch from which the Spaniards took the lead."*

Further angered?? Was there some sort of gratuitous flaunting of pepperami bars or green and white straws that went unreported by the media? Is there any kind of Rangers supporter other than a permanently raging one??

I'll need to look that one up in the Laptop Loyal rulebook too – a free-kick is not to be awarded if it is deemed "soft". Maybe someone should take Mr Lindsay aside and diplomatically say "Look son, I know your hurting badly because your team got pumped rotten, but a free-kick is a free-kick". In any case, the Spaniards did not take the lead directly from this free-kick. The ball was played square to winger Jesus Navas who had the freedom of Govan to cross it into the box, and with Davie Weir dreaming about relaxing with a bag of Werther's Originals, Sevilla striker Konko had the easy task of heading past "£10million-rated" bevvy merchant McGregor.

And another thing - this "*soft*" free-kick was more of a foul than that which earned Pascali of Kilmarnock a red card against Rangers the previous Saturday, but mysteriously a slight tug of an opponent's shirt has metamorphosed from a yellow card offence to not even a foul within a period of a few days. OK, a "soft" foul, which isn't actually a foul at all. Answers on a postcard as to why that might be to... *K Jackson, Daily Ranger, Doublethink Department, Central Quay, Glasgow.*

Away from the Beeb for a second, Jim White, ably supported by Neil McCann on Sky, commented that "*it was only a small pull of the jersey though Neil wasn't it?*"

Watch out for the new FIFA rule book which says small pulls of the jersey are no longer illegal conduct. A variation of this new law has been in force in Scotland for decades in circumstances involving teams in blue shirts with RFC crests which clearly confused White in his despondent feeling of having been transported back to 1996.

Back to Lyndsay and his hurting bear act "*Rangers had the better of the first half*" Who cares if a game lasts 90 minutes? And just for good measure, a photo of Naismith's U-571 act is accompanied by the caption "*The result may have been different had Rangers been given a penalty*"
Yes it might have been 4-2 to Sevilla. You really have to pinch yourself and remember it's only Celtic fans that are paranoid.

Another interesting point to note (unless you are a Scottish media employee) was that the crowd at Ibrox was 40,572 for a Champions League tie. A few questions arise from this that will be suitably ignored by the Scottish media:

How does that affect the "*guaranteed*" £17 million Champions League windfall much crowed about in the Laptop Loyal since Rangers won the league last season, which was very much based on three full houses?

Why is this ignored when less than capacity crowds at Celtic Park have been highlighted by the media this season and used for every negative angle of speculation you could think of, from Celtic falling £10million into debt next year to a fan's vote of no confidence in Tony Mowbray?

Ibrox is **twelve thousand** below capacity for a **Champions League tie** and **no comment whatsoever** is made on this by the Scottish media.

Must be bias to the O*d F**m again.

Meanwhile, the Herald's Graeme McPherson won a Moniteau Comedy Festival award for his player ratings:

RANGERS   1-4   SEVILLA

Rangers 4-5-1
ALLAN McGREGOR 6
STEVEN WHITTAKER 6
MADJID BOUGHERRA 7
DAVID WEIR 6
SASA PAPAC 6
KEVIN THOMSON 7
STEVEN DAVIS 6
LEE McCULLOCH 6
PEDRO MENDES 6
JEROME ROTHEN 6
STEVEN NAISMITH 7

Sevilla 4-4-2
ANDRES PALOP 6
ABDOULAY KONKO 6
JULIEN ESCUDE 6
SEBASTIEN SQUILLACI 6
FERNANDO NAVARRO 6
JESUS NAVAS 6
LOLO 5
DIDIER ZOKORA 6
ADRIANO 7
LUIS FABIANO 7
FREDI KANOUTE 7

RANGERS 69 SEVILLA 68

So having had their arses skelped 4-1 we are told that actually Rangers were the better team. I believe someone once said *"there are none so blind as a hurting Establishment hack"*. McPherson also showed his true colours and with it his credentials for one day taking over from Bentfoot as chief Herald bluenose with this little anecdote about Jesus Navas who provided the cross for Sevilla's first goal - "*Winger suffers from chronic homesickness so popped into Bairds Bar for a pint just to hear people talking about Seville again*". Hilarious Graeme. I'm really glad your team got pumped.

First "Honest Apology" of the season

4th October 2009 – Craig Thomson (he of the vicious vendetta against poor wee Kevin Thomson) apologises for not awarding Celtic at least one blatant penalty at Mordor. Davie Weir chops Maloney down in box in the first Us V Them game of the season but Thomson waves play on and Rangers go up the park and score. STV website and various media report *"Old Firm referee Craig Thomson has admitted he's 'disappointed' at getting his decision wrong when he decided not to award Celtic a penalty in the 12th minute. Hugh Dallas said: 'Craig and I have had our post match de-brief. Whilst I would compliment Craig for his overall handling of yesterday's encounter, he is disappointed at his error of judgement when he decided against awarding a penalty to the visiting team in the 12th minute."*

Whilst it was good of them to touch on the matter there is a distinct lack of righteous indignation from the Laptop Loyal, such as would be seen if these decisions had gone against their beloved Rangers, for example if Pedro Mendes or Kevin Thomson had been correctly sent off.

After his team suffered a wee "honest mistake" or two at the hands of the MIBs, paranoid Motherwell manager Jim Gannon said : *"Right now there is a question mark over the standard of our refereeing, and it affects the SPL table. After the last Old Firm game Hugh Dallas had to defend the referee* [Craig Thomson]. *But the result of that match might have been different had the ref got the big decisions correct"*

Two penalty claims turned down when David Weir blatantly fouled Maloney and Wilson. Maloney booked by Thomson to compound matters. The Daily Mail said this – *"Maloney, in particular, seemed harshly dealt with after being chopped down by David Weir with the score at 1-0 and was accused of simulating another tumble in the box following a challenge from his Scotland team-mate. TV pictures later suggested Craig Thomson got both calls wrong."*

Kyle Lafferty adds 'thug' to his list of talents alongside 'cheat', with a flying hitch kick to Zeng Zhi's groin. See photo above and consider the referee's clear unobstructed view of the incident and, once you've worked out why he didn't take any action (remember, you're not allowed to consider bias to Rangers), you can get back to the simpler problem of working out how to achieve cold nuclear fusion.

HONEST MISTAKE NO.8 Penalty not given for blatant foul by Weir on Maloney in the box.

HONEST MISTAKE NO.9 Penalty not given for blatant foul by Weir on Maloney in the box. Maloney booked for diving.

HONEST MISTAKE NO.10 Lafferty catches McManus with a late headbutt no card.

HONEST MISTAKE NO.11 Lafferty kicks Zhi in the groin – no card. Could be a red on its own, but added to previous incident Lafferty should be off the park. The Daily Record prints a photo of the incident with the caption "Welcome to Glasgow, China". Aye it's a great laugh isn't it.

HONEST MISTAKE NO.12 Novo deliberately handles when on a yellow card. No second yellow card. If you think red cards aren't dished out for this sort of thing see, Sutton C. Rangers v Celtic Nov 2004.

HONEST MISTAKE NO.13 Weir stamps on McDonald's knee and follows up with a knee to the back right in front of the referee Craig Thompson who had a clear view. Free kick awarded but no booking and no video review panel for Weir, despite the offence being more serious than the one McDonald was cited for in May 2009.

POSSIBLE EFFECT Two penalties denied. Weir, Lafferty, Novo could, and probably should, have all been sent off. Two converted penalties and Rangers reduced to 10 or 9 men. High probability of at least a 3-2 win for Celtic.

(Rangers -5 [-3], Celtic +5 [+3])

Mr Dignity: Bullet Proof

20th October 2009 Rangers 1-4 Unirea Urziceni

The silence from the sycophants masquerading as journalists in this country has shown once again what hypocrites they truly are with their whitewash of Walter's tactics in this game, in which his team that he assembled over a 3 year period, lost in a woeful, abject manner against a Romanian team lucky to have even a tenth of his budget at their disposal. According to the tabloids and the radio pundits it was all the fault of the players who need to have a right good look in the mirror. No blame can be apportioned to Man with Nosurname.

Amazing – from the same press corps who are quick to savage other managers (Gordon Strachan for a completely random example) and pick through the carcass of abject defeat when it comes to Celtic and who proudly justify their personal diatribes by saying that it is their duty to ask these questions and demand answers on behalf on "*the fans*".

What happened to their sense of duty at the Unirea post-match press conference? Where is their sense of duty in today's newspapers? Probing questions? Balanced criticism? Don't be daft, it's Walter (Never just "Smith" by the way), we can't give him any cheek or even stand up to him. So what is it, respect or shameful fear? To be truthful it matters not one iota because the dereliction of duty our hacks have shown in this whole sorry affair would make your skin crawl. They have all, to a man, rallied round the Man with Nosurname, subjecting us to talk of his players having to have a look in the mirror and the paucity of the resources available to him (as opposed to a team who were in the Romanian third division six years ago). At this juncture it might be interesting to have a look back at what the same media had to say about the previous worst result for an SPL side in Europe – Celtic's loss away to Artmedia Bratislava. The following article from the Guardian captures the tone nicely:

"With one mishandled game in Bratislava Strachan and his players have wiped up to £10m off the club's income in the year ahead. Celtic cannot have anticipated that worry when they granted him a transfer budget of £7m, which is 10 times greater than the combined expenditure of the other 11 members of the SPL

A transitional season was inevitable for Strachan but, while there was no golden inheritance for him, he did squander what resources he had on Wednesday. **His tactical decisions in Bratislava were grossly misjudged. With Celtic 2-0 down and the game in a dull phase, he brought on an extra attacker.** *"We gambled with three up and it didn't work for us," Strachan remarked, with the understatement of a man in shock.*

The enterprising approach taxed his noticeably unfit team and Artmedia, an otherwise undistinguished group who do know how to hit on the break, scored three times in the closing quarter of an hour. Strachan may have been undone by his starry-eyed view of the Celtic post. On the eve of the match with Art media he spoke of a need to ditch the damage-limitation mentality that was appropriate to Coventry and Southampton. It will now have occurred to him that, at the start, he should have been as cautious as ever.

Strachan is an intelligent manager who has spoken well at Celtic **but it is his decision making that fell into disrepute on Wednesday** *and now he has to show that he can be wise under pressure. Ruthlessness is also essential. While the centre-halves and his new left-back Momo Camara must have appalled him, action is called for elsewhere too.*

In buying the Poland attacker Maciej Zurawski and the Japan playmaker Shunsuke Nakamura, whose £2.7m transfer from Reggina should be completed after a medical today, Strachan has favoured men who can ease a pass through a defence but at the same time he has continued to select

John Hartson, a forward currently too immobile to capitalise on a through-ball.

Strachan broods on bad results and, following one calamity, became so lost in thought during a walk that his wife had to drive and collect him many miles from their house. By tomorrow, at Fir Park, he will have to be far more sure of where he and Celtic are going".

Compare and contrast the treatment and invective used on a man in his first game in charge of Celtic with a man who has been Rangers manager for almost 3 years, plus the 7 from his previous stint.

Why did the press slate Strachan when they should have simply slated the players?

Jim Traynor questions the integrity of honest pros?

So the post mortem continued into the weekend. By the Saturday afternoon the Scottish media had yet to emerge from its official period of national mourning, with a minute's silence rumoured to be scheduled for Tuesday evening at 8:22pm to coincide with the moment Steven Davis missed their penalty, which incidentally, put a new light on all this "we would've beat Sevilla if we'd got the penalty" talk.

On the Saturday afternoon on BBC Radio Scotland, leading Laptop Loyal figurehead Jim 'No Neck' Traynor did his bit to keep things in perspective and ensure that the manager Walter Nosurname was held to account for his share of the blame. Discussing the matter with ex-Hearts striker John Robertson, No Neck stated that sole responsibility lay with the Rangers players who had "*cheated*" the fans and their manager by failing to give 100% in the Unirea game and that they should be held to account.

This got me wondering…

Was this the same Jim Traynor who fearlessly slaughtered Chris Sutton in 2003 for having the temerity to suggest Dunfermline players failed to show 100% commitment in a game against Rangers, and called for Sutton to be banned for at least 9 matches for "*this scandalous slur on the integrity of honest professionals*" and stated that he "*has demeaned Dunfermline and the Scottish game*"?

I for one can't wait for No Neck's disciplinary hearing and 9 match ban.

The Laptop Loyal's Selective use of Statistics: The Worst Record of a British Team in the Champions League

For reasons that remain inexplicable to the non-paranoiac, no-one in the Scottish media raised the subject of the dreaded 'Worst ever record of a British team in the Champions League' after the Unirea defeat. It would seem an apt time to have mentioned it with Rangers sitting on 1 point from three games and two more away matches to come. For more reasons that remain unexplained this was something of a hot topic the previous season (2008/09) with Hugh Keevins alone bringing it up on Radio Snide just the dozen times whilst salivating in anticipation at the prospect of Celtic earning this 'honour' with anything less than a win over Villareal in our final game. By complete coincidence Flanders managed to avoid mentioning the identity of the current record holders, who as it happened managed to go on and lower the bar with regard to that particular record in 2009/10 season. Give them another star to put on their badge.

Union Jack flown at Battle of Manchester Sold at Christie's

A giant shot, urine and buckfast-scarred Union Jack that was flown at the Battle of Manchester has sold at auction for nearly 390 empty ginger bottles and a £5-off Farmfoods voucher, more than 20 times the pre-sale estimate.

The 11ft by 7ft flag (3m by 2m) from *HMS Bridgeton Loyal RSC* was bought by an anonymous collector by the name of Alastair Johnston (no, I haven't heard of him either) bidding against the National Front Museum and other would-be buyers from around a wee part of West of Scotland stuck in a centuries old time warp.

The new owner of the flag, which is believed to be the only surviving Union Jack to have flown at Manchester — 500 days ago yesterday — paid a total of 384 empty ginger bottles when his RFC credit card was declined for part of the payment.

In the short term however, it may become the object of a battle to prevent it leaving Bridgeton. Patrons of the Crimson Star public house are considering pooling their giro money and fake disability allowances together to prevent this piece of Rangers history residing in a place where it may come into contact with Eggs Benedict, pepperami or green and white drinking straws

The flag was made from 31 pieces of "We Are the People" bunting by the regulars of The Louden Tavern shortly before the victory over the Spanish and Russians at Barcelona in 1972. The flag subsequently led Rangers Orc tribes to victory in many famous battles including Birmingham 1976, Dublin 1984, Sunderland 1990, Birkenhead 1998, Eindhoven 1999, Rotterdam 2002, Villareal 2006, Pamplona 2007, Barcelona (again) 2007 and finally saw its greatest triumph as Manchester was over-run and sacked by rampant Orcs in May 2008.

After the battle it was taken down and presented to Lieutenant Bill 'Tiny' William McBillyboy of *HMS Bridgeton Loyal RSC*, a singular honour for one of the Red Hand Brigade's junior officers. The flag has remained in McBillyboy's family since, despite the best efforts of Manchester Constabulary to locate and apprehend him. McBillyboy decided to sell the flag after footage of him rampaging in Manchester was shown throughout the UK on Crimewatch, resulting in plans to move to Orange Free State in South Africa to avoid apprehension by the authorities.

The flag is riddled with holes from shot, splinters, cigarette burns and pointy hats and still has a pungent smell of buckfast, urine and vomit. News of its sale attracted interest from "private" handshaking institutions as well as the mentally unbalanced.

Charles Miller, the London auctioneer who sold the flag, said: "*It was all quite exciting. We are a small auction rooms and we were packed in like sardines. Most of the crowd were Scottish football journalists on mobile phones muttering "yes Sir David, no Sir David, certainly your Divine Lordship" and bearing physical evidence of having come straight from Walter Smith's rectum. Fortunately, having eaten the sweetcorn out of Wattie's shite many times in the past, none of us were particularly perturbed, quite the opposite in fact. When the hammer eventually came down there was a huge round of applause and cries of "We Are the People" and "Go on home Timmy, the Famine is Over*" ".

"*The price is way above anyone's expectations but does reflect the historical importance of the flag and the battle in which it got pished and puked on over a year and a half ago, not to mention the ability of Rangers supporters everywhere to beg, steal and go round people's doors asking for empty ginger bottles when they put their minds to it. Some Glasgow families of a Timmy persuasion even resorted to putting green and white straws on their doors to prevent Rangers fans breaking in and stealing their valuables*".

Mr Miller then became incensed and threw a chair at a passer by in a Celtic top whilst shouting a flurry of expletives peppered with multiple uses of the word "*fenian*".

However a spokesman for the Department for Culture, Media and Sport cast some doubt on the authenticity of the flag's history. Many historical scholars, originating exclusively from the Scottish media led by "Hearts" supporter Ewen Cameron, have claimed that many of the military victories credited to HMS Bridgeton Loyal RSC and other Orc tribes were in fact the work of English armies such as *Chelsea Headhunters, Millwall Hooligans and West Ham Casuals.*

"*They claim that the travels of Rangers Orc armies have been completely benevolent, and in fact have played no part whatsoever in the brutality which by some bizarre and completely coincidental anomaly has just happened to follow them around Europe for over 35 years. Therefore, we cannot definitively verify the authenticity of the historical links of these military victories to Rangers Orc armies.*"

Despite this official Government line, it is well known outside the circles of orange spectacle wearing apologist lackey Scottish journalists, that the proud history of rampage and violence attributed to the Rangers Orc tribes is genuine, and that Ewen Cameron is as much a Hearts fan as Zsa Zsa Gabor.

One claim that is yet to be verified however, is whether this particular Union Jack was present in one of *HMS Bridgeton Loyal's* finest moments – a "Red Hand" salute spectacular in the heart of Israel in 2007, although disappointingly for the Rangers tribes present no violence broke out. The flag is expected to take pride of place atop the marble staircase of Der Fuhrerbunker, Ibrox, Kinning Park, Glasgow, although rumours persist that the buyer Alastair…erm… Thingwy, has a long term plan to flog the thing to a gullible American collector for thousands of pounds to appease his bankers.

Translation of Rangers FC statement on shares

26th October 2009

THE Board of Directors of The Rangers Football Club plc ("Club") is aware of the recent speculation and various comments in the media over the weekend.

Watty blabbed

The Club's board has been advised by its principal shareholder, Murray International Holdings Limited ("MIH"), that it is considering options regarding its shareholding in the Club and this may or may not lead to MIH disposing of some or all of its stake in the Club to a third party.

We are trying to flog the spoiled goods

These considerations are still at an early stage and may or may not lead to any offer for the issued shares of the Club.

We've not found a mug yet but are currently chasing a lead in South Africa

Under the provisions of Rule 8.3 of the Takeover Code (the "Code"), if any person is, or becomes, "interested" (directly or indirectly) in 1% or more of any class of "relevant securities" of the Club, all "dealings" in any "relevant securities" of that company (including by means of an option in respect of, or a derivative referenced to, any such "relevant securities") must be publicly disclosed by no later than 3.30 pm (London time) on the London business day following the date of the relevant transaction.

This requirement will continue until the date on which the offer becomes, or is declared, unconditional as to acceptances, lapses or is otherwise withdrawn or on which the "offer period" otherwise ends.

When we dae find a mug we'll tell everybody.

"Interests in securities" arise, in summary, when a person has long economic exposure

This huz happened cos we're skint

27th October 2009 Rangers 3-1 Dundee Co-op Cup

Dundee denied two strong penalty claims with the score at 1-1.
Jocky Scott on BBC -"*We had two stonewall penalties, how the referee Dougie McDonald didn't give them I don't know? The second one – a blind man could have seen it!*"

The Scotsman "*I don't care what anyone says. For the first one, Craig Forsyth says the goalkeeper definitely touched him. There was no reason for him to go down as he would have been in a position to score. Unsurprisingly, Smith did not concur with his close friend's assessment of the incidents. "I didn't see the first one, **because my view from the directors' box was obscured by a pole**," said Smith.*

HONEST MISTAKE NO.14 Craig Forsyth brought down by Neil Alexander in the box. No penalty.

HONEST MISTAKE NO.15 Leigh Griffiths brought down by Sasa Papac in the box. No penalty.

POSSIBLE EFFECT No impact on SPL. Both penalties would potentially have put Dundee 2-1 / 3-1 up. Rangers would have been struggling to stay in the Co-op Cup which they would go on to win.

Laptop Lapdog Iain King still spinning on behalf of Sir Minty

28th October 2009

A good old fashioned piece of Laptop Loyal poodle-speak in the Sun today, the poodles are still out in force.

"*An insider* [i.e. we made this up] *said: 'There's no way David Murray* [what no Sir?] *will let the club go at a knock-down price'* "

Oh dear. Sir Minty holding the great Glasgow Rangers to ransom with his unreasonable demands, preventing a clean break and a minimal outlay for any prospective owner to allow them to maximise any remaining capital to improve the team. After all the Scottish tabloids have been full of bleating about how unreasonable Lloyds are to have the temerity to seek £1 for every £1 of debt owed. I mean, a business seeking to get fully paid for debts owed to them. How unreasonable is that??!! So presumably Iain King thinks Sir Minty is being a tad unreasonable, or at least acting against the interests of Rangers.

Em, no...

"*His main concern will always be, as he has stated before, that the club ends up in the right hands*"

They missed the bit about the right hands that can pay the most money. I don't quite get how selling at a knock-down price is at odds with the club ending up in the right hands. Surely the less paid to Moonbeams the more remains to sort out the team? No? David Murray still retains a core of loyal lapdogs in the press. There's life in the old dog yet.

Balanced articles on Mowbray, Smith, McCann and Murray in the Scotsman

Pressure on Tony Mowbray simply not adding up
By Andrew Smith The Scotsman 30th October 2009

"*More than that, it hardly computes that when Rangers toil, sympathy is understandably extended to Walter Smith over the failings of players he signed, but when Celtic toil, Mowbray is flailed for the failings of players he did not.*

This is nothing short of Laptop Loyal sacrilege. Andrew Smith won't be getting a job at a Scottish tabloid or a gig on Snide or Fake Radio.

WHEN he was a Celtic player Tony Mowbray must have dreamed of finding himself in the sort of 'crisis' that now envelopes him as Celtic manager. Especially one precipitated by a first League Cup defeat for the new man at the helm – as he suffered on Wednesday with the 1-0 home loss to Hearts in the quarter-finals of the Co-operative Insurance Cup.

In November 1994, Mowbray played in an altogether more historic League Cup loss as Raith Rovers edged-out Celtic on penalties in final of the competition – to become the first lower division side in 100 years to triumph over the Glasgow club in a domestic decider. Then, Celtic just also happened to be eight games in to an 11-game winless league run that stands as the longest such sequence in their history. It left them in a lofty fifth position. And none of this brought pressure to bear on the six-months-in-the-job Tommy Burns comparable to that being presently heaped on a Mowbray whose team are top of the SPL.

That is partly because we live in a far more hysterical age and partly because 15 years ago it wasn't uncommon for Celtic to be out of the top three. But still there is much about the mauling of Mowbray in media and supporters' circles that don't add up. Right off, though, it must be said that two home victories in nine home games does add up to one honking statistic.

Yet, even within that, Hearts – whom Celtic pilloried for the final half hour on Wednesday they twice hit the goal frame before Georgios Samaras spurned two glorious openings – are the first winners in the east end of Glasgow this season who really should have had Mowbray squirming. Even when the reverse represents no less than Celtic's fourth home domestic cup loss in the past three years. Dinamo Moscow, Arsenal and Hamburg are teams this current Celtic squad are capable of losing to whatever the venue. And that has little to do with the man struggling to shape them in to an effective unit.

Mowbray fares acceptably when you compare his start with the previous two managers. Not least in a European context. And that is his problem. If only, first out, he had suffered the club's worst defeat on the continental stage – a la Gordon Strachan with Artmedia Bratislava in 2005 – then his early record would not have been scarred by playing sides superior to any Scottish opponents thereafter.

If only, as with Martin O'Neill in 2000, he had the relatively gentle introduction of such as Jeunesse Esch and HJK Helsinki then more home wins might have been easier to come by in Europe – the club exiting that year's Uefa Cup through losing at home to Bordeaux, incidentally.

If Celtic register a home win against Kilmarnock tomorrow, then their points total over the first quarter of the league season will only have been outstripped once in Strachan's three title-winning terms.

From some of the intellectually-challenged inanities expressed, you'd think Celtic were threatened with relegation under Mowbray. They are merely exhibiting the same shortcomings that have reared up regularly across the past two seasons. Which is as it should be considering the personnel remains largely unchanged during that period. Yet Celtic's play isn't as soulless as it was in the final of months of the last campaign. A time when they found both goals and wins in the league harder to come by than they are now, it should be noted. It might be sloppier but, considering between January and April of this year no Celtic striker other than Scott McDonald scored, it again shouldn't be so puzzling that, when more chances come their way, Celtic's forwards are finding more ways to foul them up.

Judgments must be reserved on Mowbray until his keynote £3.8m purchase Marc-Antoine Fortune is fit and playing regularly – as he hasn't in more than two months – and there is more than Danny Fox, Landry N'Geumo and Zheng Zhi as his recruits. It is a real curiosity that the Englishman, a true decent sort, isn't being cut any slack until he at least has the January window to coax more transfer-market remedial action out of his Celtic board. More than that, it hardly computes that when Rangers toil, sympathy is understandably extended to Walter Smith over the failings of players he signed, but when Celtic toil, Mowbray is flailed for the failings of players he did not.

There is one respect in which Mowbray really does fall down when set against his immediate managerial predecessors, however. In attack, midfield and defence, O'Neill inherited Henrik Larsson, Paul Lambert and Johan Mjallby. In attack, midfield and defence, Strachan inherited John Hartson, Stilian Petrov and Bobo Balde. And in attack, midfield and defence, Mowbray must now seek turns from such as Samaras, Barry Robson and Stephen McManus. Indeed, probably not since Burns has any Celtic manager been bequeathed so meagre an inheritance.

Hypocrisy rules as McCann and Murray swap places
Glenn Gibbons   The Scotsman 31st October 2009

Glenn Gibbons writes the only sensible appraisal of the relative merits of Fergus McCann and David Murray that I have ever read in a Scottish newspaper:

"IF NOTHING else, events at the Old Firm over the past 15 years confirm that few sideshows are more bizarre – or captivating – than the sight of football chroniclers scurrying to distance themselves from past mistakes. This is an exercise that invariably has no place for contrition, an admission of guilt or even a semblance of acknowledgement of previous misjudgements, but it does accommodate a shipload of hypocrisy.

When revisionism sets in, those who, like David Murray at Rangers, were once exalted, had better be prepared for an unaccustomed rough ride. For those who have been routinely vilified – in this case Fergus McCann at Celtic – the reappraisal is, almost without exception, made too late.

In the years following the little Scots-Canadian's rescue of the Parkhead club on the day it was due to be declared bankrupt in 1994, nobody was more consistently castigated by a media whose agenda was certainly not shaped by a proper scrutiny of McCann's work. It was, instead, in most cases inspired by the Iago-like whispered lies of former hangers-on who had been slighted by McCann's decision to jettison them on the perfectly sound premise that they had nothing to offer.

This media-led campaign against the Celtic managing director was so appallingly effective that the club's own supporters jeered him as he unfurled the league championship flag – Celtic's first in ten years and the one that denied Rangers a record tenth on the bounce – in 1998.

The derision was widespread and profound, despite the evidence of McCann's work: a colossal new stadium taking shape, improvements in the team's fortunes and a staggering increase in season ticket sales and in the club's annual turnover, making them the perfect business model in the eyes of properly-qualified analysts.

By the time of the tenth anniversary of McCann's accession – five years after his departure – in 2004, many of those reporters, readily abetted by sports editors, who had crucified him during his tenure were, quite shamelessly, proclaiming him the founding father of the modern Celtic, a visionary to whom a statue should be erected and after whom Celtic Park should be re-named.

In one or two quarters, however, there remains a residual resentment, marked by a refusal to recognise McCann's achievements. Indeed, on Tuesday of this week we were told by one newspaper that it was Brian Dempsey who had saved Celtic. By the following day, another had informed us that David Low had actually formulated the business plan that took the club out of the abyss. Fergus must be very grateful.

Now, in the last few months, it has been possible to detect a subtle shift in the media's treatment of Murray at Ibrox.

While he has avoided outright hostility from his 'friends' in the business, it has become clear that he is no longer regarded as infallible, a man editors and their minions believed should be humoured and accommodated.

Instead, the conclusive evidence of his reckless fiscal policies have clearly taken Rangers into the dark place vacated by Celtic 15 years ago and there is now, inevitably, a penalty to be paid. It seems obvious, however, that Murray's previous influence on a scandalously compliant media has been so strong that, so far, he has been given a relatively easy time. His severest critics are to be found on forums among the club's supporters.

Perhaps, as the true extent of Rangers' problems unfold – and deepen the longer they go without a buyer – the former chairman will be subjected to the kind of institutional opprobrium McCann had to endure for work that, ultimately, brought his club unprecedented prosperity. Not that Murray should be especially discomforted by the unusual experience of being publicly harangued. With his main business, Murray International Holdings, having declared liabilities of £760 million, Rangers are probably the least of his worries. This tendency among football commentators to present personalities in a misleading light extends in the present circumstances to the Rangers manager, Walter Smith.

One of the most puzzling aspects of the recent happenings at Ibrox has been the readiness of several media outlets to portray Smith as the kind of victim whose plight could catch the attention of Amnesty.

It is a picture in need of serious re-working. Smith himself would bridle at the idea of his having been unfairly treated by Rangers, an institution whose willingness to pay him handsomely for his services over the ten years of two terms has helped – along with notable success in his businesses outside football – make him sufficiently wealthy to be impervious to hardship.

At the moment, the manager certainly has more money than his club.

Smith re-affirmed his personal welfare last week, when I asked if he was concerned that his employers would ask him to take a pay cut when his contract expires in January.

"As I think I've said before," he replied, with a knowing smile, "I don't have any concerns".

He would agree without hesitation that Rangers owe him nothing. The other bewildering element of Rangers' headline-friendly plight is the role to be played by Dave King, the South African entrepreneur. King has already been nominated by a number of papers the only man in the world with the money and the desire (he is said to be a lifelong fan) to buy the club.

Curiously, one of the pieces which proclaimed him the likeliest new owner also reminded us that he was facing 322 charges of criminal fraud and that his passport had been impounded by the South African authorities.

Quite apart from any possible "fit and proper person test", Dave would appear to have a serious problem with actually getting here."

Celtic and Rangers press conferences: spot the difference

1st November 2009

Tony Mowbray would have to learn pretty fast about the agenda pushed by the football media in Scotland. He had the temerity to leave a press conference following a 0-1 defeat to Hearts in the prestigious CIS Cup, before hacks had finished grilling him - cue headlines declaring that Tony Mowbray "*walks out of press conference*"

Quite how a person is supposed to leave a press conference in any other manner is not explained by the drooling hacks who pen this shite, but contrary to some of them, The Man with Nosurname does not levitate from the room, he only does that trick when passing over water (unholy). Of course the insinuation here is that the Celtic manager threw some sort of tantrum because grubby hacks deemed that the time he devoted to answering their agenda-ridden leading questions was too brief.

On the other hand, in the wake of two 1-4 humpings at home in the Champions League, failure to beat Hibs at home in the SPL and the club being mired in dire financial difficulty, placing its very existence in some uncertainty - when asked about the most serious difficulties affecting a Scottish club in the past 15 years, Nosurname came out with the eloquent Wilde-esque response "*Gonnae just pack it in. Otherwise I'll just walk away*". No dissenting voice in the press about this fragrant lack of respect or perceived succumbing to pressure that was implied in the case of Mowbray.

As it happened the Rangers manager did indeed leave the media room mid-question, after one naive poodle forfeited all Winalot rights by asking "*Did you ever think you would see a time when Dundee were spending more money than Rangers?*". Nosurname simply got out of his seat muttering something incoherent as a deep shade of purple spread across his cheeks and steam began to emanate from his ears. Still no aspersions cast at the Dignified One though, for this little show of impertinence.

Nosurname had even managed to slip in a subtle piece of sexism by accusing one hack of putting a "*female twist*" on a question which he deemed unworthy of an answer. You may recall the furore after Gordon Strachan likened a female hack's inability to understand the emotions experienced as Celtic manager to his inability to perceive the pain of childbirth (possibly the very same hack), resulting in furious demands for an apology from the club and compensation for the subsequent injury to the poor little flower's feelings. But this is Sir Walter, so nothing to see here, move along quietly.

A look at recent press conferences involving Celtic (Tony Mowbray, Barry Robson) and Rangers (The Man with Nosurname) give an interesting insight to the Laptop Loyal agenda.

To set the context - each of these press conferences took place in the immediate aftermath of:

Rangers losing 1-4 at home to Unirea Urziceni, beating Dundee 3-1 in the CIS Cup then drawing with Hibs 1-1 at home. Attendance at the home Champions League game was an extremely disappointing 12,000 below capacity, the team were roundly booed throughout the match and there was mass exodus of fans in the second half.

Celtic had lost 0-1 to Hamburg at home, beaten Hamilton Accies 2-1 away and lost at home to Hearts 0-1 in the CIS Cup. The attendance for the Hearts Cup tie was only 19,000, albeit for a much less prestigious competition than the Champions League and there was some booing at the final whistle.

So very similar circumstances surrounding both clubs, other than the fact that one is in complete financial meltdown with no guarantee of its survival, but I'll just pretend I'm Chick Young and gloss over that for the moment.

For those unfamiliar with Orwellian Laptop Loyal speak I have provided a translation of each question

Tony Mowbray post-match interview questions following defeat to Hearts in the CIS Cup:

"*Bad result for Celtic what was your overall assessment of the match?*"

I'm just easing you in gently Timmy

"*What was your view of the penalty incident*"

A great chance for some 'sour grapes, manager loses it under pressure copy' if he questions the decision. He doesn't. Damn. I'll try again.

"*Both teams created chances, did you feel that your team created enough chances to win?*"

This is the kind of inane question that would get that wee shite Strachan wound up. Celtic only had about 20 shots on goal as opposed to 3 from Hearts. Hopefully Mowbray will get all flustered as well, giving me the chance to write some 'bad-tempered manager losing the plot' copy. He doesn't bite. Damn. Time to bring out the big guns.

"*You said before about the lack of quality that you have in your side, was that a case of it showing itself again tonight?*"

I know this is completely out of context and basically a downright lie, but I've got to get some sort of reaction out of you to make you look really bad to get some good 'club in crisis' material.

[I think BTM's response is worthy of inclusion here, and demonstrates that he is well up to speed with the media agenda in Scotland]

"*No I've never talked about a lack of quality in my side, I think the team's got a lot of quality in it.* **I'm constantly misrepresented by the media in Scotland**. *What I've said on given days is that we lacked quality in certain areas and that's always been from me on specific days.* **Mischievous journalists** *want to say that I've questioned the quality of the footballers. I've never done that. But that's fine, listen... I accept and work under the environment I'm working with*".

[Back to Laptop Loyal speak:]

That was close, but not quite good enough for some 'Celtic paranoia/Mowbray blasts the media' patter. One more big push to get the bastard.

"*There was plenty of boos at the end there, we all heard them* [although certain other chants like Famine Songs, Jock Stein slurs and racist chanting we have a bit more trouble hearing for some reason]. *What do you say to the fans who aren't buying into the Tony Mowbray revolution?*

Great. Get him to have a wee dig at the fans just like when Strachan said they don't know anything about the game, produce a few banner headlines and that'll soon get the Celtic fans on his back. Damn. He didn't rise to it. I'll just have to make do with a "Mowbray storms out press conference headline".

The Man with Nosurname post-match interview questions following defeat to Unirea Urziceni in the Champions League:

"*Walter. Don't know where to begin with that. Could you explain what went wrong?*"

Walter. I am as gutted as you are your Eminence. I'll start with a suitably vague question which will allow you to expand at length with any excuses and avoid any specific questions about tactics or your own shortcomings. Blame the players if you want. That'll work.

"*Dan Petrescu said that the missed penalty was the turning point of the game. Would you agree with that?*

See what I did there? A completely inane questions about what might have been, that allows us to say that the result boiled down to one incident in the match and was basically a result of pure bad luck. Again this easily avoids territory that might cast some doubt on your magnificent tactical decisions your Lordship, and if we want to really push the boat out, we could claim that really we kind of deserved to win the game like we did against Sevilla.

"Is that a low point for you as manager of Rangers, the lowest point?"

I'm playing out of my skin here. It'll be succulent lamb to go with the Winalot this week. To follow follow up the previous inane question, a question completely irrelevant to tonight's game which allows the Dignified One to ramble on about whatever he likes and avoid any responsibility for tonight's result.

"How do you think that leaves you in terms of qualification from the group?"

Always finish on a positive. Remind the teddy bears that mathematically they can still qualify from the section even though this is less likely than Rangers signing Danny La Rue in January and him to scoring the winning goal in the Champions League final in May. Appeasement of the fans is top priority so that Walter and Sir David are never held to account and I can get my tummy tickled in Sir David's office over a nice Bordeaux.

Barry Robson pre-match interview questions a few days after defeat to Hearts in the CIS Cup:

"What's the story with the home form?"

Celtic are shite aren't they? Come on Barry. They're shite aren't they? Oh, and by the way when it comes round to the return game against Hamburg we'll be starting on the shite away record in Europe again too.

[Random stat which demonstrates how easy it is to make something look really negative to fit your agenda: Rangers last 3 home Champions League games - P3 W0 D0 L3 F2 A11 PTS 0 Somehow this wee stat has escaped the attention of the Scottish media]

"Is it harder on those nights when the stadium is a third or a quarter full and you can hear everything that's coming off the seats?"

Come on Barry. Say something bad about those plastic paddy fans of yours. After all you used to be one of us.

"How frustrating is it when you go on these sequences, what is it, 2 out of 9

you've won at home. You come back into training, what can you do to vary it?"

I know that 4 of these 9 home games were against European teams like Arsenal who could give Hamilton Accies a run for their money, but we are the media and we have teams of researchers who can go away and dig up all this shite to be used in evidence against you. I think Celtic are coming up for the longest ever period in Scottish Football without scoring from a corner and I'll get Cecil to check that out straight after this interview so we've got ammo for the next one. Hopefully those gullible Sellik fans will sap all this in and start getting on your case.

"*Do you think, in the current climate, the problems of the Old Firm are exaggerated when you don't win a game?*"

Time to take the foot off the gas a wee bit to provide "balance". See how I mentioned "the Old Firm" there, to make it look like Celtic's financial problems are just as bad as ours... I mean Rangers? I'm no daft eh.

"*Do you think the strikers are going through a confidence crisis?*"

My pen is poised, ready to pounce with a 'Celts in Crisis' headline. Damn. Seems like Barry is no daft either.

"*Have you noticed a difference in the manager over the past few weeks when things haven't been going well?*"

Well I can't get you to say anything negative about the Celtic fans or your team-mates so now I'll start on the manager. After all, that is some shitey run of form you've had over the past few weeks that has seen Celtic plummet to the top of the league.

"*From your point of view, is it maybe a problem that the team hasn't had a settled eleven for a number of games?*"

If at first you don't succeed... There's a 'Robson blasts Mowbray headline' here, I can almost touch it!

Damn.

I'll have one last go at a 'Robson blasts Celtic fans' headline

"*You did say that a lot of fans had come out and supported you, but at the end there was some booing. What would your message be to the fans who are maybe a little restless?*"

Nothing. I guess we'll just have to concentrate on the 'Dave King set to save

Rangers in squazillion pound deal' headlines.

Nosurname's pre-match interviews a few days after home draw with Hibs and win over Dundee with the club continuing to experience financial turmoil:

"If you can get a winning run together would this help bring the squad together?"

Come on Wattie, We know you can do it!

"Walter, did you learn anything about the three young guys who started in Dundee that you didn't know already?"

Give us the nod and we'll fill our papers with hype about the latest batch of young Gers superstars that Sir Alex/Big Eck/Mark Hughes are going to swoop for in a £3million deal. This'll keep the fans distracted for a while.

"Would you be more inclined to play him (Danny Wilson) in an SPL match now?

I'll ask anything but questions about finance, low crowds, fans leaving early or fans booing Master.

"The *youth system is arguably more important than ever. Are the crop of young guys coming through, are you now seeing the real benefit of Murray Park these days?"*

You didn't quite give me enough to work with re the superstar wonderkids headlines your Lordship. I've also given you a chance to bum up Sir David and waffle about how brilliant Murray Park is and more better and more expensive than any other training ground in Scotland ever ever.

"*I think you used the word 'stagnation'* [these hacks are never quite so vague about statements made by Celtic managers are they?] *a week or so ago in the sense that you haven't been able to bring in new players. Is the enthusiasm that comes with bringing these young guys in a way of avoiding that?"*

I am playing an absolute blinder here! I am a certainty for my succulent lamb and claret this week. I've asked you a potentially quite tricky question, although framed in such away that you are in no way responsible for the situation, and then I've gone and provided you with the answer!! All you have to do now is waffle on about how there are some good young players coming through but how it's important not to rush them. This allows you to manage the expectations of the fans by presenting just enough of a tantalising glimpse of a much improved future, whilst at the same time playing down the immediate impact these players might make before they are flogged to the likes of Brentford.

"Difficult game last week and then a difficult game this week. Come the end of the season do you expect Rangers and Celtic will still be in the top two"?

I'll give you a wee rest by asking a frivolous question a 5 year old could answer and has no relevance to immediate problems of severe urgency besetting the club. Again you will be afforded the luxury of rambling on at will. I'll cough loudly if you begin to fall asleep mid-sentence Master.

"Do you feel that it's harder now for Rangers or Celtic to win the league because the gap has narrowed?"

Oh dear, I'm not sure if I've overstepped the mark between acceptable sycophancy and sheer laughing stock. I can assure you my intentions were pure Sir Walter. I was only trying to appease the fans by emphasising the challenge facing you, in the face of competition from huge spending Unirea, Hibs, Motherwell and Hamilton Accies.

End of press conference
Now to re-cap, both sides have had disappointing results recently, reduced crowds, disgruntled fans booing events on the park although the problems are worse for one particular side where booing was a constant feature of the whole game and in which more than half the fans left the ground well before the end of the game. This club is also mired in an almost unprecedented financial crisis given the extent of the debts in question.

So let's score the performance of the Scottish media in raising these issues:

CELTIC
In two interviews, the media refers to:

Booing from the crowd - 3
Low attendances - 2
Possible managerial frailties - 2
A potential crisis - 1
And misrepresenting the manager's comments - 1

RANGERS
In two interviews, the media refers to:

Booing from the crowd - 0
Low attendances - 0
Possible managerial frailties - 0
A potential crisis - 0
And misrepresenting the manager's comments - 0

Must be "O*d F**m bias" again.

8th November 2009 Falkirk 3-3 Celtic

HONEST MISTAKE NO.16 Celtic score an injury time "winner" away to Falkirk only for it to be wrongly disallowed.

Daily Record – "*Celtic fans **yelped in frustration** and their mood would not have improved when television replays showed assistant Lawrence Kerrigan was **wrong** to flag for offside when Samaras was played in behind the Bairns defence in injury time. His shot may have been blocked by Olejnik but it dropped to McDonald who poked the ball into the net only to see the flag fluttering along his line of vision. To be fair, Celtic players kept their protests to a minimum.*"

The Sun – "*TV pictures showed that linesman Andy Tait was **wrong to flag**"*

Both newspapers quote different linesman but what is not in doubt is that the decision was obviously incorrect

ALMOST CERTAIN EFFECT Celtic denied two points, having to settle for one for the draw rather than three for the win. (Rangers -5, Celtic +7 [+2])

The Man With Nosurname Speaks, The Laptop Loyal reveres

20th November 2009

It was a time, more than ever, that every Scottish News sports bulletin became nothing more than a " wisdom of Wattie" update. Tonight (20/11/2009) STV was at its pro-Rangers crawly bum lick best/worst. Raman announced breathlessly that the one with no surname will explain why he doesn't want the Scotland manager's job. This is actually the top STV sports item. It is the be-all and end-all of the story. Nothing about Craig Levein, other contenders or who else might be interested. The BBC were also in raptures at the proclamation of their master but at least couched it in terms of "*the ongoing search for the new Scotland manager*", whereas STV were only interested in sifting through the Cardigan's shite to pick out the sweetcorn.

Nosurname doesn't want the job. That's all we need to know. Fantastic, let's get on with talking about people who DO want it.

STV bulletin begins "*It was widely expected that Walter would not be interested in the Scotland job and the Rangers manager made statements to that effect, so it was no great surprise when he confirmed today that he wouldn't take the job*". Cue several minutes of wisdom from the great wise one.

Brilliant. So STV's top news story is about something that was never going to happen... not happening. Is there a brain cell anywhere to be found at STV?

Next up, Steven Whittaker telling everyone who will listen about what great players Greegsy, Boydie and Captain Unbookable* are, and pleading with the new manager to bring them back into the Scotland squad. You couldn't get a more neutral view then one of their team-mates

*(except in England and Europe)

Two Sides of the Same Coin?

You can put money on one cast iron certainty, when the phone calls of protest from Mr and Mrs Outraged of Larkhall flooded the switchboards one second after the completion of the minute's silence at Falkirk, those doing so would be guilty of a rather impressive selective morality. Regardless of the inane behaviour of those chanting outside the ground during the silence, for Rangers supporters to sputter and fume, venting their indignation in a manner reminiscent of Captain Mainwaring from Dad's Army, is a little hard to take. Fine, you expect that in football rivals will try and exploit every failing, actual or merely perceived, but when it comes to our Dark Brethren the realisation is unavoidable that this isn't just rivalry, these loonies actually mean it!

After all if Rangers and their supporters were pristine pure, a club stuffed full of fine, upstanding citizens who went to bed in starch-saturated pyjamas buttoned up to their necks and never contemplated an unclean thought, well I guess it would be tolerable. I need hardly mention that isn't the case, far from it. Yet when the mood is upon them Rangers supporters could put Hyacinth Bucket to shame for sheer gratuitous pomposity. Often, and this is the hilarious bit, unofficial Rangers sites will inevitably carry such stuffed-shirt outrage alongside other articles that would send Bernard Manning into a shocked swoon. On one site two 'Outraged of Larkhall' examples nestled either side of a bizarre short story on the subject of Graham Spiers being buggered by Gerry Duffy. Often these missives from the Offended Bus are unintentionally hilarious, combining as they do high-ground pontificating with own goals that would put Tom Boyd's effort at Dens Park to shame.

Let's look at one example entitled "*TRUE COLOURS - The Celtic Minded Show Theirs Yet Again*" by the brilliantly monikered 'Pro Patria'. In this simply fantastic tribute to accidental comedy, the author starts in rather standard fashion before the first punchline comes racing alone: "*It is a fundamental principle that everyone is allowed a point of view and the right to protest. And as much as it pains me to say it that includes people of all denominations, creeds, cultures or religions no matter how much you disagree with them or their principles.*" Not exactly a ringing personal endorsement of the right to protest, not if it pains Mr Pro Patria for that right to be exercised, and indeed, the author appears a little bit confused regarding the whole subject.

"*The other issue I have with this protest was the particularly offensive chant of 'F*ck the Queen*", he waffled. "*Now correct me if I am wrong but the Queen is not only our Head of State but also head of the Anglican Church thereby making her a religious leader as well as a Spiritual Leader. So therefore is it not reasonable to assume it is a Sectarian offence (not to mention treasonous) to shout 'F*ck the Queen'. Why no arrests from the Police if that were the case?*" You'll notice the lack of a question mark at the end of the second last sentence. Obviously Mr Pro Patria fails to realise that it is indeed unreasonable, for the simple reason that if his definition were to be accepted then anyone arguing in favour of republicanism could be deemed to have committed a sectarian offence. As for the accusations of treason, even Captain Mainwaring would be rolling his eyes at this point and making twirling motions with one finger next to his ear. Pro Patria is obviously one of those Rangers supporters who have never quite come to terms with the fact that the 17th Century has ended.

Opposition to the monarchy is hardly down to some kind of dislike for the quaint and rather harmless Anglican church. My dislike of the monarchy for example is entirely due to its undemocratic position in the stifling hierarchy of this blighted nation, its role as a PR exercise by the British Establishment in order to detract attention when the going gets rough, and the fact the idle parasites suck up £millions of tax payers money and then have the gall to lecture the rest of us on how we should lay our noses on the grindstone. Yet according to the aforementioned genius, my position should be deemed sectarian simply because the Queen is the head of some minority religion, and not forgetting the object of adoration by a shower of forelock-tugging buffoons who are forever locked into a world view that was fashionable a couple of centuries ago.

As I said though, the eloquence of any justified ire caused by what was, in my opinion, a depressing act of mind-numbing stupidity is soon put into its proper perspective when the darkness that inevitably bubbles away just below the surface comes to the fore. You don't have to read far to saunter across an attempt to justify the cloying bigotry of the Famine Song. The author selectively quotes from a Jim Traynor article in the Daily Record where he claims Traynor wrote: "*These people need to understand we are Scottish with no wish to be dragged back into the past. We don't want to be become Irish. Those who do should catch a ferry from Stranraer and leave the rest of us alone.*" Really? Gosh. This is then following up by Pro Patria snickering: "*Now I could be slightly naughty and say that Mr Traynor could be inferring what many of us think and indeed what many fans were branded racists for saying....'Why don't you go home'.*"

The problem is, of course, that for the author to reach this conclusion a bit of editing had to be undertaken in order to arrive at the necessary 'quote'. What Traynor in fact wrote was: "*These people need to understand we are Scottish with no wish to be dragged back into the past. We don't want to be Little Englanders. And we don't have any desire to become Irish. Those who do should scramble over the Wall or catch a ferry from Stranraer and leave the rest of us alone.*" Not only that, the quote followed a paragraph in which Traynor denounced both the Falkirk stupidity and the violence in the Ghencea Stadium. So why did Pro Patria feel the need to take Traynor's comments out of context and expunge the parts he didn't like? Well, its obvious, otherwise he wouldn't have managed to find even a feeble excuse to justify a deplorable song that's rightly attracted the racist label.

Did Traynor mention the events at the Ghencea Stadium? Why yes he did, and as it happens what did Pro Patria, this fine upstanding defender of decency have to say about those disgraceful scenes? "*Only last week Rangers were involved in a situation in Bucharest that could have led to innocent Rangers fans being hurt or killed due to the actions of thugs masquerading as Stewards,*" he squealed. "*I cannot condone the actions of someone deliberately breaking seats to throw at stewards but the points being glossed over and indeed ignored by ALL the Scottish Media is why these fans felt so compelled to engage in such actions in the first place.*" Ok, so let's have a look at that shall we. According to the apologist, and there are many of his ilk, there can be no possible justification for singing songs **outside** a football ground during a Remembrance Day Silence, but there **can** be justification for acts of violence inside a stadium that includes assaulting stewards and wrecking seats, so much so, that the game came close to being abandoned. The Rangers supporters were "*compelled*" to commit acts of violence you'll note.

No Riot Ensued

Is it just me or is there something peculiar about this mindset; a rather selective morality, a very curious concept of dignity? What was the flashpoint for the violence inside the Ghencea after all? Allegedly, and with this bunch you'll have to order a few tons of salt, someone threw an Irish Tricolour onto the Perspex shielding behind which the Rangers supporters were penned.

One Rangers supporter claimed: "*I then noticed a Tri-colour which was hanging off the top of the perspex wall at the front of the pen. I personally didn't see how it got there but others around me were adamant that it was a result of a steward on trackside trying to throw it into the Rangers fans. Things quickly escalated as fans suddenly rushed forward and started trading punches with stewards who were still in our section down the front.*" Yes I see, and at this point we have the obligatory old gent getting waylaid by ruffians. "*I was later told from someone who witnessed it that it was the result of a elderly Rangers fan walking up to an steward to complain about them goading the Rangers fans with the Tri-colour, I was told that the guy was punched full in the face and then set upon by about 6 stewards as he hit the ground.*" Like I said, a few tons of salt.

Other articles by Rangers supporters are a bit less constrained, screaming indignantly about the fact the poor Bears were taunted by a "*highly offensive article*". My God they're a sensitive bunch. Fast forward twenty four hours to Celtic's game in Hamburg, and the lumpen morons that comprise the home support indulged in a rather ironic tifosi display where one upper stand was devoted to a rather off-colour Union Flag and a banner which ran the full length proclaiming the slogan "*No Surrender*". Imagine if the same had occurred in the Ghencea, with the Union Flag replaced by an Irish Tricolour and a banner reading "*Tiocfaidh ár lá*". I guess Pro Patria and his fellow apologists would now be finding ways to justify genocide and the end of civilisation as we know it. You would have thought at this point that someone, somewhere amongst the Brethren would have pondered over why they would react in such a hysterical manner when presented with the flag of a neighbouring EU state. Ha! Such a comic notion.

Now before I progress further on this subject, let me just state that I have been in several grounds where Celtic supporters have been goaded, or should I say, attempts have been made to goad, with a Union Flag. On every single occasion the perpetrator has been met with derisive laughter. Be it a midweek game in Dens Park (God that one was funny), Hamburg itself or Ewood Park, every time the reaction has been far different from that witnessed whenever the Forces of Darkness have found themselves having to cope with terrible, soul-destroying exposure to an Irish tri-colour. Perhaps that's the reason Celtic supporters can venture all over the world and receive plaudits for their behaviour, and God knows I know we're not all angels, while Rangers supporters totter from one scandal to the next.

Yet where is the condemnation of this behaviour from the same people who will snotter on at length about the disrespect to Remembrance Sunday? As Graham Spiers stated: "*Villarreal, Pamplona, Manchester, now Bucharest. Why is it that, when Rangers FC and their spineless supporters' spokesmen start groping around for excuses, the common themes of 'heavy-handed policing' or 'these are not real Rangers fans' are forever trotted out?*" You'll remember that after Rangers supporters crapped, pissed and trashed

Manchester city centre into a third world disaster zone, the bold defenders of dignity at the RST launched an investigation into..... the police. We're still waiting publication of their devastating dossier on the culpability of the Manchester plod - guess we're be waiting a while.

One of our favourite contributors to Follow Follow, the definitely certifiable 'Little Boy Blue', displays the mindset of these Rangers supporters quite succinctly when he seeks to justify the violence in Bucharest: "*Some Bears hadn't taken too kindly to being locked out of the ground because not enough turnstiles were open*". He explained, well that's ok then, except no one was locked out they just had a queue a bit longer than expected - still, justified reason for lamping a steward eh? Next we have the reaction to the carnage that occurred in Manchester, the devastation of a city centre described thus: "*the post-Manchester (08) demonisation of our fantastic support.*" You'll note he has to put year dates after the event so we know exactly what particular disgrace he's referring to. Now read on: "*Inevitably, Manchester has reared its ugly head again. Yes, the 'riot' and 'rampage' of 18 months ago, when something like 200,000 Rangers fans poured into the city, leading to just FORTY-TWO arrests, none of which resulted in a conviction for anything other than a minor misdemeanour, is again being thrown in our faces.*" Poor little diddums.

OK, again we have a rather selective attitude to facts in the that statement. For one thing the most serious charges had at that time not gone to trial, as the Manchester Evening News reported: "*Thousands of drunken Rangers fans fought running battles with police as they rampaged through Manchester city centre in more than five hours of trouble. In separate incidents, two police officers became separated from their units, surrounded by hooligans, knocked to the ground and kicked and stamped on.*" In the end **twelve** supporters were convicted and sentenced to **jail sentences** ranging from eight months to two and a half years – although one fan was give a suspended sentence for pleading guilty. Judge Andrew Blake summarised the case as "*the worst night of violence and destruction suffered by Manchester city centre since the blitz*".

So the claim that the **forty two** arrests have resulted in no serious convictions is just a little bit disingenuous since the main trials hadn't taken place at that point and none of us has a crystal ball. Should we be surprised? Not at all, the Rangers mindset is a marvellous device for altering reality to whatever they prefer. Sticking with Little Boy Blue again we're told that "*If our club had spoken out against the Hack Pack's speculation, innuendo and blatant lies, not to mention the Keystone Cops masquerading as a legitimate police force, Rangers would be in front of UEFA next Thursday with a well-nigh impeccable record.*" Yes you read that right. I would venture further into constructive criticism of this opinion, however I'm simply too gobsmacked by sheer incredulity. So, Rangers problems in all these European away games are simply down to what? A shoddy PR effort by the club and a pan-European conspiracy by the continents' police forces? Nothing to do with the support at all? All of this smacks ever so slightly as paranoia from where I'm standing. The answer to everything put in front of the dignity crowd seems to be an unflinching "*oh no, it isn't!*". Has there ever been a group of people so unfairly maligned? Don't laugh.

The impressive ability to deny the obvious and their inability to admit their failings, leaves Rangers supporters absolutely excluded from the ranks of those entitled to criticise others. Yet, as we can see with their hysteria over the Remembrance Sunday "protest", they appear to be indifferent to the charges of hypocrisy, instead howling and bawling at everyone and anything voicing criticism of their behaviour; even their own club. Martin Bain will have earned the seething contempt of the Brethren by his comment following UEFA's latest punishment: "*The moronic conduct of these individuals was wholly unacceptable and flies in the face of what we stand for as a football club.*" Well Martin, maybe what you stand for now, but what Rangers stood for in the past encouraged these types to flock to your club. According to The Herald though, Rangers are so desperate to rid themselves of this oppressed '*minority*' that they even had their fingers crossed for a devastating punishment rather than the mild slap on the wrist they received from the Zurich Gnomes. "*The Herald understands there are some senior figures within Ibrox who sank into their seats when the UEFA decision was presented to them,*" wrote Darryl Broadfoot. "*Bluntly, having exhausted every avenue of re-education and spent hundreds of thousands of pounds in a promotional campaign to weed out the remnants of sectarianism that scar the club's image at home and abroad, UEFA coming down hard was the last hope.*" Doesn't your heart bleed?

You'll note though that it isn't just looney-tune sites that are bouncing around full of rage and/or denial, the Hyacinths at the Rangers Supporters Trust broke off from penning letters demanding apologies for imagined slights, to begin another dodgy dossier: "*The RST has been contacted by a number of our members with detailed stories of what really happened in the Steaua Stadium in Bucharest. At the same time, several RST Board members have also given accounts of their experiences. This information will form a report which the RST will produce and send to the Club and the relevant football authorities.*" Not dissimilar to the RST reaction following the Manchester riot where condemnation of violence was slight and indignation over the injustices suffered by the poor Bears so great that I had to check to see if the Manc plod had instigated a vicious pogrom. A culture of denial is firmly rooted amongst the Brethren, a reaction of course propagated by the realisation that bad news is here to stay unless, by some miracle, the 21st Century is belatedly embraced.

It would be nice at this point to break off and bask in the warm glow of yet another Rangers PR debacle, however that would be to ignore the other part of this article, Falkirk and the previously mentioned "protest". Let's be clear about one thing first though, Remembrance Sunday has been hijacked by a deeply loathed Government desperate to stem the unpopularity of its military adventures. The gutter rags, especially the Daily Mail, have enthusiastically responded to the call to arms, turning what was, and should be, voluntary participation, into an obligatory summons where public figures and organisations are hounded and vilified if they fail to take part. The Government for its part quickly grasped at the annual remembrance event when it all started to go pear-shaped in Iraq, attempting to parasitically leech the emotions generated by the sacrifice of two World Wars onto their own shabby imperialist escapades. Consequently the line between remembrance and support for "our boys" in Afghanistan and Iraq has been blurred, and the event has gained unwelcome connotations. Let me be blunt, since 1945 the British state has not involved itself in a single conflict that could be termed "just", quite the opposite. Only the determination of Harold Wilson kept Britain out of Vietnam, which otherwise would have given us the full set of disgraceful adventures.

Participation therefore in Remembrance Sunday has quickly gained a political perspective that did not exist before. Many will be oblivious to that perspective, for others though the event has become somewhat sullied due to the machinations of opportunist politicians and the hysteria of the tabloid press. When the government insists on politicalising Remembrance Sunday, I'll admit to a deep feeling of unease. Oh sure I feel for the victims of another British imperialist folly, but that goes for the Afghans and the Iraqis as well as our own. Moreover those participating in the current conflicts are there through choice, fighting not for freedom and the nation but for the interests of the global corporate elite. Participation in such conflicts may be excused by sentiments such as "It was not their choice which battles they fought as they simply obeyed orders", however the Nuremberg Principles were quite clear on using such a justification: "The fact that a person acted pursuant to order of his Government or of a superior does not relieve him from responsibility under international law, provided a moral choice was in fact possible to him."

So I can understand why individuals would wish not to participate in Remembrance Sunday, however there are ways to protest, some dignified and some plain moronic. Those who decided to vocally protest should have understood that despite other events, whether in Kenya, Ireland or Afghanistan, the dead of two World Wars are commemorated during Remembrance Sunday; a total of approximately 1,382,000 individuals. Aren't these deaths deserving of some kind of respect? Yet there was no respect on show at Falkirk from those **outside the ground** who elected to bawl throughout the minute's silence, as a pathetic form of protest it's difficult to top. Of course the "protest" was seized gleefully by those ever desperate to remove the latest Rangers embarrassment from the back pages, and others who for some reason insist on trying to balance the charge sheet. Of course I'm maybe overestimating those who took part in the "protest", attributing a political aspect which in all reality probably didn't extend any further than the bottom of a Buckfast bottle.

So we have our own embarrassing element, however despite frantic efforts by some in the media to drag the Celtic support down to the level of our fallen cousins there really is no valid comparison. An undignified and embarrassing protest is hardly on the same level as events in the Ghencea Stadium after all. Sure there are occasions when football supporters will be confronted with overzealous or thuggish policing, and tempers will boil over, however when that happens on a serial basis in country after country, then questions have to be asked. One of the questions might be, "why is this only happening to Rangers supporters so frequently?". Dismissing the statistics as the work of a poor PR department or a European-wide plod conspiracy is a soft shoe shuffle into the Twilight Zone. Not that you'll find questions asked on Rangers websites, a litany of excuses and conspiracy theory teat suckling is preferred, which makes the pompous hysterics over the Falkirk "protest" rather ludicrous; it's like Rose West writing to the Bristol Evening Post to complain about littering.

I'll leave the final word, nearly, to the unusually perceptive Darryl Broadfoot, no doubt the real one has been the subject of a fairy raid and a changeling left in his place: "*The dreaded question now is: what will it take for UEFA to recognise a club in a state of utter helplessness when it comes to controlling an uncontrollable and vile appendage to their audience? Of course, apologists will cite an element of provocation: the time-honoured heavy-handed policing, an insufficient number of turnstiles and supporters being herded in like cattle. That does not excuse the ripping up of seats or the grotesque sight of salivating, bare-chested fans preparing for battle with the authorities. Rangers can only hope it does not require bloodshed or, heaven forbid, a fatality until it dawns on European football's governing body that the club has a problem which, for all their hard work, they alone simply cannot cure.*"

So let's hear no more of this *"two sides of the same coin"* nonsense, it is simply not justified by the evidence.

Why Rangers fans hate Graham Spiers

Graham Spiers *is a Scottish sports journalist who writes for the Scottish edition of The Times newspaper. He was brought up as a Rangers F.C. fan.*

Spiers can also be critical of the club:

"I have always happily ignored one of the traditional and cowardly rules of Scottish sports journalism - the rule which says, always apportion equal blame to Celtic and Rangers when talking of bigotry - by pointing a much bigger finger of blame at Rangers, the club I grew up supporting."

Spiers has been a prominent critic of the club's leadership and supporters. He has highlighted many incidents of racism and sectarianism. In

September 2008, he wrote "For years now Celtic Park – unlike Ibrox – has been largely free of sectarian or racist chanting." In the aftermath of the 2008 UEFA Cup Final riots Spiers called Rangers "a club with poison at its core."

The above is an excerpt from the Wikipedia page devoted to Graham Spiers, a football writer actually deserving of the title 'journalist'. This does not mean to say I agree with absolutely everything that rolls off Spiers' pen, however I think it is fair to say that as a journalist he has largely resisted the forces and agendas that afflict 99% of other Scottish football writers. Of course there is also his gig on Radio Snide Supersnoreboard, but he is by and large a fair and balanced journalist and certainly as fair as we are going to get in Scotland along with Gibbons, Smith and English at the Scotsman.

The reason for highlighting the above excerpt is because this page is flagged on Wikipedia as being "in dispute". The "dispute" concerns various Rangers fans snottering with rage at the ostensible fact that Graham Spiers is a Rangers supporter, or at least was brought up as one. Apparently they know better than the man himself, and in a fit of truculence, accuse Spiers of being some sort of double-agent Celtic propaganda peddler posing as a Rangers fan through his contribution to the book *It's Rangers for Me?*, to which he contributed a chapter on his experiences of supporting the club. Paranoia anyone? Even taking into account their fantastic talent for denial, self-delusion and laughable moral high-ground claiming, one might wonder why this is such a point of contention among Rangers fans?

Well, the answer of course, is because if Spiers is acknowledged as being at least someone of a Rangers background, his criticisms cannot simply be tossed aside as yet more of Paranoid Timmy's Fenian Conspiracy. The fact that Spiers himself is a Rangers fan lends substantial credence to his views on the culture among the club's supporters, which has led them a merry dance, arm-in-arm with Chelsea and Millwall fans, into calamity and disgrace on more than a few occasions. I read a few of the reviews of *It's Rangers for Me?* on Amazon and a common theme was the disdain with which Spiers is held by Rangers fans, with one pointing out that the journalist is generally popular among Celtic fans and loathed by their Rangers counterparts, holding this up as some sort of proof that he is not what he claims to be. Others rant on, calling him a "Rangers-Hater", presenting his criticism of the club, or more accurately the club's supporters, as evidence that he has no love for Rangers, and is in fact a closet Celtic fan.

Being critical of a club is in itself evidence of nothing, particularly when such criticisms arise from unignorable and catastrophic events such as the Manchester Riots, or the sick mindset that wishes to propogate slurs against the deceased. The agendas are easy to spot when it becomes obvious those doing the criticising are trying to dredge up every little piece of negativity they can find, as is the case with the Scottish media at large and their coverage of Celtic. However the subject matter Spiers has raised in recent years (in contrast to his peers) – repeated hooliganism, the Jock Stein slur and The Famine Song – can hardly be considered petty, frivolous or vindictive.

In October 2007 I got an insight into the way a Rangers fan like Spiers might feel watching events such as those at Manchester in 2008, when that halfwit ran onto the Celtic Park pitch to tickle the AC Milan goalkeeper Dida on the chin. I was angry. Angry that the actions of some idiot could have serious repercussions for our club, and potentially undo one of the greatest results in Celtic's history. Although his actions could hardly be termed violent they were indefensible and thankfully UEFA's judgement was that a financial penalty would suffice. Incredibly, another fan without a brain cell repeated the trick, minus the chin tickling, against Man Utd just over a year later. Again, UEFA opted for a fine, although I suppose if a fine is all that is deemed appropriate for riots on the scale of the Manchester carnage then it doesn't leave much room for more severe action elsewhere. But I was incredulous, that in light of all the publicity around the "Dida" incident, some numbnut could still be stupid enough to invade the pitch again. Quite frankly I could have no sympathy for either of these clowns and anything the courts would subsequently throw at them. Of course, some of the punishments called for by the blue-tinted glasses brigade (egged on by the media it has to be said) were ridiculous, such as points deductions and having to play matches behind closed-doors, these being justified by comparison with an incident where, coincidentally, Dida was struck by a firework in a Milan derby. However, pointing out that such punishment would be absurdly draconian and based on fallacious comparison, is not the same as denying all liability and claiming that those involved were justified in their actions and were in fact the innocent victims of infiltrators and circumstances outwith their control; defences offered in relation to much more serious instances of crowd disorder involving Rangers fans.

I can imagine someone who cared about Rangers FC, watching lumpen morons laying waste to what little remains of the club's positive image, and feeling anger and a desire to somehow inject some semblance of sense into the perpetrators, so that they may see the error of their ways and the possible consequences for the club they purport to love with a view to preventing such calamity in the future. Someone in Graham Spiers' position has the means to do so, although it is hardly conceivable that many of the "FTP brigade" will be picking up copies of The Times any time soon. But to his credit, unlike the Ewen Camerons and Keith Jacksons of this world, he did attempt to address the issue in a way that would deal with the club's ills in the long-term, rather than the short-sighted 'sweep it under the carpet and it'll go away' approach of the rest of the Scottish media.

To my mind, the following article is written by someone who genuinely cares for the club concerned and who wants to see these problems resolved, whether it be in the capacity of a fan of the club, or someone who simply cares about one of Scotland's major clubs in the context of the overall health of Scottish football. Certainly, addressing the issue head-on is the only way the problem will be resolved, rather than the customary "Whattaboutery", bleating about "heavy-handed" policing or compiling as many MINORITY reports as you can muster. The article certainly paints us as no angels, and I think only the most blinkered of Celtic fans would say we are absolutely whiter than white, but then again, what club is? Just ask Mark McGhee. But the article also gives us credit where credit is due, which is more than can be said for the rest of the Scottish media:

Time for Martin Bain to speak out about the sectarian chants of Rangers' fans
By Graham Spiers 22nd September 2008

Even when things get as mad and agenda-driven in the sectarianism debate as they did last week in Scottish football, some aspects remain crystal clear in their need of condemnation. That is, if people have the courage to say so.

Celtic, streets ahead of Rangers when it comes to cleaning up their act, nonetheless will find it hard to fully divorce themselves from their benighted city rivals unless that clump of idiots in their away support who croon about the IRA can be silenced. The Celtic Park club, and in particular their chief executive, Peter Lawwell, have spoken out about it before, but perhaps another public push on the matter is essential.

The fact is, the IRA chanting is galling for Celtic, given that the club have led the way over the past 15 years in eradicating bigotry from the vast swath of their support. For years now Celtic Park – unlike Ibrox – has been largely free of sectarian or racist chanting.

Over at Ibrox, the latest favoured chant to pollute the air deserves open condemnation from Martin Bain, the Rangers chief executive, if only he can find the guts to do it. The so-called Famine Song smacks of a brain-dead racism of the type too many Rangers fans simply cannot leave behind: anti Irish and anti Catholic. No wonder Strathclyde Police are now threatening to make arrests at Ibrox for racist behaviour. And it is inconceivable that, in private, Bain does not deplore the song, though he can't bring himself to say so publicly.

I have only one measure of sympathy for Bain, who in every other sense is a decent man and a talented football executive, and it is this: he must be weary of the prejudices of the white underclass which continue to infect a large minority of the Ibrox support. Rangers have suffered humiliation upon humiliation in recent years – in Villarreal, in Pamplona, in the Uefa prosecution over bigoted chanting, and most recently and shockingly in Manchester. Just what must it be like being this club's chief executive?

That, however, does not excuse Bain's timidity last week over the Famine Song. Of it, without a word of condemnation, he said: "Clearly some of our supporters feel aggrieved that a song they believe to be no more than a 'wind-up' of Celtic supporters should be singled out like this..."

I'm sorry? Unfairly "singled out" and a mere "wind-up"? Given the recent tradition of the bigotry problem at Rangers, I fear this latest dirge about "Irish" or "Fenians" being sent back to Ireland deserves something slightly more withering than Bain's folksy "wind-up" claim. The song is trash, it is racist, and he should find the guts to say it.

Back in 1972 – yes, it goes this far back – when the Rangers fans rioted in Barcelona and got the club flung out of Europe, you didn't find the then Ibrox manager, Willie Waddell, indulging in this sort of obfuscation. On the contrary, facing his own supporters and with the steam coming out his ears, Waddell went straight for the jugular in condemning those who embarrassed his club.

"It is to these tikes, hooligans, louts and drunkards that I pinpoint my message," Waddell said. "It is because of your gutter-rat behaviour that we [Rangers FC] are being publicly tarred and feathered." Every football club chairman or chief executive, like Bain, needs to keep reasonably "on-message" with his own customers. But racism and sectarianism need to be condemned, not shirked.

The madness of last week, involving BBC Scotland headlines and pages of the fall-out in many Scottish newspapers, had its own peculiar evolution. We have now reached the stage where organised bodies of Celtic and Rangers fans, often via those modern lunatic asylums called fans websites, are in a race to land the first propaganda blow.

I must admit, when last week's story first broke about alleged "Irish diplomats" poking their noses in by "getting in touch" with the Scottish Government about the chanting of Rangers fans, something wasn't quite right about it. Just who was stirring which large pot here? There was something strained and farfetched about the way the story developed. Personally, it made me suspicious, and it only fed the now-rampant paranoia that goes with wearing a Rangers scarf.

Then, predictably, something even more ludicrous happened. A group of Rangers fans, voraciously casting around to find someone – anyone – to make a similar complaint about Celtic, came up with the dubious figure of Gregory Campbell, a Democratic Unionist MP from Northern Ireland, who duly expressed his inability to venture to any Celtic game due to some supporters' unsavoury singing.

You could almost hear the underground clamour: "Quick lads, we've found an equaliser, get this Campbell bloke on to the TV stations!" And so the whole daft scenario unfolded, tit for tat, jibe and counter-jibe. In terms of addressing sectarianism, last week was not one when our media covered itself in glory.

One other fallacy needs to be debunked here. No one is suggesting that football chants should have either a squeaky, Mary Poppins air about them, or that they should be strictly football related. On both counts, of course not. Football largely enjoys the colour and daftness of its fans, and any killjoys in this regard should be kept well away from the debate.

But neither bigotry nor racism is funny. If only someone, somewhere, could teach a section of the Rangers fans to love themselves, rather than hate others, a huge step forward would be taken.

Scottish football "expert" Craig Paterson

2nd December 2009

Why am I never invited to appear on TV or radio to offer the watching/listening public the benefit of my insightful opinions and observations on Scottish football? This is a question that I almost never ask myself.

Ostensibly the reason is, that I am not equipped with the necessary expertise, experience and encyclopedic knowledge of the Scottish game that is possessed by such former journeymen footballers as Billy Dodds, Fraser Wishart, Derek Johnstone, Derek Ferguson or Craig Paterson (spot the common link). These are individuals who are a veritable fountain of wisdom on the Scottish game. The latter has a particularly high profile at the moment, making regular appearances as a summariser on BBC Scotland TV and radio.

The ex-Rangers centre half is held in such esteem that his expertise is now much sought after among our illustrious Scottish tabloids. Witness the following pearls of wisdom which appeared in an Evening Times piece ghostwritten by the inept Thomas Jordan. The article made reference to the Hibernian-Rangers SPL match scheduled for 27th December (Yes I know St. Andrew's day is barely out the way, but any excuse to talk about the Rangers) and Paterson is quoted:

"Hibs, of course, haven't been beaten all season at Easter Road and Celtic is, without doubt, the toughest away game of the season for Rangers. But if Rangers can emerge from these games with a healthy amount of points then it will give their title hopes a massive boost going into the second half of the season."

Here's hoping Craig.

This is all very well of course and I'd be the first to advise Mr Paterson that he needs to hike up his fee for such stunning insights, however there is one minor wee detail that slightly contradicts Paterson's verbal diahrroea – Hibs **had** been beaten at Easter Road already that season, **twice** in fact:

Tuesday, 22 September 2009
Co-operative Insurance Cup
Hibernian 1-3 St Johnstone
Stokes (1) Swankie (7)
Millar (76)
Morris (82)

Sunday, 30 August 2009
Clydesdale Bank Premier League
Hibernian 0-1 Celtic
Samaras (41)

The match involving Celtic is of particular irony considering Paterson and his BBC Radio colleagues put CSI Miami to shame with their forensic dissection of the McGeady "diving" incident in that game. This was rather a contrast to diving incidents involving 'Boydie', offside goals by Novo, elbows in the face and karate kicks by McCulloch and assorted other unsavoury stuff involving the Establishment Team, that simply escaped the attention of the BBC cameras, as well as their equally hopeless STV counterparts.

In any case, all I can do is dream of the day I will have acquired anywhere near the footballing expertise of Mr Paterson and his fellow hacks. I wonder how much money he's on for this pish? Can I have some money please or is my pish not up to the necessary standards of utter pishness?

The BBC on poor attendances at Celtic Park
2nd December 2009

Top news story on BBC Reporting Scotland, a forensic analysis of Celtic's poor attendances this season with a bold prediction that they could fall below 35,000 soon. Many interviews with fans featured - is it because of the recession? No it's because the manager and team are boring/pish/shite (take your pick) is the conclusion. Thank you for that morale boost just before a European tie BBC. Always support the Scottish team right enough.

Now, the reason there hasn't been a story like this on BBC or STV about Rangers is because Ibrox has been full to the rafters every week this season. Oh no wait...   Must be an "honest mistake"

12th December 2009 Motherwell 2-3 Celtic

HONEST MISTAKE NO.18 Samaras blatantly chopped down in box at Fir Park. No penalty. Celtic do get penalty but only on the third strong claim, two of which were stonewallers.

The Guardian – "*Celtic did have a legitimate claim for a penalty when Samaras was tripped by Reynolds. Another two poor decisions from referee Charlie Richmond denied them penalties after McGeady had equalised*"

HONEST MISTAKES NO.19 & 20 At 3-2 Charlie Richmond adds several minutes onto the initially allotted injury time with Motherwell applying pressure to the Celtic goal, however then Celtic hit on the break and with Fortune **clean through on goal**, he blows for full time

POSSIBLE EFFECT Celtic win the game so no points issue, however goal difference likely to have been increased by 2 or 3 goals if penalties had been scored and/or Fortune converted if allowed to carry on. Very unusual for a referee to stop the game at the point of a scoring opportunity, usually the referee will wait until the ball is in a neutral area of the pitch before blowing up, although this is not a law of the game.

Rangers (-5), Celtic (+7)

3rd January 2010 Celtic 1-1 Rangers

HONEST MISTAKE NO.21 Perfectly good Marc Antoine Fortune goal disallowed by 'no longer controversial' Steve Conroy.

Sky Sports Moment of the Match – *"Marc-Antoine Fortune's wrongly disallowed goal could have changed the game and the title race."*

News of the World – *"Richard Gough reflecting on the disallowed goal "Look at the last game, the one where Celtic have had the Fortune goal disallowed. I admit that it does look like a goal. The referee (Steve Conroy) has not ruled the goal disallowed because he's a Protestant or a Catholic. He's made an honest call and guys make mistakes"*

HONEST MISTAKE NO.22 Kyle Lafferty commits appalling foul on Andreas Hinkel deliberately stamping on the full back's shin with speed and momentum. Tony Mowbray is seen squirming with his hand in hands at the sight of this "tackle". This was easily a career threatening act.

Daily Mail "Then came the Lafferty-Hinkel incident, arriving after the Rangers player had earlier been **lucky to escape a booking for three fouls**. This time, Lafferty slid in, studs up, in a shocking challenge that fully impacted on Hinkel's shin, one which had the Celtic fans **howling** for a red card. And **Conroy should have administered it**."

Two months later Herald - *"The tackle is not in my head any more,"* said Hinkel yesterday. *"It's still on my shin, though. I still have the mark there."*

POSSIBLE EFFECT Celtic goal potentially makes the score 2-1 and Lafferty sending off would make it very difficult for Rangers to come back. High probability of Celtic gaining 2 points and Rangers losing the point they picked up.

Rangers (-6 [-1]), Celtic (+9 [+2])

The Wisdom of Waldo

4th January 2010

Celtic and Rangers draw 1-1 at Celtic Park and among other "incidents", Kyle Lafferty commits an appalling foul on Andreas Hinkel. Lafferty was booked for which, to most onlookers and by the laws of the game, was an automatic red card offence. What pray did Mr. Dignity himself – the man known throughout the land as the most dignified of football statesmen, selflessly defending the honour of the game single-handedly by slapping wage-saving fines any players who fall below his exacting standards of moral behaviour – have to say about that?

'The referee dealt with it and we should all move on' was the gist. Oh right. No noble acts of censure to uphold 100 years of unsurpassed dignity blah blah waffle waffle? No, apparently we should all just forget about it. In much the same way in fact, as Nosurname does over decisions made by Tom Murphy. Or when one of his players gets sent off. Or in relation to fixture scheduling. Or when a linesman runs 60-70 yards…etc etc etc

The fact that Lafferty was given a yellow card is not a reason for his tackle not to be reviewed by the Review Panel. Last May Scott McDonald's tackle on Lee Wilkie which the referee saw and judged not deserving of any censure was reviewed by the Review Panel. Why and under what authority?

The referee, Stuart Dougal, saw it and his judgement was the tackle was not violent conduct and did not merit a red card. Somebody at the SFA, prompted by the media no doubt, obviously thought otherwise and asked the Review Panel to look at it, presumably after a word with the referee even if only out of courtesy. It was a clear breach, by the SFA themselves, of the double jeopardy rule that football normally strives to maintain to protect a referee's authority.

This being so, one can only conclude that the nature of McDonald's tackle was so serious it was seen by somebody at the SFA (who exactly, and under what process and authority has still to be clarified) as the kind of violent conduct that merited an appropriate sanction which McDonald had escaped.

There is no reason for not subjecting the Lafferty tackle to the same process. The two cases are exactly the same in principle (ie the "crime" did not get the deserved and appropriate punishment) and the technicality of the yellow card does not excuse a similar process not being applied to Lafferty's "tackle".

It was clearly violent conduct, the referee did not mete out the appropriate punishment, so why is the case not being referred to the Review Panel, or have the SFA rewritten the rules or invented a new set whilst Celtic wait clarification of what they actually are? This is not a sour grapes or paranoia issue, it is about the fair application of the same rules and their underlying principles to everyone regardless of whose agenda it suits. With their silence on The Famine Song, Jock Stein slur (about a former national team manager) and the Review Panel "rules" the SFA look to be more and more guilty of favouring one club in Scotland over all others. The evidence mounts up with every day of their silence, evasion and obsfucation.

Of course fast forward to October 2010, and after Rangers goalkeeper Allan McGregor was referred to the SFA Review panel for kicking out at Aberdeen's Chris Maguire and subsequently banned for one game, the Scottish press took a sudden keen interest in asking questions about the mechanics of the process (as if they didn't know). "Who is responsible for referring these matters to the panel?", "Why did this take 10 days to come to the SFA's notice?" howled the rags. The Evening Times handed over it's back page to the RST to list seven questions they "*demanded*" the SFA answer, under a piece titled "*Fans call on SFA to explain McGregor ban*". Tell you what, while they wait, I'll have a wee go at attempting to explain it to them – he was guilty of violent conduct; violent conduct is an offence which must be punished by a red card, therefore he was given a retrospective red card resulting in a one match ban. There you go, nothing too complicated I think you will agree.

As it happens, these seven questions were almost identical to the ones raised by Celtic at the time of the Loovens and McDonald incidents 17 months prior, but of course that was all total paranoia and deranged conspiracy theories, whereas the RST simply made a sensible request "*for clarification on the timing and process relating to the one-match ban handed to Allan McGregor*". For extra paranoia value, the RST's last question asked for a precedent where another player has been banned and 12 penalty points added to his record. Well leaving aside the utterly transparent and paranoid "you're just picking on our poor wee goalie" angle to this, my reply would simply be in the form of four words… "Alan Thompson Peter Lovestodive". I'm sure you know what I'm getting at. You could ask Scott Brown if you're still unsure.

The icing on the paranoid "we cannae see the woods from the trees" Establishment club cake came from the Divine Cardigan himself. Venting his spleen at the injustice of it all, Nosurname accused the SFA of having hastily convened a disciplinary panel to ensure Kenny Miller missed a Celtic-Rangers game. I am not playing with, or twisting words here, the exact quote is – "*Last season, they (the SFA) quickly organised a disciplinary hearing for Kenny Miller's appeal, **so that he would miss the Celtic game**.*" (15/10/2010). So where is the media's howls of derision at a manager making disgraceful claims of favouritism, bias and, dare I say the forbidden word – conspiracy? Under the carpet somewhere no doubt. Such is the prerogative of the manager of the Establishment team who was a servile media at his disposal to mould every utterance into a thing of statesmanlike dignity.

Of course as Celtic fans well know, the supreme irony of this is that the SFA convened a hearing as soon as they got back off the plane from the Bahamas to ensure McGregor would see out his ban against Motherwell and be available to play against Celtic. Add to this, the haste with which they were able to exonerate… sorry… give an objective hearing to… the "kicking the goalie's head" case of Madjid Bougherra the season before which conveniently allowed him to play in the last game SPL decider against Dundee Utd in 2008/09 season. In contrast, back in February 2002, the SFA managed to take nearly three weeks (18 days) to give Bobo Balde a two-match ban on the basis of footage referred to the video review panel. By a happy coincidence the drawn-out nature of proceedings ensured Balde missed a game against Rangers on March 10th that year. Hurrah! We should remind the SFA that Celtic were in the "clarification" queue first.

Time to Get Rid of that O*d F**m Tag

The press in this country has willfully tried to ruin our reputation time and again and are ramping up the heat to temperatures rarely experienced before, merely to deflect some of the heat from Rangers in their time of financial fiasco. Their biggest weapon has been the Old F**m tag, and the view that both clubs were "as bad as each other". The Celtic support is unhappy at the company we keep, and wants a change. More than that, we understand another term, a far worse one. It's called "guilt by association", and as long as there is one person out there who believes in that, the collective Celtic support would like some distance between us and unnecessary trouble.

In short, Celtic **must** formally ditch the "Old F**m" tag once and for all. Get it gone, get it gone now and forever. If there are financial consequences then let us pay them. The tag now actively hurts us. I imagine a lot of their fans would have no objection to being rid of the tag either. Large numbers of their supporters actively despise us and everything we stand for. I would imagine they'd be more than willing to dump us overboard if the chance came along. They are the stupid ones, of course, because if there's one thing which becomes clearer the more one looks at Rangers' present plight it's this; they need the Old F**m tag like never before. Without it, they are in serious trouble, which is all the more reason for us to be rid of it, in my view.

Rangers have a clear financial stake in the maintenance of the status quo. It would be massively damaging to them, in terms of prestige and in finance, if we were to go our separate ways, and remove the absurd element of what looks like collective bargaining from the equation. When Alastair Johnston became chairman of Rangers he admitted as much, in an interview to The Sunday Mail, on August 27th of last year.

"*It is extremely important that there is the competition between Rangers and Celtic on the field,*" he said. "*That's what gets the juices of the fans going, and is the lifeblood of the game. But off the field, there is more that unites Rangers and Celtic than separates them - both are dealing in the same economy with the same circumstances and parameters.*"

The last part of his statement "*the same circumstances and parameters*" was disingenuous at best; at worst it was a wholly misleading statement designed to deflect the truth. One would imagine the businessmen on our board, all qualified and capable people, would see through this transparent nonsense, unlike the Mail journalist who wrote it up and the editor who put it in print without questioning it.

Celtic and Rangers do not face the "*same circumstances*"; we are financially sound, with an evolving business strategy and multiple revenue streams, which have taken our turnover above and beyond theirs. They are riddled by debt, unable to tap new marketplaces, even now, operating at nearly their maximum season ticket capacity. We do not face the "*same parameters*", because although, yes, we are both stuck in Scottish football, at least for the foreseeable future, we have expanded our business model outside of these shores. Channel67 now broadcasts our games across the world, and unlike domestic football rights, these belong solely to the club. No-one denies now that we were wise to retain our multimedia rights when Rangers sold theirs to NTL, in a much hyped deal. Of course NTL offered their deal to both clubs, and as everyone is aware, Celtic's directors turned them down flat, and were derided for it in the press at the time whilst Murray was lauded as a "visionary" of "unrivalled business acumen", even though anyone with half a brain could see Internet football streaming was going to explode in the UK and beyond over the next decade. The Celtic board realised that there was value in going it alone, that it made good commercial sense, that there was a vast and untapped market out there which could net us big money in the long run.

On this occasion, our board knew the value of going the other way. I would say, with Rangers facing financial calamity, the time has come to make that official policy. There is no mutual benefit to be had. Celtic are better off going it alone, the only benefits of the present "arrangement" are those which accrue to the Ibrox club. In this desperate time of theirs, with the future of their team looking murky, companies which have to negotiate with them will be highly unlikely to pay top dollar for a product which might be past its sell-by date. Ranger's plight is now out there, in the full public view; they are desperate, and no business which has dealings with them will be unaware of that. In much the same way as they can no longer command high transfer fees for their dross, their negotiating position in the wider world is weakened too. What are Rangers going to do if major companies offer less than they believe they are worth? Play hardball?

Their hunt for a buyer, despite proclamations in June that they are no longer seeking one, seem likely to drag on for a while yet. A club whose best hopes lie with a man facing hundreds of fraud charges do not make good bedfellows for a company trying to secure a major deal. The reputation of their supporters – large sections of which continue to defy all understanding or appeals to change – makes them a pariah no reputable organisation would wish to be associated with. Their long-term future is uncertain and in doubt, and their ability to expand and broaden their base beyond Scotland is limited firstly by money and secondly by the narrow confines of the image they have wrapped around themselves during the era of David Murray; an image tied to Britishness, insular "traditions" which define them as a club with limited appeal to outsiders.

Going hand-in-hand with Rangers makes us look as if we need the "O*d F**m" tag to justify ourselves outside of the environment we are in, when actually this could not be farther from the truth. There are serious issues of "guilt by association", particularly when one considers the enormous and extraordinary lengths the press goes to in order to protect Rangers, its fans and its players from negative publicity. There is no issue as important to our fans as this, because we have one of the best reputations in the game, and outside of Scotland everyone knows we are a different type of support, not just the flipside of a coin.

The press in Scotland never stops putting us under the spotlight, subjecting us to negative publicity whenever they can, and it leads others to question that reputation; after all, if you are an Italian who knows the reputation we enjoy across Europe and then are subjected to the coverage we routinely receive in our own country, you would naturally wonder which image is true. After all, who knows us better than our own press? You might be forgiven for drawing all sorts of wrong conclusions.

We are constantly subjected to the "just as bad as each other" parrot call, a familiar call to arms for Rangers men like Ewen Cameron and Bill Leckie. They even managed to use that tag in connection with the Manchester Riots. What do you know, in amongst all those Chelsea, Millwall and West Ham casuals were a few Tims too. The Old F**m tag is never more widely used than to drag us into the gutter Rangers frequently find themselves occupying. When the UEFA first started to take an interest in the festering sore of their battle hymn book in 2006, every media outlet in the land shrieked "What about Celtic?!!" Celtic, whose fans had won European and FIFA Fair Play awards only a few short years before and have brought credit to the whole of Scotland on each and every foreign excursion. The press willfully tried to ruin our reputation, merely to deflect some of the heat from Rangers. Their biggest weapon was the Old F**m tag, and the view that both clubs were "as bad as each other". One of the men who pushed that myth was Gordon Smith, now head of the SFA, who alleged an "agenda" against Rangers when it comes to highlighting sectarianism. He is one of the pushers of the idea that both clubs are "as bad as each other", a view which is useful in staving off the empty threat of SFA sanctions against clubs who's fans engage in bigoted or racist behaviour. After all, if you accept the premise, how can you fine Rangers or dock them points when Celtic fans are "just as bad"?

In February 2010, the News International chain, through its News of the World rag, ran one of the most biased and nakedly defamatory acts of recent years; they attempted to put our club at the centre of a date rape allegation involving a Rangers player. As we now know, these allegations centred around Allan McGregor and the relevant authorities have decided that no further action is required. Now, one can understand the need for anonymity, but what I can't buy is – why the need to plaster a **Celtic** crest and image of **Celtic Park** all over the story. Quite simply our "friends" in the press had quite deliberately, attempted to bind us to this story, first with the use of the Old F**m tag to hide the fact the player in question plays for Rangers and, more seriously, to actually use a picture of our stadium in the story in a further effort to mask the truth and, far worse, to willfully give the false impression that the suspect could have been a Celtic player.

Some will argue that no real damage has been done, that the name of the player involved was always going to get out, and thereby clear our club of any involvement; I refute that utterly. Stories like this have appeared in the press from time to time, involving other high-profile individuals, and in most cases the names never become public and the accusations remain neither countered nor proved. Had such a thing happened in this case – as was very likely – our club's name would forever have been tied to this event because of the way the story was framed; the Old F**m tag narrowing it to one of two clubs. Every single player in our squad would have had that hanging over their head, and our reputation would have taken a hit.

The Old F**m tag has followed us now for more than half of our existence as a football club. Whatever benefits it might once have brought us, now it does us nothing but harm. It has bound us, inexorably, to the worst elements at Ibrox. It has allowed the press a stick to beat us with, allowing them to drag us into issues which were none of our concern. Politics and business holds fast to the view that perception is reality, that people judge first on how something looks rather than going deeper, to find out what something actually is. A salesman who is failing does not go out to work in a broken down car, but pays a deposit on a new one to give people the outward appearance of success, giving him credibility with the customer on the doorstep or in the factory.

As long as people perceive Celtic as being one side of the coin and Rangers the other, those who don't know any better will treat us just the same. The neutrals will judge us not only on what we do, but on what the club across town gets up to. The media will use that stick to beat us whenever Rangers are feeling the pain, even as they use any example of negative publicity which has our name on it to bludgeon us without mercy. Neil Lennon was a "Celtic star" when he had his personal problems some years ago and Artur Boruc was never referred to as an "Old F**m" keeper when his own personal life was splashed all over the tabloids. Can you imagine the Daily Record plastering the Rangers badge and stadium all over the Thugs and Thieves story? Let's get this "Old F**m" millstone off our necks.

10th January 2010   Hamilton Accies 3-3 Rangers

HONEST MISTAKE NO.23 Rangers are heading out of the Scottish Cup at 3-2 down to Hamilton Accies when they are awarded a ridiculous penalty as Kenny Miller kicks the ball off a Hamilton Accies defender's arm whilst he's lying prone on the ground. The player (Stuart Elliott) actually tried to pull his arm away from the ball.

The Times "*Rangers also got lucky to a degree — the penalty awarded to them after 61 minutes, when Stuart Elliott was judged to have stopped the ball illegally while lying on the ground, looked harsh.*"

Scotsman – "*They needed a touch of good fortune to equalise when referee Charlie Richmond rather harshly penalised Hamilton debutant Stuart Elliott for handball, awarding the spot-kick from which Kenny Miller converted.*"

16th January 2010   Celtic 1-1 Falkirk

HONEST MISTAKE NO.24 Celtic should have had a penalty when Fortune was fouled by Brian McLean in the box. Eddie May admits this to the press.

Mail on Sunday – '*Falkirk manager Eddie May said: "Overall, I thought it was a fair result. But I think they should have had a penalty."*'

Daily Mail – '*Alan Muir denied the Parkhead club a late penalty claim – when Brian McLean **tangled** with Fortune – in the 1-1 draw with Falkirk on Saturday*'. Note that McLean '*tangled*' with Fortune and this was a '*claim*' for a penalty.

HONEST MISTAKE NO.25 Artur Boruc is penalised for handling the ball two yards INSIDE his box. This has to be the most ludicrous free kick given since the inception of the SPL, and to add insult to injury it was only 20 yards from goal in a potentially goal-scoring position for Falkirk. This is an extremely rare infringement to see, and even rarer to see penalised, although it helps if the infringement was actually committed in the first place of course. The free kick was given by linesman Francis Andrews with five minutes to go and the score at 1-1.

Daily Mail "*Hinkel was also unhappy about Celtic keeper Artur Boruc being penalised for apparently stepping out of his area late on. "It's not really my thing to say something about referees but, once again, we had some very strange decisions," said Hinkel. "Not even just the penalty – look at the situation when Artur had a free-kick given against him."*"

POSSIBLE EFFECT Celtic denied a penalty to win the game 2-1. Falkirk given the chance to score a winner near the end of the game through a nonsensical error by the linesman (see below). High probability of Celtic winning if the penalty is given, resulting in a two point swing.

Rangers (-6 [-1]), Celtic (+11 [+2])

The Scottish media, neither neutral nor objective

His latest piece in the Evening Times, entitled "No more bets for Tony Mowbray if results do not improve" is like Bad Journalism 101. Martin (McGuire) does not support his assertions with facts, he re-hashes rumours, goes on flights of fancy and makes assumptions, all in the space of 17 short paragraphs, and less than 500 words.

A few weeks ago, when Tony Mowbray's first major falling out with the press resulted in his accusing them of pursuing "agendas", Mark Guidi, on Radio Clyde, dishonoured his profession by threatening to cast aside objectivity entirely. "The gloves are off," Guidi said, ominously.

There was a time when sports journalism in Scotland was important, when it commanded respect. There was a time when sports journalism in this country had credibility, because those who worked in the profession knew their business, and knew their responsibilities and took those seriously. We are a long way from that benchmark.

Martin (McGuire) might not realise it, but he is a symbolic figure. His two principle media roles – his Clyde Super scoreboard "commentary" slot and his Evening Times column – are demonstrable proof of how far the standard has fallen and about how low the profession has sunk.

Martin (McGuire) has become a joke figure in Scottish football circles. Over in the blue corner, Rangers fans detest him – I don't think that's overstating the case – believing him to be a gossip merchant and teller of tall-tales. In fact, they'd go further, and call him an outright liar at times. Their hatred of Martin (McGuire) is indicative of their hatred for anyone in the media who criticises their club, but it has an extra edge because they believe that he is a Celtic supporter. They are right. He is a Celtic supporter, but Rangers fans should look past that. After all, if we can do it, so can they. They see any criticism of their club from this man as proof that he's out to get them, when actually the explanation is much simpler than that. Martin (McGuire), like his Clyde colleague Hugh Keevins, is in the business of sensationalism, not journalism. No right-minded person can take someone like that seriously, whichever team they call their own.

Celtic fans have long since looked past Martin (McGuire), knowing what he is about. He is one of a number of "Celts in the media", a group including Keevins, Nicholas, Walker and even Craig Burley, who's behaviour is such that they are hated by their fellow Celtic supporters. When Celtic fans are asked to choose hate-figures from the press, these guys often feature on the list, alongside rent-a-quote Rangers men such as Hateley, Johnstone, Chick Young and Jim Traynor, the latter two of course claiming to support other sides. Young, allegedly, is a St Mirren fan, who according to some sources needs a map and a guide to find their home ground, whereas Jim Traynor is supposed to be a follower of Airdrie United. Oddly, for a neutral, he seems to have a strange fascination with what goes on at Celtic.

The word neutral is used deliberately in this context. It is used because it's what so many in our media claim to be. They are broadly grouped together in two categories; Rangers fans who wish to pretend they're not, and Celtic fans who are trying to deny they are. Amongst that number is our friend Martin (McGuire), who long ago decided that "neutrality" meant slamming us hard, every chance he got. He thinks this makes him look as if he isn't taking sides, as if he is above the fray, and in a sense he is, which, if you'll pardon me for saying it, is the problem.

There are those in the media who basically are what they are. They are the sports journalists who are hopelessly partisan. Take Mark Hateley for example, he is very plainly, simply, unapologetically, a spokesperson for Rangers. His column for the Record is indistinguishable from the content in the Rangers News. At times, the tone of his articles, especially those about Walter Smith, veers into outright veneration. Derek Johnstone, on Clyde, is similar; he is unashamedly biased in everything he says, they are what they are. They do not pretend otherwise.

Sports journalists, in the main, strive to be one of two things; they must be either neutral or they must be objective. As Scotland houses two huge sides, and as both have a disquieting habit of drawing even non-supporters into their orbit, it is hard to find anyone who can maintain true neutrality. The people who can genuinely stand above the fray are a rare breed; rarer still are those who can look at the game and apply cold, hard logic to it, therefore objectivity is almost unheard of in Scottish sporting circles, and it's that which we need the most here.

This is the area where so many, Martin (McGuire) and his cronies included, utterly fail to make the grade. They claim to strive for the first, but because they don't possess the latter they can't quite make it. Neutrality means not taking any side in a debate, but in presenting both sides of a case, no matter how ridiculous one of those sides is, and for those who are pretending to be neutral that is their Get out of Jail Free card, their back-stage pass to play at being respectable members of a respected profession. Under the guise of neutrality they can hide what they really are, which is to say that they are cowards. If they weren't cowards, perhaps then they'd be capable of at least attempting to be objective.

This means that when controversy rages, or when, say, the Rangers fans engage in singing racist songs, those times when we need someone objective to call something what it is, the assorted hacks can put on their "neutral" hats and pretend to be outside the debate. This appalling lack of conviction, this ignorance of their wider responsibility, has hammered the credibility of the Scottish sporting media into pulp. The damage this does to the whole of the game is bigger than that which affects one club, and is the reason these people can be simultaneously hated by Celtic and Rangers fans alike. The contempt this inspires in their listeners and readers leads to their word being distrusted by everyone, and this weakens the standing of not only their respective media outlets but to the media profession as a whole. It's not for nothing some are universally loathed; they do nothing to inspire faith in their word, or respect for their views.

Objectivity is a holy word in journalism, and a misunderstood one. Often mistaken for neutrality, in its purest form it is the opposite. Objectivity is about the search for truth, and it veers away from neutrality at any point where the facts or the truth mean taking one side or another. It is truly impartial, it sincerely stands above the fray, analysing and commenting on, and illuminating, the Search for Truth. In such an endeavour there is an ultimate loyalty, a loyalty to that higher standard journalism is supposed to represent. It is the antithesis of sensationalism, the silver bullet fired in the cause of informing the public – not entertaining them, as much of the news media is geared towards today.

Take the situation regarding Rangers efforts to find a buyer, and their being a creature of the Lloyds Banking Group.

An objective look at the whole picture, based on the facts, would lead to any independent observer concluding that the bank is entitled to reclaim the money it is owed. Rangers successes in the 90s, indeed their successes last season, as well as their present league lead, were built on spending money that did not belong to them, money that, by rights, by logic, they should be expected to repay. At a time when companies are going down and people are being thrown out of work or out of their homes, it is simply unreasonable to expect the banks to allow an exemption for a football club which got itself into difficulty through its own fault.

Further, any objective observer would conclude, through a simple process of fact-checking and analysis, that any talk of Dave King saving the club is simply impossible. His position as a virtual prisoner of his legal problems in South Africa is absolutely unequivocal. Indeed, the government itself has made this abundantly clear, in no uncertain terms, stating, for the record, that his assets remain frozen.

There is no need here to go out of the way to appear neutral, to try and find both sides of the argument; these are undisputed facts, or they would be if the sports media in Scotland was capable of viewing them in an objective way. Instead of acknowledging these truths, we see instead propaganda pieces on why the banks should bend their rules to let Rangers off, even as hard working men and women are expected to pay what they owe and well established firms are shutting down daily, and fantasies abounding about the South African coming to the rescue with a bag full of money under one arm and a new contract for Kris Boyd under the other. This is the same thinking that let David Murray continue to evade questions when Rangers debt was rising in the first place, and which follows him to this day, and has resulted in embarrassments to journalism like the spectacular own goal that was the £500 million "redevelopment of Ibrox" plan.

The sports media appears to operate under a different set of rules, as our former manager Martin O'Neill, who was forced to sue them – and more than once – can testify. So too can the players slandered in the Thugs & Thieves story. No-one lost their job over the fantasies which were the genesis of those famous legal battles, and I wouldn't imagine Keith Jackson will lose his job over his latest fiction-passed-off-as-fact, the recent tale about Scott Brown. As I said above, this kind of thing is indicative of the standard which Jackson and his ilk operates according to.

For the vast majority of the Celtic support, two things about the affair rang out loudly. First, his assertion that Celtic fans would be shocked by news that Brown might be up for sale was so erroneous as to render the whole point of the piece moot; most Celtic fans barely whimpered. Brown has not been a tremendously successful signing, and his absence in the team at crucial periods in the last three seasons has had minimal effects on our form. Some have suggested his absence in season 2007-08 was a key factor in our seven match run towards the title.

The other thing which stood out was the denial from Tony Mowbray, who the piece had specifically named as having told Scott Brown he was free to find another club. Jackson made sure that there was no dubiety at all in what he had written; this was not Peter Lawwell telling Brown, not John Reid nor a phone-call from Dermott Desmond. This was not little notes left in his socks, not anonymous messages on his mobile phone or a poison pen letter dropped through his letterbox saying GO AND GO NOW. This was our manager, Tony Mowbray himself, in a sit-down with the player, telling him he did not feature in his first team plans.

Tony Mowbray's statement contains no dubiety either, no room for doubt or evasion at a later date; his language is clear, absolutely unambiguous and straight to the point. *"The story is absolute nonsense,"* he said *"I never told Scott Brown that I want him to leave the club. Scott is a huge player for Celtic and absolutely part of the future plans of this club."*

We are now in murky waters, as far as our relationship with the press goes. They are not neutral, because some are blatantly and unashamedly biased and others like to use that as a convenient cover for their lack of backbone. They are utterly without objectivity, tending to ignore facts in order to reach the conclusions they want, and their veracity is seriously questionable. The issue of whether we believe Jackson or our manager does not even factor into this; everyone who knows Tony Mowbray speaks first and foremost of his integrity. He would not lie, and in this case he would have no reason to. The sale of Scott Brown would not be a catalyst for the supporters burning the stadium to the ground. If Mowbray genuinely wanted to get rid of the player what would be the sense in denying this and stating that Scott Brown is *"a huge part of the future of this club"*? This would be a very strange way to seek out a buyer.

Jackson, on the other hand, is a slippery character who writes for a paper with a long history of mendacity and bias against our football club. The situation is not a difficult one to judge, and most of our fans reached their conclusion even before the club issued its now famous denial. That denial has threatened legal action. Today, the paper all but dared us to take it. I hope the board calls their bluff and does so.

When he gave his pre-match interview to Celtic TV in preparation for the coming weekend, he was in bullish form, "The story of Scottish football really isn't big enough for the newspapers that are out there and they try to create an agenda that can run for a few days and can cause a bit of unrest," he said. "It gets reaction from supporters, it gets letters pages going, it gets the back page the following day because there's reaction. It doesn't affect me but I know it affects our supporters." In this, he is correct; it makes us angry.

"Why do I speak to the press?" he asked, "Really to talk to our fans - that's the only reason that I talk to the media. If it were down to me solely, I would probably end up doing all our media stuff to our supporters through mediums like Channel 67 and the Celtic View. Maybe there's a proportion of our fans who don't have access to Channel 67 or have the opportunity to buy the View, and their only knowledge of Celtic Football Club is through the daily newspapers. That, in my mind, is why I give the courtesy to talk to the newspapers." It is a courtesy more than they deserve. "I've spoken to the last two Celtic managers," he said, "who told me, 'don't get over-concerned about it ...... every Celtic manager gets that'."

He ended on Scott Brown, on the story of the week, and how the press has crossed the line and broken its own golden rule. "People just can't make stories up and write them," he said. It shouldn't be allowed to happen, which is why the club are taking action, I think."

A few weeks ago, when Tony Mowbray's first major falling out with the press resulted in his accusing them of pursuing "agendas", Mark Guidi, on Radio Clyde, dishonoured his profession by threatening to cast aside objectivity entirely. "The gloves are off," Guidi said, ominously.

Catastrophic decline in Scottish football journalism standards

Ah, Jim Traynor. Once upon a time a respected, articulate, fair-minded sports reporter for the venerable Glasgow newspaper, The Herald. His career path aptly sums up all that has gone wrong with sports journalism in this country.

Whereas once we had genuinely brilliant writers (step forward Hugh McIlvanney), and knowledgeable, if slightly annoying, broadcasters like Bob Crampsey and Archie MacPherson; now we have....

1. Embittered old controversialists. Traynor, Keevins, McNee epitomise this group. Ironically all good writers, in a previous generation they would have been the wise old men of the press, writing leisurely for the broadsheets and spending the rest of their time in the Ubiquitous Chip debating the collapse of Lehman Brothers and the rise and fall and rise of Dutch football, and other such topics. But commercial pressure has forced them into tabloids, where the remaining money is. In order to survive here, they have to surf from one controversy to the next, and if there aren't enough controversies, they have to create them. McNee did this infamously with "The Fields of Athenry", the septugenerian Keevins tries to fan the flames every morning on his amateur-hour radio station, and Traynor is reduced to peddling idle gossip dressed up as news in his thin and getting thinner rag.

These poor old souls are a little better than the second group...

2. The Boys. The Boys consist of approaching middle-aged boys like Keith Union Jackson and Spewing Cameron, late thirty-somethings who in vain adopt the ridiculous wide-tied dress sense of their football playing idols, and can be spotted hanging onto the coat-tails of Krissy-Krissy and Bammy in garish nitespot "29".These boy-men know little outside of football, and their knowledge of the game does not generally stretch further back than Souness' arrival at the Death Star. Almost incapable of writing in English, they communicate in cliché, and trade in dressing-room gossip.

3. The Wee Boys The Wee Boys are almost straight-out-of-Uni journalism grads – Darrell King, Darryll Broadfoot, Matthew Lindsay. In the past, these boys would have spent the next five years making Traynor's tea and absorbing knowledge of the game and how to articulate it in print. Now they are given a big tie, a few "make your accent mid-Atlantic" voice lessons, and thrust in front of an autocue. The result is often car-crash telly and the further impoverishment of our sports media. "You can literally see what he was thinking there", no you can't Dawwyll.

Almost without exception, every post on websites such as Celtic Quick

News, Celtic Underground and E-Tims is better written and more insightful than all of the banal cliché-ridden drivel in the tabloids, which is a testament to how articulate your average fan can be, and a damning indictment of how badly served we all are by our sports media. Sadly, I cannot see that changing in the near future.

Jim Traynor on The Famine Song – "Ditty Vacant"

It is difficult to know where to start on James Traynor's article in The Daily Record on 22 September 2008. After you read it you either conclude that he has not read all the words in what he calls the "*Ditty Vacant*" or if he has read them has made one of two choices, but in none of the various possibilities does he come out with any credit whatsoever either professionally or personally

The most charitable conclusion is that he has not read all the words in which case only his professional competency comes into question, how can he possibly comment on a ditty that he has failed to examine in totality?

Or

Less charitably he has read them but what he has written raises questions about the personal character, integrity and judgement of a man who fails to see anything wrong with charges of paedophilia against a large group in Scottish society hailing from a particular demograhpic as well as one of footballs greatest managers, now deceased, and then still thinks it acceptable to tell them to go away because they do not see things as he does.

Or

He does deplore the words but in the interest of creating controversy and selling newspapers he chooses to bury his personal principles.

In the case of the first two his suitability for purpose as a responsible journalist comes into question on grounds of lack of professionalism or poverty of character. In the case of the third, one cannot question his suitability for purpose, it does sell papers, but we can condemn his lack of ethics.

On the article itself he makes a number of unbalanced, unproven or untrue statements all of which suggest lack of professionalism or judgement at best or malice at worst.

Lack of Balance
He dresses up his main argument that preventing this song being sung represents an attack on free speech, but totally fails to say that the right to

free speech comes with associated responsibilities to use that freedom wisely. Since he has not shown any signs of such responsibility or wisdom in his article, it would have been a miracle had this counter point entered his head, because if it had and had he been a man of integrity, his article would have been still born.

His argument that Celtic fans are wrong to take offence at The Famine Song (TFS) might have more weight if we thought the person making it had pursued a similar argument with those Rangers supporters who were offended by Boruc blessing himself or even his one fingered salute at their abuse. I cannot recollect any argument put forward by Traynor presented with quite the same vigour as the TFS one. Happy to be corrected on this point but my recollection is that Boruc was the focus as the offender not the Ranger's support for being offended. Does white man speak with forked tongue?

Lack of Judgement.
Traynor cites a number of present day issues that should disgust us more than the chorus of the Famine Song and if it were only the chorus, there is an argument that the present day issues are as, if not more, important. But it's not the chorus that offends; it is the song in its entirety. If he thinks that unfounded charges of complicity with paedophilia against an individual or suggesting that an identifiable group in society with its roots in another country indulge in paedophilia as a matter of course is not as present day as any of the other issues, then for a journalist he is not very current.

Interestingly on what gives offence, I heard a Rangers supporter on Clyde on Tuesday night phone in to object at being classified as racist because of the singing of TFS. My thinking was I can understand what you are saying, but how would you feel about being called a paedophile? Would that not offend you just as much, if not more? I would also tell that supporter that I was not calling him a racist but that is a judgement of society that has been attached to him by what people are singing in his name. At least my objections are not the result of actions done in my name, but false accusations made by others against me. We are not calling Rangers supporters racist, that is a consequence of what they sing and until they take responsibility for those consequences they are bound to endure them. That man's objections were aimed at the wrong folk and if I can put myself in his shoes to understand his anger, why can he not put himself in mine?

Missing The Point
Traynor says " *if any politician even attempts to tell Rangers fans to drop it we'll be entering into dangerous times*" A bit of news Jim, politicians said this a couple of years ago when McConnell's anti sectarian policy was adopted. All that is lacking is The Police/SFA/SPL implementing the consequences of that policy by saying "we warned you again and again, now we are going to make arrests/deducting points." The fact that Rangers fans are clearly in

breach of rules (whether they make sense or not) is something being overlooked in the murky stoor kicked by arguments such as Traynor's.

Lack of Intellectual Discernment
Again missing the point, he suggests that banning the singing of TFS would be an imposition of one set of will over another's. If it were the will of the others that singing this song is ok, it would not have fallen foul of a law that was brought into being in a democratic society. Singing TFS is the opposite of what Traynor argues, the will of the majority has been and is being flaunted whilst this song continues to be sung. To infer that stopping TFS is akin to something like, imposing Sharia law on UK law is bad enough, but to fail to understand that it is Scottish law that the song challenges in the first place suggests lack of intellectual discernment on his part.

A Man Sees What He Wants to See
Like Martin Bain he draws his attention to what Celtic fans dare do. Our occupying the high moral ground appears to annoy him. He has seen no denunciation of the Novo song and has seen disgusting and horrible chat on (Celtic) fans message boards. He must be looking in the places where he finds what he wants to find. I have seen the Novo and songs referencing the IRA denounced lots of times and I have read more enlightened and civil exchanges of views on message boards than I have in the printed press. We do speak from a higher moral ground because we aspire to occupy it. If that is a fault, it is one I gladly hope we continue to aspire to. We should have been alarmed at the Novo threats he says. We were Jim, we were, because we knew from what **actually happened** to Neil Lennon that such threats if carried out could lead to death. If we appear to Mr Traynor or others to occupy the high moral ground, that perspective can come from looking up from lower ground.

Finally, the last paragraph about going to find a better place to live if you do not like where you are, is what one would expect to hear from the very folk Traynor is trying to defend. Surprising that eh?

Well Mr Traynor, we got news for you and your ilk, we ain't going anywhere we're staying to drag you lot kicking and screaming up to the higher moral (but still imperfect) ground that we occupy.

That is what makes the difference between us and those singers of TFS that think their song is anything other than what it is to anyone occupying the higher ground.

Traynor loses the plot with a caller
The caller, Ian, was English and was making the point about how obviously one-sided the media is in this country, citing Graham Spiers as an exception, to which Traynor became quite bitter saying, *"don't talk to me about that lickspittle"*, and ending the call by shouting at the caller *"you're paranoid,*

you're paranoid, you are an idiot!". A most eloquent and devastatingly effective denunciation of the allegation of media bias from No-neck there, in contrast to the obviously mentally disturbed caller.

Ewen Cameron bases a week of anti-Celtic "paranoia" jibes on a call from a Rangers fan

20th January 2010 – I don't listen to Spewing Cameron's ..em... spewing, on his shitey radio programme, but I do get updates from friends unable to find the 'off' button on the radio (as opposed to simply not finding the 'on' button in the first place, like me). One such friend, who has a strong masochistic streak, told me one day last January about "John the Establishment caller". As many of you will be aware, this character was a caller to the show who was essentially cannon fodder (a Straw Man if you like) for Cameron to rip apart and use as the basis to characterise all Celtic fans as crazy paranoid loonies, and ergo label any points put forward by Celtic fans about the statistical anomalies of the season's "honest mistakes" (and the rest) unfounded paranoid delusion without having to engage in any significant exploration of the points raised. As my mate described John's poorly articulated and wildly exaggerated claims of behind the scenes meetings in darkened rooms with Masonic handshakes all-round, I remarked that this sounded suspiciously like a Rangers fan on the wind-up; in fact not only did it sound like a wind-up designed to smear Celtic fans, this appeared immediately to be the most logical conclusion. Later that day I had the unpleasant experience of a cream bun acquaintance – the kind who only wants to talk about football after Rangers have won but claims to support Airdrie – sidling up to me smugly and launching into a blow by blow account of "Establishment John's call who, to this disciple of William, was an accurate representation of the Celtic support in general i.e. a rambling paranoiac rabble. I replied that this sounded like the work of a Rangers fan on the wind up and was of course met with a wave of derisory laughter at yet more "paranoia" and an offer of the X-Files theme on mp3. I prefer Quantum Leap anyway.

The next day my mate sent me a link to the notorious Follow Follow website indicating that I would be interested in the content. It turned out that he had been leading a sleazy double life whereupon after the respectable people of the world had retired to bed for the night, he would occasionally embark on the illicit thrill of perusing the comedic rants of the mentally unbalanced on the world's most extreme right wing website. Unfortunately, or rather fortunately, I did not have an account with this particular online organ, therefore to view said link I would have to create an account, which I did, submitted to the site admin for authorisation, and then retired immediately to the bathroom with some industrial strength cleaner and a wire brush. Four days later, after eventually assuming that I had been blackballed for having a suspiciously 21st century sounding surname, the site admin validated my log-in and I had the all-clear to read about the latest goss on ferry timetables, paedophile lists and the great fenian Coronation Street scriptwriter conspiracy.

It transpired that the link led to a thread dedicated to Spewing Cameron's week-long bore-a-thon on Royal Radio consisting of relentless repetitive schoolboy jibes about "shadowy figures" and the playing of X-files theme music, in response to "Establishment John" the unbalanced and "paranoid" Celtic supporting caller. Subsequent callers making perfectly reasoned points backed up by compelling evidence were swatted away by the infantile host, masquerading as an unbiased supporter of Scotland's Other Shame. The "paranoia" parrot-call veto served its purpose yet again.

Except of course, the thread on Follow Follow (see below) revealed that this was not paranoia at all. Some member of the Rangers intellectual elite (got Standard Grades in Music and PE which come in handy in the marching season) going by the monicker 'Compare the Trophies' had the stunning and completely original idea of posing as a Celtic fan on a phone-in to take the pish out of us. Personally I think 'Compare the Riots' or 'Compare the European Cups' has a better ring.

Now, either Cameron was completely taken in, or simply didn't care as it provided the ammunition for a week of gloating, unfunny jokes and snide remarks at the Celtic support's expense. One would expect no less from a Media House poodle. An excerpt from the relevant thread is available below in all it's monsyllabic and mis-spelled glory

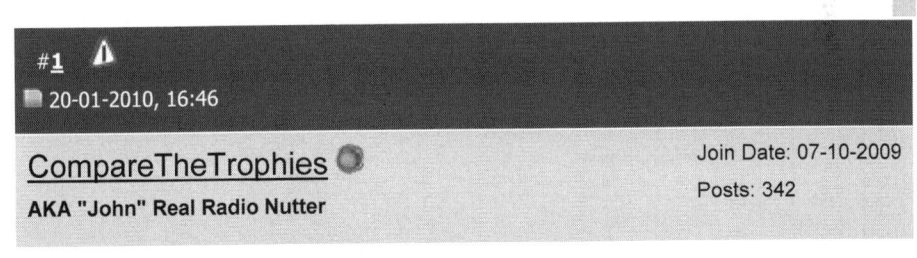

Wednesday Night's Establishment Phone in Meeting

#1
20-01-2010, 16:46

CompareTheTrophies
AKA "John" Real Radio Nutter

Join Date: 07-10-2009
Posts: 342

Wednesday Night's Establishment Phone in Meeting

As we gear up to 6 o'clock, "John" is working on his script... *cough* speach for tonight RR phone in.

He is wondering if any of the bears have ideas of "evidence" that could be used to fuel his arguement.

For those not understanding who "John" is... Listen to RR "Listen again" feature and listen to 18th Januarys Show...

Here's hoping we will get another good laugh tonight....

#2 — 20-01-2010, 16:56

lechatnoir
watching inscrutably

Join Date: 15-11-2009
Location: The Medicine Way
Posts: 145

I for one cannot wait...the amount of dhims I've spoken to who are outraged by this...is quite frankly superb. Some were even plotting a protest tonight while the establishment meeting was in progress.

#3 — 20-01-2010, 16:59

Geo 1972
Malcolm Tucker's apprentice

Join Date: 06-05-2008
Location: The Establishment HQ
Posts: 1,599

Tell them it goes as far back as Jim Farry delaying Jorge Cadette's registrartion which made him miss some crucial games. That will get them going.

#9 — 20-01-2010, 17:07

stoob
WATP

Join Date: 05-05-2008
Location: GF2
Posts: 225

lol i will be listening

#22 — 20-01-2010, 17:49

manse On The Bench

Join Date: 09-11-2006
Posts: 311

These people take paranoia to a hole new level.

#**24**

20-01-2010, 17:51

CompareTheTrophies
AKA "John" Real Radio Nutter

Join Date: 07-10-2009
Posts: 342

If i get on tonight.... I will mention my own name on here... CompareTheTrophies

#**29**

20-01-2010, 18:10

CompareTheTrophies
AKA "John" Real Radio Nutter

Join Date: 07-10-2009
Posts: 342

Got through... i might be gettin a phone back to go on....

#**33**

20-01-2010, 18:14

CompareTheTrophies
AKA "John" Real Radio Nutter

Join Date: 07-10-2009
Posts: 342

Im onnnnnnnnnnnnn!!!!!!!!!

#**34**

20-01-2010, 18:15

colcho
* * * * *

Join Date: 29-07-2006
Location: Laughng at celtc
Posts: 2,810

John on now

andrew_2010
FF Squad Member

Join Date: 04-11-2006
Location: A champagne supernova Livin 4ever
Posts: 966

he's on!!!!!!!

#37
20-01-2010, 18:15

1988Ger
Trialist

Join Date: 13-01-2009
Posts: 83

Here he is haha

#38
20-01-2010, 18:16

BeardyBear
1st Team Regular

Join Date: 15-04-2008
Posts: 1,314

Yasssssss mate wind them up something awful

#39
20-01-2010, 18:16

WATP51
Oh baby i was born with a fast fuse.

Join Date: 28-07-2006
Posts: 1,176

Brilliant!! Ewan has fallen forthis big time

#41
20-01-2010, 18:18

ger4life
blue and proud

Join Date: 01-01-2007
Location: Alloa
Posts: 1,442

john is funny as f*ck..

#42
20-01-2010, 18:18

cumbernauld loyal
Nature Is The Law

Join Date: 21-09-2006
Location: Sittin' on a cornflake....
Posts: 20,184

Absolutely brilliant

#44
20-01-2010, 18:19

cumbernauld loyal
Nature Is The Law

Join Date: 21-09-2006
Location: Sittin' on a cornflake....
Posts: 20,184

Get compare the titles in

#45
20-01-2010, 18:19

colcho
*****

Join Date: 29-07-2006
Location: Laughng at celtc
Posts: 2,810

Roughy asking who is the establishment

great stuff in store again

#46
20-01-2010, 18:20

WATP51
Oh baby i was born with a fast fuse.

Join Date: 28-07-2006
Posts: 1,176

Did you cut you off?

#47
20-01-2010, 18:20

CompareTheTrophies
AKA "John" Real Radio Nutter

Join Date: 07-10-2009
Posts: 342

Was cut off before i could go on.. had some real good stuff aswell

#48
20-01-2010, 18:20

nottinghambear
Trialist

Join Date: 05-11-2006
Location: nottingham
Posts: 92

superb. classic radio.

#49
20-01-2010, 18:21

CompareTheTrophies
AKA "John" Real Radio Nutter

Join Date: 07-10-2009
Posts: 342

The Establishment have cut him off....

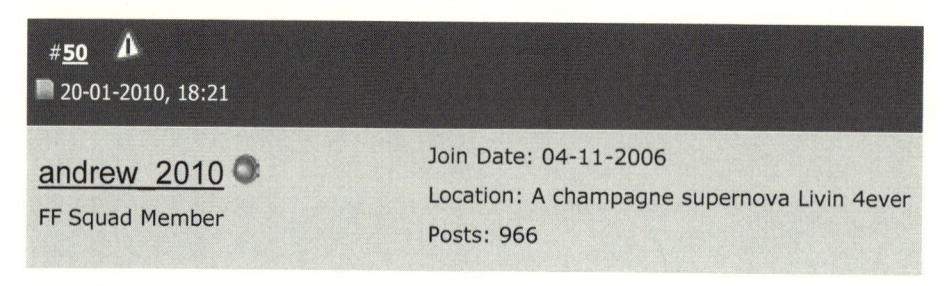

#50
20-01-2010, 18:21

andrew_2010
FF Squad Member

Join Date: 04-11-2006
Location: A champagne supernova Livin 4ever
Posts: 966

you got enough in mate to wind up timmy. well done!

28th January 2010 Celtic 1-2 Hibernian

HONEST MISTAKE NO.26 Celtic goal disallowed against Hibernian. It is unclear as to why it was disallowed, presumably for a "push".
The Scotsman – "*Celtic toiled to get back into their stride, although they did seem harshly dealt with on the stroke of half-time when Darren O'Dea stabbed the ball into the net, only for the goal to be disallowed for a foul on Smith **which was not easy to identify**.*"

The Scotsman's entry for The Master of Understatement Award 2010.

The Herald – "*They thought they had regained the lead just before half-time when Marc Crosas's free-kick into the box was jabbed into the net by O'Dea but referee Iain Brines saw something – **either offside or a shove** – and disallowed the "goal". That stoked the atmosphere around Parkhead*"

Either offside or a shove? Or maybe a pair of blue glasses?

POSSIBLE EFFECT Celtic equalising goal disallowed. Probability of a one point swing. Rangers (-6 [-1]), Celtic (+12 [+1])

Media using old stories to bum up Rangers

30th January 2010 – In the Evening Times, they have Andrew Little telling fellow youngsters Wilson and Fleck to sign their contract offers. That's at least three articles in the last two weeks from different sources urging these guys to sign up to "the cause", always with the pretence that they are simply interviewing another Rangers player/ ex-Rangers "legend"/ an average ex-Rangers player/ Walter Smith's paperboy / someone who went to a Rangers game in 1985 [delete as appropriate].

When Gary Caldwell refused to sign his contract offer, Celtic were "*intransigent*", the club's offer was derisory, wasn't good enough and we were disrespecting our captain. But with Wilson and Fleck – "it's a good offer, so get it signed".

News websites are talking up Rangers with outdated articles, they aren't even subtle about it. Newsnow has two very positive Rangers stories from the STV site marked as top stories from the last 24 hours. These are actually articles from September 2009 and one dated December 2009 on how fantastic the new wonderkid Fleck and his only slightly less wonderful sidekick Wilson are. One even suggests Man Utd are falling over themselves to buy these two for a combined £3million. The financial situation at Mordor must be getting really desperate. BBC and STV are also pulling out all the stops for Rangers. Nothing new but the Laptop Loyal really are surpassing themselves this season, they deserve an award this year for services to Hundom. Or something else.

James Traynor trying to take the moral high ground with Tony Mowbray absolutely laughable

25th January 2010

In response to Jim "No-neck" Traynor's Daily Rectum article entitled *"WHAT'S YOUR AGENDA TONY?"*

Jim,

You work for a populist newspaper that understand its sports section has to kow-tow to its constituents in its reporting, rather than comment insightfully or even contextually on events. You seem to have an audience for this type of product so why change?

I'll put forward how I think the editing the sports section of a populist newspaper works. The Sunday and Monday match reports are framed to please the people likely to buy the paper (the people who support the team which has won). During the week "stories" are naturally framed, either manipulated or conjured, or simply made up, to please the largest section of the crowd which is likely to buy the paper - Rangers fans.

In terms of numbers of fans in Scotland, the largest denomination to which the Record would frame its stories to please, is Rangers fans. The paper can try to manouevre quickly in its editorial style to reflect the vagaries of the two biggest sides' fortunes (because fans of Celtic might buy more papers when Celtic win - the run to Seville being a particularly nauseating example, notwithstanding the Record's rampant support for Souness's Blackburn and various other opposing teams along the way), but the default position, if I had your job Jim, would be to please Rangers, who have more fans (in this country).

For what it's worth, I think you long ago sold out any right not to be associated with idiocy, or to be confronted with melodrama in your everyday life - you write for a tabloid. You long ago sold out any right to create a piece slating somebody else for whipping up melodrama and hysteria when this is, in my opinion, the de facto editorial orientation of your newspaper and radio show.

It's a shame Jim, because from what people say you were once quite a good sports journalist, potentially in time capable of being mentioned in the same breath as McIllvanney. Were you to adopt a different editorial stance and try this style of reporting, however, I think your constituents would simply howl with derision (See the career path of Spiers, G for an example), and I believe your owners and advertisers know it as well.

I think it's a bit hypocritical to slate Tony Mowbray for creating hysteria, then continue to whip it up yourself in some self-aggrandising piece on you and your paper's fantastic reportage. Tony has to try to put together a football team that will sell tickets, you have to try to sell newspapers. You'd look a little less ridiculous if you stopped trying to pretend you are on some sort of higher moral plain. Just a little.

30th January 2010 Hamilton Accies 0-1 Celtic

Over the space of a few weeks, several players leave the field of play to celebrate goal. Only Celtic players are booked for this.

Morten Rasmussen was correctly booked for leaving field of play to celebrate with fans after scoring the only goal of the game against Hamilton Accies.

HONEST MISTAKES NOS. 27, 28, & 29 Two weeks later Steven MacLean scores against Celtic, takes off his shirt, jumps the advertising hoardings along with half the Aberdeen team and celebrates with the fans at the Dick Donald Stand. No second yellow card issued by Brines. In the same game Darren O'Dea is booked for leaving the pitch after McGeady's goal and is later sent-off for a second bookable offence. McGeady himself is booked for kicking the ball away

The following day Steven Whittaker scores a goal for Rangers and runs to the fans at the East Enclosure. No booking issued by Conroy. 10 minutes later, with the score at 1-0, Whittaker puts in a challenge that is deemed a bookable offence so is given a yellow card which if the earlier infringement of the rules was dealt with properly would have been a red.

Three days later in the Scottish Cup replay against St Mirren at Mordor, Kyle Lafferty kicks the ball away **and is given a lecture by referee Iain Brines**. Honest Mistakes is one thing, but seeing an infringement and failing to apply the relevant sanction is, well, someone can try to explain it to me any other way than bias to Rangers.

SAME OFFENCE – CELTIC PLAYER BOOKED. OPPONENT OR RANGERS PLAYER NOT BOOKED

HONEST MISTAKE NO.30 Fortune tries to control a bouncing ball in the box, Diamond comes through from behind and kicks Fortune in the chest. Penalty to Celtic or play on? Referee's decision? Free-kick to Aberdeen!

POSSIBLE EFFECT MacLean should have been booked but this in itself would not be likely to change the result of the game. Although he kicked Fortune in the chest, Diamond was attempting to play the ball so a penalty would have been harsh.

New SPL rule: Rangers supporters to vet team lines

12th February 2010 – Following the revelation that Mark McGhee was scandalously considering utilising his playing resources to the maximum benefit of Aberdeen rather than the great Glasgow Rangers the SPL today introduced a new rule. Henceforth all SPL managers must submit their team lines to the Chief Thingwy of the many Rangers Supporters Associations and Sunday Boys Clubs for approval 24 hours before a match. In addition, any manager found to mention the word "Celtic" more than once in the same week will be severely dealt with. The Laptop Loyal will be closely monitoring this disgraceful use of the term "Celtic" and taking the appropriate action against those shown to be disloyal to the cause. This word is almost as provocative as brazenly brandishing a pepperamis bar in the Govan stand.

Commenting on the matter, Chief of the Rainjurs Supporters Association and self proclaimed spokesman of Ra Peepul, John "I want an apology from Martin O'Neill" MacMillan said "*I'm not biased or bigoted*". The rest of us said "*Well you **are** definitely a total clown*". Next it'll be the old "Aberdeen only try against us" chestnut again. Rangers paranoia right enough. Incidentally, Matthew Lindsay the hack who covered the "story" is clearly raging at the prospect as well. Hell hath no fury etc etc…

Rangers fans' chief: 'Weak' Aberdeen are out of order
Exclusive by Matthew Lindsay
12th Feb 2010

"Fuming Rangers fans' chief John Macmillan today called on the SPL to take action against Aberdeen boss Mark McGhee if he fields a weakened team against Celtic tomorrow. Gers supporters are incensed after former Celtic striker McGhee revealed he would rest some of his top-team stars against his old club in ESPN's live televised match at Pittodrie.

*Walter Smith's side dropped three points when they lost 1-0 to an Aberdeen team **featuring all their best players** on their last trip to Pittodrie back in November."*

Evening Times poodle Matthew Lindsay having encyclopedic knowledge of the Aberdeen FC squad and relative strengths and merits of all the players who can be neatly categorised in a hierarchy from 1 to 22, through best player and best fighter down to the diddy that ends up in goals watching the jaikits.

"And Macmillan, general secretary of the Rangers Supporters' Association, feels the governing body would be entitled to **punish McGhee** for his **controversial actions**."

He said: "*I am very unhappy about this, but not surprised.*"

*"Since he was appointed Aberdeen manager, **Mark McGhee has mentioned Celtic in his comments to the media on numerous occasions**. He was foolish enough to say Celtic was his first love when he was appointed.*

*"I am not a biased or bigoted person whatsoever, but **the number of times McGhee has mentioned Celtic** since he has been appointed Aberdeen boss **does make you wonder**."*

This is priceless basketcase stuff – the paranoiac outrage at the mention of the proscribed word "Celtic", followed by the guilty protest about not being biased or bigoted. Bigoted? Probably. Biased? He's the head of a Rangers supporters organisation for feck's sake! In a league where at least 50% of the managers are from a Rangers background, they seem to get a bit over sensitive about the ones who aren't; paranoid almost.

So much for fielding a weakened side anyway as Celtic hold the mighty Dons to a 4-4 draw. Celtic's defensive performance was shambolic, topped off by Braahfields's Rogan-esque concession of a penalty via an inexplicable deliberate handball, however the practically ever-present helping hand of the "honest mistake" was in evidence yet again but the press were suffering from temporary blindness.... yet again.

Consider:

McGeady kicks the ball away = yellow card.

Steven MacLean kicks the ball away = carry on, nothing to see here.

Darren O'Dea celebrates McGeady's goal by going to the Celtic fans = yellow card.

MacLean scores against Celtic and goes into the crowd for the longest celebration since Porto in Seville. He also removed his shirt = no yellow card.

By the letter of the law McLean should have been sent off, though personally I'd have said a yellow card was sufficient.

Iain Brines provided perhaps the finest "honest mistake" of the season so far. With Fortune well-placed in the Aberdeen penalty area to take control of a bouncing ball, Zander Diamond came in from behind with a swinging boot and kicked the Celtic forward in the chest, before punting the ball upfield. Brines had a decision to make – a penalty to Celtic, or play on. His decision? A free-kick to Aberdeen. You have to laugh or you would cry.

Two weeks before, Morten Rasmussen scores the winner against Hamilton Accies and goes into the crowd = yellow card (correctly).

A few days after the Aberdeen debacle, Rangers are at home to St Mirren, Kyle Laughable kicks the ball away and gets a wee talking to from the referee about how if Laughable does that another five times he might have to think about booking him.

Of course none of this is to detract from the fact Celtic would struggle to have constructed a defence even if Mowbray had signed Ironside, Rumpole, Matlock and Perry Mason as our back four. But if we are going to drop points, it would be nice to at least lose or draw fairly. After all, when the fans of the nice wee teams start on their moral high horse crap about all the decisions going against them when they play the "O*d F**m", I've yet to meet one who accepts "Well St Mirren are shite anyway so quit moaning and sort yer team out" as a valid answer.

10th February 2010 Celtic 2-0 Hearts Aiden McGeady kicks the ball away = yellow card. Robbie Keane flagged offside wrongly FIVE times.

10th February 2010 Motherwell 1-1 Rangers

HONEST MISTAKE NO.30 Goal for Motherwell chopped off against Rangers. No need for various views of this one. No marginal decision or checking replays. Forbes was at least **three yards onside**. Former Rangers players summarising on ESPN Terry Butcher and Colin Hendry agreed the goal was clearly onside.

Daily Record "*Craig Brown last night accused bungling linesman of costing Motherwell a famous victory over Rangers. The furious Fir Park boss had to be dragged away from John Gilmore at full-time as he protested the controversial decision to disallow a second-half Ross Forbes goal for offside. Forbes poked home Stephen Craigan's knockdown to seemingly put his side 2-0 up and on the brink of a first home win over Gers for seven years. But Gilmour flagged despite TV pictures later clearly showing the goal should have stood. Well boss Brown was in no doubt his side had been robbed and said: "I've seen the TV evidence and it indicates the goal was OK".*"

POSSIBLE EFFECT This glaring "mistake" by the linesman prevents Motherwell going 2-0 up. The high probability is that Motherwell would have gone on to win the game. Two point swing against Rangers.

Rangers (-8 [-2]), Celtic (+12 [+1])

14th February 2010 Rangers 3-0 Hibernian

Steven Whittaker leaves the pitch after scoring the opening goal, covered elsewhere.

HONEST MISTAKE NO.31 Kris Boyd elbows Zemmama in the face. Incredibly the booking is classified as "obstruction". Any other classification for the booking would have meant Boyd would be suspended for the upcoming Celtic game. The verdict of obstruction was not consistent with Steve Conroy's signal at the time of the decision. However, amazingly, when the referee's report emerges it is revealed that Conroy ruled this on offence of obstruction. This decision is even more laughable than the Boruc handball.

The Herald: "*Merouane Zemmama last night **claimed** Kris Boyd went for his face with his elbow and **would have been sent off in other countries**. The Rangers striker was booked after his arm **caught** Zemmama. Walter Smith, the Rangers manager, said he believed the caution had pushed his striker though the 18-point disciplinary mark, **thus meaning Boyd would be unable to play against Celtic in two weeks**. However, Steve Conroy, the match referee, **later confirmed that the booking would only amount to two points for obstruction, leaving Boyd one point shy of suspension*"

HONEST MISTAKE NO.32 Kenny Miller falls theatrically in the penalty area under no contact and wins a penalty which is converted by Boyd to make it 2-0.

POSSIBLE EFFECT By the time of the penalty, Whittaker should have received what would have been a second yellow card if he had been given the appropriate censure for his goal celebration. Boyd's "obstruction" meant he was clear to play against Celtic on the 28th but made little impact in that match. Although Rangers received the benefit of three honest mistakes in this game it is would be no more than a 50/50 chance of Hibs equalising so the benefit of the doubt would still lie with Rangers. No points swing.

Graham Spiers says it's time for hacks to come clean

Graham Spiers
The Times
16 February 2010

The loathing of the Old Firm across Scotland, obviously outside of their own two, vast tribes, remains highly visible. At a Q&A session I did with Craig Levein, the Scotland manager, in the Byre Theatre in St Andrews recently, there was mild cheering across the audience when I noted that not many Rangers or Celtic fans were present with us. It was almost as if the evening was purified as a result.

Of course this is nothing new – Manchester United are resented across England, and Real Madrid are loathed in every other region of Spain. In football, as a rule of thumb, the big, rich clubs are detested. Even so, the contempt for the Old Firm in Scotland is still striking. There is quite a perverseness about it, too, given that Scottish football might hardly be on the map were Rangers and Celtic not to exist.

Mark McGhee, the Aberdeen manager, and a self-proclaimed Celtic fan as a boy, got into trouble last week by hinting that, when his team faced Celtic at Pittodrie in the SPL on Saturday, he might rest certain players to save them for Aberdeen's Active Nation Scottish Cup replay against Raith Rovers on Tuesday. **No doubt the newspapers' "spin" of what McGhee actually said contributed to the furore,** but the Dons manager felt wounded by the episode.

McGhee faced not just suspicion as a traitor among his own fans – let alone those of Rangers – but also outright venom: how dare he even hint at weakening his team before facing one of the horrible big two? For McGhee it became a very touchy subject.

On the road covering Scottish football, as I discovered in St Andrews, you find the Old Firm being regarded as tawdry, unrefined and even loutish. Whenever Rangers or Celtic wash into town the local denizens react as if there is a need to hold their noses and look away, as the uncouth mobs arrive. Of course, the stupid politics of Ireland, which will not leave either club, is a further reason for this loathng. There is almost a perception of a social or political backwardness among the invading Old Firm hordes.

This tarring of belonging to either Rangers or Celtic is at its funniest when viewed across the Scottish media. There are hundreds of us involved in the coverage of the Scottish game, **yet you are hard-pressed to find more than a few in my business who will openly admit to being a Rangers or**

Celtic fan. One or two colleagues even visibly squirm in their seats if you casually ask them if they have an Old Firm allegiance.

The point is hit home further by the sheer noise and repetition of those reporters who will loudly proclaim their love of Airdrie, St Mirren, Falkirk, St Johnstone or whomever. In their keenness to assert their allegiance to one of Scotland's provincial clubs what they are actually saying is: "Look, I'm clean, I'm clean!" It is a standard joke of Scottish football that supporters are now extremely cynical of commentators who confess in this way.

OK, well let me come clean, then. Having written like this, it wouldn't do to then skive off without relaying my own football background. For the purposes of a book about Rangers which came out three years ago, I had to sit down and work out how many times I visited Ibrox as a boy between 1969 and 1982, and was taken aback to tot it up at in excess of 200 visits with my father to watch Rangers.

Ever since this confession was made I have had to live with an element of flak as a consequence - as if I had once confessed to a murder. Ah well, tough. If you were brought up in the west of Scotland, and you loved football, then the chances are that Rangers or Celtic would be your boyhood team.

I presume, in writing this, no banning orders will now be served on me in Edinburgh, Perth, Kilmarnock, Dundee or Aberdeen as I follow the lovely Big Two for The Times.

Funnily enough, Traynor took up the subject on Radio Shortbread later that day and was very vocal in trying to force Kevin McCarra of The Grauniad to admit he's a Tim, but had no compulsion to force cathartic confessions from any other hacks with "loyalties" to the Dark Side.

The Rangers Dressing Room, Ibrox Stadium, Glasgow, 12.25 Sunday 28th February 2010

The players are gathered for their team talk.

"Right lads I want 110% commitment from the word go against these bastards. Remember they are all fenian scum, tattie munching, tarriers from Ireland *spit*. I don't care if you kick, head-butt or feign injury [wink at Laughable] to win this match. The whole existence of the Establishment club is at stake. Now go out there and get intae them. Good luck and God Save the Queen"

At that point Walter Smith says *"Thanks Mr McDonald, I'll take it from here"*

The Dougie McDonald Show and Hateley's objective opinion on Celtic's concerns

> Bougherra's walking a tightrope now

> Don't worry Boogie I've got you

28th February 2010 – Celtic head to Mordor needing a win to keep their already faint title hopes alive. A Rangers win will practically guarantee the championship, putting them 10 points ahead with a game in hand. What followed was entirely predictable, but only to those of us who are completely paranoid. Bougherra is booked by referee McDonald for a late tackle from behind on Keane in the opening minutes, along with Celtic's Marc Antoine Fortune for an accidental handball. Bougherra goes on to commit seven more fouls, each one just as serious, if not more so, than the one he was booked for, yet astonishingly (if you're not paranoid) receives no further reprimand. Midway through the first half a Maurice Edu goal is correctly disallowed for a handball in the build up by Kenny Miller. Unlike Fortune, Miller is not booked.

Much is made of this "disallowed goal" after the game by the media in an attempt to "prove" that these "honest mistakes" even themselves out. It just goes to show how perverse the mindset of some Rangers supporters is, and how much the media pander to Spoilt Child FC, when you consider how often they go bleating to the media about **correct** decisions given against their team. Talk to one of them about how incredible it was that Bougherra stayed on the park and he'll hit back with "*aye but we got a goal disallowed*". Yeah it was a handball, can't understand why that was disallowed. They seem incapable of grasping the concept that if the laws of the game are infringed in the act of scoring a goal it is incumbent on the referee to disallow it, even if that "goal" is scored by Rangers. The classic example was Big Feck giving an "ashen-faced" interview on Radio Shortbread in 2005 after his team managed to scrape a 3-2 win at Fir Park despite Barry Sideways getting himself sent off for punching Richie Foran in the face, or as the BBC and the rest of the media reported it "*raising his hands*". A greetin faced, but dignified, Rangers manager told Chick Young "*this proves that Rangers don't get all the decisions*". So, getting a player sent off for gubbing an opponent is now some sort of injustice is it? Spoilt Child FC right enough.

In the second half, with Bougherra fouling Celtic players left, right and centre with impunity, it was a nice wee bonus for referee McDonald and the rest of the Rangers supporters when one of these fouls was committed on Kamara inside the penalty area allowing him to deny Celtic a penalty. If the award had been given, as per the laws of the game, no doubt the media would have subjected us to talk of a decision going against Rangers and how "controversial" it was. But the best was yet to come. In the 65th minute, Kyle Lafferty grabbed Scott Brown around the neck and as the players "tangled", Brown's head made the merest of contact with Lafferty's chest, causing the cheat to collapse spectacularly to the ground holding his **face**. From a line of sight obscured by several players, Dougie McDonald sprinted over to send Brown off in a manner resembling Usain Bolt on amphetamines. Lafferty, the initial aggressor, was not even booked or spoken to, and was left to check his nose for imaginary blood. Up to that point Celtic had not been playing particularly well but neither were they under the cosh and the game was finely balanced. We can never know how the game would have panned out but for McDonald taking the bait of Lafferty's cheating, but from that point onwards Celtic never looked like winning. They just about held on for a draw but lost a goal in the final seconds of the game, when Edu scored after Artur Boruc parried a shot by.... you guessed it, Madjid Bougherra. Of course, as the media would never tire of telling us, the referee played no part in determining the outcome of the game, the defeat was all down to Celtic's inadequacies, despite the winning goal coming as a direct result of a shot by a player who should have been sent off long before that passage of play.

Go back to sleep Scotland, you're media has worked out how it all transpired...go back to sleep Scotland, and congratulate yourself on living in the land of a fair and transparent football establishment... you are free to lose as we tell you... you are free to lose as we tell you...go back to sleep Scotland.

HONEST MISTAKE NO.33 Fortune booked for handball. Kenny Miller handballs in the build up to a disallowed goal. No booking.

HONEST MISTAKE NO.34 Madjid Bougherra booked for foul from behind on Robbie Keane. Bougherra commits **seven** more infringements but is not given a second yellow card. Former referee Kenny Clark said: "*I've got to say that I did note a couple of times about Bougherra living dangerously, and I think he was on his very last life, as it were. He was treading a very thin line. On another day he might well have been red-carded, but he got away with it. I think he was very fortunate to remain where he was*". Question: Is it only Rangers players who get these lives?

HONEST MISTAKE NO.35 Bougherra trips Kamara in the Rangers penalty area. No penalty and no second yellow card for Bougherra.

HONEST MISTAKE NO.36 Brown sent off for clash with Lafferty. Lafferty grabbed Brown by the neck and Brown moved his head towards Lafferty's chest making minimal contact. No action taken against Lafferty.
The Scotsman : *Striker Kyle Lafferty has admitted Scott Brown was unlucky to be sent off by referee Dougie McDonald in Sunday's Old Firm derby. Celtic have appealed against the red card dished out to their captain after a clash with Lafferty. Rangers went on to seal victory thanks an injury-time goal from Maurice Edu and went ten points clear of their rivals. Northern Ireland international Lafferty, now preparing to face Albania in a friendly tonight, said: "To produce a red card was harsh but it is the referee's decision and is* **nothing to do with me!**"

I'm sure collapsing to the ground holding your face might have helped convince the referee Mr Laughable.

POSSIBLE EFFECT Although Celtic were not playing particularly well, the probability is that they would have held out for a draw with a full compliment of players. With Rangers reduced to 10 men after Bougherra's fourth or fifth foul Celtic may well have had the upper hand but given the uninspiring nature of play from both teams a draw would seem the most likely result. Two point swing from Rangers, one point swing to Celtic.

Rangers (-10 [-2]), Celtic (+13 [+1])

With no shortage of talking points from another "controversial" Us v Them game, who better to take an objective look at the season so far than Mark Er Um Er Hateley. With the Rangers News rejecting the following article as being too partisan, the Daily Record was only too happy to print it. Hateley's hatred for Celtic is palpable as the poison practically wafts off the page:

Daily Record
11 Mar 2010 By Mark Hateley

Don't make him** [The Man with Nosurname] **angry. You wouldn't like him when he's angry.

I'm sure Kevin Gallacher, Chick Young, Mixu Paatelainen, Steve Conroy, Connor Sammon, Tom Murphy, George Drummond and a host of other referees and linesman would agree.

*Walter has had steam coming out of his ears for some time now because of **a stream of insults** and excuses spewing out of Celtic Park and he has responded like a man possessed.*

Lies. No-one connected with Celtic has insulted Mr Dignity, far less launched a "*stream of insults*". Whether the factors that Celtic fans have quoted as having an effect on the title race are "*excuses*" depends on your viewpoint, and we all know where Hateley's loyalties lie. Personally I happen to think that having goals disallowed, penalties not given and opponents not sent off as a result of **blatantly incorrect** decisions – mistakes which repeatedly benefit one particular team – had a more than marginal effect on the outcome of the season, but then again, I'm paranoid.

They've blamed the refs, they've blamed the SFA, they've blamed the state of the pitches.

Lies. Celtic have raised concerns about refereeing decisions which even hundits in orange specs such as Hateley would agree were incorrect. We've asked for clarification about these decisions only to be confronted with mass hysteria from clowns like Hateley and a dogmatic insistence that it's all just honest mistakes which even themselves out. Whether they will even themselves out any time before the year 3010 is not explained by these obstinate apologists though. We've been over the pitch allegations earlier, the irony of course being a certain Glasgow club would go on to throw a hissy fit at being "forced" to play on a "difficult pitch" for the third time that season; and the club in question wasn't Celtic. As far as the SFA goes, answers on a postcard as to what Celtic are supposed to have "*blamed*" on them, but why let that get in the way of a good anti-Celtic diatribe.

All this crap about the "establishment" conspiring against them left a bad taste in the mouth of anyone who cares about the Scottish game. That is the kind of paranoid pap only the most deranged of supporters would cling to.

Lies. As if Englishman Hateley gives a shit about anyone in the Scottish game other than his paymasters at Ibrox. A club that has continually undermined the interests of the Scottish national team since they tapped up the then Scotland manager and have since gone through a schizophrenic ritual of complaining about the "demands" placed on their players as a result of being called up for Scotland – to complaining about their players not being picked and then banned from the national team – back to moaning when their players are picked for the Scotland squad again – with, of course, the Scottish press 100% behind them every step of the way. Now that's what I call deranged.

*Celtic have mounted a **sustained and sinister campaign** to cast some kind of doubt over the integrity of this entire Scottish set-up. And that is **simply unforgivable**.*

There's that "sinister" word again. More lies. Here's a far-out notion – perhaps this *"doubt over the integrity of this entire Scottish set-up"* has something to do with spectacularly wrong refereeing decisions constantly benefiting the same club? But in the manner of a cheating husband who blames the person who spilled the beans to his wife for his predicament, rather than his own duplicitous behaviour, Hateley (along with the rest of the Scottish media) is enraged at Timmy having the temerity to defend himself rather than to know his place and slink back into the corner and take it lying down.

*They have thrown accusations around on a seemingly weekly basis. The excuses they have come up with for their own shortcomings get more and more ridiculous by the day. **They have attempted to blacken the reputation of the entire Scottish game**.*

Here we go again with the "defender of the Scottish game" shite. More lies. Hateley is interested in nothing more than the narrow self-serving agenda of the club that pays his wages which is a sad reflection on the current state of Scottish football journalism, when a Rangers mouthpiece like this can find space in a so-called national newspaper to spout his venom. If he was in any way interested in truth, fact or objectivity, rather than anti-Celtic propaganda, it would be easy enough for Hateley to ascertain that these *"weekly" "accusations"*, if they actually existed, correlate exactly with horrendous refereeing errors favouring the Establishment club. Celtic have no interest in *"blackening the reputation of the entire Scottish game"*, Rangers, referees and the Scottish football authorities are doing an excellent job of that without our help.

*But they were right about one thing. There is indeed something rotten in the state of the SPL - **and it's festering away in Glasgow's East End**.*

What can you say about this? Spoken like a true bigot. Such a statement would be too strong for publication in the Rangers News, but the Daily

Record has no qualms publishing this hate stuff which tells you all you need to know about that rag.

*Because of Celtic's attempts to deflect attention away from the real reasons why they are in such an awful mess, they have shown utter contempt **for the magnificent achievements of Smith and his players**. **Rangers have been phenomenal this season** and the way they have been playing in recent weeks suggests to me they have taken Celtic's **nefarious smear campaign** very personally indeed.*

Hateley sprinkles on a liberal dose of the customary Rangers sycophancy before attacking Celtic again, this time using a word he doesn't actually know the meaning of. The Rangers lickspittle leaves us with the final irony of accusing Celtic of conducting a smear campaign, having just gone over the line of smear campaign into outright slander and vilification of our club. Still nothing the Laptop Loyal have to offer should surprise us by now.

Ewen Cameron: A Police Announcement

1st March 2010

Clearly relishing the Dark Side victory that pretty much secured the SPL league title (sponsored by Honest Mistakes), Spewing Camerhun launched into a childish skit on his radio show the next evening about police being on the lookout for a man called Robbie Keane who had gone missing in the Govan area, and was last seen in Davie Weir's back pocket. Hilarious stuff. One wonders why you haven't managed to carve out a career-path as another Frankie Boyle, Billy Connolly or Richard Curtis, instead of pretending to be a talentless hack reduced to making a living by winding up punters and pandering to sectarian knuckledraggers on a radio version of the Sun newspaper.

To run with this theme, I wonder if anyone could assist the relevant authorities with regard to the following appeal:

Police are concerned about a local man, Ewen "Spewing" Cameron, who has gone missing and was last seen on Monday evening in the Charlotte Square area of Edinburgh disappearing into David Murray's blazer pocket in pursuit of a bone and a can of Winalot. Cameron had been out celebrating Rangers victory over rivals Celtic the previous day. Police believe he had consumed a considerable volume of alcohol as he was heard gloating and baiting Celtic fans with incoherent rambling about Davie Weir being better than Robbie Keane on local low-brow radio station, Fake Radio.

Cameron describes himself as a Hearts fan, but police have dismissed this line of inquiry as a smokescreen, after receiving numerous corroborated witness reports of the "journalist" railing against Celtic. These include - getting pals to phone up his Fake Radio show pretending to be Tims so he can slag Celtic fans for their blatant "paranoia"; quoting a "dossier" of penalty and red card "statistics" lifted straight from the Follow Follow forum as gospel fact and using it as another excuse to get tore into "paranoid" Celtic fans; slandering the greatest club captain in Scottish football history Billy McNeill and accusing him of being "paranoid"; dragging Celtic fans into the Manchester Riot abomination by saying they are just as bad as those responsible, contrary to all empirical evidence; saying that Neil Lennon brings violent assaults at the hands of bigots on himself, and making a big show of congratulating Hearts' fiercest rivals Hibs after they beat Celtic in an important SPL game, which by complete coincidence allowed Rangers to move to the top of the table.

Police have been unable to find evidence of Cameron behaving in such a way towards the Establishment team so have moved quickly to reject the "Hearts fan" conspiracy theory which has taken root amongst the unhinged Follow Follow community, commonly known as the mainstream Scottish media. Cameron's preoccupation with paranoia has also led to concerns about his mental condition which detectives believe may be linked to his disappearance.

Cameron is in his mid-to-late thirties and his physical appearance is described as a cross between Super Mario and Phil Mitchell. His hair is beginning to recede at the front due to years of forelock tugging to Sir David Murray, Martin Bain and other Establishment club officials, and his stout build is believed to be a direct result of a rich diet of Winalot, succulent lamb and the finest red wines. Detectives are linking the demise of his idol and puppet master, Sir David "Moonbeams" Murray, to recent events. They believe this led to a disruption in Cameron's supply of Winalot and succulent lamb and that the Fake Radio "journalist" has had to revert to the same diet of bitter oranges he endured through his pre-fame years leading to an adverse psychological reaction.

Cameron gives his occupation as "journalist", but sources with access to secret police files confirm that in reality he has moved between a number of job roles from Establishment Mouthpiece to Murray Poodle over the course of his all-not-too brief career.

Police are confident that Cameron will be apprehended within the next 48 hours as it is highly unlikely that someone with no backbone and a bellyful of Winalot and Cabernet Sauvignon can move swiftly enough to evade capture for long. After being taken into custody, Cameron will be placed in a caring Poodle Pound for retired Laptop Loyalists, to spend the remainder of his days with a never ending supply of his favourite Winalot among such past greats as Gerry McNee and Ken Gallacher.

Fraser Wishart and the selective agenda of the Laptop Loyal

Fraser Wishart is an ex-Rangers player and chief executive of the Scottish Professional Footballers Association (SPFA). As such he is responsible for representing the interests of **all** professional players in Scotland. However Wishart has demonstrated a curious selectiveness in the cases which he chooses to highlight in the media.

Allow me to illustrate:

February 2008 - Celtic awarded a disputed free-kick against St Mirren. The Celtic player involved, Shunsuke Nakamura, is pilloried on radio phone-ins and TV. Newspapers carry headlines referring to Nakamura as "CON MAN" and "CHEAT"

Wishart makes no statement on the matter to defend the player. Maybe Naka was behind on his subs.

March 2008 – Rangers v Celtic. Kevin Thomson of Rangers is bizarrely carried off after a pathetic attempt to win a penalty by throwing himself to the ground in the penalty area and deliberately making contact with Georgios Samaras with his trailing leg. Although the press coverage is almost universally sympathetic to the player, Wishart launches a vigorous defence of Thomson through comments which are enthusiastically published in the media.

One specific statement is of particular interest - "*What I would say is that in many instances players lift themselves off the ground when they think the tackle is coming, then the tackle doesn't come*".

May 2008 - Fraser Wishart, a man paid as a trade union official under the umbrella of the GMB, actively supports a season extension, without consulting his members, even though it is against the interests of players from 11 of the 12 SPL clubs who pay his wages.

August 2008 – A Rangers goal is wrongly disallowed against Aberdeen (swoon!), prompting NoSurname into a mental (but dignified) rant about how they also got a goal disallowed against Dundee Utd as well but never complain about these things… whilst..em… furiously complaining about getting a goal disallowed. Cue total outrage among the Scottish media. On Clyde1 an Aberdeen fan phones in to point out that Rangers' goal in the same game came from a free-kick which should never have been awarded. Wishart dismissed this, helpfully pointing out that "*Aberdeen still had a chance to defend the free-kick*". You know the kind of comment that he, or any of his poodle Establishment colleagues, failed to make when Celtic were awarded a disputed corner against Motherwell towards the end of the 2007/08 season, an incident which brought Darrell King to the point of an anuerysm.

August 2008 - Scott Brown, Aiden McGeady and Darren O'Dea are involved in a fracas in nightclub. Newspapers carry witness reports that "*A few guys were winding them* [the Celtic players] *up but as the night went on it started getting nasty....* "*The players started to leave but as McGeady got outside he was jumped by a gang who set about him*". Curiously the newspapers seemed very reluctant to name the aggressors as Rangers fans, instead referring to them as "*A few guys*" and "*a gang*".

November 2008 - Aiden McGeady is attacked outside a nightclub. Despite reporting "***It's believed** the 22-year-old Celtic winger was subjected to a volley of vile sectarian abuse by three cowardly yobs*" and "*There was about three of them and they started dishing out some abuse, it was pretty heavy stuff*" and "*It's understood they branded him a "Fenian b*******" before landing two hefty blows*", the Sun can't quite manage to identify whether they are Rangers supporters or not. Funny that. The Sun is also at pains to stress that Rangers players have also suffered at the hands of thuggery, with one having his car daubed with "*Celtic slogans*" [I guess it's a fair cop then] and another scandalously having his address published on the Internet. Among all the subsequent anguish and gnashing of teeth among the Scottish media at these "crimes" obviously committed by Celtic fans, no-one feels the need to point out that none of the predicted violent attacks on the player's property came to pass. Hmmm, another strange one.

At no point in all of this does Fraser Wishart feel the need to decry Rangers fans and bemoan the inability of players to go out without being attacked for "*the colour of jersey they wear on a Saturday*". Maybe Wishart's concern was for tolerance of crimes against fashion?

August 2009 - Aiden McGeady is sent off against Hibs for diving. Fraser Wishart is mysteriously absent with any public proclamations of support for the player along the lines of "*What I would say is that in many instances players lift themselves off the ground when they think the tackle is coming, then the tackle doesn't come*"

February 2010 - Fraser 'Judge Jury and Executioner' Wishart decries an "assault" on Rangers goalkeeper Alan McGregor "*just for the jersey he wears on a Saturday*". Maybe he should be called as a witness as McGregor himself was reported to have told police he did not know what happened or even where.

Despite all this, no-one in the Scottish media has queried Wishart's role or, for example, his publicly disavowing the actions of his own members when they happen to play for Celtic.

Alan McGregor

The Alan McGregor case is another case that shows the staggering disparity in the Scottish Media's treatment of Celtic and the Establishment club. Now I am a pretty liberal guy and am a firm believer in "innocent until proven guilty". However the reluctance to address the allegations against this guy is very out of character for tabloids for whom this kind of stuff is their bread and butter. Any concern over due process doesn't wash when you consider the trash these low-lifes have published in the past (see Boruc, A). The sexual assault allegations have been roundly buried by the media and have been completely absent from discussion on the recent "assault" story.

It is not difficult to imagine the rainforests which would have been decimated over the past couple of months if Artur Boruc had been the subject of a similar complaint. The Daily Ranger/Sun etc would be digging up lapdancers, ex-girl friends and wee lassies from Poland who's pigtails he pulled when he was 6 years old, to fill up front, middle and back pages of their rags with lurid stories. They would be demanding Celtic sack the player and he be made an example of.

Paranoia? Consider the front page splash in the Sun back in September accompanying a photo of Boruc straightening a woman's hair with a pair of hair straighteners. All sorts of lurid accusations were levelled at Boruc which were found to be completely false forcing the paper to print an apology.

But in the case of McGregor... the rags print a photo of the CELTIC stadium in relation to the original sexual assault story, the whole thing is allowed to die within a couple of days, then weeks later when the player appears in public with a black eye under mysterious circumstances, no links are made between the two events and his poor bird is blamed for wasting police time. The press simply accept the implausible story put out to deflect attention from one of the Establishment team's prize assets – **that no-one at all** was responsible for the assault and his girlfriend called the police presumably out of spite or some sort of memory defect. Maybe McGregor is suffering from the same mental condition as Edward Norton's character in Fight Club.

Then of course we have Walter the Dignified One. After having made noises about McGregor being unfit/ having to buck his ideas up, Nosurname acts decisively to..er.. do nothing and keeps the errant player in his team for the game against Celtic. Such decisive and effective leadership skills as demonstrated by the Rangers manager being absent from Celtic Park when it came to McGeady who was actually dropped from the team after conflict with the manager. No, in that case Strachan was out of order and the player was a niggly wee shite. In fact, in their glee the Scottish media couldn't make their minds up who they wanted to put the boot into more, although I reckon Strachan shaded it with the "Strachan Out if Celtic lose the next game even though they're top of the league" stories. Anyway, consider the logic applied to each case and try to work it out.

Billy McNeill

Radio Clyde - caller berates Billy McNeill for having the viewpoint that decisions have been going against Celtic for 50 years, caller is cut off as he start to get abusive.

McGuire responds
"*Billy is a legend, and he is allowed an opinion, its just that an opinion*"

Big Fat Derek adds "*every team gets decisions against them, but its just honest mistakes, I got a penalty against me in the 77 cup final, the ball hit my thigh, not my arm, and the referee gave a penalty, wrongly, and to be honest, I had forgotten about it 5 days later, I didnt go on about it*"

OK so you're not mentioning it 33 years later then Derek? And thats the first time you have mentioned it since five days after the final? Utter pish. I am not old enough to have watched this game live, but am well aware of the circumstances surrounding it as every time Celtic and Rangers are involved in a Cup Final, Johnstone is wheeled out to whinge on about the penalty that never was contrary to the evidence of everyone else's eyes. As any fair minded person would tell you fatso, the ball hit your arm. Anyway, one decision against them in 33 years. They've got it hard. Next they'll be on about a dodgy corner we got in 1965.

Walter's schizophrenia

Wattie the Cardigan says Rangers were let down by the referee on Sunday (28 Feb Rangers 1-0 Celtic, The Dougie McDonald show) and they should have had a penalty for Hinkel not doffing his cap and saying "after you m'lud" to Edu. Is this the same Cardigan who said the referee had a good game?

"I thought the referee handled the game very well," said Smith
heraldscotland.com 28/02/10

*RANGERS manager Walter Smith has sent a stark reminder to Old Firm rivals Celtic that they are not the only victims of **questionable** refereeing decisions.* (Here we go again with the comparing "*questionable*" decisions with **blatant errors**)

"We should have had a penalty, for example, when Maurice Edu was taken down in the box." Daily Record 03/03/10

I think we have some selective memory problems for the soon to be pensioner. So if he is so concerned about the poor refereeing, and being such a dignified guy and all that, will he be doing the decent thing and say he is supporting Celtic in their appeal of Scott Brown's red card? Thought not.

How the SFA appeals process works

SFA Press Release:

Following the decision not to uphold Scott Brown's appeal for his sending off at the hands of Brother McDonald we would like to take this opportunity to clarify the appeals process –

The referee who sent a player off reviews his decision and decides that 'yes I was right to send him off', after being publicly backed for sending him off by every rent-a-gub ex Scottish ref you could find (unless of course he happens to be an English ex-ref with a suspiciously Irish sounding name who said it wasn't a sending off [Dermot Gallagher]). *He's not gonna say 'no I was wrong' and look like a prat after being backed by the whole of the media, the Scottish refereeing fraternity and that halfwit Winter from down south is he? Not unless it's an Algerian centre half, in which case the full weight of the entire Scottish media machine will be screaming at you and demanding you rescind your decision.*

Of course there was no mention of the external pressure applied to the referee to uphold his decision by the newspaper and media reports declaring Brown *"technically guilty"* on the say so of an openly Rangers supporting ex-Premiership referee. On the other hand there was mass hysteria and apoplexy, over the pressure applied by *'unknown Celtic source'* prior to the game. That pretty much sums up what Celtic are up against with this appeals process. On the other hand, if you're Boogie you get your red card rescinded no questions asked.

More media lies over the Falkirk pitch

Gordhun "Celtic got a dodgy penalty against Falkirk in 1987" Waffle has a strange pre-occupation with attacking all things Celtic. For someone who portrays himself as a virtuous defender of the wee teams against the big bad O*d F**m, he is mysteriously reluctant to have a go at Rangers, and on the rare occasions he is forced to do so, he invariably drags Celtic into whatever shameful situation the Establishment club find themselves mired in, just to be "balanced" of course. Keep an eye out for where Waffle manages to drag Rangers into this tawdry episode, which he either managed to dredge out of his own fevered imagination or copied from Keith Jackson. You'll be needing your electron microscope. Oh by the way, he's a Falkirk fan. Honestly. Yes, seriously.

Celtic spark new row after complaining Falkirk's pitch isn't good enough Mar 5 2010 Exclusive by Gordon Waddell

*CELTIC have **sparked** their **second war** in two weeks after **complaining to the SPL that Falkirk's pitch isn't good enough for them to play on**.*

A Hoops official called the top flight's beaks yesterday afternoon to ask for an independent investigation into the quality of the Bairns' playing surface ahead of Sunday's live TV clash.

So not saying anything becomes *"asking for an investigation"*, which in turn becomes *"complaining that Falkirk's pitch isn't good enough for them"*. This follows a familiar pattern where hopeless and vindictively biased "journalists" like Waddell, take an unremarkable statement from a Celtic player, manager or official, and concoct fantastical scenarios of foaming-mouthed paranoia and unfounded attacks on a range of poor wee innocent victims. Apologists for the likes of Waddell and his peers would say that this is simply a journalist creating a story according to the tabloid modus operandi. However this assertion falls apart when you look at their reaction to the many **genuinely** paranoid statements that have emanated from Ibrox over the years (*"nobody will do anything to help us, everybody's against us, the split fixtures are always unfair to us, that linesman ran 70 yards just to get my player sent off, the SFA brought forward that hearing so Kenny Miller would miss the Celtic game etc etc etc*). In each and every case, the Scottish media reaction is to take one of two stances, or a combination of both –

a) Underplay the rampant paranoia i.e. "a *disappointed* Walter said... a *frustrated* Martin Bain said...". Suggestions that the Man with Nosurname/Baldy etc have accused anyone of cheating, bias and/or conspiracy is avoided at **all** costs

b) Outright support i.e. Nosurname/Baldy's comments are reported as undisputed fact ... "*Rangers have been hampered by an unfair fixture list... Incredibly the referee sent Bougherra off... Miller will miss the Celtic game after the SFA hastily convened their Review Panel...*"

But when it comes to Celtic; in Laptop Loyal land asking a few questions about refereeing decisions is akin to starting a war. You'll actually find that in reality, it's the media who have launched a war against Celtic in a blind desperate fury of denial and cover-up. If Celtic's "paranoia" was so wide of the mark surely all of this hyperbole to discredit the club would be unnecessary, everyone else could just roll their eyes and make wee twirly motions with their fingers like they do when Romanov goes off on one. But no, the media's behaviour bears all the hallmarks of the false rage of someone who's opponent has come dangerously close to exposing the truth, therefore smear, denial and deflection are the only tactics available, because to actually address the subject matter would make their position untenable.

But last night **fuming** *Falkirk boss Steven Pressley hit back at his old club. And in a thinly-veiled blast he* **questioned their bottle for the title battle** *if they needed* **diversionary tactics to deflect attention** *from their team.*

Celtic **stoked the fires** *of last week's Old Firm match by complaining to the SFA over refereeing decisions. The timing of that move* **sparked outrage** *- and Falkirk are equally upset.*

And on it goes – big bad Celtic "stoking the fires', "sparking outrage" and conducting "wars". There's nothing like a neutral commentator keeping things in perspective with a nice piece of objective journalism. It's a pity we live in Scotland though and are served by such wee bitter, jaundiced hacks like Waddell who serve up this kind of biased crap day in, day out.

Pressley told us: "They are obviously concerned about being able to adapt to the pitch. I have no concerns about my own players. Regardless of the condition of the pitch my players will be physically and mentally ready for Sunday's game."

Answers on a postcard as to where Pressley "*hits back*" at Celtic, or "*questioned their bottle for the title battle*" or mentioned their "*diversionary tactics to deflect attention*". I guess that bit must have been the result of a few wee "honest mistakes" from the kid-on journalist there. I hear there's a lot of that going around at the moment.

Falkirk spokesman Keith Hogg said his club received a phone call on Wednesday seeking permission for an independent expert to inspect the pitch.

"We find there's nothing wrong with that; we're quite open here at Falkirk Football Club," he said. **"It's just part of the SPL's looking after the state of Scottish football and making sure that all our pitches are up to spec.** *To be honest, we're quite happy about that."*

Back in the real world, the quote from the Falkirk spokesman ties up with an official statement released by Celtic on the matter:

Further to erroneous reports in today's press, Celtic Football Club can confirm that it did not make any official complaint about the Falkirk pitch and did not ask for any pitch investigation or inspection.

This is supported by a Scottish Premier League statement which reads: "We keep an eye on all our pitches and monitor them over the course of the season through our delegate reports.

"The weather has had an impact on pitches up and down the country, but as things stand all our games are good to go for this weekend."

The Daily Record's take on this is "nah nah nananah! we can't hear you!". In another uncredited piece on the same day, the rag quotes the SPL statement but blithely carries on accusing Celtic of "*intervention*":

The Parkhead side expressed concerns about the condition of the playing surface at Westfield to the SPL, who **insisted** this morning they were carrying out checks on a number of pitches **as a matter of course**.

A league spokesman said: "We keep an eye on all our pitches and monitor them over the course of the season. The weather has had an impact on pitches up and down the country but, as things stand, all our games are good to go this weekend."

The SPL sent independent expert Bill Gillespie to the Falkirk Stadium yesterday afternoon after the Bairns were asked to make their pitch available for inspection.

Celtic's intervention *comes just a week after they expressed concerns about the quality of refereeing this season ahead of the Old Firm derby.*

The un-named hack has dropped a clanger here. He or she, writes Celtic "*expressed concerns*" where clearly this should have been "*waged war against all referees, past, present, future and deceased till the end of time as part of a their paranoid fatwah of hatred and bigotry*". Chief football scribbler Union Jackson would not approve.

So let's recap – Celtic's "intervention", that doesn't exist, comes just a week after they had the temerity to make a factual statement that the club had been the victim of a number of glaring refereeing errors over a series of games against Rangers. How dare they.

The Daily Ranger carried on in their "we'll just believe what we want to believe and say what we want to say" manner. Union Jackson was still at it in his match report of the game:

"*It was Keane's cool head and costly class that proved the difference between the sides – which is as it should be,* **even if Celtic seem determined to prove the existence of other murky factors behind the winning and losing of matches***. The failings of Mowbray and his players have in fact all been down to* **referees with rancid morals***. Or in yesterday's case – had it not been for Keane – it could even have been blamed on a playing surface that seemed in* **sinisterly poor condition**".

Couldn't get a more neutral viewpoint than Keith "Rangers TV" Jackson could you? Talk about overegging the pudding. Yes we get it Keith, Celtic have accused everyone including refs of bias and even complained about Falkirk's pitch. Except Celtic did no such thing.

Neither Celtic nor Tony Mowbray have accused anyone of bias and they did not complain about the pitch despite the press reporting that they had, however, Jackson - who seems to know an awful lot about what goes on at Celtic for someone who's hardly out of the Rangers TV studio - has failed to grasp even the most basic of information, perhaps because it does not suit his agenda.

Somewhat ironically, on the very same weekend of all this unsavoury Celtic paranoia and disgraceful slurs against other team's pitches, a certain other manager was getting his cardigan in a twist after his team were the beneficiaries, yet again, of a refereeing "honest mistake", this time Davie Weir not even booked by Charlie Richmond for a last man foul on Michael Higdon of St.Mirren:

"*Everyone wants people to get ordered off, everybody wants penalties against us, everybody wants everything against us*"

Still, what's a wee bit of paranoia between a lapdog and his master?

We've established that Rangers are in fact the ones who are paranoid, given that every aspect of Scottish football from the SFA, to the SPL, to the Scottish national team, to the media – is without exception, set up to please whatever whims the Establishment club take, and yet **still** they howl and whine about injustice and "lack of sporting integrity". One thing they haven't done is complain about the state of other team's pitches though. I'm sure a fearless crusader who's so impartial in his loathing for both of the O*d F**m clubs, like Gordhun Waffle, would have drawn it to our attention by now; in the interests of balance of course.

To check that out, let's take a wee trip back to April 2008.

The scene: Spoilt Child FC are battling on four fronts in their bid to win an "unprecedented-quadruple-that-Celtic-already-eclipsed-in-1967". The Scottish media are all very excited and are doing their upmost to get the authorities to change their rules mid-season to help their favourite team win everything. Dignity FC have just been rather fortunate to overcome First Division St Johnstone in the Scottish Cup semi-final, beating them 2-0 after extra time. The downside though, is that Steven Naismith, who they recently signed from Kilmarnock for a tenner in 50p installments, ten empty ginger bottles and a Farmfoods £5-off voucher, has torn cruciate ligaments after coming off injured only to be told not be such a poof by his dignified manager and to get back onto the park. Naismith then broke down with an injury that would keep him out for 8 months. One would have thought the media might have questioned the wisdom of a manager sending an injured player back out onto the pitch resulting in said player picking up a more serious long-term injury than the one already suffered.

Before we start getting all paranoid though, I should point out that there's a perfectly logical explanation as to why the media didn't question Uncle Waldo's possible role in this serious injury to a young star player, that doesn't involve them being a shower of servile lickspittles.

It was all the pitch's fault you see:

Steven actually hurt his knee twice. At first he thought he was going to be OK but when he went back on he caught his foot in the ground. I've said publicly our own pitch is not a good one this season but for the National Stadium that one is in a shocking condition. By all accounts they can't water the pitch here before games for some reason. I don't fully understand why. Our own pitch is suffering this year but for the National Stadium this pitch is poor" (19/04/2008)

But surely we can allow the most dignified football manager to walk the face of the earth since Bill Struth, a wee rant now and again can't we? After all, it really is a one-off for Dignity FC to be complaining about other team's pitches:

That has riled Bain, who has seen his team play on a "difficult" pitch at Fir Park twice as scheduled. "Celtic are not being asked to go and play on the difficult surface at Fir Park when they have only played there once this season," he said. "Does that equate to 'sporting integrity'?" (13/04/2010)

I'm not sure Baldy, but I am sure it equates to a dummy spitting tantrum.

Strangely though, no stories appeared in any Scottish newspaper accusing Dignity FC of disrespecting other teams, making any accusations, launching any attacks, deflecting from their own deficiencies or lacking bottle for their title challenge. Funny that.

Honest Mistake no.666

"Honest mistake" number 666 in the much publicised Falkirk v Celtic match. To be fair, a really difficult call for the linesman, what with the attacker being several feet behind the ball. I mean what self respecting Scottish linesman wouldn't flag this for offside? Still yesterday's "Honest Mistake" at Ibrox proves that it isn't just Celtic who suffer from bad decisions ...according to Jim Traynor. In a journalistic "Honest Mistake" Traynor missed out the bit about it being basically any team playing against Rangers that suffers. Then again Walter the Dignified One says we should all be good enough to overcome these wee trivial obstacles and get on with it, so I suppose that's fair then.

HONEST MISTAKE NO.37 – Robbie Keane wrongly flagged offside despite being *yards* onside

HONESY MISTAKE NO.38 – Davie Weir *not even booked* for pulling Higdon of St. Mirren's jersey thereby denying him a goal-scoring opportunity.

BBC – *St Mirren boss Gus MacPherson was angry Rangers' David Weir was not punished by referee Charlie Richmond for a foul early in the Buddies' loss at Ibrox. "I'm not wanting players booked or red-carded but there are laws to the game, David Weir impeded Michael Higdon in the process of shooting, he affected how he was shooting. There's a decision to get made there. No decision was made". MacPherson feels guidelines set down at the start of the season are not being adhered to. "It's compulsory that we must go to a meeting at the start of the season, it's not optional, and we're set down guidelines," he said." And during the course of the season, these guidelines change. I'm not just talking about St Mirren games, I'm talking throughout the game as we see it. We watch games, we go to games and we see clips on the BBC and* **we see a different set of rules getting applied. None more so than when we're coming here** (to Ibrox*)" *Note – not the O*d F**m

POSSIBLE EFFECT Celtic beat Falkirk so only a slight goal-difference implication. Rangers and St Mirren are level at 0-0 when Weir commits his foul. St Mirren go on to open the scoring. There's a high probability that they would have gained at least a point after going one goal up against ten men. So two point swing away from Rangers.

Rangers (-12 [-2]), Celtic (+13 [+1])

Scottish Press in Full-On Gloating Mode

10th March 2010

Bryan Young from the Metro is clearly a right big Rangers man.

His back page on last night's win for Rangers over the Ayrshire Huns proclaims the headline "*Our lead's this big*" accompanied by a photo of Kenny Miller embarking in a fairly typical open arm aeroplane-style celebratory gesture.

Your lead's that big is it Bryan? I'm glad you're happy.

The piece opens "*Kenny Miller thinks 13 is his lucky number as he illustrates just how big Rangers lead at the top is*".

Or maybe he's just put his arms out in celebration and reading anything more into it is evidence of paranoia or an unbalanced mind?

Good to see our neutral newspaper writers refusing to get carried away. All that's missing is a "Wearra Peepell!'

Graham Spiers acknowledges historical bias against Celtic in the course of deriding a caller

12th March 2010

I heard Graham Spiers on a phone-in whilst in a taxi on my way home. He said something that grabbed my attention in the context of bias against Celtic.

His was in the midst of ridiculing a caller who espoused the view that there is bias against Celtic from officials in Scotland and there always has been. Spiers asked the caller if he really believed that referees got together in secret wee groups to discuss how to make decisions that would prevent Celtic from winning, using the tired old "darkened room conspiracy" smear to great effect - observing that such meetings or collusion would be necessary to facilitate such a conspiracy. He laughed a few times while making this point although the Radio Clyde producers stopped short of playing the X-files theme.

However he went on to drop the ball rather incredibly, by making another statement in the same conversation, that was not followed up in any way whatsoever by any of his quick-witted and fearless journalistic colleagues on the panel. He said that there was little doubt that there **was** bias against Celtic 40 years ago, but that it had long since disappeared. I found myself asking the car radio, in lieu of not being able to ask the man himself, how does he arrive at that conclusion?

Does he have information proving collusion between officials in the past?

Was he suggesting anti-Celtic bias was institutionalised back then and therefore there was no need for 'darkened room' conspiratorial meetings?

Was he suggesting rogue individuals were responsible?

Was he suggesting referees acted like others in position of authority at that time and applied discriminatory practices in line with their prejudices?

Was he suggesting the SFA applied discriminatory practices?

Was he right in his timescales, as that takes us up to 1970?

It's astonishing that such a statement could be casually dropped in to the discussion and **no-one** asked him to elaborate (the caller was cut off before he could do so of course). This is particularly so when furious reflex denials and derision are immediately poured on anyone of Celtic persuasion who makes such an assertion. Just ask Billy McNeill.

Spiers' mockery of the caller was totally undermined by this one statement. He had just acknowledged that bias existed 40 years ago among officials and the football authorities, therefore the next logical step is that there is no inherent reason why there could not be such bias or conspiracy today. He had acknowledged that bias could, **and has**, existed therefore the old "darkened room conspiracy" or "collusion" argument seems not to be such an immovable obstacle after all.

However the Scottish media continues to dismiss as ridiculous the possibility that one team could unfairly benefit from decision-making by officials or the football authorities, however much evidence is presented, or however likely the statistical probability as suggested by that evidence. The standard tactic of the media is to weave images of comical conspiracy scenarios that can easily be ridiculed to "disprove" the notion. Of course it is naiveté of convenience to assert that bias must involve elaborate mechanisms and formal protocols to succeed, such as clandestine meetings and coded messages. If a referee has leanings towards Rangers, or any other team, he hardly needs Hugh Dallas/Walter Smith/the ghost of Bill Struth to visit him in the dead of night and give him precise orders on the exact minute of the game Rangers should be awarded the penalty. Why would a meeting be necessary for a referee to give a dubious decision in favour of Rangers? Why would he need to refer to anyone else before doing so? The chances are, when a close-call has to be made, that official will err on the side of giving the benefit of the doubt to the Establishment team.

How likely is a referee to have leanings towards Rangers? Well it is logical to expect that any referee has a keen interest in the game and therefore had an affinity to a specific team at one stage. It is more than likely that such an affinity would stay with him even when he became a referee. As mentioned previously, Rangers are the most widely supported team in Scotland, therefore the probability of Rangers-supporting referees being active within the Scottish game at any given time is very high. It should be said that such an affinity does not preclude a referee from handling games involving that team objectively. But the other side of the coin is that bias cannot be dismissed out of hand without due consideration, in spite of the furious denunciations of such a premise invariably thrust upon the public by the Scottish media in a manner that resembles an impassioned defence of a member of their own family.

This stance is all the more ironic when you consider the naive perception that investigative journalism is supposed to be the stock in trade of the media. One would've thought that systemic bias in Scottish football would be the story of the century and therefore one that would at least be subject to the most cursory of inquiries by those who kid-on at being journalists in Scotland, considering the bountiful journalistic rewards that could potentially be won. Instead what we see is an obstinate refusal to even countenance the notion, akin to the denial of a parent refusing to contemplate that her child has committed some dishonest act despite being caught red-handed. It's not as if the SFA don't have previous on this score – Jim Farry, Jorge

Cadete and Fergus McCann spring readily to mind. To their eternal dishonour, the Scottish media steadfastly refused to investigate the "Cadete Affair", choosing instead to castigate the Celtic chief executive and slaughter everyone associated with the club for their "paranoia". Many of this same shower of clowns are still dishonourably employed within the ranks of the Laptop Loyal today and regularly pontificate on Celtic's "paranoia" and "war on whistlers" without a hint of embarrassment.

When the "Dougie, Dougie" saga broke in October 2010, it emerged that Steven Craven had been marked down by the SFA for the "incorrect" booking of Kirk Broadfoot and for Stephen McManus not being sent off for a "last-man foul" in a cup tie against St Mirren. Think about who these decisions favoured, and who they went against, and you begin to get a picture of the message being sent to officials – "give Rangers and Celtic's **opponents** the benefit of the doubt or face the consequences".

The vast majority of people are going to follow the "party line" established by higher ranking officials or managers, this is simply human nature. It is an easy concept to grasp, i.e. if I enthusiastically applaud all of my boss's ideas and proposals publicly in team meetings I am likely to be looked upon favourably and this will increase my chances of progressing within the organisation. On the other hand, my boss doesn't have to explain to me it would really not enhance my career prospects to criticise him in a public forum. This is readily understood. These are exaggerated examples, but they outline the dynamics of the way people are kept in line in this manner. We see what happens to our colleagues – who moves up the greasy pole and who falls by the wayside – and pretty quickly we can work out what behaviours are likely to be acceptable and which unacceptable, and therefore we can adjust our behaviour accordingly. In this way officials such as Dougie McDonald, Andy Davis and Willie Collum know that if mistakes are made to Celtic's detriment and/or Rangers' benefit the Scottish media and the SFA will back them to the hilt, no matter what. In contrast, they just need to have a look at "controversial" Steve Conroy for a taster of what lies in store from the media if a mistake is made the other way. In fact look up Kevin O'Donnell and Jim Callaghan to see what happens if you really step over the line, or are "too fair" in your refereeing as "Big Eck" might put it.

Another irony is that conspiracy is exactly what we are seeing in relation to the manner in which the Scottish media are handling the subject of refereeing decisions. They very quickly fall into line in agreeing the main soundbites that are selected and highlighted from press conferences and which therefore determine the "story" for the day. Almost without exception this involves agreeing to follow subtle and unsubtle direction from Walter Smith and David Murray on the manner in which stories are framed. Walter is "*frustrated*" and "*disappointed*" as Celtic "*seeth*" and "*rage*". Walter "*demands answers*" while Celtic "*launch astonishing attacks*". Walter comments wisely on what is wrong with the Scottish game, whilst Celtic bleat and moan about ridiculous conspiracy theories.

Graham Spiers himself has commented many times on this media collusion - which by definition equates to a conspiracy - but he has now, for the first time as far as I'm aware, acknowledged a bias against Celtic from match officials in the past. I believe he has a duty to elaborate on this and clarify why he holds this view. He may find, if he is honest with himself, that theories of the past hold true in many cases for the present. This whole episode can be summarised by a passage from Tom Campbell's excellent *Celtic Paranoia: All in the Mind? –*

"He [Jack Ramsay, the Grand Secretary of the Orange Order in Scotland] *also claimed comments* [in relation to bitter anti-Catholic and anti-Irish sentiment] *by James MacMillan and Frank Roy, a Lanarkshire Member of Parliament, were: "unadulterated nonsense. They are describing some Scotland that used to exist in the 1950s". When I showed these comments to a devout Catholic he commented bleakly: "When I was growing up in the 1950s I was told that discrimination against Catholics in Scotland was something that existed in the 1920s – and I should not be paranoid"*

14th March 2010 Rangers 3-3 Dundee United

HONEST MISTAKES NOS.39 & 40 Rangers are awarded a ludicrous **second** penalty in the match after Kris Boyd dives again. Note this one down for future reference - the first penalty comes as Pernis, the United goalkeeper, makes the slightest of contact with Kenny Miller, **after touching the ball away**. Miller fell spectacularly to the deck after appearing to lose control of the ball anyway, having hit it too far ahead of himself. So having been 0-1 down in this Scottish Cup quarter final, Rangers were awarded **two** very soft penalties.

BBC: (Peter Houston)*"I am disappointed and I just wonder if the penalties would have been given at the other end. I hope they would have been,"* said the Dundee United manager. *"Dougie McDonald is an honest referee **in normal circumstances**, I think he is one of the best in Scotland. But I was disappointed that he got there early to give the penalty kicks."* And the United manager added: *"The second one, if we are going to give penalty kicks for that, we'll get penalty kicks left, right and centre on a regular basis*

A rather intriguing cryptic reference to *"in normal circumstances"* there, what could that possibly mean? I would be tempted to substitute the words "except at Ibrox" but of course I am totally paranoid in spite of the evidence.

Scottish referee in danger of looking biased to Rangers shock!

Graham Spiers refuses to countenance anything untoward in the running of the Scottish game, however at least he has the gumption to desist with the bias to the "O*d F**m" pish, unlike peers like Ronnie Esplin.

The Times By Graham Spiers 16th March 2010
Dougie McDonald, one of Scotland's leading referees, has to tread very carefully from now until the end of the season, for the sake of his own reputation. Within the space of two weeks McDonald has given a whole series of contentious decisions to Rangers - two of those against Celtic - and even neutrals have started to worry that it doesn't look too impressive.

First, two weeks ago at Ibrox, McDonald sent off Scott Brown of Celtic, when almost everyone now agrees (including Walter Smith) that Brown's heated tussle with Kyle Lafferty at best warranted a yellow card.

Indeed, replays of the incident showed that Lafferty was just about as guilty in that handbags tussle, yet McDonald showed red to Brown and nothing at all to Lafferty.

The big, lanky, £3.5 million Rangers striker had even performed his old trick of collapsing to the ground, his legs mysteriously giving way beneath him, but even that piece of feigning didn't cause Mr McDonald any duress.

By a minor miracle, in the same game, Rangers defender Madjid Bougherra somehow managed to stay on the field for the whole 90 minutes, despite having been booked in the first ten minutes, and, arguably, having fouled Robbie Keane enough thereafter to earn a second yellow. But McDonald, again, demurred on that decision.

Then came last Sunday at Ibrox, and two penalties awarded to Rangers against Dundee United in the Active Nation Scottish Cup, from which United had to heroically fight back to earn a 3-3 draw. In the first case, Dusan Pernis, the United goalkeeper, seemed to have got a touch before colliding with Kenny Miller in the box, but McDonald was having none of the debate - penalty.

Then, ten minutes later, Sean Dillon collided with Kris Boyd in the box, and once more, in the TV replays of the incident, it looked a 50-50 call by the referee. In the press gantry Craig Paterson, the former Rangers centre-half and now a BBC match analyst, said it wasn't a penalty, though again, McDonald gave Rangers the decision.

Now let's be clear about this. I have never argued - indeed, I have repeatedly lampooned the idea - that there is a pro-Rangers leaning among referees in the SPL. And I stand by that. In lovely, Presbyterian Scotland we have many flaws, but football corruption cannot be cited among them. Our referees, in the main, are good guys, Dougie McDonald among them. It's just that, right now, they are going through a terrible slump in form.

But having said that, McDonald now stands under a special, self-inflicted scrutiny. If he keeps up this momentous form of giving every 50-50 decision Rangers' way then even neutrals among us are going to feel a certain disquiet. As someone once said, it is not just the act, but the perception, that matters.

McDonald, in the near future, could really do with coming upon a 50-50 moment which he somehow decides not to give to Rangers.

Daily Record condemns Celtic's Rasmussen but not Kilmarnock's Clancy

The likes of the Daily Record, Sun and Evening Times are easy targets when it comes to picking off their unabashed bias to the Establishment club, but it's not every day they're complacent or daft enough to display their blatant hypocrisy in one article. Such an article appeared in the aftermath of Celtic's 3-0 win over Kilmarnock in a Scottish Cup tie in March:

Daily Record
March 15 By Anthony Haggerty and Neil Cameron

CELTIC striker Morten Rasmussen and Kilmarnock defender Tim Clancy could be forced to appear before the SFA Review Panel. Record Sport understands both players will have to answer the case for two separate incidents that occurred during Saturday's Active Nation Scottish Cup quarter-final which Celtic won 3-0 courtesy of a Robbie Keane hat-trick.

*In a bad-tempered first half Clancy **appeared** to stamp on Hoops hitman Rasmussen with the Dane later **elbowing** Kilmarnock defender Frazer Wright off the ball, **amazingly escaping punishment**.*

Some nice unbiased reporting there eh? It's as clear as crystal to this pair of Rangers toadies just what Rasmussen's intentions were, but they suddenly come over all vague and confused when it comes to Clancy. Through their blue glasses he only "*appeared to*" stamp on the Dane and did not "*amazingly escape punishment*" unlike the Celtic player for his dastardly elbowing of Frazer Wright.

Killie defender Wright insists the SFA should throw the book at Rasmussen. Wright did not believe the Dane's explanation that he was just trying to get some space for himself inside Killie's penalty box and the centre-half would like to see justice being done.

When asked about the incident, the Killie star said: "He swung an elbow at me. I asked Sky's David Tanner about it when we came off at half-time after someone else said the telly showed it was quite obvious he had done it. I wasn't happy about it but he just said he was trying to get free from me. He said, 'You shouldn't be close to me', so I said, 'Sure, I'll let you stand and score.' He definitely caught me. If he meant to do it, it's not very nice. Hopefully it's something which will be looked at.

Perhaps Rasmussen should have said "Ach, it was only a wee slap". Remember this clown is the one who hit Shunsuke Nakamura in the head after Celtic were given a penalty against Kilmarnock in September 2008 and justified it by telling the media "it was a just a wee slap". Funnily enough there were no howls from the media, or anyone at Celtic for that matter, for the SFA Review Panel to "have a look at it".

"I think if it was one of us who had done the same thing it would be picked up on."

What? Just like his own "wee slap" and his team-mate Clancy's "apparent" stamp?

"Someone has to have a look at it. If TV pictures prove he's done it then I'm all for him being done, he did catch me. The result hurt Wright in more ways than one and he said: "I got caught in the head trying to clear the ball and went off for stitches. When we got to the medical room the door was locked. Eventually someone found the key and I got stitched."

Give me a minute while I go away and get my violin. Predictably this pair of lickspittles don't bother to ask Rasmussen for his opinion and give him the chance to launch into some ramble about the injustice of it all. Of course, if by some aberration they had they would have simply slaughtered him for being paranoid.

Clancy "appearing" to stamp on Rasmussen

Co-op Cup Final red card spin and how the Laptop Loyal paints a picture of thugs and saints

21st March 2010

Craig "*McGeady and Nakamura have hardly had a touch and that's great*" Paterson thought Danny Wilson shouldn't have been sent off in the CIS cup final because:

a) Rangers had already had a man sent off

and

b) Because he's a young boy

The man is an idiot. How in god's name did he get that job? I think we all know the answer to that one. Aside from being obviously biased, it's like watching a cardboard cut-out of Craig Brewster. I know that by law, it has to be a former Rangers player, but please BBC, give us Billy Dodds with a wee sign saying "the referee got it just about right".

As you will recall, Kevin Thomson was sent off for a violent foul on Steven Thomson of St Mirren, as was Danny Wilson for pulling an opponent's shirt when last man. Paterson said of the Wilson incident "*I thought since Rangers are a man down the referee might have settled for a yellow*". Yes, only in Scotland are the FIFA Laws of the Game malleable depending on whether the Establishment team have already had a man sent off. As it turns out, the Scottish media have also written another law into the rulebook with the rest of us unawares – a limit on the number of times you can send off the same player. Read on to find out more.

The media were very keen to push some sort of conspiracy against Kevin Thomson – yes, the same media who constantly vilify us for our "paranoia" – by reminding us forcefully that Thomson had now been sent off three times by Craig Thomson over the course of his all too long career thus far. The Scottish Sun's Roger Hannah was particularly keen to emphasise this point:

Once, Twice, Three Times is Crazy

The Sun By Roger Hannah 23 Mar 2010

*KEVIN THOMSON has **slammed** Co-op Cup Final ref Craig Thomson after he sent him off for the THIRD time. **Rangers ace Thommo is raging at the 'poor' decision** by Scotland's No1 whistler and Treble-chasing Gers are ready to challenge the red card for Thommo's **wild lunge** on St Mirren's Steven Thomson.*

Kevin Thomson was sent off for a violent two-footed tackle that could easily have ended the career of Steven Thomson of St. Mirren, yet the Sun hands over its pages to spin this as some sort of injustice against the poor hard-done by Rangers thug.

Thomson said: "It was a lunge and I never got much of the ball"

You can say that again, so what are you complaining about??

*"There certainly **wasn't any malice in my tackle** yet that's the third time Craig Thomson has sent me off now. I thought the decision was poor."*

And we're back to the old "intent" fallacy that the media are willing to peddle to create the illusion of big bad refs giving incorrect decisions against their Rangers heroes. I will not labour the point as I've already laid out the rules on violent conduct earlier in this tome, but needless to say, the only criteria is excessive force which endangers the safety of an opponent and was emphatically the case with Thomson's "lunge". The question remains whether the media are hopelessly biased, or merely hopeless, when it comes to understanding the laws of the game, although the complete lack of anything resembling a similar staunch defence of Loovens, McDonald, Brown or any other Celtic player within their rags speaks volumes.

"I spoke to the boss about it and we were both disappointed with the red card. The sending-off ruined my Cup Final and I'm really disappointed with how it panned out."

Well don't try and break opponent's legs then! Simples.

*It was the fourth dismissal of his career, **the third by ref Thomson**. He was red-carded by his namesake earlier this season for a foul on Ian Black at Hearts.*

Which was another shockingly violent lunge which by sheer luck didn't make contact with the Hearts player otherwise it may have been goodnight career for Mr Black. Even the Man with Nosurname gave the game away by complaining that Black *"wouldn't have been able to carry on in the game in the manner he did if the challenge had made contact"*. You can say that again... again.

Now you can't help but think if the player in question was Balde B, or Lennon N, or Brown S; the limelight would not be shining solely on the referee as it was in this case, insinuating some terrible vendetta against the poor wee player. No it would be, get *"hard-man* Balde", *"fiery* Lennon" and *"tough-tackling* Brown" up in front of the panel immediately to add a few more games onto that ban.

Thomson was also dismissed by Scotland's top ref playing for Hibs at Dunfermline in 2004.

So the conspiracy against him started six years ago when he was at Hibs because Craig Thomson knew he was going to sign for Rangers three years later? This is all starting to sound a bit crazy and paranoid.

The Gers star added: "I was very disappointed. I felt if the referee had blown for the foul on me to start with then it would have stopped my challenge from happening."

Ah, so his two-footed assault was the referee's fault was it? Glad to get that straightened out. And there's another Rearrangers rule change for FIFA to note – retaliation is AY-OK for players in blue jerseys who are the victims of innocuous fouls.

*"I get on quite well with Steven Thomson and I had a wee bit of banter with him in the game. **I'm pretty sure he knows there was no intent**. I'm a winner and I like to think my style reflects that."*

The intent pish again. Right, OK, we get the picture, you're a good wee boy really.

"The day was a bit of an anti-climax for me because I feel I let everyone down, even if the boys dug it out."

Aw diddums. This statement begs the question – if he's such an innocent party, merely the victim of a cruel and malicious vendetta; why would Thomson have any reason to feel guilty? Maybe it's because, deep-down Thomson realises this is all just jaundiced pish and excuses, even if the press is all too keen to promote the party line. The reality that Kevin Thomson actually deserved all three red cards and is a hot-headed wee thug with a temperament problem, cannot be contemplated by the media.

You will note that Rangers players don't get tagged with the same lovely wee prefixes that Celtic players do, such as – "*fiery* Lennon"," *hard-tackling* Balde","*combative* Brown". For the media it's all about planting wee seeds you see, painting scenery in the background, so that the next time something similar crops up, we no longer remember the detail, just a vague characterisation which colours our view and hence our judgement. So in the case of Scott Brown we remember '*that hot-headed wee eejit who tried to header Lafferty*', but when it comes to "Thommo", our recollection is of '*the poor wee lad who keeps getting sent off for no reason, give the boy a break ref*'.

Propaganda disguises and deflects, it doesn't deal in detail. It skips over facts such as Kevin Thomson fully deserved the red card at Tynecastle. We are only presented a hand-picked selection of the relevant information that promotes a particular agenda i.e. the same player being sent off three times by the same referee is a statistical anomaly. Yes it probably is, although over a six year period, not that much of an anomaly. Check the stats on David Elleray and Roy Keane, or even Alan Thompson and various diving Rangers players. However, the real anomaly is that Kevin Thomson chose to commit serious fouls in three games which **coincidentally** Craig Thomson happened to be refereeing. The **fact** that these decisions were all **correct** is conveniently left out of the propaganda picture. Because of course, propaganda is specifically designed to distract your attention from the detail which may inadvertently lead you to the truth that must be avoided at all costs. Instead it paints a vague picture which does not resemble anything near the truth, and the beauty of it is – over time the details are naturally forgotten and in a few weeks or months, all that remains in the memory is the lie of the distorted watercolour, painted by the press, which lingers on in our minds. So for example, the infamous 'THUGS AND THIEVES' Daily Ranger front page can still be found on the most extremist Rangers/anti-Celtic websites held up by arrant bampots as irrefutable "evidence" of some sort of flaw in the character of those connected with Celtic. The **fact** that the story was baseless, and that the Rangers mouthpiece of a newspaper which spewed it forth into the world had to pay Neil Lennon substantial damages for unsubstantiated claims, along with a painful and begrudging apology, is forgotten by everyone not connected with Celtic. As the saying goes – mud sticks.

So next time you have the misfortune to find yourself reading the sports pages of a Scottish newspaper or their on-line equivalents, think about the adjectives that are being used and whether there is a discernable pattern – e.g. A Rangers player guilty of a violent foul usually "catches" an opponent, or "raises his hands". His Celtic counterpart will invariably be described in a much more direct manner, he will "barge / take out / elbow / kick / bring down". On the other hand, Rangers will be "denied" penalties, even if video evidence proves otherwise, and their players are "brought down / tripped / fouled" in the box. In contrast, Celtic make "claims" or "holler" for penalties, or where a Celtic player is blatantly fouled this is reported as a "suggestion of a foul". Our players "go down / tumble / fall / topple / go to ground" in the box. Incidentally, the same holds true for opponents of the Establishment club. Obviously there are exceptions that prove the rule, however if you are really paranoid (like me), keep a record of how often this observation holds true and you might be surprised how the imbalance stacks up. Even if you're paranoid (like me).

Spiers on RST buy-out plan

23rd March 2010

"The sheer farce of this attempted Rangers buy-out by supporters is beginning to tax every football fan's patience – not least the more sane among those of an Ibrox persuasion. Almost as swiftly as it is being exclusively revealed that a "Mr Big" is on the brink of riding to the club's rescue, it is being exclusively revealed (more often than not by the same newspaper) that the self-same Mr Big, in fact, is not riding to Rangers' rescue.

All the while a group of festering Rangers fans, duped on notions of being at the very gates of the Bastille, issue their internet bulletins daily saying: "Almost there lads … one more heave … the club will be ours." I have to say – and it is a condemnation of the sort of media we have today – that gullibility has been a recurring theme of this Rangers saga.

The latest victim is poor Jim McColl, by all accounts a fine guy, a Glasgow man who happens to be worth, literally, hundreds of millions of pounds. Because the punting of his name as Rangers' next saviour had that familiar reek of rushed excitement about it over the weekend, you'll forgive me for having written in The Times on Monday that, with McColl's reported interest in bailing out Rangers, it all warranted "yet another large dose of caution" and that "we are nowhere near closure" in this desperate bid to find a Rangers buyer.

It then transpires that, over the past 24 hours, McColl calmly, if with a little pique, is forced to point out that he has no such intention of getting involved with the ailing Scottish club. Oh well, on to the next target. Who else might be hanging around Glasgow with some spare millions?

One problem with this Rangers FC tragedy has been the role of the Rangers Supporters Trust (RST), a well-meaning bunch of guys but with a well-known lunatic fringe. The RST dreams daily of a "membership model" for Rangers, in the same vein as Barcelona in Spain, where the club will be in the very ownership hands of its supporters. In such a scenario some of the more extreme members of the RST aim to take Rangers back in time a few decades, re-introduce some of the old "traditional" (ahem) anthems to Ibrox, and, in the fine traditions of a junta, have a number of journalists, who have dared to criticise the club for its bigotry problem, banned and flung out of Ibrox. (I just hope I'm not one of the guys to be taken up in the helicopters).

Mercifully, none of this will happen, for two simple reasons. First, the Rangers board will not give houseroom to the wackier side of the RST – too much nonsense has occurred over the past few years for that to happen.

Second, the "membership model" of Barcelona has one serious flaw – the Catalan club is said to have a worldwide fan-base of nearly 40 million and is saturated with self-generated TV monies. Rangers, under a similar model but with their own Scottish impoverishment, would lurch along in relative poverty, and would have to severely downsize. Yet it remains a pipe-dream that causes some Rangers fans to perennially hallucinate.

A fans' co-operative would work for Rangers only in one way – if it had a sugar-daddy at the heart of it; in other words, if it really wasn't a co-operative in the traditional sense at all. That is why men like Jim McColl and others find themselves being forever dragged into this. Otherwise, the arithmetic doesn't stack up. The latest plan is for 20,000 Rangers fans to cough up £1,500 each, thus raising £30 million with which to buy the club. Twenty thousand subscribers has been blithely spoken of as an attainable target, whereas in fact 5,000 Rangers fans being willing to cough up such a sum may be a more realistic figure.

Another problem in all this is a degree of apathy – for all their passion – about the Ibrox fans. The Manchester United Supporters Trust (MUST) has a membership of nearly 140,000. The RST, with more than a few being put off by its loonier image, is said to have a membership of just 2,000. There isn't just dreaming, and some mad reporting, in this Rangers fuss. There is also a severe lack of reputable political muscle."

24th March 2010 Dundee United 1-0 Rangers

HONEST MISTAKES NOS. 41 & 42 Scottish Cup quarter final replay and with three minutes remaining Dundee United score to go 1-0 up but the goal is wrongly disallowed by Dougie McDonald. Earlier in the game McDonald refuses to give United a penalty after a blatant handball from Kyle Lafferty diverts the ball away from goal.

The Scotsman – "*In a frantic finale, Goodwillie had the ball in the net but was denied by a marginal offside decision.*" Despite the "*marginal*" comment, TV footage showed that Goodwillie was onside.

The Guardian – "*The visiting midfielder Kyle Lafferty appeared to clearly handle a Daly header inside his own penalty area but the referee, Dougie McDonald,* **opted not to award** *United a spot-kick.*"

BBC "*Kyle Lafferty handled in the Rangers box in the first-half but escaped the award of a penalty against his side. However, despite strenuous penalty appeals from the United players, referee Dougie McDonald awarded a corner to the home side and booked Garry Kenneth for dissent towards the assistant referee*"

3rd April 2010 Rangers 1-0 Hamilton Accies

HONEST MISTAKE NO.43 A perfectly legal Hamilton equaliser is chopped off with 10 minutes to go for "offside". TV footage proves it was clearly onside.

Sunday Mail – *"ANGRY Accies boss Billy Reid last night blasted the officials for denying his side a deserved draw at Ibrox. Hamilton were trailing to Mo Edu's first-half opener when James McArthur knocked home Alex Neil's cross 12 minutes from time. But linesman Steven Craven flagged for offside against sub Joel Thomas – **even though McArthur was well onside**. And ref Stevie O'Reilly chalked the goal off to hand Rangers a 1-0 victory. Raging Reid said: "I don't think anyone could deny we deserved a point. "I haven't seen McArthur's goal on the monitor but I don't need to. I knew Joel was offside when the cross came in but James wasn't. He came from deep, timed his run well and I'm told he was three yards onside. I was celebrating the goal so I'm disappointed it wasn't given. I had a word with the ref but he had a hard decision. Some they get right, some they get wrong. He called this one wrong."*

Sunday Herald - *"Rangers doing just enough to win, with a dubious officiating call thrown in: **this game was like the 2009/10 SPL season in microcosm.**"*

POSSIBLE EFFECT With only 10 minutes to go, there is a high probability that this mistake cost Hamilton Accies a point and ensured Rangers picked up three points when they should only have earned one.

Rangers (-14 [-2]), Celtic (+13 [+1])

Possible Effect of "Honest Mistakes" On Outcome of Season 2009/10

The final tally stands at -14 points to Rangers and +13 to Celtic, which is a staggering **27 point swing**. However, it is highly unlikely that **all** of the penalties that should have been awarded would have been converted, and likewise, that **all** of the goals disallowed and red cards decisions would have changed the results of games to result in swings against Rangers and for Celtic. But with Rangers winning the league by a final margin of **6 points**, what it **does** demonstrate, is that the season's "honest mistakes" presented a huge disadvantage to Celtic across the season, a disadvantage that may have been significant enough to make the difference between Celtic and Rangers over the whole season. Although Celtic played well below the expected standard for much of the season, the compound effect of the cumulative pressure from constantly trying to make up ground and of having to "*score two goals more than them*", as Davie Hay would suggest, or "*be good enough to deal with it*" as The Man with Nosurname would say, cannot be underestimated. Its impossible to crunch numbers and say with 100%

certainty that X or Y would definitely have happened, but what is clear from an objective view of the statistical spread of "honest mistakes" in favour of one particular team, is that these played a big part in who ultimately won the SPL title in season 2009/10.

Rangers' paranoia over SPL fixtures. Again.

Martin Bain has taken a <u>cheeky pop</u> at comments made by Celtic chief executive Peter Lawwell in 2008.
STV 13 April 2010

Rangers chief executive Martin Bain has dredged up previous quotes from the Scottish Premier League and Celtic chief executive Peter Lawwell as part of his argument against an uneven set of post-split fixtures. Although Rangers sit a mere six points away from clinching this season's SPL crown, **the Ibrox club have been dealt an unusual set of games**, *which will see them play three consecutive away matches against Hibernian, Dundee United and Celtic.*

Celtic meanwhile will benefit from the changes *made to the fixture list in order to try and give each team an equal number of home and away matches. The potential Champions League participants will welcome Motherwell to their home ground for a third time this campaign, instead of having to travel through to Lanarkshire.*

That has riled Bain, who has seen his team play on a "difficult" pitch at Fir Park twice as scheduled. "Celtic are not being asked to go and play on the difficult surface at Fir Park when they have only played there once this season," he said. "Does that equate to 'sporting integrity'?"

The reason that Rangers were given three away fixtures on the bounce was to allow the maximum number of Rangers fans the chance to see their side win the title and then the trophy presentation, who knows maybe a few SPL blazers were hoping to get tickets. Once again we have a situation where the SPL or SFA have bent over backwards to accommodate the Establishment club only to be met with dummy spitting and hissy fits from Spoilt Child FC.

With the title almost in the bag the SPL anticipated Rangers clinching the title in their first post-split game against Hearts then bringing the curtain down on their season with the trophy presentation on the final day against Motherwell; both home fixtures for them. However Rangers could only draw with Dundee United in their last pre-split fixture preventing that scenario materialising and meaning the title clinching game came the next weekend at Easter Road.

The events of season 2007/2008 seemed to have psychologically scarred Bain and Nosurname despite the season being extended to assist Rangers' bid to win their "unprecedented" quadruple, as well as the postponement of a fixture to give Rangers extra time to prepare for a Champions League tie. It's convenient to gloss over facts with the passage of time therefore some issues require being brought to light before they become distorted even further, especially with the ever vigilant Scottish media's strange reluctance to include these facts in any critique of the situation, instead promoting the myth that the SPL did nothing to assist Rangers who were the innocent victims of the resultant fixture pile-up, not to mention the evil machinations of Timmy.

While Rangers were picking and choosing their fixtures through December 2007 Celtic played **eight** matches including one away to Hearts which was played in a seven day spell that included Champions League ties against Shakhtar Donetsk and AC Milan. Celtic became the only Scottish side to play two Champions League games in a week. As well as sticking to their schedule of fixtures Celtic used a free midweek date – December 11 – to play a postponed game with Falkirk recognising this as the price of competing for trophies on several fronts. The Falkirk game had been postponed to help Scotland's preparations for the Euro 2008 qualifier with Italy in November and Rangers were due to play St Mirren the same weekend but never got around to playing that match until **May 15**, a full **six months** later **when St Mirren had nothing to play for** and would therefore, as professional as their approach would be to the game, not be as highly motivated as they would have been back in December, a time when their form was good enough to draw 1-1 with Celtic at Parkhead.

It was no surprise then that Rangers won the re-arranged fixture easily 3-0. This game incidentally, despite all the hyperbole from Spoilt Child FC and their media puppets was the only one where they had less than the customary three days preparation time afforded by the traditional Saturday-Wednesday-Saturday football calendar. The game was played on a Monday, following a 1-1 draw with Motherwell on the Saturday, leaving a three day rest period until the final league game at Pittodrie on the Thursday (22nd May). Rangers' last league match of the season was their **eighth** of the month, exactly the same number of fixtures Celtic played without complaint in December, dropping **nine** points in the process. Rangers did play a ninth fixture that May, the Scottish Cup final after the SPL season had concluded, but this was obviously immaterial to the outcome of the SPL championship. And that's the rub – despite all the howls of protestations from Spoilt Child FC and their media acolytes, their demands for a **further** season extension had nothing whatsoever to do with upholding the nation's honour in the UEFA Cup final and everything to do with naked self-interest in trying to manipulate the fixture list to allow them the best opportunity to win everything on offer.

That St Mirren fixture is the **only** time that a pre-split fixture has been allowed to be played after the split. Rangers were also the only side in the history of the competition to be allowed to complete a replayed Scottish Cup tie (v Hibs), after the fixtures for the **next round** of the competition had already started. Spoilt Child FC the only club to be given such dispensation in both cases; need I say more?

Looking back, one wonders if Celtic would have been wise to ask for a postponement of their match at Hearts, but there is always a feeling that asking for postponements is flagging up concerns over a particular fixture which can have an adverse psychological effect by subconsciously inflating the size and difficulty of the task at hand in the minds of the players. Perhaps if Rangers had concentrated on getting the results required – or as Jim Traynor might have said if it was Celtic in the same position, "Shut up and get on with it" – without all the complaining and pleading, they might just have pulled it out the hat. After all it's not as if they had to win all of these games. After they drew 3-3 with Dundee Utd on 6th April they only needed 14 points from their remaining 8 matches, equating to 4 wins and a couple of draws. With Celtic up twice before any fixture congestion kicked in, any points taken from these games would further reduce that points target.

As it happens Aberdeen later tried the same trick ahead of their UEFA Cup tie with FC Copenhagen, obviously naively thinking that the SPL's kow-towing to Spoilt Child FC had set a precedent that would be fairly applied to all Scottish clubs. How naïve can you get? This request was thrown out by the SPL quicker than you could say "it's in the best interests of Scottish football for all our teams to do well in Europe". Oh well, "Old Firm" bias obviously.

By the turn of the year Rangers were two fixtures behind Celtic and as the season unfolded, and Spoilt Child FC proved unable to beat teams in the Scottish Cup without replays, the decisions made in December that saw Rangers play two games less began to get problematic for the SPL with any spare dates being swallowed up by Rangers European run and Scottish Cup replays. Eventually, after much canvassing by the Scottish media, and at the expense of the other clubs in the top six, the SPL season was extended by five days to accommodate Rangers meaning that Celtic and the top six clubs had to wait 11 days between their final two matches.

Despite this extension there were further noises made about extending the season even further with suggestions that the Scottish Cup final between Rangers and Queen of the South could be put back into midweek to extend the SPL season by a further two days. Queen of the South were far from happy with this, as **four weeks** already separated the end of their league campaign and their cup final appearance. There was also the issue of their flag day, family day out being moved from the traditional Saturday afternoon to a Wednesday evening which would have been far from convenient for fans traveling from Dumfries. Anyway, who cares about them.

The other clubs unanimously indicated that they wouldn't accept a **further** extension, leaving the Rangers mouthpieces in the media, furious at this insubordination, portraying it as being purely down to Machiavellian forces unleashed by Celtic. When the post-split fixtures were announced Rangers were faced with three consecutive away games to see out the season. On the surface of it, this seemed a bit unusual and a little unfair. However there is a perfectly rational explanation for all of this, one that doesn't involve any unfairness to Spoilt Child FC, just the opposite in fact. Going into the split (bringing forward the postponed St Mirren game remember), they would be required to play **seven** of their **nine** remaining fixtures away from home due to a remarkable imbalance of home and away fixtures earlier in the season, which just happened to coincide with the autumn months when Celtic and Spoilt Child FC were both still competing in the Champions League. Of the seven weekends immediately following their respective Champions League qualifiers and group stage games, Celtic were faced with away fixtures in five of these games and were at home only twice, with Rangers' having the advantage of the opposite and less demanding schedule of home fixtures on five occasions.

Prior to April of that season, Celtic had been required by the fixture list to play consecutive away games **three** times, in each case going almost a month between home league games. In contrast, prior to April, Rangers had **never** had to play two consecutive games away from home in the SPL. So again, this is merely a case of the favouritism shown to Rangers catching up with them. By the time of the split, Spoilt Child FC had five of seven remaining games still to play away from home. It would have been possible for the SPL to have given Rangers a programme of – two away, one home, two away, one home, one away – to avoid the dreaded three-in-a-row scenario, of away games at least, if not titles for Celtic. But instead the SPL decided strangely to front load Rangers' remaining home matches – two away followed by two home and then the vindictive three away games to see out the season. If you were paranoid you'd almost think the SPL were hoping Spoilt Child FC would get the necessary points in the bag to tie it all up before having to make the difficult trips to Fir Park and Pittodrie. If this was the plan then it backfired on them.

These decisions clearly still annoy everybody connected with Spoilt Child FC even though the problem could have been avoided if Rangers had played a similar schedule to Celtic through December and the SPL had been more even handed in their scheduling of home and away fixtures over the first half of the season. Dragging up issues from **three** seasons ago when the SPL went out of their way to assist Rangers is poor judgement. Since the split was introduced the SPL has given Celtic and Rangers 19 home and away fixtures with the derby matches evenly split. The split will always create an imbalance of fixtures but is there any real difference between three away games against Dundee United and one with Aberdeen and two away games at each club?

But facts and logic don't come into the equation when it comes to the Daily Record and their beloved Spoilt Child FC. The propaganda offensive was ramped up when The Man with Nosurname let rip with a dignified rant in the manner of a senile auld Granpaw who can't remember what day it is. It took two of their crack hacks to write this shite:

Rangers boss Walter Smith demands answers from SPL over split fixtures row

Daily Record
Apr 19 2010 Craig Swan and Gary Ralston

(Note that the Man with Nosurname doesn't make "astonishing outbursts" like the mere mortals who manage other SPL clubs, no Mr Dignity "*demands answers*" as he can never be wrong).

WALTER Smith last night revealed Rangers will **demand answers** from the SPL **for a decade of unfair treatment in the split**. *The Ibrox boss' patience has snapped as he rages against a system he believes has given his team a raw deal since the end-of-season scheduling began a decade ago.*

*Smith was already unhappy at his team being asked to play their next three successive fixtures away from home this season against Hibs, Dundee United and Celtic having been told in the past that would never happen again. But a deeper analysis of post-split planning over the past 10 years has cranked up his anger and the manager wants an explanation, although the SPL last night **insisted** there is no bias in favour of Celtic.*

*Since the split started, Rangers have had nine examples of an imbalance in their fixtures against top six compared with five for Celtic. On seven of those nine occasions, the Ibrox men have played a top-six club away from home three times in the one campaign and only once at home. More **astonishingly**, Celtic have never been asked to play a rival in the top-six away from home three times since the split started.*

On closer examination this "*decade of unfair treatment*" turns out, like so much of the Daily Record's pro-Rangers drum banging, to be another statement built on rotting foundations stacked atop a mound of dung floating on a lake of diaorrhea.

2000-2001

Rangers play **6th** placed Dundee 3 times away.

Celtic play 7th place Aberdeen who finished a whole 2 points behind Dundee twice away. Rangers only once. Is there a big difference here?

2001-2002

Rangers play **6th** placed Dunfermline 3 times away. Dunfermline finished 4 points ahead of 7th placed Killmarnock, who Celtic had to play twice away, Rangers only once. Is there really any great imbalance here?

2002-03

Fixture symmetry for both clubs.

2003-2004

Rangers play **5th** placed Dundee Utd 3 times away. United finished a huge 3 points ahead of 7th placed Dundee, who Celtic had to play twice away, Rangers only once. Again, any great injustice here?

2004-2005.

Rangers play **4th** placed Aberdeen 3 times away. Still won the league anyway thanks to Andy Davis.

2005-06

Fixture symmetry for both clubs.

2006-2007

Rangers play **6th** placed Hibs 3 times away. Rangers were given a third home games against 4th placed Hearts who finished **12 points** ahead of Hibs. Hibs finished 1 point behind 7th placed Falkirk, who (you guessed it) we had to play twice away, Rangers only once. Why did Rangers not have to play Hearts and Hibs an equal number of times home and away?

2007-08

Fixture symmetry for both clubs.

2008-2009.

Rangers play **6th** placed Hibs 3 times. Once again they had 3 home games against Hearts who finished 3rd, **12 points** ahead of Hibs. Hibs finished 1 point behind 7th placed Motherwell (a pattern is emerging) who we had to play twice away, Rangers only once.

2009-2010

Rangers had to play 3 away games to 3rd place Dundee Utd, with the post-split fixture being a meaningless game after Rangers had already won the league.

The fact is, in seasons where Rangers have been "*unfairly treated*" and had to play a side from the top 6 three times away, the SPL have been left with no choice but to do so, and have consistently tried to appease them by giving them this third away game against the statistically **weakest** of the top six sides as in seasons 2000/01, 2001/02, 2006/07, 2008/09, and against the 5th placed team in 2003/04 and 4th place side in 2004/05. This means that Spoilt Child FC are howling and complaining about having to play sides like Dunfermline and Dundee three times away in one season, sides who finished a couple of points ahead of the Kilmarnocks and Motherwells of the SPL. Any club in Europe would be quivering in their boots at having to travel to East End Park and Dens Park to play meaningless games wouldn't they? It should be noted that in only two of these seasons (04/05 and 08/09) has there actually been anything to play for in terms of winning the title, and in one of these seasons (2008/09), the split actually **favoured** Dignity FC as the SPL inexplicably sent them to Easter Road for their so-called "unfair" third away fixture instead of Tynecastle to play a much stronger 3rd placed Hearts who finished 12 points ahead of Hibs. Like they say, figures don't lie, but liars can figure.

So, why is it anyway that poor down-trodden "everybody has made it quite clear they won't do anything to help us" Rangers have had to play top six teams three times away from home and Celtic haven't? Well there's a quite simple explanation although perhaps not simple enough for Bain and a Rangers manager heading into his dotage to understand.

In any give season:

• Rangers have 5 games after the split (same as everyone else)

• Rangers (and Celtic) always have 19 home and 19 away games over the whole season

• Celtic and Rangers will be scheduled to play each other twice at home and twice away

This leaves four more fixtures to schedule after the split:

If, of the four remaining teams who have qualified for the top six, Rangers (or Celtic) happen to have played three of them away from home twice already, Rangers (or Celtic) will have to play one of them away from home for a third time to ensure 19 home and 19 away games overall.

It's as simple as that.

No mental, paranoid, or indeed, dignified, conspiracy theories are relevant, it's down to sheer chance as to which other four teams qualify for the top six, although seemingly no-one in the Scottish media has the intellectual capacity to make this simple deduction or maybe its just honest mistakes. So they're either thick or biased, and neither conclusion reflects well on them. It just so happens that this chance set of circumstances has happened to Rangers but not Celtic over the past decade, although it should be noted that when this has occurred the SPL have gone out of their way to make this third fixture against the lowest ranked team possible. We can be sure that, if and when Celtic find ourselves in the same position, the SPL will do the same for us. Aye right…

Celtic get a "break" according to Walker and Provan as referee doesn't disallow legal winning goal

17th April Celtic 3-2 Hibs.

Celtic score what proved to be the winning goal late in the game against Hibs. Andy Walker screams for offside. The referee awards the goal. Andy Walker is apoplectic - "*Celtic got a break there*" he indignantly howls. TV pictures prove the goal was legal (see over page). Andy Walker is a dick.

On Sky, Davie Provan was also at it, managing to get a word in between Ian Crocker salivating over "Rangers' title party", to announce emphatically that the goal was offside and Celtic were the beneficiaries of a mistake from the officials. He then revises his opinion to *"there was a hint of offside there"*.

Message for Davie Provan in best Master Yoda impersonation:

"There is offside or no offside. There is no 'hint of offside'."

"No matter how desperately you want a Celtic goal to be disallowed"

The importance of being humped in the Champions League

26th April 2010

Consider this...

Nick Clegg turns in a polished, Blair-esque performance in the first UK Election Leadership debate. In these phone-voting reality-show times, this raises the prospect of the Liberal Democrats making serious inroads to the Labour-Conservative duopoly of the UK political system.

The Murdoch Empire/ Daily Mail & co now regard Clegg as a major threat to a Conservative return to power so immediately commence a smear campaign based on information they have held for years but have chosen not to publish. Until now.

Q: Why would Clegg be a target for these particular newspapers?
A: They pander to tradional Tory/Middle-England/floating-voter readership.

Q: Why now?
A: There is an election to win.

Q: Would anybody who came to the above conclusion be classed as paranoid or a conspiracy-theory-phile?
A: No. In fact this would be conventional wisdom.

It is a widely acknowledged fact of life that media outlets, particularly the written press, promote their agendas and biases according to their owners' corporate interests and the demographic they wish to target when it comes to issues as important as UK politics in general, and particularly in the lead up to a General Election. However, suggest that undue influence may have been brought to bear on referees and officials by a Scottish tabloid media keen to pander to its largest demographic - supporters of "Scotland's Premier Sporting Institution" © D Edgar - and this is dismissed immediately as unhinged paranoia.

In the face of such potentially catastrophic consequences of failure, we are expected to believe that all of those media 'pundits' and 'experts', referees and SFA officials (Hateley, Johnstone, Dodds, Paterson, McCann, King, Young, Jackson, McInnes, the other King, Broadfoot, Smith, Wishart, Dallas, McDonald, and the rest) with their allegiances and vested interests, were nothing more than steadfastly neutral and indifferent to circumstance? Anyone commenting on the remarkable proliferation of ex-Rangers and Rangers-minded individuals within the media and Scottish football circles is derided as being afflicted with an absurdly paranoiac mindset.

They do protest too much I think.

Another contention that will have them phoning for a white van and offering use of a jacket that buttons up the back, is to speculate that last season (2009/10), more than any other in the entire history of the Scottish game, Rangers **had** to win that SPL title **at all costs**. I need not elaborate on the details (much like the ostrich-esque Scottish press over the years); suffice to say the debt position at Establishment FC was, and remains, grim, particularly when one takes into account HMRC waiting in the wings with whatever delightful little grenades they have in hand to lob into Der Fuhrerbunker. We will never know the full extent of the consequences had Rangers failed to secure that £10million or so guaranteed pot from Champions League participation, but it is not unrealistic to ponder that the club would have been in danger of liquidation. In the real world – i.e. not the one inhabited by undead zombie football hacks who lurch from one "exclusive" to another, regurgitating verbatim the wisdom of the Master of Moonbeams – this presents motive, to add to means and opportunity.

But don't take my mental paranoid delusional word for it – none other than the Rangers chairman and CEO more or less confirmed this themselves:

Bain said: *"I know Walter has been quoted before that he was told he had to win the league last year **and that's right**.*

*"**However, the pressure at the start of this season** [2009/10] **was 10-fold compared to last year, because securing Champions League football for next season would be a massive, massive step for us**.*

"If you have Champions League football then it does transform things for you. It's a massive injection of cash to the club."
Martin Bain BBC website 15/04/10

"Obviously at some point in time you have to reinvest. We need to reinvest in the infrastructure of Ibrox, you have to reinvest in the team in some form or other and that's the challenge now."

"The impact of winning the title and qualifying for the Champions League is so material given our fragile financial status."
Alasdair Johnston 29/04/10

In February, Rangers, who are seeking new owners, announced half-year profits of more than £13m, thanks mainly to Champions League involvement.

*"**It's huge, it's absolutely huge**," added Bain.*

*"It's where our team wants to be, it's where the supporters want to be and as Scottish football finds itself in times when maybe it's not so easy to qualify, **to actually qualify for it this season is hugely important to the football club**."*
Martin Bain, BBC website 26/04/10

What wasn't so "*huge*" or "*important*" to the Scottish press, was to actually investigate the issue of Rangers' finances in the interests of presenting an honest and accurate appraisal to their target demographic – Rangers supporters – as personified by Darrell King's take on the situation, published

251

in an Evening Times article under the headline "*Poison Pill That Killed the Party*" on 27th April 2010:

*"Untangling Rangers' finances and breaking them down into layman's terms for those who matter most – the club's supporters – is not a straightforward task and much of the information this paper has obtained in the last two days **was, understandably, retained until such times as the league championship was won as it was felt it would not serve any good to further muddy the waters when the team was on the cusp of the title**."*

So Darrell King and the Evening Times were saying that the, "*understandable*", priority for their so-called unbiased organ of news and current affairs, was to ensure that none of their stories impinged on Rangers winning the title or distracted their fans from enjoying an SPL title party, by bringing to light such minor details as urgent and serious financial matters that could potentially bring their club to the edge of oblivion?! Incredible.

This from a media that has done everything in its power at every opportunity to detract from almost every success Celtic have achieved, from crying into their beer at Celtic qualifying for the 2nd round of the Champions League "*by the back door*", to printing double-page spreads on why Jimmy Calderwood thinks Rangers deserved to win the league in 2008, to inventing stories about Celtic players abusing poor wee retiring Rangers fans after a 3-0 win at Mordor. It is simply inconceivable to imagine that any Scottish newspaper would sit on such a story to "*understandably*", let Celtic concentrate on winning the league and their fans to enjoy an unspoiled title party. Perhaps if this was the case, they might have sat on the 'Wim Jansen exit clause' story back in 1998, coming as it did, in the middle of a closely fought run-in when Celtic were "*on the cusp of the title*". But nope, they were delighted to trumpet that one from the rooftops, compelled by that keen journalistic killer instinct which drives them to keep the public informed… of negative Celtic stories. Of course, journalistic convention dictates that they had every right to publicise the Jansen story but their barely concealed glee and brazen double-standards where it comes to equivalent circumstances involving Rangers demonstrates clearly that journalistic integrity is the least of their priorities.

Neil Lennon "quizzed" at press conference to confirm his appointment

9th June 2010

Neil Lennon was confirmed as Celtic manager today to flag-waving and a blaze of congratulations and well-wishing from the Scottish media.

Only kidding. No, of course Lennon's first press conference as permanent Celtic manager was a predictable exercise in the media trying to discomfit him with loaded questions designed to manufacture negative headlines. David Tanner from Sky Sports was at the forefront of this mission with the questions he put to our new manager:

Did the club approach Trapattoni?
Are you concerned about lack of experience?
Are you concerned about only being given a one year contract?
Were you worried you wouldn't get the job?

Basically he went fishing for:

Not first choice
Not ready for the job.
Not got full confidence of the board.

Nakedly anti-Celtic stuff even by the usual standards, especially considering the occasion. The last question is particularly inane. I can't work out where he was going with that one, even in terms of a negative headline, although I'm sure the Laptop Loyal would have dredged one up if Lenny had given them enough rope. Funnily enough it took an English reporter to ask a couple of reasonable questions.

Now it's not too hard to imagine the contrast in tone that would be evident if this was a press conference to unveil the return of the Man with Nosurname, or the coming of Le Saviour. We can look forward to as yet unseen levels of 'how come you're so good' sycophancy when the fat cheeky chappy TV presenter takes over at the Death Star next year. Tanner can be seen below in an illustration of the standard of lickspittlery that will likely be in evidence.

The Expert Knowledge of Mark Hateley: World Cup 2010

Taken from Hateley's crayon scribblings in the Daily Record

Can England Top the World? May 26, 2010

Capello made Mike Bassett look more like Sir Alf Ramsey June 29, 2010

I haven't seen this much unjustified confidence, hype and hypocritical hindsight since Le Guen's time at the Death Star.

Hateley on Rooney, Gerrard, Lampard and Ledley King:

May 26 - "*I also forecast that Ledley King will be the star defender at this World Cup and I expect Frank Lampard and Steven Gerrard to play out of their skins because this might be their last chance to win the tournament....Then I mix in Wayne Rooney - a genuine global superstar.*"

June 29 - "*Yes, Steven Gerrard looks like a superstar at Anfield when playing next to Xabi Alonso but look what happened last season after the Spaniard moved to Real Madrid. All of a sudden the Liverpool skipper looked a lot more ordinary. Don't tell me Frank Lampard doesn't look like a better player when he's surrounded by guys like Michael Ballack, Deco and Michael Essien. It's the same with Wayne Rooney at Man United.*"

Hateley on England's chances of winning the tournament :

May 26 - *Hateley's done the maths* [he's been to the Early Learning Centre and picked up 'my first abacus'] *and his belief is that two games hold the key to England being able to emulate the legends of 1966. He explained:* "*If all goes according to plan then we'll face France in the quarter-finals. If we win, then the Brazilians will await us in the semis. And if you get past them then anything can happen.*"

Like maybe Elvis swooping down out of the night sky atop Pegasus, showering the crowd with mana from heaven.

June 29 - "*Now let's be straight here, I never did buy into all the hype regards Capello and England. I know my compatriots are guilty of building their team up every four years and then being struck dumb by shock when they get booted out and realise they weren't world-beaters after all. I knew England were never going to win this one but they were even worse than I expected.*"

Hately makes another error here. His compatriots (but not himself, of course) are guilty of building up the England team every **two** years, allowing for the odd occasion when Steve McLaren can't qualify them for the Euros.

Hateley on Capello:

May 26 - *The odds on all of that happening lessen in Hateley's mind when the man in charge belongs to what he calls the "Golden bunch" of European coaches. He said: "Capello's like Jose Mourinho in my mind. You get what you pay for and Fabio's proved he has the credentials to be called a managerial great."He's the strongest point in England's favour because he's made a disjointed team into a unit. "The qualification campaign was well nigh perfect and Capello's already on record as saying he's going to South Africa to win the World Cup. "He gets inside the England players' heads and can have the same effect on the manager of the opposition".*

Hatelely almost getting a bit carried away there. So carried away I half expected him to say that Capello is better than Walter Smith. But that would be taking it too far.

June 29 - *"In truth he's made Mike Bassett (the fictional boss in the comedy movie) look like Alf Ramsey. From his relationships with the players to his tactics, team selections and systems, Capello made one almighty balls up of being England manager and now he is likely to pay for it with his job.*

Even so, Capello ought to have made a far better fist of it than he did. He failed because he wasn't good enough to build a team capable of dealing with the likes of Germany and made a catalogue of blunders.

Capello formed no bond with his players and appears to have rubbed many of them up the wrong way. It would also have helped if he hadn't thrown on Emile Heskey when we needed to score three goals in less than half an hour. Yes, there really is no case for Capello's defence."

So much for getting *"inside the England players' heads"* then. Seems like they had the blinds down and made him as welcome as a door-to-door double glazing, timeshare, religious cult salesman.

Hateley on the Premiership:

May 26 - *"England has a team drawn from the Premiership - quite simply the best league in the world."*

June 29 - *"The English truly believe they have the best league in the world. I'm not so sure about that but there is no denying the Premiership is jam-packed with top-quality players. The problem is very few of them are English."*

Roll on EURO 2012!

Gers through to World Cup Final

7th July 2010

Daily Rectum

by Jack Keithson and Tim Jaynor

Gio Van Bronckhorst last night blasted Glasgow Rangers into their ninth World Cup final in a row with a sensational 30 yard strike against a poor and frankly, Timmy looking Uruguay team. Unknown fringe men Wesley Schneijder and Arjen Robben scored two goals to seal the win, but the glory belonged to the dignified Gers captain who set up all three goals and single handedly kept the unseen cowardly hand of the Uruguay forwards at bay, apart from two lucky offside strikes, which the Romanist referee disgracefully allowed to stand.

The victory was masterminded by Frank De Boer, who is aiming to lead the Gers to a totally unprecedented fifth septuple of World Cup, European Cup, UEFA Cup, Europa Cup, Stanley Cup, Ryder Cup and most prestigious of all, CIS Cup, in five seasons. After last night's game De Boer didn't say he owes all of his success completely to the benevolence of our Great Grand and Dignified President Moonbeams Murray; so I will. Truly the Gers couldn't have achieved this without our Great Leader and Master shuffling all of those figures across from one bit of paper to another… sorry…I meant funding our great club directly from his bottomless pockets. By the way, don't believe anyone who tells you his troosers are also bottomless now.

With only the outsiders of Germany or Spain standing in their way, Rangers look set to become the first team playing in blue outside of Larkhall in the World, to win the World Cup for a tenth time in the febrile imagination of a Scottish laptop lapdog. Unknowns such as Bastian Schweinsteger and David Villa will surely be no match for a Rangers team of Big Gio lining up in a 0-1-0 formation with Big Frank playing the flute from the bench.

To commemorate Rangers' achievement another seventeen stars will be added to the club crest which will mean they have won millions more CIS cups even than Real Madrid and Manchester United put together. A special tangerine European fifth strip will also be commissioned featuring 280 stars on the crest, the very thing to be seen in down your local tangerine lodge this summer.

Rangers' latest unprecedented winning of every trophy this season and in the world ever for the rest of time, is also expected to lead to the return of Rino Gattuso to the light blue jersey featuring as many stars on it as there are stars in the universe. The Italian superstar has been constantly begging Moonbeams to take him back to Ibrox since being bundled into a taxi after breaching Pepperami protocol back in 1999. Our Great President now believes the time is right to grant the best player since Gio Van Bronckhorst his dying wish, 60 years before he dies.

From here, Rangers can only go from strength to strength. The gap between Scotland's Premier Sporting Institution and the rest of Scottish football, even their Auld Firm rivals – Them – will move from a gulf to a yawning chasm. Domination of European and World football followed by the Inner Solar System is only a matter of time once Mr Murray's plans for a new Super-Casino-Dome-Stadium-Death-Star-Floating-in-Space are signed off by Glasgow City Council in the year 2066.

But for the time being, neutral journalists who only write about Rangers and appear on Rangers TV like myself, can look forward to opening the marching season as World Cup winners thanks to Gio and Big Frank.

Keith Union Jackanory loving a temporary return to the good old days

I want to follow in Moravcik's footsteps and be star at Celtic, says transfer target Vladimir Weiss
Daily Record 16 Aug Gavin Berry

*CELTIC target Vladimir Weiss last night **admitted** he is desperate to move to Parkhead - after being sold on a switch to Glasgow by Hoops legend Lubo Moravcik…. "Lubomir Moravcik rang my dad and then I spoke to Lubo myself. Lubo was all positive. He's a legend at Celtic".*

This story appeared in the Daily Record on 16th August 2010 suggesting Slovakian international winger Vladimir Weiss was close to signing for Celtic in a loan deal, although the hack's choice of words was strange – "*Weiss last night **admitted** to being desperate to move to Parkhead*", as if this was some sort of shameful secret. Perhaps the shameful secret on Berry's part was actually penning a vaguely positive Celtic article.

However, any Celtic positivity from this story quickly vanished as the player ended up signing for the Dark Side:

Rangers land Celtic transfer target Vladimir Weiss - as Nikica Jelavic threatens Rapid walkout to land Ibrox move

Aug 19 2010 Exclusive by Keith Jackson

*Rangers last night completed a **stunning swoop** from under the noses of Celtic for Slovakian World Cup star Vladimir Weiss. Record Sport can reveal the 20-year-old Manchester City winger will report to Murray Park this morning to sign a season-long loan deal.*

Ah, the return of the old "stunning swoop"; all that's missing is the private jet. After two years of Ellis, Lloyds and "refusing to be held to ransom", Union Jackson's head explodes with two years worth of pent-up literary diaorrhea vomiting onto the page in reverence of Bain and Nosurname's audacious capture. But Jackanory didn't reach his nadir of pro-Rangers sycophancy till the following day:

Why I snubbed Celtic bid to join Walter Smith
Aug 20 2010 Exclusive By Keith Jackson and Craig Swan

Vladimir Weiss last night revealed why Celtic's **last-ditch attempt to lure him away from Rangers failed**.

That's funny, because four days before, the Daily Rectum was reporting that Weiss was on the verge of signing for Celtic, so surely if anyone was doing any underhand "luring" it had to be Dignity FC?

Also, the Retard staff appear to have gotten a wee bit mixed up about this one, as Weiss isn't in fact signing for Rangers at all. Note the headline – the boy is actually signing for the Man with Nosurname himself, maybe to do his gardening or something.

The Hoops' bid to **hijack** *Weiss' one-year loan move came yesterday morning but the Manchester City winger* **snubbed** *the Parkhead side's advances because:*
- **Rangers came up with the cash** *to force through the deal*
- *He believes he will learn from Walter Smith's experience and from playing in the Champions League*

Here we go again, the old Celtic attempt to "hijack" a Rangers transfer target line. Celtic have a long track record in this evil trade in human trafficking, having callously kidnapped Paul Hartley, Barry Robson, Scott Brown, Georgios Samaras and Glenn Loovens totally against their will in previous seasons. Of course when Dignity FC do it, it's called "*a stunning swoop*" and Celtic are left "*snubbed*" by the player, unlike in the opposite circumstance where Dignity and the player are both innocent victims of Celtic's evil machinations.

He is convinced Gers can win every SPL game this season on the way to the title.

Watch out this guy could be the new Lorenzo Blaw without the hair.

And in an exclusive interview with Record Sport the 20-year-old Slovakian revealed: "I still had the option to go to Celtic in the morning. I spoke to people from the club but I didn't want to wait any longer. Rangers **were prepared to pay what Man City wanted** *and got the deal done."*

The move is **another huge transfer blow to Celtic boss Neil Lennon** *who has missed out on a number of big-name targets. As late as yesterday afternoon Weiss was still on Lennon's radar but Celtic had no idea he was set to move to their rivals.*

So in actual fact it's not Weiss who "*snubbed*" Celtic, if anyone was "*snubbed*" it was Weiss because, as he has admitted himself, Celtic were not willing to pay his full wages for the year and a transfer fee for a loan signing. In fact under other circumstances, say perhaps, if a certain other Glasgow team were involved, no doubt the talk would have been of "not being held to ransom" and "pulling the plug on the deal". But Weiss has made himself look a right tit with his prattle about being "*desperate to sign for Celtic*" then going to Rangers and furiously back-tracking on his previous comments. To be fair, he's just a young lad and probably doesn't give a shit about whether Celtic or Dignity came up with the wonga to sign him, but clowns like Jackson and Swan would do well to can the "*snubbed*" and "*huge blow to Neil Lennon*" pish. I don't recall any of the numerous players Celtic "*hijacked*" from under the aprons of Dignity FC being described as huge blows to Sir Wally. Maybe that's just down to my memory, but I doubt it.

With the Weiss hyperbole out of the way, we can step back into our DeLorean and back to that Gavin Berry article of 16th August to pick up on the story of their other superstar from Vienna:

And while Ibrox chief executive Martin Bain was finalising the move late last night, Walter Smith's other top target Nikica Jelavic was considering walking out on Rapid Vienna ahead of their Europa League clash with Aston Villa tonight.

Jelavic has pleaded with the Austrians to let him fly to Glasgow to finalise a £4million move that will see his wages increase from around £3000 a week to a sum nearer £20,000.

Bain now hopes to be finally given the go ahead to sign the Croatian star this morning even though **Rapid continue to dig their heels in**. *But while that standoff continued Weiss was making arrangements to travel north to join up with the Light Blues.*

I just love it when these Rangers lickspittles in the press; those disciples of the Ibrox big money men led by Sir Moonbeams the ultimate capitalist captain of industry; come over all 'power to the people' when it comes to some foreign journeyman heroically going on strike to win a transfer to the team he always supported as a boy growing up on the streets of Zagreb/Kansas/Saigon/Alice Springs. Of course they don't quite feel the same when it comes to Pierre Van Hooijdonk or Mark Viduka for some reason I can't quite fathom.

But to summarise the Jelavic story according to the Laptop Loyal – Dignity FC won't be held to ransom by Johnny Foreigner clubs and their intransigent demands that the huns pay them a fair transfer fee for their player, on time and not in an instalment plan extending into the 25th century. Wantaway star Nikica Jelavic has issued a "get me out of here" plea to his boyhood heroes, who he has always supported as a wee boy kicking a tennis ball about the back streets of Capljina. However the unreasonable and totally outrageous insistence by Rapid Vienna that he is their player and they will play him in any games they see fit looks set to scupper Jelavic's dream move.

Unfortunately the Daily Record is not widely read in Vienna constraining the Laptop Loyal's ability to launch a successful "let's make thus guy a hun as soon as possible" campaign as per the one that caused Kilmarnock to capitulate after several months of media harassment and therefore allow

Steven Naismith to move to Mordor for six empty ginger bottles and a 10% off at Matalan voucher in 2007.

Incidentally, Austria is predominantly a Catholic country and was the birthplace of Hitler, grim facts which are not lost on the Ibrox men as they staunchly pursue their man – although we will say that Walter didnae want him anyway because he's rubbish and James Beattie is much better if he doesn't get him.

The Walter Commission Report into the McGregor Assassination

by Jim Garrishun

It's the question everyone on the face of the planet knows the answer to – where were you at 12.30pm on the 22nd of August 2010, the exact moment when a great young statesman with an eye for the ladies was cruelly cut down in his prime by a sniper's bullet? Events on that fateful day in Easter Road shocked the world, but none more so than among female rohypnol users across Scotland, who for a few terrifying seconds faced the prospect of having to go to that wee guy off Big Brother for their nat king cole in future. The brave young goalkeeper's body was still warm in the ground when the Establishment authorities leapt into action. There could be no room for allegations of cover-up and collusion; an investigation would have to be carried out with integrity and over 100 years of unsurpassed dignity to establish the facts and crush timmy-esque theories of conspiracy.

LICKSPITTLES

So it came to pass that The Walter Commission was appointed by the nation's highest wanking.... sorry, ranking sports writer James Traynor at 2.15pm that same afternoon, less than two hours after the sniper's bullets echoed throughout no witnesses' eardrums. Chaired by the Man With Nosurname himself, the Walter Commission consisted of such illuminaries as Richard Gordon, Chick Young, Derek Johnstone and senator for the Kinning Park area of Glasgow, Keith "Union" Jackson. These uprectum…sorry, upstanding dignitaries, were aided by various other dependable media lickspittles from the lowest echelons of the Scottish Establishment.

THE INVESTIGATION

Years, nay decades, of dignified lickspittlery meant that this crack team could proceed apace with revealing the true truth of events; not the real truth as betrayed by the lying eyes of the watching populace. The first phase came immediately after the incident itself whereby Commission members Alistair "Goal fur Raaaaaiiiiinjjjjuuurrrrrs!" Alexander, Billy Dodds and Craig "Nakamura and McGeady haven't touched the ball and that's great" Paterson, who were themselves witnessed to the scene of the crime, avoided all reference to it for the remainder of the match. So much so, that listeners tuning in after half time were left completely unaware that a despicable attack had even taken place. The second came in the form of a solemn eulogy from Dickie Gordon on BBC Radio Scotland at the end of the game, who expressed disappointment and regret at events, stating sombrely "this is the kind of thing we don't want to see in Scottish football".

Years of experience in presenting the correct kind of truth to the public, allowed Dickie to skilfully avoid expressions of indignation, accusations of cheating and calls for draconian punishment of the type advocated by the self same people following last season's unsuccessful assassination attempt on Aiden McGeady at the same Easter Road venue. Gordon knew that such behaviour would prove counter-productive in this unique and complex case involving an Establishment club player (cases involving the Establishment club invariably are much more complex and always involve mitigating factors, such as when a player kicks an opponent in the head and the resulting red card is described as "ridiculous"– see lickspittle King, Darrell. Clearly a bullet has to be involved before a red card for a Rangers player is justified). Furthermore Gordon would have been fully aware that such utterances would have dire consequences for his future Winalot privileges.

The next phase of the investigation passed to Chick Young, a veteran and leading global authority on sycophantic interview and oral rectum probing techniques, perfected over the past 20 years and half a dozen Rangers managers. Perhaps Young's finest hour came after the Man with Nosurname saw his team pumped 4-1 at home by a Romanian team who's name sounds like a type of bladder infection. Chicko made sure that in the aftermath no awkward questions were asked; and let's face it in those circumstances, ANY question would have been awkward. The resounding success of that mission is testament to the great man's talent.

"WE HUVNAE ALLEGED ANYTHING"

Following a few pleasantries and compliments on Nosurname's choice of cardigan and with his voice positively exuding trepidation and meekness, Chick got down to the unpleasant and entirely alien task at hand – asking the Rangers manager a question with the potential for an incriminating answer. However this is where Young showed his true blue world class toadying credentials by slipping in the world "alleged", thereby allowing Nosurname to bark back at him (in a dignified manner of course) – "we huvnae alleged anything!". Wiping the perspiration from his brow our valiant lickspittle was able to accept Nosurname's guttural retort as a valid response, leaving the rest of us to wonder if McGregor had suddenly realised he'd forgotten to set the Sky+ box for the Red Hot freeview and suffered a spontaneous paroxysm of anguish. Such is the cynicism of the paranoiac timmy mindset in the face of the irrefutable Bill's truth. Of course the same traitorous timmy mindset will have observed that the Man with Nosurname subjected to Young's advanced rimming techniques and the Nosurname chairing The Walter Commission are one and the same and then no doubt try to read some form of sordid innuendo from it, where it is emphatically clear none exists.

FINDINGS

By 2.45pm on 22nd August 2010, the Walter Commission had concluded its investigation and revealed its findings. Those of a timmy paranoiac mindset were disturbed by the seeming undue haste with which proceedings had been conducted and abruptly terminated, but "let them stroll on" was the media's dignified response.

LONE NUT GUNMAN

The Walter Commission's conclusion was that McGregor was mortally wounded by a headbutt from the grassy penalty area immediately in front of him by a lone nut spikey haired gunman. The perpetrator was identified as one Del O Riordan, a pathological maniac with sordid connections to timmy as the report's findings revealed he spent nearly two years as a resident and employee of the Parkhead piggery, before giving up football altogether and taking a menial job with the Hibernian Shite Footballer Depository (HSFD) overlooking Easter Road. This was found to be compelling and conclusive evidence of motive beyond all reasonable doubt. O Riordan was also condemned in the eyes of Commission chairman The Man With Nosurmame on account of his suspiciously Irishey sounding surname. However his commission colleagues were not keen to dwell on this evidence due to doubts surrounding the validity of a Man With Nosurname commenting on someone else's surname.

PRIME SUSPECT ELIMINATED

Luckily… sorry, unfortunately, The Walter Commission were unable to interview the prime suspect O Riordan in the course of their investigations, as he was eliminated himself before they could do so by a purely accidental blow to the kidneys from misunderstood gangland nice guy Madjid "Eight fouls" Bougherra. It is understood that Eight Fouls was so enraged by O Riordan's timmy treachery, and knowing he had at least another seven fouls in the bank before a yellow card would be administered thanks to an obliging Mason in Black, decided to take matters into his own boot. Speculation abounds amongst paranoid timmies of how Bougherra happened to be in the part of the pitch where O Riordan was fatally injured and that the MIB may have played some sort of role in this in an attempt to cover up certain umpalatable truths, but that's timmy for you.

PUBLIC SPECTICISM AND NO FUCKING CONTACT

Despite the lucidity of their findings, The Walter Commission has since come in for severe criticism from outside Hunnite and Establishment circles after the release of the controversial Youtuber film 24 hours later, taken by Abraham Youtuber from a vantage point only yards away from the grassy penalty area. The damning 7 seconds of footage, shot on Youtubers state of the art Nokia N900 smartphone, clearly shows McGregor's head being flung back and to the left after no fucking contact whatsoever. This has led to over 80% of the Scottish public embracing the "He's just a cheating bastard from a club with a track record of shameless fucking cheating" theory. Other theories have since emerged linking the McGregor assassination to the shooting of compatriots Kyle Laughable by lone-nute Charlie Mulgrew (back at the piggery, say no more) and Kevin "I can't get a broken leg without contact but my leg's not broken" Thomson (shot by Georgie the Greek, a gangster name and a timmy into the bargain, case closed) as an all pervasive and ruthless conspiracy to perpetuate and extend the power of the Hunnery-Industrial complex.

CLASSIFIED DOCUMENTS

To date, no credible evidence has been presented in public to support such claims. Well, at least nothing that Ewen Cameron, Bill Leckie or Jim Traynor will admit to. The Walter Commission and other classified SFA documents are not due for public release until 2075 and are exempt from Freedom of Information legislation in the absence of the correct funny handshake.

Rangers' "impressive" European Record
15th September 2010

Anyone perusing the sports pages of the Daily Record, Sun or any other Scottish newspaper this week could be forgiven for thinking they have been living in an alternative universe for the past few years. Prior to last night's bore-a-thon between Man Utd and Rangers, the aforementioned rags were full to the brim with platitudes to the Man with No Surname - *"Sir Alex: Walter's the only boss I fear"* - that sort of shit, and slavvering praise of the Huns' *"impressive"* away record, with token reference to their *"disappointing"* home record. Much was made of the fact that both of Rangers' two points in last year's Champions league were garnered away from home.

Incidentally, that tally of two points is another record that the Scottish press can't bring themselves to mention, the lowest ever points total of any British side in the Champions League, although Jackson, Traynor, Keevins & co were foaming at the mouth when Celtic played Villareal in December 2008 needing a win to avoid taking that dubious distinction from the Govan Orcs. The win was duly secured although with great emphasis placed by the

Scottish media on the under-strength team fielded by the Spaniards and their apparent lack of commitment, the media displaying all the traits of bitter huns enraged at a Celtic victory. Of course we can console ourselves in the knowledge that if Rangers ever pull off a good resultm say a 0-0 draw, against a big-name team fielding a weakened line-up, picking a hypothetical example totally at random, say – Man United – equal emphasis would be placed on this fact. [ahem] Anyway… all mention of this particular entry in the history books disappeared into the ether with Celtic's victory to be brought out again only if the Celts ever face the same prospect again, although Rangers seem determined to go on lowering the bar as far as that particular record is concerned.

But let's take a slightly closer look at the claims made by the Central Quay Rangers Supporters branch. So Rangers had an "*impressive*" away record in last year's Champion's League did they? Two points from a possible nine. Fuck me, what a sensational record that is. Picking up 22% of the points available is not something most of us would describe as "*impressive*".

Now, we all acknowledge that Celtic's away record in the Champions League is pish. Keith Union Jackson and his cronies love nothing more than to revel in this and rhyme off the stats. "1 point in 15 attempts… 1 point from 16 games yadda yadda yadda". Such references are punctuated with words such as "dismal", "abysmal" and "appalling". It doesn't even need to be an away game for this to be dredged up. Jangle began his match report on Celtic's 2-0 win over Villareal with "*people who say Celtic's away record is rotten have a point but usually Celtic don't*", the semi-literate Jackson having given up a promising stand up career touring Orange Lodges to scribble pish like this in Scotland's Establishment rag.

Now to be fair, as I mentioned, the rags did make a token reference to the Dignity's shitey performances at home last season, although these were described as "*disappointing*". Terms such as "appalling","dreadful" and "shocking", as well as cracking the jokes about three point plugs in Europe, are reserved for Timmy.

So how does this record stack up?

DIGNITY HOME CL RECORD SEASON 2008/09
Played 3, Won 0, Drawn 0, Lost 3, F 2, A 10, PTS 0

Add on Dignity's two previous home games from the previous season's CL:

DIGNITY HOME CL RECORD LAST 5 GAMES
Played 5, Won 0, Drawn 1, Lost 4, F 2, A 14, PTS 1

1 point from a possible 15, goal difference = minus 12.

If that's not "appalling", "dismal" or "dreadful", I don't know what is. "Disappointing" is not the adjective any objective observer would use.

And yes, I realise I have selectively left out the Dark Side's opening CL victory of season 2007/08, but if the Scottish media can selectively ignore season 1997/98 on a technicality in an effort to bum up the Fat Monster Much Eater at the expense of Henrik Larsson then I can do the same, with much more justification.

Finally, a lot has been said about the outstanding tactical abilities of the Man with no Surname. The Scottish press have laughably attempted to convince us that Alex Ferguson is in some way intimidated by the man who led Rangers to humiliation at the hands of such illustrious teams as Grasshoppers, Strasbourg, Kaunas and Unirea Urziceni, whilst at the same time painting a picture of these "giants" of the game engaged in mutual fellatio given their achievements in the gamem though in the course of their sycophantic zeal they don't explain how many CIS Cups is equal to a European Cup.

Anyway, let's have a look at this record that has Sir Awex keeching his Ys:

Played 31, Won 5, Drawn 11, Lost 15. Won 16%. Last 12 games in Europe without a win.

So you might be now able to see why I find today's lectures from the Orc minions on what it takes to get a result in Europe as akin to George Michael giving advice on how to remain celibate.

History Lesson no.101: The Scottish Media – PR arm of the Scottish Football Establishment

With a regularity that seems to correlate with the severity of their financial difficulties these days, the question of refereeing bias towards Rangers explodes onto the back pages of the Scottish press, flares for a brief moment then gradually recedes to dampened embers largely due to a concentrated effort on behalf of the Scottish Football Establishment to submerge the issue in a vat of cold water. Without exception, when such controversy rears its head following the familiar experience of a sustained period of highly dubious decisions aiding the Forces of Darkness, a counter attack is led by the nation's press aided, of course, by a vanguard of retired players in the pay of the same media and retired referees, some of whom were involved in equally controversial pro-Rangers decisions during their careers. The sports hacks from the Fourth Estate (as it would like to call itself) are, believe it or not, all rabid cheerleaders for the Dark Side by nature, although many certainly are, however to make it in the mainstream media a certain amount of personal compromise must be adopted to enable career progression.

The situation is best summed up by the media watch project, Media Lens. Referring to the ability of journalists to present officially promoted fiction as fact, the website FAQ states: "*We believe that the all-too-human tendency to self-deception accounts for their conviction that they are honest purveyors of uncompromised truth. We all have a tendency to believe what best suits our purpose; highly paid, highly privileged editors and journalists are no exception. In any case, professionals whose attitudes and opinions most closely serve the needs of corporate power, whether in media institutions or elsewhere, are more likely to be filtered through to positions of authority within such institutions.*" In other words those who toe the line are far more likely to climb up the greasy pole of career progression. During controversies, mainstream media journalists invariably adopt a neutrality facade in order to present the corporate line as their own objective opinion. Media Lens rightly regards such 'neutrality' as a sham: "*We believe that media 'neutrality' is a deception that often serves to hide systematic pro-corporate bias. 'Neutrality' most often involves 'impartially' reporting dominant establishment views, while ignoring or marginalising non-establishment views.*"

In the context of Scottish Football, pro-corporate bias can be seen in the dedicated efforts to protect the reputation and interests of the sport's governing bodies and its minions by promoting the Establishment line in the face of overwhelming evidence. It results for example in the vociferous response from the corporate media to Fergus McCann's refusal to walk away from the Jorge Cadete registration scandal, and the outpouring of sympathy for Farry following Celtic's vindication. Despite an independent commission finding beyond doubt that the SFA chief executive deliberately delayed Cadete's registration until after the 1996 Scottish Cup semi-final against Rangers, which Celtic lost 2-1, the corporate media took great pains to attribute the event solely to Farry's penchant for officious bureaucracy or a simple personality clash between McCann and Farry. Farry was the lone gunman on the Park Gardens grassy knoll. The fact that prior to the commission finding, the SFA's internal inquiries amazingly, but inevitably, exonerated Farry, was brushed aside. The SFA had resorted to the standard tactic of any institution found guilty of corruption, blame it all on one "rogue" person of evil spirit acting alone to serve their own agenda, independent of the organisation. This simply doesn't wash. It is inconceivable that Jim Farry could have lasted three years obstructing and obfuscating, with the full support of the media in such a case where Rangers were the injured party. Farry was able to operate within a culture amenable to progressing an agenda against Celtic and to blame everything on one individual; however culpable he clearly was; is utterly mendacious.

Only one newspaper really questioned the lone accidental gunman theory, The Scotsman on 2 March 1999, "*A Fall Guy Named Farry*", pointed out the impossibility of Farry alone dragging out the investigation process for three years: "*At the very least, the office bearers, John McBeth, of Clyde; Chris Robinson of Hearts (both vice-presidents) and George Peat of Airdrie (treasurer), should have insisted on examining all pertinent material and accelerating the process. Their lack of action is at least the equal of Farry's, even if the chief executive, as the man in charge of administration, was the starting-point for the improper handling of the matter."* The article continues: *"The former Lord Dervaird, for example, would surely have questioned how internal inquiries into the business at Park Gardens could possibly have exonerated Farry on a previous occasion when the case presented by Celtic proved to be unopposable."* A lone voice in the corporate media wilderness, and McCann's summary that the whole episode pointed to an "institutional bias" was of course not given the time of day.

Added to the Establishment cheerleading there is an almost deferential attitude to certain Scottish figures that practically eliminates the possibility of any real critical comment or assessment. With David Murray for example such veneration allows the most fantastic nonsense to be swallowed by corporate journalists then vomited onto the back pages. Who can forget the incredible media celebration over Murray's laughable Ronaldo PR stunt, or indeed the near universal acclaim heaped onto the Rangers owner by the corporate media when he emerged from honorary chairman purdah in 2004 to present his Cunning Plan to restore Rangers finances? The Cunning Plan you may recall involved nothing more than some vague idea about "trading out of trouble". Despite the poverty of Murray's scheme, which had been promoted breathlessly for a full week leading up to the Grand Announcement, very few hacks bothered to ask any troubling questions, or indeed any questions at all, simply presenting this wafer-thin stunt as another magnificent Murray coup. If you wish to look for evidence of a total lack of 'neutrality' when it comes to Rangers and David Murray, look no further than this national embarrassment.

To further understand the relationship between the Scottish Football Establishment, of which the mainstream media is part, and Rangers, the fact has to be recognised that for most of the 20th century up to the present day, Rangers were and are the adopted team of the Establishment. Only through the patronage of the Establishment could Rangers maintain their infamous sectarian employment policy for so long, with silence from the SFA and practically the entire mainstream media, with a few notable exceptions, being absolutely deafening. Not until UEFA started to take an interest in the late 1980s and Graeme Souness, to his credit, showed the necessary willingness to break the sectarian lines, did the barriers reluctantly come down. Similarly it was only when UEFA embarrassed the SFA by explaining their decision not to punish Rangers for the bigoted chants of its supporters during their game against Villarreal in 2006 that Park Gardens began to move on the matter, if only to keep up appearances.

As Roddy Forsyth of The Telegraph reported following the successful appeal against the original UEFA decision not to punish: *"Uefa appealed against the decision of the control and disciplinary body - an autonomous committee within Uefa - after Rangers had been acquitted on the grounds that the game's authorities could not be expected to clean up problems effectively sanctioned socially by custom and usage."* Although this was bizarrely trumpeted by Rangers supporters as a complete exoneration (which reveals much about their thought processes, or lack thereof), UEFA had basically stated *'why should we do something about this when Scottish authorities, including the SFA, are doing zip?'* It should be noted at this point, that when faced with a growing demand to end Rangers' protected status, the SFA chief executive, ex-Rangers player Gordon Smith, in October 2007 whined as he launched into an appeal to leave Rangers alone: *""Rangers are going through a hard time at the moment and to a certain degree there is an agenda against them. Celtic have always thought that people were against them, but now Rangers are starting to feel the same."* Diddums.

The corporate media either treat accusations of official bias with lofty disdain, ridicule, or when the evidence against Rangers is overwhelming, by adopting the 'neutrality' approach which accuses both Celtic and Rangers of equally gaining from officials at the expense of other teams. The latter also aids in maintaining the fiction of "wee team" support in the media, that as Graham Spiers pointed out is a laughable con. A typical example of this 'both as bad as each other' approach would be STV's Ronnie Esplin's effort following sustained criticism of pro-Rangers decisions. Suddenly the controversy also involved favouritism to Celtic: *"Are Scottish referees really biased towards Rangers and Celtic? Ronnie Esplin considers the logistics of referees favouring **the Old Firm** after a month of 'mistakes' by officials."* In this article Esplin offers the examples of Kris Boyd's absurd yellow card for "obstruction" and Ross Forbe's wrongly disallowed goal against Rangers as to why the subject is a hot-topic of the moment. Answers on a postcard as to the justification for including Celtic in the controversy.

Esplin is by no means unique in trying this on, yet while it is true that **all** clubs occasionally benefit from match officials mistakes, the sheer volume in Rangers' favour either forces each "balancing" article into vague generalisation, or alternatively, the adoption of marginal or uncontroversial decisions as evidence, such as the now legendary Kris Boyd "disallowed" goal against Motherwell. Walter Smith too, isn't shy of including less controversial decisions on the rare occasions when faced with questions about match officials favouritism. In his after match press conference following Rangers draw at Fir Park in February, Smith responded when asked about the aforementioned Ross Forbes' disallowed goal which would have put the home side 2-0 up: *"But I think if I can remember correctly we had a goal knocked off in a [previous] match here, a goal by Kris Boyd. So sometimes they go for you, and sometimes against you. If you wish to cast your mind back, we would have won that game if we had got that one. So it balances out. I thought? I would remind you of that."* Indeed, maybe someone should have reminded Smith that a goal can't be scored after the referee's whistle has blown for an infringement, offside in this case. In the game in November 2008, which ended goalless, the linesman's flag and subsequent referee whistle meant that play had largely stopped by the time Boyd thumped the goal into the next, an act described by the Daily Mail as 'frustration'.

In short the mainstream media have a corporate inclination to lend unwavering support to the football Establishment regardless of the evidence, although there's an important exception to this which we'll look at later. As an example of the media wagon-circling in the face controversy, we can look at the then Dundee United manager Craig Levein's withering attack on notorious referee Mike McCurry following a truly outrageous performance by the match officials when United visited Ibrox on 10th May 2008. In the course of that game United were denied the most obvious of penalty awards which would have seen David Weir sent off, had a goal disallowed for a ludicrous offside call, and Kirk Broadfoot and Daniel Cousin avoided reprimand for punching Noel Hunt and headbutting Mark De Vries in the face respectively. A selection of Levein's after match quotes –

"**It's impossible to win here in important games**. *The referee bottled it because he knew if he'd given the penalty Weir had to go. He knew it was a penalty but the game was so important to Rangers he couldn't give it. The assistant probably had a better view than the ref but he won't put his head above the parapet, will he?"*

"It's Rangers at Ibrox. You can't win that. An important game, a title decider? We can't have Dundee United winning that game. Who gives a toss about United, eh? Swanson's goal is a good one as well. It hits Weir and goes in. We deserved to get something from the game - but you cannot win"

"I said to the ref we'd be as well not turning up. What's the point? Mike could have phoned me this morning and said: 'Look, Rangers are going to get the points, tell your lads to stay in the house. But people don't think about that. It's all about the pressure on Rangers. The importance to them."

"And if you give a decision against them you get hammered. **Can you imagine if this was the other way round? McCurry would never referee another game.***"*

After the [CIS Cup] *final I did my best not to have a go at the referee* [Kenny Clark] *for denying us a penalty* [when Cuellar blatantly pulled back Kalvenes in the penalty area]. *Maybe some people have mistaken kindness for weakness on my part.*

There's no doubt if you add what happened today to the cup final then I've every right to be furious. Noel Hunt got punched in the face at the [disallowed] *goal. He has a split tongue - a deliberate punch by Broadfoot. And Cousin head-butted Wilkie. The referee should control the Rangers players."*

Incredibly it wasn't McCurry who incurred the media's wrath, it was Levein. In the face of an intense media backlash, Levein later toned down his criticism, and United owner Eddie Thompson attempted to calm troubled waters by resorting to the "balanced" bolthole, bizarrely claiming that McCurry's performance was proof that match officials are biased in favour of "*the Old Firm*" and, in the lack of anything approaching an equivalent circumstance involving Celtic, desperately resorted to calling Scott McDonald a diver. George Peat, SFA president, reacted to McCurry's shocking performance by lambasting Levein's comments as "*criminal*" without elaborating on which laws Levein was supposed to have violated. Clearly, under the Scottish Football Establishment model of law and order, a rape victim would be committing a crime by making a complaint against her attacker.

The corporate media's inability, or unwillingness, to objectively report can be witnessed in the reporting of the events in the two games against Rangers in season 2009/10 which led to Celtic making official representations to the SFA over the actions of match officials. When news of these discussions was leaked, media reports of George Peat's knicker-wetting outrage carefully avoided mention of the cause of Celtic's concern or rigorously downplayed the relevant information. It took a non-Scottish source, World Sports Network website WSN.com, to report the issue with any semblance of objectivity: "*Both Old Firm games this season have seen major decisions go against Celtic, including several penalty claims during their 2-1 defeat at Ibrox in October, most notably when David Weir felled Shaun Maloney without punishment from Craig Thomson. Marc-Antoine Fortune had a goal controversially disallowed by Steve Conroy in the 1-1 draw at Celtic Park on January 3 for a foul on Rangers goalkeeper Allan McGregor.*"

Compare the WSN quote to the reporting of the same story in that infamous rag, the Daily Record: "*Celtic **believe** they were denied at least one penalty in the first Old Firm derby of the season at Ibrox in October - a match which Rangers won 2-1 - and also **insist** they were denied a legitimate goal during the 1-1 draw New Year's Parkhead fixture.*" Craig Thomson's admission of a "mistake" regarding the Maloney penalty claim is ignored by Keith Jackson when reporting on the 2-1 match, and the near universal confirmation that Fortune's goal was legitimate is reduced to Celtic alone insisting the goal was legal. In none of his reporting will you find mention of concerns over the fact that Kyle Lafferty was allowed to remain on the pitch at Celtic Park after a horrendous "leg-breaker" two-footed tackle on Andreas Hinkel.

You'll have noted a running theme here, of referees admitting to more than the usual number of "mistakes" benefiting Rangers. McCurry also admitted to "mistakes" after the aforementioned Dundee United shocker. Even when mistakes in Rangers favour are acknowledged, there is no follow-up to join up the dots or attempt to investigate just why it is Rangers benefit from match official's "errors" far more than any other team. Such a topic, that should be ripe for exploration by any self-respecting investigative journalist, isn't touched with a bargepole by the corporate media for reasons already outlined. The most that can be inferred is concerns about the general standard of refereeing, or the smokescreen of "Old Firm" bias. Yet incompetence would surely manifest itself in a general sharing of injustices amongst clubs to a similar degree? That clearly does not happen so how can such a defence be maintained?

To underline the propaganda offensive, Celtic were criticised during the spat with Peat after the game against Rangers on 28th February for not taking up an offer to meet with Hugh Dallas, the SFA's Head of Referee Development, "*despite the fact that at the start of the season Dallas made clear his door was open to any aggrieved manager*". Again the fact that 'impartial' Hugh Dallas featured in several controversial incidents involving Celtic, including the infamous 1999 league clincher for Rangers at Celtic Park where he clearly lost the plot and may as well have donned a Rangers top, is blithely ignored. Would Dallas have thrown up his hands and offered a mea culpa shedding bitter tears asking forgiveness for those match officials whose integrity has been compromised by such unbalanced "mistakes"? I doubt it very much. It's a bit like making a complaint to the "Independent" Police Complaints Commission who then instruct the police to investigate themselves – a waste of time. After all, one game filled with pro-Rangers decisions would be unfortunate, two in succession is getting beyond a joke, but three? If Hugh Dallas needs a visit from Tony Mowbray or Neil Lennon to bring his attention to the smell of decomposing herring then he's deliberately blocked his nostrils.

Yet what of the SFA, can they really be instructing referees to act in a nefarious manner? Isn't such an accusation so ludicrous that it merits the hooting and braying from the corporate media? Well, perhaps if there was no evidence for prior form on this, but there is. To fully understand the situation in Scotland, and to wholly appreciate the ability of the game to be warped in favour of one team, you need look no further than the circumstances surrounding the treatment of Paul Gascoigne during his Rangers career. Similarly to appreciate that accusations of bias regarding match referees are not just the produce of gripe and girn, one only needs to look at the events of season 1997-1998 and the behaviour of one Bobby Tait. First though let's ponder Gascoigne's interesting relationship with match officials.

In 1995 Paul Gascoigne joined Rangers for a fee of £4.3m, his signing was proclaimed a great coup for Murray and consequently Scottish football. The journalist Gerry McNee revealed on STV's Scotsport programme that the SFA had instructed match officials to protect the player and to show leniency due to his notoriously volatile temperament (the theory being that sneaks would provoke the big bairn into temper tantrums). Any doubt over the validity of McNee's claim dissipated as Gascoigne was allowed to rampage through season after season, mixing incredible skill with brutal thuggery, while miraculously avoiding a red card. No other player has managed to accumulate thirteen yellow cards in one season without encountering a red somewhere along the line. The issue was covered by Bryan Scott in the Daily Mail following Gascoigne's eventual overdue dismissal in November 1997. "Cynics might wonder at this point why, prior to Wednesday, no Scottish referee had ever red-carded Gascoigne, who courts trouble on a regular basis by using his arms and elbows as a dubious means of protection," he said. "Were they afraid to risk attracting the notoriety of being the first to deal severely with the biggest-name player at Scotland's biggest club and, if so, might Rowbotham have rid them of their inhibition?" No one asked if they were merely obeying orders.

Rowbotham not only committed the cardinal sin of actually red carding Gascoigne, he awarded enough legitimate injury time for Celtic, through Alan Stubbs, to grab a late injury time equaliser which contributed in no small way to Celtic winning the league title and stopping Rangers ten-in-a-row bid. Walter Smith afterwards accused Rowbotham of lacking impartiality, presumably referring to the slating Rowbotham received when he failed to take action against Gascoigne in 1995. On that occasion the lovable rogue inflicted five stitches on Aberdeen's Paul Bernard's face and head-butted John Inglis in the chest. Gascoigne wasn't even booked for either incident, however such was the level of mayhem at the game that the Procurator Fiscal asked Strathclyde Police to examine 'certain incidents' during the match. Probably panicking due to Rowbotham's strict interpretation of the Hands-Off command, "Gazza and defender John Brown were hauled before the SFA on the strength of ref supervisor Don McVicar's report and given one-game bans". Rowbotham had a career "stall" after the game but found himself in Coventry after red carding Gascoigne, although quite why is anyone's guess as he clearly followed the rules on that occasion. Maybe that was his mistake.

Another referee who found himself in a bit of a pickle due to Gascoigne and the no sending off rule was Jim McGilvray. During a game against Partick Thistle in February 1996, McGilvray followed the rules, however stupid, and booked Gascoigne for leaving the pitch to celebrate his goal. So that's Gascoigne on a yellow, which means that from now on nothing can be done against him for the remainder of the game, and that's just how it turned out. Despite two further bookable offences, including stamping and wrestling, McGilvray failed to hand Gascoigne a second caution. Afterwards McGilvray justified his behaviour by laying the blame on the SFA, huffing that their rules regarding leaving the field of play during goal celebrations forced him to harshly book Gascoigne, and then the poor mite felt unable to dish out a second yellow in case the harshness of the original decision caused a riot amongst the followers of Dignity. Yes you read that right. Leaving aside the fact that the third bookable offence should have removed any moral qualms, McGilvray felt no similar inner turmoil or fears for public safety when it came to Partick Thistle's Roddy McDonald in the same match. McDonald walked due to two yellow cards, the first which most missed as it was issued as the player left the pitch at the end of the first half.

According to Partick Thistle, McDonald was cautioned for crossing himself as he left the pitch, a regular trait. "*Rod was completely innocent, I am convinced of that. He crossed himself, as he does during every game,*" claimed Murdo McLeod the then Partick Manager. "*And there no way he was trying to incite.*" An unnamed player stated: "*Rod was very upset at the end of the match. He just couldn't understand why he'd been booked, then sent off.*" McGilvray you'll note had no problems with booking someone for blessing themselves, but felt the goal celebration rule was a bit harsh.

Interestingly enough McGilvray did not witness the heinous act committed by McDonald, instead two Rangers supporters complained to Plod who then drew the referee's attention to this perilous assault on civilisation as we know it.

Sixteen days after that game McGilvray resigned, blaming the SFA for imposing restraints on match officials that were making the job impossible. Initial crisis management of the decision quickly fell apart with McGilvray the object of intense media attacks and no some amount of gaitling gun attack by the SFA Chief Executive, Jim Farry. One unnamed "Grade one" match official was quoted by the Daily Record hissing: "*Jim's talking rubbish when he says he didn't want to send Gascoigne off because it would have caused a riot. All he's doing is trying to justify the decision he took not to send him off. But what he HAS done is reinforce the myth that there is one rule for Rangers and another for the rest - which is utter rubbish.*" McGilvray's real crime was to give the game away, can't have that at all. Tellingly, McGilvray did not come under this sustained media barrage for his actual performance at Firhill, rather for his criticism of the SFA. You may wonder what was the greatest offence, failing in his job or having a spat with his ex-employers, clearly the corporate media came down heavily on the latter which says a hell of a lot about their perspective. Moving on we come to another period of intense

In an ironic but predictable twist, McGilvray was later rehabilitated by the Daily Record following Hugh Dallas's 1999 spectacular, the same newspaper that carried headlines in 1996 such as "*McGilvray's gone from a referee to a whinesman*" (geddit??) and "*Bottler Jim let us all down*". The bold Jim was trooped out as an ex-top grade one official to give Dallas' performance a clean bill of health and to condemn accusations of bias thrown at the unfairly maligned referee. Moving on we come to another period of intense bias in favour of Rangers by match officials, their Ten-in-a-row build up

Now as Celtic supporters we are used to having to cope with referees and their assistants pulling out all the stops for Rangers in their time of need, but season 1997-1998 will be remembered for many things including the sight of Bobby Tait throwing all caution to the wind for the cause. Prior to his penultimate performance Tait had officiated at two highly controversial games that season involving Celtic and Hearts. In February 1998 Celtic played Hearts at Tynecastle in a game of huge importance, a win would see Celtic go top of the league by two points. Tait got into this stride by first disallowing a perfectly good Morten Weighorst goal, described by Glen Gibbons of The Scotsman thus "*Referee Tait indicated that he had controlled the ball with his hand, but, to the naked eye and, relying on Wieghorst's vehement protest as a guide, it seemed a pretty severe judgement*", then manufactured several minutes injury time at end of the second half despite a lack of stoppages to account foe this. With Celtic leading by a single goal, and with Tait checking his watch several times (no doubt wondering how far he could push it), a deflected Quintongo goal deep in injury time levelled the scores. Celtic restarted the game by driving at the Hearts box, and with Weighorst bearing down on goal Tait blew for full time.

The next encounter at Parkhead in March, had Tait overseeing a bruising encounter between the two teams, yet only one side was penalised while the other appeared to be authorised to rampage at will - I'll leave you to guess which of the two teams. On this occasion with Celtic pressing to break the deadlock, Tait brought the game to a close after adding a mere 47 seconds injury time, despite several lengthy stoppages for injuries during this "tousy" encounter. When news broke that Tait had asked the SFA for, and was allocated, the last home Rangers game of the season versus Kilmarnock to officiate as his farewell appearance (bizarrely this happens apparently), black clouds of suspicion descended in the minds of Celtic supporters, if not the see-no-evil-hear-no-evil media. The league was balanced on a knife-edge and could go either way. With Rangers requiring three points from this vital game the decision to hand it to a well-known Rangers supporting referee would be viewed with incredulity in most countries. Not here though. In what was possibly the greatest moment of karma in Scottish football, Tait played four minutes injury time in the first half and a further four in the second despite nowhere near this amount of time being taken up by injuries, only for Kilmarnock's Ally Mitchell to grab a winning goal deep into injury time at the end of the match, leaving Celtic needing just one win from their last two games to win the league and stop the ten.

The possibility that a referee could have acted the same way in relation to Celtic and for it to have gone without critical comment by the media is simply beyond plausibility. Similarly does anyone seriously believe that if Paul Gascoigne had signed for Celtic, match officials would have shrieked at the possibility of showing a red card for his elbow and head-butting antics? No, it's simply not credible. Only Rangers could have enjoyed such benevolence and as Rangers' need grows so too does the ability of that club to benefit from match official eccentricities and "mistakes". Back in the nineties it was Rangers burning desire to reach Ten-in-a-row, an event probably heralding Armageddon, now it's their desperate attempts to extract themselves from the financial mire. Whenever the call goes out, the Scottish Football Establishment can be relied upon to respond and act accordingly. Equally the corporate media can be relied upon to act as a propaganda wing, ignoring and deflecting the injustices, muddying the waters and lambasting those daring to voice dissent. When the league is effectively over and Rangers are safe, match officials can safely throw Celtic a bone in the shape of a couple of "dodgy" decisions to allow journalists to claim things have "evened out".

Aiden McGeady was subject to show trial by media following his comments on the Dougie McDonald show at Ibrox in February 2010. *"The comments before the game might have played on his mind,"* said McGeady at the weekend. *"It's safe to say he wasn't impartial the other day. Of course it didn't look like a red card for Scott Brown."* Considering the fact that McDonald certainly did not deal with the Brown-Lafferty incident impartially as one was red carded and the other let off without even a caution, it really is an act of intellectual acrobatics to construe such a comment as being controversial, however this is an area that the Scottish media excels with years of experience in twisting and spinning stories to pander to Rangers. Tony Mowbray defended McGeady by claiming the player had found the word lying in the street and didn't actually know what it meant, no doubt seeking to defuse the situation with a wee dash of humour. However the Scottish media suddenly rediscovered their keen investigate faculties for some unknown reason and STV took great delight in informing everyone that McGeady was a clever cookie, revealing his high school grades and informing an astonished nation that his father is an English teacher. Clearly McGeady has no defence and we must brace ourselves for his public flogging when the SFA's general purposes inquisition demands his appearance. Not everyone who questions match officials is punished of course, especially if they are called Walter Smith.

Let's recall at this point that Rangers sent a "*sharply worded letter of complaint*" over the appointment of Rowbotham for the midweek derby match in November 1998. And what do you know... the word "*impartial*" was used. "*Because of events following the game against Aberdeen two years ago there was no way he could be **impartial***", the letter stated. "*He was under extreme pressure and the bottom line is that this time he should not have been appointed in the first place.*" Rowbotham it seemed could not be impartial due to a match that had occurred two years previously, despite having refereed **three** Rangers games in the meantime. Rangers of course were not punished or asked to explain this accusation, by either the SFA or the Scottish media. Rowbotham on the other hand didn't get off so lightly. More recently Walter Smith questioned the impartiality of linesman Tom Murphy following the so-called disallowed goal at Fir Park in November 2008, by girning: "*I think it is shown quite clearly that Boyd was onside. Mr Murphy was quick to allow a Scott McDonald goal at Celtic Park last season and he was quick to disallow that one tonight.*" With a name like Murphy he has to be a biased Celtic supporter right? You'll not be surprised to hear that Smith escaped SFA punishment. Escaping punishment at the same time was Falkirk striker Michael Higdon who accused referee Iain Brines of being a Celtic fan.

Rangers are a club who have benefited from Establishment favour for nigh on a century. Nothing has changed nor will it do so unless changed is forced upon the Scottish game. The sheer extent of the dishonesty in season 2009/10 reflects the Establishment's confidence in their invulnerability, and will remain so unless confronted. Match officials may not have won Rangers the league by themselves, Celtic's own deficiencies hold no small responsibility, but they certainly have contributed. Such a situation should be considered an embarrassment in a civilised society where sport is governed by rules and structures designed to ensure fair play. In Scotland clearly that ideal exists as nothing more than an abstract concept. One club is placed above and beyond the rules, whilst the others, and certainly their only real rival, are expected to accept injustice in silence.

"Dougie, Dougie" and the Definition of Conspiracy

con·spir·a·cy

[k*uh* n-**spir**-*uh*-see]
–*noun, plural* -cies.

1. *A combination of persons for a secret, unlawful, or evil purpose*

2. *Any concurrence in action; combination in bringing about a given result*

"Conspiracy" is a word that gets banded about a lot these days, but you get the distinct impression that those who wield it as a weapon to belittle the arguments of opponents, have little understanding of the actual meaning of the word. The chances are – if you are lucky enough to be employed in these hard economic times – your place of work is a conspiracy. You and your fellow employees conspire, some more effectively than others no doubt, to ensure as best you can that the goals of the organisation are met. This model is replicated across the length and breadth of the country in tens of thousands of organisations. There is nothing underhand or sinister about it. There is no need for surreptitious meetings in darkened rooms or for speaking in code in hushed voices – although you may be unfortunate enough to have to endure the odd sleep-inducing team meeting. Instructions are given, received and understood, and many codes of acceptable behaviour are observed without the need for a diagram on the wall or for everyone to get together and plan how they're going to behave in meticulous detail.

Managerial styles vary from workplace to workplace, and even from manager to manager within the same workplace. It is not uncommon to find that more latitude may be available from one manager to the next. Jimmy might be OK with you coming back from lunch five minutes late, whilst Senga comes down on you like a ton of bricks. This is learned quickly through first-hand experience or by observing the experience of others. It is not necessary for all of the workers to gather together and formulate an elaborate plan involving everyone coming back five minutes late from lunch on Jimmy's shift. This happens because Jimmy tolerates it, and everyone is quite capable of reaching this conclusion independently, and from there, acting in their own self-interest, which just happens to coincide with those of their fellow workers i.e. to have a fly extra fag, to get one last bet on in the bookies or to get an extra hand of cards in; because we know Big Jimmy won't mind a wee extra five minutes before we get back to work. On the other hand we know that Senga is not someone to be messed with, so we won't be able to hang around for the result of the 1.35 at Kempston if we want to still be in a job by the end of the week.

Humans are social animals. It is estimated that 90% of human communication is non-verbal. We pick up on all sorts of signals and subtle shifts in mood to gauge a social situation. In your workplace you will no doubt have a clear idea of what kinds of behaviours and opinions are likely to curry favour and which should be surpressed if you want your career to progress, or even to keep your job. No-one has talked you through every single scenario that could possibly arise, but you may observe how Wee Jeanie has destroyed any chances she had of promotion by challenging management directives once too often. Her card has been marked. She is not management material. The management team have not held clandestine meetings with Jeanie's truculence at the top of the agenda and from there gone on to hatch a nefarious plan to ensure she never gets promoted. But each individual manager knows her personality, and more importantly knows the managing director's opinion of her, and they know the difficulties they would have in keeping the staff in line if her rebelliousness was ever rewarded with promotion to a position of authority – they are online with the message. She is not a company woman.

If this is a scenario that almost all workplaces can readily identify with, why should the SFA, or the BBC, or the Daily Record, or referees, be any different? Many of us have worked in shops, fast-food outlets or pubs where we've had to adapt our behaviour to meet the vagaries of the customer's whims. Why should the Daily Record be any different? If the Daily Record knows the lion's share of their customers are Rangers supporters and supporters of other clubs who are basically a watered down version, why would they not adjust their behaviour (i.e. their reporting) to meet the whims of their customer base? Similarly, if you are a referee and you see Steve Conroy being hounded and branded "controversial" for quite reasonably sending off a Rangers player, but in stark contrast, Mike McCurry and Dougie McDonald defended to the hilt by the same media after numerous abysmal glaring errors, surely it would only be human to take the path of least resistance when a "50-50" call comes around next time, even if it turns out to be a blatant "honest mistake"? After all, you know that your peers and the whole of the Scottish media will rally to defend you – as long as the correct team benefits from your "honest mistakes" of course.

I know if I was a referee, and I saw Gary Hooper falling in the penalty box under a defender's challenge and I wasn't quite sure whether there was contact or not, I wouldn't need a briefing before the match with Peter Lawwell to give Celtic the benefit of the doubt and award a penalty. I may have to forfeit my career as a Grade One referee mind you, but I wouldn't need any Celtic-minded co-conspirators to prompt me to give Celtic the odd dodgy penalty here, and disallow the odd good goal for their opponents there, and vice-versa when it came to Rangers.

Referees and journalists are the product of lobby systems, whereby it is necessary to ingratiate yourself with (i.e. 'lobby') your superiors or the Establishment to progress or even maintain your standing. This system weeds out those who fail to conform, only allowing those who are willing to operate within strict confines of the acceptable to progress to positions of responsibility. Even those mainstream media figures we know as mavericks, such as Graham Spiers, operate within these boundaries, taking great care not to cross lines so avoiding a terminal career stop. Therefore Spiers can talk of Dougie McDonald skirting with the **perception** of being biased to Rangers, but is careful to emphasise his opinion that this refereeing "*form slump*" is in no way related to favouritism in any shape or form.

Journalists operate within such boundaries, not through naked coercion, but as a part of a system that restricts career progression to those able or willing to follow the rules. David Edwards, a political writer specialising in analysis of corporate media, said of the mainstream political commentator Andrew Marr:

"*To listen to, and believe, mainstream journalists like Marr - who is undoubtedly an honest and sincere individual - is to be stifled and bemused by a necessarily superficial, misleading and confusing version of the world that cannot make sense because it cannot address the real issues. Marr is not a liar and he is not a crude propagandist; he is the unwitting product of a system that selects for the ability to talk intelligently and convincingly about anything and everything,* **so long as it is not genuinely costly to power.** *The crucial factor is that individuals are able to do this sincerely and with the firm conviction that what they are saying is the uncompromised, freely-expressed truth.* **This, in the end, is the real genius of the modern system of thought control** *- it is very subtle, invisible, and its greatest victims are often not the deceived but the deceivers themselves.*"

What Edwards is describing is a natural bias, a natural perspective applied to world events distilled through a lens of pre-conceived dogma, in Marr's case, the notion that the UK and other Western states are fully democratic nations, guided by the will of their electorate, and that our foreign policy is entirely benign and configured for the common good of the people who's nations we have to selflessly invade. In this way, the idea that Tony Blair could be a war criminal cannot be countenanced as he merely made, well…"honest mistakes", borne of pure benevolent intentions to deal with a tyrant and to bring freedom to poor oppressed masses – and nothing to do with oil or staying on the coat tails of our superpower ally, or some would say, master. Britannia rules the waves right enough.

This level of denial allows journalists to talk passionately of bringing freedom to the Iraqi population, of our armies leaving just as soon as "free elections" can be held (to install a puppet leader), and other lofty motives; whilst at the very same time these self-deceiving words are being uttered, our armies are rushing off to secure oilfields and pipelines, and the US is building permanent military bases.

The dynamic at play here is that mainstream journalists are naturally biased for a number of reasons, the major one being that they have observed enough of the subtle and not so subtle signals over the course of their experience to ascertain the parameters within which they can comment (i.e. Tony Blair can be accused of well-intentioned blundering mistakes but nothing more serious – does that ring a bell?). They know that overstepping these boundaries will mean the stalling of their career, if they still have a career to stall. This means that the desired bias and doctrinal beliefs which are sought by elite corporate managers and political spin masters, have been subtly ingrained within them as they climb the greasy pole. After all, self-denial and self-delusion are powerful forces – we all need to sleep at night. For political commentators this may be a problem, but I can't see many hacks who earn their crust from the relatively trivial world of Scottish football having to take a strong Ovaltine of an evening to get to the land of nod.

The same dynamic occurs with football journalists as it does with any other. The editorial stance of any Scottish newspaper is to ingratiate with its prime market. In Scotland that is Rangers fans and fans of many other Scottish teams who's values, whilst being fairly watered down, are more convergent with the – to quote Graham Spiers – 'Presbyterian' outlook of Scotland in general, including latent anti-Catholic and anti-Irishness attitudes. In this sense, whilst rivaling Rangers for the title of biggest club in Scotland, Celtic have the peculiar status, in a marketing sense, of being a minority concern for the Scottish media. In fact, as the chief rival of the object of their patronage, Celtic actually become a target with which to score points against, and curry yet more favour with their priority market. So, in the same way that the right-wing national media pander to the Tories and right wing rhetoric, whilst going after the likes of George Galloway and the "looney left"; the Scottish media eulogises all things Rangers and attacks and condemns Celtic at every turn. This dynamic is underpinned by the fact that where there is bias, conspiracy follows naturally and without the need for formal planning. Put simply, if the media and SFA are full of Rangers fans and those who have learned to toady in with them, they're hardly going to be inclined to give Celtic a break are they? That's what it boils down to – the conspiracy is that "complex". If all of this is lobby system stuff sounds a bit too mental, paranoid and far-fetched for you, consider the fact that the corporate media in Scotland are only too willing to buy into it when it suits them i.e. when it can be used to defend their precious upstanding referees:

Scottish refs are too ambitious to be dishonest, claims Killie boss Paatelainen

Daily Record Nov 5 2010 By Anthony Haggerty

MIXU PAATELAINEN reckons refs are so hell-bent on climbing the greasy pole they wouldn't dare jeopardise their ambition by making biased decisions. And he has slammed claims officials are bent.

Paatelainen said: "I don't believe referees are dishonest.

"I don't believe they try to influence the game so his favourite team wins or gains an advantage. In the refereeing profession they are ambitious and want to do as good a job as possible because they want to try to get on to the UEFA and FIFA lists to do Champions League matches and international games."

"They would be found out very quickly otherwise so every referee should be respected."

Of course this presumes that, in order to be "*found out*", those running the show don't also share the same biases, which you'll forgive me for saying, is quite an assumption. Nah, it all sounds a bit X-Files to me.

es·tab·lish·ment

[ih-**stab**-lish-m*uh* nt]
–noun

1.(*often initial capital letter*) the existing power structure in society; the dominant groups in society and their customs or institutions; institutional authority (usually prec. by *the*):*The Establishment believes the war is crucial to our national security and is worth any tax money spent.*

2. (*often initial capital letter*) the dominant group in a field of endeavour, organisation, etc. (usually prec. by *the*): *the literary Establishment.*

Now think of the word "conspiracy" and no doubt your mind immediately conjures up images of shadowy figures in darkened smoke-filled rooms. This is not a coincidence. It is a consciously created smear, the result of something far bigger than the petty world of football rivalry. It is one way Governments and Elites maintain their grip on "conventional wisdom" and the doctrinal norms that run the world today. Anyone who questions the findings of the barely credible Warren Commission investigation into the JFK assassination, or who believes our armies are in Iraq and Afghanistan for any reason other than a selfless benevolent wish to spread freedom and democracy, is immediately referred to as a "conspiracy theorist". This is so ingrained in the modern psyche, that often even those sympathetic to such views, use this terminology themselves. Regardless of who is saying it, this immediately puts the burden of proof on the "conspiracy theorist" and is subliminally already a black mark against their character. No matter that 80% of Americans armed with over 40 years of evidence believe the "conspiracy theory" about the JFK assassination over the official findings of the case; no matter that first call for US-led forces in Iraq was the Ministry of Oil and to then set about securing oil fields and pipelines rather than showering the natives in flowers and confetti whilst handing out UN aid packages. The very fact that you've made the effort to garner facts about these issues independently marks you down as someone of unstable character. You should be a good boy and go back to your state of zombie-esque unthinking compliance, where the issue most likely to inflame anything vaguely resembling passion within you, is who gets voted off X-Factor.

Language has been tarred with supplementary meaning to frame the already limited debate. This is immensely useful to Elites and the Establishment. A "conspiracy theorist" may make all sorts of lucid and compelling factual observations, but at the end of the day, he's a "conspiracy theorist" and to that end, he might as well be walking around with a sign saying "I'm clinically insane" hanging from his neck – or worse, "I'm paranoid".

There is no need to engage in debate with such a person to any meaningful extent, as all this person has to offer is "conspiracies", "theories" and conjecture, whereas the Establishment apologist deals in "fact" and can parrot off conventional wisdom to which everyone else simply nods. This is underpinned by what Noam Chomsky calls "Concision". That is, when you enter a debate with someone within a time constraint, like for example – a radio phone-in show – where easily digested rhetoric and soundbites need to be provided within a few minutes either side of commercial breaks, or for however long the host will allow before cutting you off – it is immensely difficult to elaborate satisfactorily on views that stray outside "conventional wisdom", because you have to provide enough background and evidence to "re-boot" the listener's line of thinking. Therefore callers can speak about Boruc "provoking" Rangers fans with the sign of the cross, Strachan being a wee smart arse deserving of no respect and Neil Lennon being a crazy madman accusing referees of all sorts of cheating and bias in contrast to the dignified Mr Smith, and everyone just nods along in agreement as we've heard it all a hundred times before.

But call up and put forward the point that Rangers in fact have filed the most complaints with the SFA of any Scottish team; that they have displayed more paranoiac traits than any other club through their squeals of victimisation whilst at the same time the Scottish football Establishment bends over backwards to accommodate them; and that the Man With Nosurname has cast more aspersions against referees than all other SPL managers put together – and you might as well be talking Swahili. You can start to recount the evidence but there is simply not enough time to build the case. But when you are simply parroting "conventional wisdom" like "all Celtic fans are paranoid" you don't need a case, everyone just agrees. That's the beauty of propaganda.

The "conspiracy theorist" is also in a Catch 22 situation in terms of the "credibility" of evidence. Without evidence to back up his assertions he can hardly be credible, yet the very act of taking the time and making the effort to assemble the requisite evidence is in itself viewed as an act of the paranoiac, and therefore such evidence is invariably dismissed. Much of this evidence, by its very nature, tends not to be found in mainstream sources, so is therefore tainted in some way in the mind of the apologist. I myself, have been accused of all sorts of mental disorders on the basis of taking the trouble to have written *Laptop Loyal Diaries* by people who have no comprehension whatsoever of its contents, having not read a page. All they know is it's about Celtic, it's about the media being biased against Celtic, therefore it's paranoia. And they genuinely believe this. This is not anti-Celtic bias in the sense that these people really believe we are all paranoid - case closed.

Isn't it ironic that Winston's tormentor in Orwell's 1984 had a suspiciously Irish surname?

The "Dougie and Willie" Smear Campaign

On 17th October 2010 Celtic beat Dundee United 2-1 at Tannadice. Celtic had taken the lead in the 13th minute after a free-flowing move involving several players, before Anthony Stokes spun on the touchline and played a fine through ball for Mark Wilson who crossed for Hooper to score. United equalised after Joe Ledley appeared to be pushed to the ground by Prince Bauben but no foul was given and the ball broke to Goodwillie whose shot deflected off Loovens and into the net. In the 70th minute we were then presented with one of Scottish football's defining moments – United goalkeeper Dusan Pernis dived at the feet of Gary Hooper and clearly took the legs away from the Celtic striker. Referee Dougie McDonald awarded a penalty kick, and to all those watching the game at the time this immediately seemed to be an uncontentious decision. However, with assistant referee Steven Craven taking up his position for the penalty, and Dundee United players haranguing McDonald, the referee decided to consult with his colleague running the line. To everyone's astonishment (except paranoid Celtic fans), McDonald overturned his decision and re-started play with a drop ball, and with no Celtic player in the vicinity to contest it, this amounted to allowing United a free clearance up the park. TV pictures later showed that the United keeper may have touched the ball a fraction of a second before making contact with Hooper, but how the referee suddenly reached his Road to Damascus moment, where the margin for error in his decision was so miniscule, is difficult to envisage. It is hard not to come to the conclusion that the furious reaction of the Dundee United players was the key factor. Celtic went on to dominate the remainder of the game and scored a deserved winning goal in the last minute through that man Gary Hooper. So with Celtic managing to secure their well-deserved victory, we could look forward to a day or two of controversy over the non-penalty award before getting back to normal service; or so we thought...

Of all the extraordinary events that followed, one thing that stood out for me more than any other, was the sheer brazenness of the smear campaign conducted by the Scottish media against everyone connected with Celtic FC. Not just Neil Lennon; not just Billy McNeill; but the fans and everyone connected with the club. Oh, and Steven Craven got it in the neck as well – I wonder why. I use that term 'smear campaign' very deliberately, as there simply isn't a more accurate description for the sheer bias and malicious spin that tainted almost every report on the issue over the following three weeks that was passed off as "news" by the media.

There are various facets to the Smear Campaign which I have loosely headed – *Rewrite history, The Crazy Paranoid Manager, All The Other Dignified Managers, Make the Perpetrator the Victim* and *The "Neutral" Character Witnesses*.

All of the techniques I've outlined in this book are evident in this Mother of all Smear Campaigns – the selective use of language, the misrepresentation and exaggeration of reasoned statement, the twisted headlines that don't reflect the quotes, presenting the views of those with vested interests as impartial, and the obligatory character assassination – they're all there. Let's have a look at each in turn:

Rewrite History

As I outlined earlier in this chapter, there is rarely any need to employ formal conspiracy mechanisms to prompt various parties to act in their convergent interests, although the "Dougie, Dougie" case would indeed involve some good old-fashioned "darkened-room"-style conspiring.

The media certainly didn't need any external prompting to move into full-on rewrite history mode, as this is something in which they are fully conversant and engage in on a weekly basis when reporting on Celtic and Rangers. It's second nature to them – if not first nature. *Rewrite History* was in full flow almost as soon as the game had ended, firstly with the Laptop Loyal's account of Dundee United's goal. This is before we even get to the "Dougie, Dougie" lie. Listening to the game on the radio at the time, the commentary indicated that it looked like Ledley had been fouled by Bauben before the ball broke to Goodwillie the goalscorer. The live text updates on SKY Sports website corroborated this [13:23 approx]:

38 GOAL GOODWILLIE! **Ledley looks as though he is fouled** *but United press forward through Goodwillie who bears down on goal and his shot deflects off Loovens and wrong-foots Forster.*

But only minutes after the final whistle [13:48], this certainty of a foul in the build-up to United's goal had morphed into Joe Ledley randomly lying on the ground for no apparent reason, at least according to Keir Murray on BBC website:

Joe Ledley was on the turf **claiming for a foul**, *when Goodwillie picked up the ball, made a bee-line for goal and tried his luck from 18 yards, his shot deflecting off Loovens past the stranded Forster.*

And by the time this made it into the newspapers 24 hours later, all mention of a foul in the build-up had been mysteriously erased from history, as per the following account by Union Jackson in the Daily Record:

And in 38 minutes his team collapsed with disturbing ease as Goodwillie's speculative drive from distance hit Glenn Loovens, wrong-footed Forster and bobbled in past the flat-footed keeper.

Of course we all know that if Joe Ledley had fouled Scott Severin before setting up Gary Hooper to score a goal, the Daily Record & co would have buried any reference to it. And we also believe that the Statue of Liberty is made of corned beef.

This is a minor detail but one that captures nicely one of the media's key anti-Celtic tactics. As Aldous Huxley said *"The greatest triumphs of propaganda have been accomplished, not by doing something, but by refraining from doing. Great is truth, but still greater, from a practical point of view, is silence about truth."*

So we move onto "Dougie, Dougie" and the penalty decision. In the immediate aftermath the media were only too happy to jump to the conclusion that assistant referee Steven Craven had initiated the discussion with McDonald on the matter, despite TV pictures clearly showing that the assistant referee had moved into position for the penalty to be taken, a strange course of action for someone hell-bent on persuading the referee that a penalty shoudn't have been awarded. Union Jackson in the Daily Record invoked his pro-Rangers/anti-Celtic psychic powers again to explain the circumstances surrounding this conversation:

Daily Record 18/10/2010

*With the teams level at 1-1 - thanks to first-half strikes from Hooper and United's David Goodwillie - McDonald pointed to the spot for a Celtic penalty **only to be talked into a change of heart by his assistant Steven Craven**.*

and

*But McDonald had seen enough. He made a great show of pointing to the spot only to have to reverse his decision **when Craven called him over**.*

I'm not sure what kind of specs Jackson was wearing, although I've a fair idea, but McDonald did not "*make a great show of pointing to the spot*", he simply signalled for a penalty in the customary manner, The only histrionics were from Dundee United players berating the official, but the media will gloss over that as it doesn't fit the jigsaw of their agenda. Jackson is clearly irked at a referee with the temerity to even consider awarding Celtic a penalty. As for the contention that Steven Craven "*talked*" McDonald "*into a change of heart*", well we can make an allowance for the fact that the "Douge, Dougie" lie had not yet surfaced at this point, although the most cursory of examination of Craven's positioning would have pointed to something fishy. But to be fair we couldn't expect a Scottish journalist of all people to have the type of inquiring mind that would follow up such a clue.

The next day (October 19th) and enter stage right Hugh Dallas to support his number one Honest Mistake merchant.

Daily Record By Hugh Keevins 19/10/2010

HUGH DALLAS last night backed Dougie McDonald's change of mind to deny Celtic a penalty at Tannadice on Sunday.

The SFA ref chief revealed the whistler had been "really disappointed" with the wrongly-awarded spot-kick that was rescinded on the advice of his assistant ref Steven Craven.

*"The officials are wired up to each other **and after an exchange of information between them** Dougie decided he had no other option but to go back on his decision.*

"Dougie's really disappointed over what happened and we'll get a report from the referee's observer in due course."

Note that the 19th of October was the Tuesday, fully 48 hours after the Sunday lunchtime match and there was nothing in this impassioned defence about the "Dougie, Dougie" lie, yet in the chronology acknowledged by all parties, McDonald had already notified Dallas of all of the facts at this point. Note also the very careful choice of words highlighted in bold. This is a strange choice of words for someone who is supposedly insisting on the truth, the whole truth and nothing but the truth. It smacks more of someone covering their back so that if something hits the fan at a later point they can defend themselves on a technicality i.e. "I didnae say that Craven called McDonald over" whilst doing nothing to dispel that misconception. After all, what prevented Dallas himself from notifying the SFA Chief Executive of the fact that the officials had conspired to lie to Neil Lennon, Jim McBurney the match observer, and effectively the public? In fact, surely it would be encumbent upon him to do so? Why wait for Dougie McDonald to blow the whistle, so to speak? And if Dougie McDonald was troubled enough by his conscience (or by the prospect of being found out on someone else's terms) to inform Dallas, why would McDonald himself not go the extra step and inform the office of the Chief Executive? Perhaps the answer to that is because the chain of command at the SFA dictated that this would be the responsibility of the Head of Referee Development?

Paul67 the author of the website Celtic Quick News, summarised the position more succinctly than I, or any journalist could, so I will not attempt to deconstruct and reassemble his words, rather I'll just present them to you here:

http://celticquicknews.co.uk/?p=3754 1st Nov 2010 [Accessed 12th Nov 2010]

In his BBC interview yesterday, Dougie McDonald confirmed that on the Sunday evening of the game Hugh Dallas was aware Neil Lennon and match observer Jim McBurney(*) were lied to, however, despite this disclosure, McBurney remained unaware of the truth and submitted the report, revealed by Celtic Quick News, on the Tuesday.

Celtic had written to the SFA asking for an explanation of the penalty events, which the SFA responded to without admission of the lie told to Neil Lennon or subsequent cover-up.

At this point the matter was contained. Dallas spoke to Radio Clyde on Monday evening, explained that McDonald had erred and eventually corrected his decision, and the observer's report was on file, complete with the undiscovered lie.

In speaking publicly on the issue Dallas should have either provided full disclosure or let it be known that an investigation into the post-match administration process was underway.

Despite failing to do this, if Dallas reported the lie to Regan and to McBurney on the Sunday or Monday morning he can claim to be innocent of any cover-

up. Due process would then take over, McBurney would record events in his report and Regan would initiate an investigation.

If Dallas failed to report the lie to Regan and McBurney by the Monday morning he is party to a cover-up. If no one escalated the issue until Steven Craven met Stewart Regan later in the week, the chief executive must ask why the two more senior officials, Dallas and McDonald, left him and the SFA exposed while they participated in a cover-up.

(*)Jim McBurney's match report mentions the "Dougie, Dougie" conversation three times, referring to it firstly as "*a brief discussion*" and secondly as a "*consultation*". In the context of the report there is nothing to suggest cover-up in the use of these terms, but the real smoking gun lay in the third reference -

In the 69th minute a penalty kick to the C [Celtic] team was awarded. Mr McDonald was immediately met by DU [Dundee United] players. **AR2 [Craven] had now positioned himself at the junction of the 18 yard line and the goal line, ready to view the expected penalty kick.**

At the immediate post match discussion when I asked why Mr McDonald ran over to AR2, **I was told that the assistant had communicated via the head set shouting "Dougie, Dougie".**

As we now know, this was not the case, therefore this constitutes the first telling of the lie. The second telling of the lie was to the face of Celtic manager Neil Lennon as per Craven's account:

Craven revealed: "Lennon came into the room after the game and asked Dougie why he hadn't given the penalty.

"We told him the version that was a lie. He seemed fine with the explanation. But, then, I suppose his side had still managed to win thanks to a late goal. I told Neil it was better to win with a legitimate goal rather than a dodgy penalty. He agreed." [Sunday Mail 31st Oct 2010]

The most logical interpretation of the comment "*it was better to win with a legitimate goal rather than a dodgy penalty*" is that it was a tactic to appease a potentially very unhappy manager, one who certainly made his displeasure known very forcefully at the time, and of course is also a simple statement of fact. The penalty award was debatable, with many Celtic partisans eventually agreeing that it was incorrect, so it would certainly be reasonable to describe such an award as dubious if it had come to pass.

But now with the truth having been outed and McDonald's original version of events now accepted as an out and out lie, or a "mistruth" as the world's worst sports journalist insisted on calling it (the buffoon Pattullo at The Scotsman in case you have happily avoided his output), we know that McDonald suddenly realised he might have "f***** up" (Craven) or "made a mess of this" (McDonald), and approached the assistant referee without any prompting to ask his advice on the decision. Now, there's no big deal in that, so why did a conspiracy then arise to concoct a spurious version of events? As The Guardian reported: "*In reversing his decision to award Celtic a penalty during their match against Dundee United, McDonald was correct. His flawed move to implicate the assistant Steven Craven, nonetheless, both during the game and in subsequent discussions with the SFA's refereeing observer remains a dubious business.*"

Why did McDonald find it necessary to shift the responsibility for the penalty award reversal onto Steven Craven, and why subsequently did others in the SFA seek to continue this charade when they knew the actual version of events? Well let's leave aside the most cynical explanation for McDonald's behaviour, which would be to attribute the startling award of a penalty in Celtic's favour by this notorious character as a momentary lapse which he sought to immediately rectify. No, let's instead accept for the sake or argument that McDonald genuinely realised he made a mistake, why the subsequent invention? According to Michael Grant in The Herald "*McDonald's motivation wasn't to cheat Celtic, it was to protect his own reputation and status. That instinct can't be uncommon*". Indeed but it's when we come to look at McDonald's reputation that the reason he was so concerned becomes rather obvious.

In the wake of a plethora of "honest mistakes" last season, most notably in games involving Celtic and, coincidentally, Dundee United, versus the Establishment team, we realise that rather than having a reputation of spotless purity as advocated by the SFA and their media Establishment poodle colleagues, McDonald is a highly controversial referee notorious for his pro-Rangers on-field performances – and this is where we come to the explanation for the "Dougie, Dougie" saga. Another match official may not have felt the need to "protect his reputation" by seeking desperately to implicate a colleague when overturning a bad call. McDonald though, lugging his baggage around like a ruptured camel, may have realised that his involvement in overturning Celtic's penalty award in such circumstances would have led to a rafter-shattering hue and cry. Consequently bringing his assistant, Craven, into the decision deflected what could have been a howling barnstorm of condemnation given McDonald's perceived leanings. Certainly the official line that a perplexed McDonald had been called over by a distressed Craven to hear the bad news had the desired effect, even Neil Lennon's anger abated somewhat following the official line explanation. "*Neil got a complete and thorough explanation and was very happy with it,*" claimed McDonald as he dismissed the "Dougie, Dougie" inclusion as a triviality. "*He knew it wasn't a penalty and he accepted that. Neil was brand new.*"

The Craven Smear

Charlie Smith, the other assistant referee for the Dundee Utd-Celtic match, would later be wheeled out to claim, as part of the inevitable smear campaign response, that the 'you would rather win with a good goal than a dodgy penalty' comment was some sort of self-aggrandising boast on Craven's part. To evaluate this we need to consider Craven's account of events and then Smith's counter-claims:

Dougie McDonald told me to lie to Neil Lennon about Celtic penalty U-turn, says quit linesman Steven Craven
Sunday Mail 31st Oct 2010 By Mark Guidi

….."I thought he had the perfect position. There was no way I could question him. He then ran towards me and said: 'I think I've f***** up. Did the keeper get a hand to the ball?' I told him I believed the goalie played the ball and that it wasn't a penalty. So he decided it should be a drop ball."

"To make it clear, **Dougie approached me. I did not call for him to come over.**

"After the game, in front of the other assistant referee and the fourth official, we spoke about it. Dougie said we should tell the referee supervisor (Jim McBurney) that I called him over to question the penalty award. He claimed it would give the decision to overturn the spot-kick more credibility."

"I went along with it because I wanted to be supportive of Dougie and back him up. That's the first time I've lied after a game. It was the wrong thing to do. With hindsight, I regret it. I'd never lie again. The supervisors have earpieces and can hear all communication between officials during games. Jim said he didn't hear me calling over Dougie but that the stadium was noisy."

Supervisor McBurney wasn't the only person the officials tried to deceive. They even lied to Hoops boss Neil Lennon when he asked for an explanation.

Craven revealed: "Lennon came into the room after the game and asked Dougie why he hadn't given the penalty.

"We told him the version that was a lie. He seemed fine with the explanation. But, then, I suppose his side had still managed to win thanks to a late goal. I told Neil it was better to win with a legitimate goal rather than a dodgy penalty. He agreed."

McDonald's controversial U-turn led to a media storm and the worried ref decided to come clean to Dallas. But Craven claims the refs supremo wasn't interested in the truth and wanted the linesman to keep taking the flak. That then kicked off a series of events that led to Craven handing in his resignation and the SFA starting an investigation.

The first part of that probe led to McDonald receiving an official warning but the investigation is still ongoing.

Craven said: "On the Monday morning there was quite a reaction in the papers. I sent Dougie a text to ask what he thought of the fall-out. He called immediately and told me he had talked with Hugh the night before and decided to come clean. Dougie told Hugh lies were told to the supervisor. He then told Hugh the truth - that I had not shouted for him to come over.

"I was then urged to tell Hugh the truth when he called me. I was happy to do so and felt quite relieved. When Hugh phoned he asked me to talk over the penalty. He said: 'So what happened after you called out for Dougie to come over? You called out Dougie, Dougie, Dougie?'

"My wife was in the room and I told him that was not the case. I told Hugh he now knew the truth. The truth was the version Dougie had told him over the phone. But Hugh repeated: 'What are you talking about, you said Dougie, Dougie, Dougie and called him over' but I told Dallas I did no such thing. Dougie came clean and so did I. But Hugh didn't seem to accept that."

"I phoned Dougie back and told him Hugh tried to make out this wasn't true and denied having the conversation with Dougie on the Sunday night. Dougie's response was he thought Hugh was just trying to test me, that he wanted to see if I would tell the truth or stick to the previous story. My reading of the situation was Hugh wanted to protect Dougie and leave me to take the flak.

"It was wrong to lie and I'm not proud that I went along with Dougie's suggestion. Rewind the clock and I wouldn't do it. But it was worse to continue the lie. I was really upset after that conversation with Hugh."

Craven then got even angrier when he checked his email and received the official match report. He was criticised for his performance at Tannadice and that convinced him it was time to get out of the game.

Craven said: "When I got my match report from the game emailed to me that proved to be the final straw. I was down-marked for getting an offside decision wrong. When I got the match report I phoned Drew Herbertson at the SFA and told him I'd had enough. I was going to quit at Christmas - but not because of my ankles, as has been reported elsewhere. It was because of all the nonsense with Hugh".

So let's pick up on what Charlie Smith had to say about all this in a piece appearing on the Herald website on 1st November under the completely unemotive and neutral title [cough!]:

'Steven Craven jumped for 20 pieces of silver' claims fellow Tannadice assistant referee'
The Herald 1st Nov 2010 By Michael Grant

...But McDonald's other assistant on the fateful day on Tayside, Charlie Smith, has questioned Craven's version of events. Smith had no part in the penalty decision and **was not privvy to the subsequent conversations between Craven and Dallas. But he accused Craven of embellishing his story** and claimed there were inaccuracies within it **which made him question his motivation for going public**.

So this third party, who was not privvy to the central issue under debate – whether Hugh Dallas attempted to manipulate Steven Craven into maintaining the "Dougie, Dougie" lie or not – is wheeled out by the Herald as some sort of authority on the matter?

"The obvious inaccuracies for me are concerning. *People don't let the truth get in the way of a good story. If he had been accurate you could say 'okay I see where you're going' but to put inaccuracies in a story to allege a cover-up is disappointing. Steven made no secret of the fact he was going to chuck it at Chrismas.* ***For me, Steven has jumped for his 20 pieces of silver."***

The obvious question here is, 'where are the inaccuracies? Smith hasn't at this stage actually challenged any part of Craven'e account.

"We entered the dressing room [at Tannadice] together and sat down," Smith said. "Stevie instigated removing the communication packs [ie headsets]. At that point Stevie asked Dougie 'what are we going to say to the supervisor?'. It was Stevie that instigated the conversation so we could clarify it to the supervisor."

There is no significance in the fact (if indeed it is a fact) that Craven instigated the *"removing of the communication packs"* and asked for clarification on what the cover story would be. Craven freely admits that at this stage, he was going along with the "Dougie, Dougie" lie, and it would only be natural for someone involved in this conspiracy to seek clarification to get the story straight. In fact, if anything, it shows that Craven was looking for McDonald to take the lead on the issue.

Smith claimed Craven was happy with the agreed version of events when Neil Lennon entered the room after the game for clarification. "It was a quiet, polite conversation. Dougie explained the situation to Neil. Steven said to Neil 'you won with a goal in the last minute, would you not rather win with an honest goal than with a dubious penalty'. That's the disappointing thing . . . ***he was delighted to take the credit at the time****. There was no cheating. There was no malice in it."*

Again, this is not contentious. Craven admitted that he was involved in the initial conspiracy and that this was the form of words he used to explain the situation to the Celtic manager. But Smith weakly attempts to get some mud to stick with a dubious interpretation of Craven's motive. As stated previously, the most logical interpretation of the 'you won with a good goal rather than a dodgy penalty' statement is that Craven was pouring oil on troubled waters. It is also merely a statement of fact that anyone could have made to Neil Lennon with no particular ulterior motive. But even if we believe that Smith has the psychic capacity to know that Craven's words were an egotistical attempt to take credit, it is still merely smoke and mirrors regarding the important issue - Hugh Dallas's role in all of this. Smith's allegation amounts to nothing more than a feeble attempt at character assassinaton, a tactic the media have been using in spades against Celtic, or anyone allied to Celtic's position, time and time again.

"I've never encountered any harassment from the SFA. I've always found them to be very fair. I was at the fitness test the day this supposed bullying

[by Fleming towards Craven] was supposed to have occurred. I was standing two feet from Steven. All the nonsense that's been said is totally untrue.

Well bully for Charlie Smith, he has never encountered any harassment from the SFA, but that has nothing to do with Steven Craven's experiences. More deflect and deny smoke and mirrors. "*All the nonsense that's been said*" refers to another part of the Craven article in which he states:

"We had to go through a fitness test but I had been off work and informed Fleming I still felt under the weather. **In front of colleagues** *he started to shout at me from five yards away. I was horrified and disgusted at his outburst of verbal abuse. I shook my head in disbelief then he got into an uncontrolled rage. He continued to shout at me."*

Note Craven says "*In front of colleagues*", not "in front of Charlie Smith". So we are expected to take Smith's word at face value – he witnessed the incident in question and Craven is lying, whilst offering no evidence other than to brand Craven's story "*nonsense*". Steven Craven has given a reasonably detailed account of an incident between himself and another individual, but we are supposed to dismiss it on the basis of Charlie Smith's word that he was there and he knows better? Someone who can't even get his biblical references correct when he's trying to smear someone. I'll let you decide who is more credible.

If we return to the beginning of Smith's views on the matter, the clear implication is that Craven simply made all of this up to sell the story to the newspapers. Jim Traynor, Sports Editor of the Daily Record and Sunday Mail, stated on Radio Scotland that Craven received no payment for his story. Perhaps Smith would care to accuse Traynor of lying too? But, in contrast to the greedy money-grabbing Mr Craven, what possible ulterior motive could Smith have for coming out and backing his boss in public and attacking someone who has become persona non grata at the SFA? Hmmm, nope can't think of anything.

Smith's psychic powers also extend as far as knowing Craven's reasons for resigning better than Craven himself, but to "prove" this, Smith merely offers up more statements that don't actually contradict the original story. Yes Steven Craven made no secret of the fact he had decided to step down at Christmas, and now he's making no secret of the fact he's stepping down for other reasons, except Charlie Smith knows better apparently. The plausible interpretation is that the initial 'stepping down at Christmas' line was the cover story, not the one that Craven has now made public.

Ultimately, nothing Smith says here confirms or disproves that Hugh Dallas tried to surpress the "Dougie, Dougie" lie, and his entry into the fray smacks of someone with a vested interest, participating in a wagon-circling exercise. His "evidence" amounts to nothing more than an attempt to taint Craven's character to cast doubt on peripheral details of his story as part of a smoke and mirrors exercise that he and his cohorts hope will taint his key claims regarding Hugh Dallas.

But Charlie Smith was not the last character "witness" to leap out of the rotting woodwork like a sewer rat to attack Steven Craven and Celtic Football Club. Martin Cryans, the chairman of Scottish Senior Football Referees' Association weighed in with his version of events – coincidentally, another version gleaned from having no involvement in any of the incidents concerning the Dundee Utd-Celtic game or the claims later made by Steven Craven. In an interview with the BBC, Cryans said – "*The guy* (Craven) *who was going* (at Christmas) *has chosen to take a pop and there's not much more to it there*". So without being party to any of the relevant goings-on, Cryans felt able to assure the BBC of what he thought was the truth, and conversely, what he thought was pure invention by ex-official Steven Craven.

Is the reputation of our referees not low enough without their trade rep sticking his nose into a dispute between two officials, telling us that some very serious allegations have "*not much more to it*" than some guy "*taking a pop*"? Rather than contradict Craven's story, this time our Establishment apologist goes for an 'och, this isnae really important at all' line. Again we have someone with a vested interest, making a poor attempt to refute what are serious claims which heve been outlined in some detail, purely on the basis of 'don't listen to that guy, listen to me'. When witnesses who are not actually witnesses, are called to give evidence, we have all the makings of a Kangaroo Court. The accusation of a cover-up has been made. A good plan of defence would be to stop making this look like a cover-up, because when we have non-involved parties telling the media what happened, and the media enthusiastically giving great prominence to these comments, that's exactly what it looks like.

Short of a court-hearing, or acquiring Charlie Smith's mythical psychic powers, we cannot be certain of all of the details of the case. Craven has made a statement, Hugh Dallas has strongly refuted it, and it is left up to the individual to draw their own conclusions. Hugh Dallas's statement on the matter makes interesting reading in the context of what Celtic fans had to put up with through all of this controversy, which takes us onto the next item of history that was rewritten – Craven's reason(s) for resigning.

The Celtic Fan Smear

The media attempts to discredit Steven Craven can be understood in the context of trying to protect the position of a key player in the Scottish football Establishment, Hugh Dallas, and the current status quo, whereby the regular pattern of "honest mistakes" which hampers Celtic, and favours Rangers, is defended strongly as a mere by-product of a refereeing "form slump"; a slump which as far as I can see, has lasted for at least the past 20 years. Billy McNeill would say 50 years, but I guess the only captain of a Scottish side to lift the European Cup is paranoid too. In fact, as Gary Hooper has proven, you only need to spend a couple of weeks in the company of Celtic players and fans and this terrible paranoia contagion will overcome you.

However the media moved to cast Celtic fans as the villains too, a move intended to deflect as much heat as possible from their SFA Establishment colleagues onto us, their perennial punchbags. Any mud that subsequently stuck would be a nice bonus for them. This was achieved through the stock 'verbal threats against the family' story, which first appeared courtesy of a Daily Record piece by Mark Guidi. The article didn't even bother with the usual charade of claiming to be from an un-named "source", instead just passing off their unsubstantiated shite as fact:

Celtic penalty row linesman on verge of quitting believing SFA are blaming him for Tannadice boob

Daily Record Oct 23 2010 Exclusive by Mark Guidi

STEVEN CRAVEN is set to quit as an assistant referee because he feels the SFA have hung him out to dry after last Sundays controversial Tannadice clash. Craven believes he was made the scapegoat for Dougie McDonalds U-turn over awarding Celtic a penalty against Dundee United.

After the game it was inferred Craven had instigated the chat with McDonald that led to the penalty not being given. However, its understood McDonald knew immediately he had got the decision wrong and, off his own back, made his way to Craven to ask for his colleagues opinion.

SFA ref chief Hugh Dallas has applauded McDonald for changing his mind. **But the lack of a detailed explanation has left Craven in the lurch.** *And Record Sport also understands he was disgusted with the SFA for marking him down in the supervisors report.*

The fallout from Tannadice has led to a week of turmoil for Craven and his family. **He has been the victim of threatening remarks and his two teenage sons have suffered serious verbal abuse.** *That will lead to him resigning and when he takes charge of a reserve game at Murray Park today it will be his final match.*

What's interesting here is that more-or-less the full story behind Craven's motivation for resigning is contained in the story, yet the "journalist" then adds the part about "*threatening remarks*" and "*serious verbal abuse*" and brazenly passes **this** off as the reason Craven resigned. Once the Daily Record's 'resigning due to threats from Celtic fans' slur was invented – because make no mistake, although Celtic fans are not named, this is the clear implication – the other rags all jumped on it, in an orgy of anti-Celtic glee. In fact the first to do so, was Guidi again in the Record's sister rag the Sunday Mail the next day:

SFA launch probe into reasons behind linesman Steven Craven quitting

Oct 24 2010 Mark Guidi, Sunday Mail

Although Celtic went on to win 2-1, Hoops fans were angry with the officials for the way they handled the incident. **Craven has since been targeted by** *angry punters and his family have endured a torrid week of verbal abuse.*

Guardian Laptop Lapdog Ewan (what is it with that name?) Murray, dispenses with innuendo and just comes straight out and blames Celtic fans for the resignation, whilst also persisting with the myth, long since abandoned by even his lapdog peers, that Craven was responsible for overturning the penalty award:

Assistant referee Steven Craven quits after abuse following Celtic row

The Guardian 25th Oct By Ewan Murray

The level of abuse Craven has received for that intervention has led him to end his refereeing career, the SFA admitted tonight. "I can confirm that I have met with the relevant match officials and members of the referee departments regarding the events that occurred during the recent match between Dundee United and Celtic," said Stewart Regan, the SFA's chief executive. "I can also confirm that Steven Craven has tendered his resignation and will no longer officiate in the professional game. I hope to conclude the investigation within the next 48 hours and will make further comment at that time."

This up and coming Establishment poodle even goes as far as to claim that the SFA "*admitted*" abuse from Celtic fans was behind Craven's resignation. Read the quotes from Stewart Regan and explain to me where he "*admitted*" this please. It is beyond me.

The Sun Roger Hannah 26th Oct 2010

Linesman Craven resigned yesterday **after being subjected to fierce personal abuse** *in the wake of that game.* **His family was also subjected to abuse**.

Daily Mail 27th Oct 2010

He was unhappy at a **perceived lack of support** *from within Hampden, while* **members of his family were subjected to verbal abuse**

Note the spin from the Daily Mail. Craven's claim of bullying and harassment mysteriously becomes, "*lack of support*", and is also only "*perceived*", whilst the "*verbal abuse*" from nasty Celtic fans is real and factual.

However the most biased coverage of the issue I have seen, emanated, not from the usual suspects, but up in deepest darkest Grampian, courtesy of the Press and Journal. Their report completely missed out the opening paragraph which explains Steven Craven feelings about being made a scapegoat and delved straight in with Regan's statement on the resignation and the juicy stuff about threats and this kind of thing posing a danger to refs and their families blah blah blah…

Sinister side of referee criticism emerges as SFA continues probe into fallout of United-Celtic game

Craven quits after threats and verbal abuse of sons
Press and Journal 26/10/2010

And they complain about West Coast bias!

So what did Steven Craven say to trigger all these fevered reports of serious/fierce/deadly/sick (choose suitably exaggerated adjective) abuse against himself/his sons/the pet dog/the souls of all of his living, dead and unborn family till the end of time? Well, nothing actually. When an interview with Craven was finally published by the Sunday Mail on 31st October this is what he had to say about the *"fierce"* and *"serious"* abuse, as well as the *"threatening remarks"* widely reported thoughout the Scottish media:

"Yes, I've had three ankle operations. But it's nothing to do with injuries [his resignation]. *I've never failed a fitness test in 14 years.* **It's also not down to family reasons**. *My 14-year-old Andrew supports Rangers and my 18-year-old Ross supports Celtic. Andrew attends a Catholic school with around 1,500 other kids. Only four or five of them support Rangers at the school. A friend phoned me to say he'd heard Andrew had been getting some stick at school because his dad had allegedly chalked off a penalty for Celtic.*

"*I asked Andrew about it.* **He told me he'd received one or two bits of verbal abuse but nothing he couldn't handle**. *I told him I'd put my kids first but* **he assured me it wasn't too bad**. *There was also a bit in a newspaper that stated refs are ready to quit because of pressure put on officials by SPL managers. That's wrong.*"

So one of his sons received *"one or two bits of verbal abuse but nothing he couldn't handle"* and he himself received no abuse at all. What Craven describes is something that goes on in playgrounds the length and breadth of the country every day, and wouldn't appear to merit the banner headlines in the press which resulted, as well as the furrowed brows and moral indignation that went with it. A bit of classroom teasing has been built up to sinister proportions of grown men foaming at the mouth with rage and having to be restrained from attacking the poor man and his family in the street.

As we have seen, the *'personal/family abuse'* story first appeared in the Daily Record on 23rd October, where it was reported as undisputed fact despite no sources being quoted. It beggars belief that this story could have come from Steven Craven himself given his robust rejection of it in the Sunday Mail. This begs the question then, who came up with the story? I guess its not inconceivable that it was simply made up by the journalist, or rather, a journalist sought out a source who could confirm that a wee boy called Craven's son a bad name at school and ergo this would justify headlines proclaiming *"serious"* and *"personal"* abuse of Steven Craven and his family, forcing him to resign from refereeing, just ignore all that stuff about Dallas and being made a scapegoat.

It's interesting at this point to consider one aspect of Hugh Dallas's response to Craven's revelations – "*I am dismayed and saddened that the reputation I have built up over 30 years could be besmirched by such unfounded *allegations. I am extremely angry and upset at the completely unsubstantiated allegations made by Steven Craven in a Sunday newspaper"*

While the SFA were busy sitting on these lies, Celtic supporters were receiving world-wide publicity for forcing Steven Craven to resign from the game, which, according to Craven, was completely untrue. This allegation was repeated on London-based radio stations and on websites as far afield as Asia and North America. My reputation, your reputation, Celtic FC's reputation, suffered. I am - to borrow a phrase - extremely angry and upset at these completely unsubstantiated allegations.

The Sunday Mail eventually revealed the allegations were untrue, although as is often the case, the corroborated rebuttal received a fraction of the coverage and no worldwide publicity. While the world reported Celtic fans were to blame for the resignation of a match official, did the SFA have written reasons for Craven's resignation and fail to alert Celtic that their supporters were being blamed for a shambles which was none of their doing? With the SFA ranks closing tighter than a camel's arsehole in a sandstorm we may never know for sure.

Speaking of closing ranks, Kenny Clark, the ex-Grade One referee, was one of a myriad of Establishment stooges wheeled out to defend the integrity of referees and Dougie McDonald in particular. In the course of painting a stark picture of salt of the earth referees unfairly maligned and put in mortal danger by heartless Celtic managers cruelly asking for explanations of their glaring errors, Clark said the following – *"Before my number was ex-directory I had a couple of abusive phone calls, and I frequently had to put up with abuse in the streets or at social occasions. There have been occasions when referees have received threatening letters, letters with razor blades contained in them, and we're aware of referees having windows smashed in their homes."*

This begs the question of our esteemed and impartial Scottish media – why are threats and abuse of referees only front page headlines when it can be pinned on Celtic fans? After all, one particular Scottish club has rather a colourful history in this sort of death-threat carry on, in respect of Celtic's current manager in particular, not to mention physical assaults. Fans of other clubs, including Aberdeen, have been convicted on charges of verbally abusing and assaulting Neil Lennon. Lennon, McGeady, Boruc and a host of other Celtic players have been met with volleys of sick abuse at grounds all across Scotland, masquerading as the whimsical banter of the wee teams. So it would seem rather far-fetched to imagine that all of the unpleasantness described by Clark could have been the work purely of Celtic fans, if at all.

Another question that points to a hopelessly biased and in the pocket of the Rangers-led Establishment media, is – why did it take them the best part of two weeks to seek Steven Craven's views? Why were the press not falling over each other fighting their way to his door for an interview the moment his decision to resign became known? After all they were going around interviewing any rent-a-gub Establishment stooge they could find in the meantime – Martin Cryans, Charlie Smith and Kenny Clark to name but a few. Surely the big prize would have been an interview straight from the horses mouth? This would have been the case, of course, if the media were investigating the issue free of agenda and spin, but I'm guessing having got this far, I don't need to persuade you that that is not the reality.

A day or two before Craven's version of the story was published by the Sunday Mail, I received text messages outlining rumours of what was in store, and this news quickly spread throughout "cyberspace", the Celtic community and beyond. But before we start congratulating the Sunday Mail on a stunning scoop representing a victory for fair journalism and a sign that they might somehow be breaking ranks with the Establishment's media stranglehold, consider a few points –

- It had taken them almost a fortnight to approach Craven
- Over the intervening period the same hack, Mark Guidi, had instigated then repeated the 'personal/family abuse' slur in sister rag the Daily Record
- In the Sunday Mail piece Guidi had the gall to state "*Inaccurate stories started to appear on a daily basis in an attempt to cover up the real version of events - and that's why Craven has decided to speak out.*" despite the fact **he and the Daily Record** were the ones who first published these "*inaccurate stories*"

Rather than some spontaneous burst of journalistic integrity from the Sunday Mail, a more plausible scenario is that once it became clear that Craven was not for co-operating in the cover-up, and it therefore became merely a matter of time before his side became public, it became a commercial imperative for them to get Craven's story. If a few small holes were going to be punched in the Establishment armoury they might as well make a lot of money from it, and in any case, a counter offensive would soon repair the damage.

The counter offensive duly arrived a few days later, after yet another glaring "honest mistake" in a Celtic-Rangers game, which you guessed it... hindered Celtic and benefited Rangers. Since the Laptop Loyal were fresh out of verbal and personal abuse stories, the situation called for a Defcon 2 'Death Threat' story. Funnily enough, keeping their title of number one for anti-Celtic fan smear stories, it was the Daily Record who came up with a suitably exaggerated account of a referee receiving sinister death-threats from those evil-machiavellian Celtic fans again – courtesy of, who else, Union Jackson:

Death threat calls made to referee Willie Collum after Old Firm clash
Daily Record Oct 26th 2010   Exclusive By Keith Jackson
OLD Firm ref Willie Collum received **chilling death threats** just hours after taking charge of the powder-keg Glasgow derby on Sunday.

The shaken official answered a number of sinister phone-calls at his Lanarkshire home with the caller threatening to "go after him and his wife and children".

It's understood Collum reported the calls to the police **but turned down the offer of protection** outside his home. The 31-year-old **outraged** Celtic manager Neil Lennon by awarding Rangers a penalty in the second half of the top of the table showdown.

Last night Collum's SFA bosses confirmed that he had been the target of death threats and added that there **was a sectarian undertone** to the calls. **Spokesman Darryl Broadfoot** said: "Willie received a number of threatening calls at his home on Sunday night, one of which was taken by his wife.

Keech has his trowel out here, as he breathlessly informs us of these "*chilling*" death threats, and "*sinister*" phone-calls. 'Sinister' is fast turning into one of Keech's favourite words these days. The offer of police protection is served up as the icing on the cake. Note that according to Rangers TV Jackson, Neil Lennon was "*outraged*" by the mere award of a penalty to Rangers, accidentally leaving out the part about it being yet another appalling "honest mistake". An "honest mistake" by Jackson himself and in no way intended to subtly smear the Celtic manager's character of course. Note also, the identity of the SFA spokesman who tearfully relayed this information to a shocked gathering of the Central Quay Rangers Supporters Club.

Yep, when all else fails, the Scottish media, usually The Daily Record or their fellow gutter inhabitants the Sun, can always be relied upon to come to the rescue with their 'Grisly Tales for Gruesome Kids', or the 'Match Official Death Threat', as it is otherwise known. Never for one second are the source of such death threats contemplated, for example it wouldn't be entirely impossible for these threats to be a set-up intended to implicate Celtic fans, provided of course they exist in the first place. Well it's easier to look up a phone-book and make a phone call than it is for hundreds of Chelsea fans to travel to Manchester/Bucharest/Pamplona and batter the living daylights out of the police to deliberately besmirch the good name of Glasgow Rangers, and the Scottish media bought that pile of excrement. If Rangers fans are capable of lifting a phone and calling Ewen Cameron to smear Celtic fans then they would be capable of doing the same with Willie Collum. Regardless though, the "death threats" are again used as a tool with which to silence dissent and to keep the bias of match officials from public discussion. Its effectiveness could be seen by the way Neil Lennon was forced onto the defensive during subsequent press conferences, reduced to mealy mouthed requests for clarification when justified outrage should have poured forth instead.

The Crazy Paranoid Manager

Coldplay's *'The Scientist'* has just started on the music TV channel I've got playing in the background, and it got me thinking of a scenario. Consider this:

You are a scientist and believe strongly in a theory that you are convinced has been proven over the course of many years of experimental trials you have conducted. You have put forward this theory to your peers but despite the evidence presented, it has been met with universal scepticism. In an effort to persuade them of the merits of this theory, you predict that errors will occur in each of a series of three experiments to be carried out jointly by you and a rival scientist. These errors duly occur in exactly the manner you had predicted. What do you think the reaction of your scientific peers would be? Would they embrace your theory, or at least consider it something worthy of further investigation?

Well if this took place in Scotland, apparently the reaction would be to dismiss the theory and the results out of hand, as a statistical aberration indicative of a random fluctuation of errors with no set pattern. Then, to set about selectively highlighting one or two trivial errors within your previous experiments to prove this "evening out" effect, and to then instigate a smear campaign against you by wildly exaggerating all of your statements to portray you as some sort of cross between the Incredible Hulk and that guy from Chewin the Fat who goes mental and breaks everything.

Sound familiar?

We all know that the current media – to borrow their own phrase – witchhunt – against Neil Lennon was only a matter of time. It happened to him as a player, it happened to Mowbray, it happened to Strachan, it happened to O'Neill and it even happened to Barnes, although to a lesser extent as Rangers were in a dominant position then and financialy at the peak of their spending. It's interesting to note that media hostility to Celtic, whilst always present to some degree, really ramped up in the post-2000 O'Neill period, which coincided with Rangers' slide into the financial mire. Paranoiacs might suggest a link between the two.

Although we knew it was coming, the catalyst for the explosion of derision flying Lennon's way would be the "Dougie, Dougie" fiasco, although with another "honest mistake" show lined up against the Establishment team the week after, the fates were conspiring to create the climate for a perfect media propaganda offensive storm. The first item on the charge sheet served up by the Laptop Loyal against Mr Lennon is that he had an outrageous outburst against the match officials following that particular Dundee Utd-Celtic match. To evaluate this charge, I'm going to ask you to play a wee game. It's called 'Spot the Raving Paranoid Manager From the Post Match Interviews' – and what you have to do is, well, the title explains it.

Which of the following managers is paranoid – A or B?:

A) "*The linesman took his position up as if it was a penalty. There was a long delay for some reason and the linesman says it's not a penalty. For me, it's another strange decision that has gone against us in the last six to eight months. The referee was adamant it was a penalty. He has made the decision he shouldn't really have to be overturned by his linesman. It's very rare you see that happen.I thought Dougie had a far better position and look at it than the linesman.*"

B) "*Dougie couldn't get his finger to the spot quickly enough. It's not the first he has given against us. I thought his performance was below average today. I've got to be honest.*

"But then Dougie McDonald **conspires** *to try to give a penalty against us. Then it transpires that it is not a penalty. What has happened there?"*

"Ki Sung-Yong went in two minutes later and went down like a sack of tatties. I've had players booked for that. I am not saying that's the reason we lost the game, but I am looking for a more consistent performance from a referee who is meant to be one of the top referees."

"Barry Douglas wins a ball against Samaras in the middle of the park. The ball goes out, the referee gives us a foul. Samaras gets up and pushes him and Barry Douglas gets booked. Where is the reasoning in that? Why are we getting booked for that? We've had a number of bookings and I have got to question that. I thought he didn't have a particularly good game."

"*Celtic were celebrating as if they won the league. I am going to start running down the track for 30 yards after we score a goal. Celtic seem to get away with it, the whole backroom staff, the lot. Every time I leave the dug-out I get the fourth official hauling me back.*"

Something tells me Peter Houston doesn't like Celtic – talk about paranoid drivel. Nobody of sound mind would expect a player not being booked for falling due to a blatant body check in the penalty area to be a reason for the loss of a game. In fact, in such circumstances the attacking team would have much more reason to feel aggrieved. Now if we were looking around for an incident that *could* have a major effect on the outcome of a game, how about, oh… an example at random… a penalty being awarded then rescinded? What's that you say… that decision went in Houston's favour? Oh well, it must mean Neil Lennon is paranoid.

As far as the 'Spot the Paranoid Manager' game goes, I guess 'Paranoid Dundee United manager' doesn't have the same ring to it for the Laptop Loyal's liking, and anyway, Dundee United are not a threat to Rangers, so the answer is A.

With the "Dougie, Dougie" story unfolding, the minor sideshow of a Celtic-Rangers game (24th Oct) came over the horizon, and with it another front for a media offensive in their "War on Celtic". In pre-match interviews, Neil Lennon's comments, to any sensible person where fairly understated as illustrated in this article in the Herald on the eve of the game:

Lennon hopes Collum gets the major decisions right in Old Firm encounter
The Herald 23rd Oct 2010 By Graeme McPherson

Neil Lennon hopes Celtic's ongoing spat with the Scottish Football Association over **perceived** *refereeing injustices* **will not add to the pressure** *on referee Willie Collum, who is officiating in his first Old Firm derby tomorrow.*

"It's a difficult one for him," Lennon said. "Considering the recent history of controversial decisions that have gone against us in these games, I just hope he has a good day and we're not talking about him after the game. I just hope he gets the big decisions right. We wrote to the SFA just for clarification about the penalty decision. So I assume the dialogue will continue but we haven't had a reply yet."

Lennon repeated his opinion that Celtic have been hard done to by referees in recent Old Firm matches, **but elected diplomatically, after a pause, to write it off as "human error"**.

"Have we had a rough side of things? Certainly, in the last year anyway. We've tried to do something about it. I think the club made the position quite clear last year, so we'll draw a line under it until 3.40 on Sunday. I put it down to human error. But you can't keep getting those decisions wrong on a consistent basis. I would like to think it's just honest mistakes being made, yeah."

Note that the Herald is careful to state that these refereeing "*injustices*" are "*perceived*". It's also interesting that the Herald reporter included the colloquial word "*yeah*" as part of Lennon's response. This is highly unusual. Quotes from football press conferences are universally peppered with colloquialisms and "ayes" and "mebbes", and these are always tidied up for publication in newspapers. I can't help but think that on this occasion, Lennon's "*yeah*" was left in as an attempt to infer a sarcastic dimension to the Celtic manager's statement. If you think I'm paranoid, just think about the number of eyes this article would have passed in front of – the journalist himself, sub-editor and editor. Very little makes it into print in a newspaper by accident.

It would be difficult for any objective sane person to find a problem with a manager expressing the opinion that he hopes the referee has a good game. One can't help but think if a certain manager with nosurname made the self-same remarks, the press would spin this into some sort of dignified pledge of support for Willie Collum – something along the lines of "Walter backs referee in the face of intolerable pressure".

Instead the Scottish press chose to see it slightly differently:

Scottish Sun 23rd Oct 2010 By Robert Grieve
NEIL LENNON last night piled Parkhead pressure on Old Firm debut ref Willie Collum. The Celtic boss **warned**: Make sure it's not about **YOU.**

Lennon **believes** Celts got a raw deal from Scotland's whistlers last season. **The Hoops even lodged an official complaint with the SFA**.

Lennon has now **demanded rookie** Collum is at his best tomorrow, adding: "It's a difficult one for him. I just hope he has a good day and we're not talking about him after the game."

301

It doesn't get any more biased than this. Of course, we couldn't think of any other clubs who lodge official complaints about such matters as fixtures or their players being subject to disciplinary procedure could we? And of course, they are also subject to furious accusations of paranoia and inciting violent responses from their fans aren't they? Anyway.... read the quote from Lennon and read the headline and the part about "*demanding rookie Collum is at his best*" again and think of a rational explanation, which doesn't involve the obvious conclusion of course, as to how this amounts to Neil Lennon "*piling Parkhead pressure*" on Willie Collum. Again, we have the notion that Celtic suffered from bad decisions spun as some sort of delusional fantasy, and trowel in hand, lapdog Grieve lays it on thick with all of this intolerable Machievallian pressure heaped on a poor wee "*rookie*" referee, who's only experience of refereeing has been FIFA Internationals and Champions League ties. Needless to say, these sentiments were echoed by the Daily Record, Evening Times et al.

Whilst the SFA were desperately trying to keep a lid on their "Dougie, Dougie" lies, they were also snottering on their website about "*unjustified and manufactured controversy*" in a thinly veiled swipe at Celtic:

Collum itching for derby debut
SFA website Friday, 22 October 2010

*After another week of **unjustified and manufactured controversy** surrounding the events of the Dundee United v Celtic game last weekend, Collum has reminded both Rangers and Celtic of their responsibilities in ensuring a memorable derby for all the right reasons.*

Unjustified eh? Manufactured? Sources say that immediately after this statement the SFA sent out an office junior to procure a crate full of Brasso for the use of SFA office bearers. Funnily enough, the latin term for neck is 'collum' – there must be a conspiracy somewhere in there.

In light of the SFA's ludicrous pontificating and moral indignation, lets have a wee appraisal of their role in this "*unjustified and manufactured*" controversy.

It took the SFA **12 days** to confirm the "*post-match administrative process was not completed to the expected standard after Celtic's visit to Tannadice on 17 October*", and that assistant referee Steven Craven did not call "Dougie, Dougie" to attract the attention of referee McDonald. Whilst the referee made a misjudgement (whichever way you look at it) over the penalty decision, it appears the observer's report, which was submitted approximately two days later, was falsified.

Within minutes of the full time whistle, assistant referee Craven was implicated by McDonald for the penalty being rescinded, ultimately leading to the assistant resigning as an SFA official. The anticipated demotion of McDonald for these indiscretions was subsequently not forthcoming.

Many questions remain unanswered. To what extent can a referee provide false information to a match observer without censure? Did observer, Jim

McBurney, speak to Steven Craven immediately after the match? Did he interview McDonald in private, or was the matter discussed in the referees' room with all the match officials present, as is normally the case?

If McBurney spoke to McDonald in private, away from Craven, why? Why did no evidence from Craven make it into the observer's report? When did Craven give his version of events to Dallas or McBurney? Did Dallas know the truth before speaking to the media two days after the match?

It strains credibility to suggest that McBurney failed to take evidence from Craven or that he spoke to McDonald in private. The SFA statement on the subject ends by saying the Referees' Association *"is to work in tandem with Stewart Regan (SFA CEO) to help develop a respect initiative"*.

A respect initiative? How about giving us the truth?

Returning to the following week's Celtic-Rangers game, whilst Willie Collum was busy reminding *"both Rangers and Celtic of their responsibilities"*, it seems he forgot to remind himself of his own responsibilities as he went on to have the customary howler peppered with "honest mistakes" coincidentally favouring Rangers, most notably awarding Rangers a penalty for a "foul" that both did not exist, and couldn't possibly have been seen from his position with his back to the play. In addition, with shades of 'Seven fouls' Bougherra, he also allowed Lee McCulloch to merrily run around comitting foul after foul whilst on a yellow card, without taking further action against the player.

The media's take on this was a dogmatic refusal to investigate the issue and simply offer a Groundhog Day regurgitation of the same old 'Celtic putting intolerable pressure on referees' theory espoused back in March following the first Dougie McDonald show at Ibrox. Now a five year old child would point and laugh at the absurdity of the media's 'big bad Celtic unfairly intimidating poor wee terrified referees into making mistakes' pish; yet grown men, supposedly fully qualified professionals with degrees in Journalism and everything, trot this guff out as undisputed truth. Yes, they expect grown adults to believe – that each having been cowed into a quivering wreck in fear of their lives by Celtic's vicious bullying – Craig Thomson, Steven Conroy, Dougie McDonald and Willie Collum had no alternative but to make glaring mistakes **against** Celtic?? In which alternative Scottish media version of reality do trembling victims of bullying and intimidation actually screw the perpetrator over as a direct result of their fear of retribution? This simply defies belief. Of course the media have no desire to introduce such basic logic to their latest anti-Celtic theatrical production.

One of the biggest proponents of this anti-logic drivel was, surprise, surprise, the Man With Nosurname himself, a direct beneficiary of the "intolerable pressure" the likes of Willie Collum and Dougie McDonald had to endure:

Rangers boss Walter Smith warns rival Neil Lennon to worry about Celtic, not referees

Daily Record Oct 25th 2010 By Craig Swan and Hugh Keevins

*But seething Smith took time out from the celebrations to open fire on rival boss Lennon - who **accused** whistler Willie Collum of handing the Ibrox club a penalty he didn't even see.*

*That withering blast followed his pre-match press conference last Friday when **Lennon ordered Collum to do his job right**.*

Note that Sir Dignity can be portrayed as "*seething*" and/or raging etc. when this is being spun by the Laptop Loyal as an expression of righteous anger against a cruel and despicable enemy. Lapdogs Keevins and Swan (yes it took two of them to come up with this biased tripe), employ the customary word play with Lennon "*accusing*" Collum of making a mistake, which it was patently obvious to everyone with functioning eyesight, was indeed a mistake. They also paint a vivid picture of Lennon with his horns and pitch-fork aggressively "*demanding*" that poor wee Collum do his job right.

I mean, how unreasonable is that? How else is he supposed to provide the "honest mistakes" to help out Ra Gers if he's expected to do his job right!?

Smith hit back: "I felt there was unfair pressure on the referee to start with and thought he handled the game extremely well. We will always have arguments about one or two decisions."

One or two!? Try dozens and dozens! Yes it's easy to be philosophical about "*one or two*" decisions that can always be relied to help you out.

"But we've now had two Old Firm games out of three where the referee has been placed under unfair pressure before the match."

This is brilliant propaganda, although I doubt Sir Dignity realises it, speaking as he does from the perspective of the self-deceiver, who is quite happy thank you very much, with the status quo. Make the perpetrator the victim, ignore the real issue and focus on irrelevant detail. Any truly objective journalist could easily explain to Nosurname that the reason the referees in each case have been put under "*unfair pressure*" in each of the last **four** Celtic-Rangers games, is actually due to the blundering incompetence of their predecessors, their mistakes, by chance of course, favouring the Establishment team.

"In all the time I have been involved, the majority of Rangers and Celtic games are won by the best team when you look at it. We had 10 minutes at the start and 20 minutes at the start of the second half where we looked the better side."

So Rangers were the better team for the 30 minutes out of the 90, that makes them the better team does it? Genius stuff Wattie. Genius.

"Willie Collum was placed under an unfair pressure. There isn't any doubt about that."

You can thank Craig Thomson, Steve Conroy and Dougie McDonald for that.

"We have to look at what is actually happening rather than blaming the officials."

What is actually happening – like Rangers being awarded a penalty for a blatant dive, or Celtic players getting sent off as a result of Rangers players diving, or Rangers players getting to commit as many fouls as they want, or Celtic having a legal goal disallowed, or not being awarded penalties for blatant fouls in the box – that kind of thing? Yes it really would be better if we just turned a blind eye to that sort of thing Waldo wouldn't it? Don't worry though, because the media and the rest of the Scottish football Establishment are doing their damndest to ensure that's what will happen as soon as they can get Celtic to shut their mouths.

"We all fall out with them and have our own ideas about decisions that go against us."

Oh, we all know you're not shy when it comes to voicing your opinion about officials, especially Irish sounding ones.

"But there comes a time where you have to look a lot deeper than that. Otherwise, there is no use in playing the game."

Couldn't agree more Waldo, couldn't agree more. If only the Scottish media felt the same.

For his part, Neil Lennon had this to say about the game and its controversial moments (from the same Daily Record article and unusually spin free) :

Lennon said: "I wouldn't mind if Rangers cut us open to win the match. But goals change the psychology of games and the penalty looked soft to me. I don't think he saw the incident properly so why did he give it?

"I feel let down by that decision and I think the referee has an obligation to explain that decision. He doesn't necessarily have to make that explanation in public but I'd like to know why he gave it."

"The referee was probably under a lot of pressure going into the match because of all that had been said and written since our game against Dundee United at Tannadice."

"But that doesn't explain anything. There was a long way to go in the match and we were only 2-1 down. Kirk Broadfoot went over easily and a penalty was awarded at a time when we were trying to regroup after going behind for the first time. When you go 3-1 down it's a very difficult road back from that deficit."

Lennon also took issue with the referee's failure to show McCulloch a second yellow card. He said: "It was a blatant case of obstruction. It should have been McCulloch's second yellow, reducing Rangers to 10 men."

But Lennon did concede Celtic had gone soft in the second half. He said: "We shot ourselves in the foot. I said to the players at half-time that we'd gradually improved over the first 45 minutes.

"Our job after the interval was to stay in the game and yet we lost a goal straight away. Hopefully they'll learn from the mistakes they made and make sure they don't make them again."

"The manner of the goals, and the way we lost them, was the most disappointing aspect of the game for me."

Quite a reasonable series of statements from the Celtic manager there. Of course, many will disagree with much of what he said, but the least that can be said is Neil Lennon expressed his opinion in a calm and sensible manner.

Not quite the way that bastion of impartiality, Union Jackson saw it in his match report in the same edition of the rag:

Keith Jackson Daily Ranger 25 Oct

They might even have been reduced to 10 men before half time when McCulloch barged down Georgios Samaras but Collum, who was now in control of the contest - took no further action. **It was almost as if the referee knew he had been too quick to card the Rangers man first time round -** *and he had - but none of that washed with Lennon* **who could sniff conspiracy in the autumn air.**

In 66 minutes the game was up when Majstorovic was suckered into a **clumsy tackle** *on Broadfoot.*

The Rangers full-back left a leg hanging to ensure contact and then threw himself to the ground, all of this happening behind the back of ref Collum who had got himself in a bit of a fankle.

His description of the penalty alone should lose him all of any credibility he might have had, why are journalists so scared to use the word 'dive' when it comes to Rangers players, and why do these sensibilities only apply to the Establishment club? Everyone knows it was a dive, why not criticise the player who cheated? I've become a leading authority on rhetorical questions these days.

This is yet more utter, utter pish from the tabloid bogroll. The most irritating thing is the consistent use of the words 'conspiracy' every time anyone associated with Celtic questions a refereeing decision. The previous weekend we had a manager (Houston), who off his own back, actually used the word 'conspire' to describe a referee's decision (which ultimately went in favour of his team, work that one out!). Yet I have never seen anything written in any paper that would suggest Dundee Utd are conspiracy theorists or paranoid. Neil Lennon answers a journalist's question about decisions honestly, and instantly is branded as *'sniffing conspiracy'*. It's the worst type of lazy and biased journalism, it ignores the fact that Lennon did not blame the referee for the result, that he acknowledge his own team's deficiencies, that he didn't mention or even vaguely insinuate 'conspiracy' and as even Rangers TV Jackson himself said, *'he had a point'*. Again, you are left in the front room with the feet up, a cup of tea and the white elephant for company, and the Scottish media scrambling around furiously trying, and largely succeeding, to discredit everyone connected with Celtic FC.

Mind you, Union Jackson's description of the penalty was rivaled for sheer laughable bias by STV's website - *Willie Collum's decision to give a penalty* against Daniel Majstorovic for a **collision** with Kirk Broadfoot in Sunday's Old Firm derby is the latest contested issue by the Glasgow club.

A collision!? If that's a collision then surely Kyle Lafferty was felled by a cruise missile fired from Charlie Mulgrew's back pocket back in May 2009.

Ewan Murray in The Guardian was a bit more subtle but a further 24 hours later, once the 'death threat' strategy had been hatched, still managed to wildly exaggerate Lennon's statements – *"Celtic have made their displeasure with decisions plain recently. The referee for Sunday's Old Firm derby, Willie Collum, was **castigated** by the club's manager Neil Lennon for awarding a dubious penalty to Rangers."*

Read Neil Lennon's comments again, then read Murray's account etc etc etc

Of course, now the 'death-threat' dimension had been introduced to the mix, conveniently distracting attention way from a few unsavoury details – 1. Many observers felt Lee McCulloch should have been sent off 2. Rangers were awarded a penalty for a blatant dive which the referee couldn't have seen, and 3. This was the third time in four Celtic-Rangers game this pattern of **glaring** honest mistake had occurred in Rangers' favour.

Instead, what the media presented us with, was a lot of hyperbole over unverifiable claims that a Celtic fan, or fans, (we can't know how many due to the media's unrivalled propensity for exaggeration and spin) threatened Wille Collum and/or his family and/or his wife (again, the media can't make up their mind whether it was just the referee, his wife or his family with different reports quoting different variations on the threat).

As I said, these threats could not be proven to come from Celtic fans, but SFA spokesman Darryll 'Rangers season ticket' Broadfoot assured us they had sectarian undertones so I guess it's a fair cop then. I mean there's no other group of fans who would want to sent threats with sectarian undertones to a man who is a Religious Education teacher at a Roman Catholic High School and who was the subject of months of rabid speculation and conjecture, including ludicrous suggestions of having a crucifix pendant attached to his whistle, on a certain well-known popular fan's website with a distinctly blue tinge. A nonsense suggestion clearly.

In fact, most Scottish journalists revealed themselves to be incapable of referring to Collum without mentioning the juicy wee detail about being an RE teacher. The fact that the Religious Education syllabus at Catholic schools is the same as that of any other Scottish school delivering the national curriculum is probably beyond these oafs and their outdated little innuendos. Incidentally can anyone tell me Dougie McDonald, Craig Thomson or Alan Muir's occupation? Seems to be that Collum is the only referee who's vocation is of interest to the Scottish media.

All eyes on 31-year-old RE teacher Willie Collum who was fast-tracked by SFA to the top
The Scotsman 23rd Oct 2010 **By STEPHEN HALLIDAY**

Allan Pattullo
The Scotsman 25th Oct 2010
As any good teacher knows, the key to a disciplined, attentive class is to crack down quickly on any silliness. **Collum, who teaches religious education at Cardinal Newman High School in Bellshill**, *was given an early excuse to lay down the law when Anthony Stokes made one of many nonsensical challenges which littered the afternoon.*

Richard Wilson
The Herald 24th Oct 2010

*A **31-year-old Religious Education teacher**, he was in some ways the central figure. Small, thin, pale, he seemed a slight representation of authority.*

Barry Glendenning The Guardian 24th October (live text updates)
7 min: Rangers have a penalty appeal turned down when Daniel Majstorovic tries to dispossess Sasa Papac in the penalty area. Referee Willie Collom waves away the appeal and replays show he was probably correct - there was non contact between the players, Papac just lost his balance. **FYI: referee Willie Collom is a religious studies teacher. You couldn't make it up.**

I wonder if any of the self-righteous idiots currently pouring their bile onto Neil Lennon for heartlessly endangering this poor young man's life, with his scandalously irresponsible insistence on answering the lapdog's leading questions honestly, would care to criticise any of the journalists who publicly revealed Collum's place of work. Probably not, and why should they? After all, we're belatedly in the 21st century, dragging the knuckle draggers kicking and screaming with us. The knuckle draggers will continue to do stupid and irresponsible things and each and Neil Lennon shouldn't be held responsible for each and every individual act by a bampot (or Rangers supporter masquerading as a Celtic bampot)

But the media preferred to blame Lennon, putting him on the defensive as per the below from the Daily Fail:

Celtic boss Neil Lennon insists Celtic are not to blame for refereeing crisis.

'It's not me who is making a big issue of referees,' said Lennon. 'I didn't do it until last week. But if I feel a controversial decision goes against us, I have the right to ask the question.

'If there is a perception that Celtic are putting pressure on referees, it is an unfair perception. Up until last week, I had never had a problem with referees.

'But when you get a decision as controversial as the one at Tannadice - and another big decision this week - we have the right to ask questions.

"I never got the opportunity to speak to the referee on Sunday. I am still not convinced he saw the incident properly. I don't know how he can be 100 per cent sure it can be a penalty. If he saw it again, I don't think he would say it was a penalty.

*"I disagreed with the decision on Sunday and I still don't think it was a penalty. **The majority of people agree with me on that**."*

A few reasoned comments here and a few factual statements there, enough for the media to blow this up to "Lennon's war on whistlers/ referee's witchhunt". Time for the Fail to dredge up an incident from Lennon's playing days, one where, incidentally, the referee lost the plot almost as much as the player:

Lennon famously clashed with Stuart Dougal *at the end of an Old Firm defeat at Ibrox as a player. But he strongly denies he's been a vocal critic of refs since moving into the dugout last spring.*

I'll tell you something though, you don't have to go back five years to get an example of the Man with Nosurname "*clashing*" with referees.

*He said: "I have been pretty supportive of referees and had a good relationship with them. But when there are decisions like that I have to answer questions as honestly as I can. And if that's a criticism of the refs then so be it. I don't have anything against the referees personally or professionally. **I'm not the first manager to complain about decisions so I don't know why it's being exaggerated so much**. It is not sour grapes because we didn't do ourselves justice in the game. That is the most galling thing."*

If Neil doesn't understand why it's being exaggerated so much, then I would certainly be available to provide a few lessons at a reasonable rate. Mind you, having been at the sharp end of it for close on ten years, I suspect Neil Lennon requires no lessons from me about the sly agendas promoted by the Scottish media.

I not so much a sly agenda, rather an in yer face "we hate you" agenda, The Sun website carried a link on their homepage consisting of a suitably snarling photo of Neil Lennon below a title of "*LIVID LENNON SLAMS CRITICS*". Clicking the snarling seething image takes us to the article, with the original photo blown up to show us the full force of his aggressive 'I want to kill the ref stance' atop a new tagline of "*BLAST…Neil Lennon*". The article itself is titled "***I'm not a Bad Bhoy*** *Neil Lennon last night rounded on his critics…*". No attempt by the paper to frame Lennon in an unflattering light there obviously…

He said: "I have been hearing this for ten years, tempers, tantrums, the same regurgitated rubbish I had as a player I'm getting as a manager, by the same people.

*"People can interpret it any way they want. I don't think I behave any differently from other managers. I don't know why I get criticised. You would need to ask the people who make an issue of it. It seems my behaviour gets exaggerated, **maybe because of who I am and who I manage**."*

Lennon is right on the money and needs no lessons from me.

On the subject of sly agendas, I came up with another new fun game. It's a variation on spot the ball, The Daily Record propaganda version. Spot where Kenny Clark uses the words "Neil" ,"Lennon" or "Lenny" at any point, as according to the Daily Record his remarks all directed at the Celtic manager and only the Celtic manager:

REF BACKLASH IS YOUR FAULT Ex-whistler Clark has pop at Lenny
Daily Record 29th Oct 2010 By Gordon Parks

*Kenny Clark last night told Neil Lennon **he IS** whipping the nutters into a frenzy with his **war on whistlers**.*

*On Tuesday Record Sport told how the **Celtic boss** flatly denied **his rage against refs** led to Willie Collum receiving death threats after his decision to award **Rangers** a **penalty** in Sunday's Old Firm showdown. **But** former top whistler Clark **has taken apart Lennon's defence - and blasted Celtic's insistence on demanding explanations** over refereeing decisions.*

*Clark said: "There is no question that what the **clubs** do stoke the fires of the fanatics. And **they don't** need to be wound up any more. It's a sorry state of affairs when **clubs** are wanting explanations about individual decisions.*

*"It would be a strange world if a referee was to ask a **club** why their star striker missed a penalty. Could he talk us through it? The striker wouldn't be able to explain how he did it. Referees are never going to get agreement on everything, with both teams happy about every decision after a highly charged game."*

*"I'd like to think **everyone** will take a step back and show a bit of restraint in the comments **they** make about match officials. If any young man was contemplating taking up refereeing, then I'm sure after this week their family are trying to dissuade them. Retaining referees is also a problem."*

*Clark also pointed the finger at **bosses** who use the display of officials to blur their own deficiencies and team failings. He said: "From time to time, there is no doubt in my mind **managers** throw up criticism of referees as a smokescreen."*

Nope. I guess I must just be shit at gullibly sapping in their doublespeak propaganda lies.

I can't wait for Lenny's next outburst in the "*war on whistlers*". Maybe something along the lines of "I thought we should've had a corner there" to really cause the SFA's heads to burst in an aneurysm of 'Timmy refusing to know his place and slink back into the corner hatred'. Similar effects can be achieved with pepperami bars or green straws at Park Gardens I hear.

With all of this unseemingly wars and witchhunts on the go, and accusations of accusations of bias, it was time for the SFA to spring into action and sort everything out:

NEW SFA supremo Stewart Regan is ready to get tough to fend off a refs crisis at Hampden.

Now chief executive Regan will seek to push through a raft of proposals aimed at safeguarding refs.

He's had crisis talks with Rangers chief executive Martin Bain over Allan McGregor's ban.

[That one sneaked under the media's 20/20 radar didn't it?]

He is still embroiled in an internal investigation over Dougie McDonald's display at Tannadice last week.

Linesman Craven resigned yesterday after being subjected to fierce personal abuse in the wake of that game.

[This was 26th Oct, five days before the media's 'personal abuse' lie was blown out the water]

Now Celtic boss Neil Lennon has demanded answers from Collum over his derby display in Sunday's win for Rangers.

The bust-ups have led to growing dissatisfaction from Grade One officials.

Not that any of these "*bust-ups*" had anything to do with appalling errors on behalf of these Grade One officials themselves of course.

Now Regan is drawing up a refs' charter in a desperate bid to rebuild shattered confidence among officials.

So what was Stewart Regan's masterplan to rid the game of persistent and endemic "honest mistakes":

- They could include an English-style BAN on gaffers talking about refs before games.
- There could also be on-the-spot fines for managers who blast officials after games. Regan's had to deal with FOUR major rows in three weeks since taking the Hampden hotseat.

These proposals are concerned merely with stifling managers' ability to criticise referees and do nothing to address the widely acknowledged "form slump". All this amounts to is put our fingers in our ears and hope Timmy goes away.

There's an interesting contrast here, between the SFA and the Establishment media's refusal to countenance any criticism of referees and their stance of blaming everyone else, in particular their troublesome rogue Timmy club, for refereeing ills – and the advice dished out to Tony Mowbray and Celtic last season, which was to forcefully insist that all the club's problems were of their own making and they should get their own house in order before pointing the finger elsewhere. Hmmmm, a slight wee spot of hypocrisy from the Scottish football Establishment? Never!

All The Other Dignified Managers

A spin off of the Neil Lennon smear campaign, was to build a utopic vision of an SPL full of well-adjusted sane, salt of the earth managers, providing a sharp contrast with the wee ginger shite © Strachan, G. This was achieved by twisting and bastardising statements from other managers to make it look like everyone in Scotland was 'tut tutting' the Celtic manager for his sheer mentalness and paranoia. An example from the Daily Record:

But Paatelainen - whose side face the Light Blues tonight - **blasted the conspiracy theorists** *and* **talk of refereeing bias** *among officials in Scotland.*

Take a wild guess at who the "*conspiracy theorists*" are? Don't bother with the fact that these "*conspiracy theorists*" have never uttered the word "*conspiracy*" or accused any referee of "*bias*". The Headline was "*Mixu Blasts Lennon*" despite the actual quotes from the Hibs manager amounting to nothing of the sort. This tactic called for the media to ask every manager they could get their hands on about "*talk of bias*" and "*conspiracy theories*"; managers who have not been at the sharp end of anywhere near the number of decisions Celtic have endured over the past year or so, and knowing full well the reason for these leading questions (i.e. to get a dig at Celtic), were therefore hardly likely to start expounding at length on the Establishment agenda against Celtic.

"*STEVEN Pressley last night refused to join the witchhunt against referees despite seeing his Falkirk side knocked out of the Co-operative Insurance Cup by a soft penalty at Aberdeen.*"

Who's "*witchhunt*" would this be then? Oh aye, Neil Lennon's that's right. It's interesting to note that whilst at the same time purporting to defend our poor wee victimised referees to the hilt, the Daily Record (1st Nov) at the same time believes that the award of a "*soft penalty*" would reasonably provide enough motivation to join a refereeing "*witchhunt*". A "*soft penalty*" now isn't really a penalty according to the new Laws of the Game according to the Laptop Loyal. There's nothing like consistency eh.

Another new law introduced under emergency powers allowing the Laptop Loyal to create new Laws of the Game in times of urgent need to smear Celtic, was to allow SPL managers to veto the appointment of referees to oversee their fixtures:

However, Motherwell boss Craig Brown revealed he has no axe to grind with McDonald being the man in the middle for the clash in the Capital. The Fir Park gaffer said: "I have no problem with Dougie being the ref for our game against Hibs. I get on well with Dougie and we have always been fine with each other. He is a good, honest pro and I'm happy with him."

Well we can all sleep in our beds soundly at night now – the manager of Motherwell has no problem with a referee who has given a series of terrible mistakes against Celtic and in favour of Rangers. What a truly dignified gent, and a lesson in how to accept decisions that have absolutely nothing to do with you for the wee ginger shite © Strachan, G.

If anyone, knows about mental rants against referees it's Uncle Walt himself – but he was unavailable for comment on the 5th of November so the Laptop Loyal turned to the second grumpiest auld git in the league, Jim Jeffries. A man who actually reported Willie Collum for two **correct** offside calls, claiming he was "*spoken to like a wee boy*", after he entered Collum's dressing room to politely enquire as to an minor point of clarification if it wasn't a terribly awful inconvenience old chap.

Now, if someone bounded into my office, F-ing and blinding at me for mistakes that didn't exist, he's be lucky to get out with his teeth in place never mind spoken to like a wee boy. Of course, all of that passed off with barely a murmur in the press. Not a "LIVID JEFFRIES" or a "HEARTS BOSS RAGES" headline to be seen for love nor funny handshake. Mr Happy had his say about it all under a headline "**Celtic get their fair share of dodgy refereeing decisions**" in the Daily Record, seemingly unaware that a decision isn't dodgy just because you happen to really, really hate Celtic and wish their goals were all disallowed. The Record once again demonstrates that they are in fact quite open to a good conspiracy theory when it suits their anti-Celtic agenda when Jeffries suggests – raising question marks against his sanity – that Dougie Dougie might end up giving Celtic a "*contentious*" decision i.e. not disallowing a goal because Mr Happy really, really hates Celtic:

"I have listened to a lot of comments and some people have concerns. I am not suggesting for a minute that Dougie might, **but if he took a game involving Celtic and there were any contentious decisions given in favour of them, what is the other manager going to be thinking**?*A lot of managers feel Celtic get their fair share in terms of decisions.*

The Scottish media then took an sudden unaccustomed keen interest in the fortunes of Hamilton Accies after they had a goal disallowed against Dundee United, the Sunday Mail giving them their first backpage splash since they got a player sent off against Celtic:

I won't rap referee over our 'goal', says Hamilton boss Billy Reid
Sunday Mail Nov 7th 2010 By Rob Fairburn
ACCIES boss Billy Reid insists his men were denied a legitimate goal but refused to criticise the match officials. Hamilton thought they had got off to a flier when Dougie Imrie headed home a Marco Paixao cross but linesman Lawrence Kerrigan flagged to say the ball had crossed the byeline before it was delivered. But Reid viewed the incident on video and is convinced it was a goal.

Disappointingly there was no reference to a "war on whistlers" or even a "witchhunt". As it turns out the main reason for Reid's magnanimous reaction had little to do with generous spirit:

Reid had little option but to back the officials after defending referees in his programme notes following the recent row over the controversial Dundee United v Celtic game.

That's what you get for jumping on the Establishment smear campaign bandwagon, get it right up ye!

And of course there was the Man with Nosurname himself, whose staunch defence of the brethren… sorry… referees, has already been well documented here. However, the world contains only a finite number of rent-a-gub SPL managers, so when the Laptop Loyal ran out of them, they simply started interviewing random players, and asking them to provide soundbites for some good "we're dignified unlike mad mental paranoid Celtic" copy:

Time to accept referees make mistakes as much as players, says Dundee United star Scott Robertson
Daily Record 28th Oct 2010 By Euan [that name again with a funny spelling] McArthur

*SCOTT Robertson has refused to join the **chorus of criticism** against referees*

What Chorus? Oh I see, Celtic's. So that's "*chorus of critcism*" to add to "*witchhunt*" and "*war on whistlers*".

However, rather than slating the 31-year-old whistler, Robertson highlighted the fact players regularly make mistakes as a reason to cut refs some slack.

Who should cut Refs some slack? Oh I see, Celtic. Carry on.

"He's seen it his way, given an honest opinion and you have to accept that."

Hmm, I suppose what he is really saying is Celtic are Paranoid?

"We are all human. We make mistakes and referees are no different. I must have made about five in the game myself."

Well there we have it, what the fuck are Celtic complaining about when some random from Dundee United unconnected to any of Celtic's issues with referees feels this way? Can the Daily Record not interview someone from Borussia Dortmund to see what they think? How about Bloomfontein Celtic, but then again with a name like that, they're probably paranoid too.

And another thing – I'm sorry but all of this "players make mistakes too" stuff is utter gash. When a player makes a mistake, only himself and his team-mates suffer. Such is the nature of a team game. However when a referee makes a mistake this has connotations for one of the teams. Now, it is absolutely true to say the average player will make four or five mistakes in a game, and this figure is probably higher for a referee given that he is involved in every passage of play over the 90+ minutes of a game. But statistically these mistakes will result in a throw-in going the wrong way, or a team being awarded a free-kick in the centre-circle. This is where the smoke and mirrors become obvious again, because Celtic's "*chorus of criticism*" concerns **serious glaring errors which fundamentally affected the outcome of games**, not piffling 50/50 throw-in or free-kick decisions.

This exposes the second flaw in this line of argument, being, that if a player had made the same number of catastrophic errors as Dougie Dougie or his brethren, that player would soon find himself out the team sooner than you could say "I thought I was allowed to kick the goalie in the head". We certainly wouldn't see the player's manager staunchly defending him in the media, and dragging out his team-mates and other players seemingly at random to state what a great player and all-round jolly nice chap this guy is. But it's obvious that the closed enclave of the refereeing Establishment operate on different terms.

Just to get the full perspective on Celtic's "*war on whistlers*", I feel I should include the official club statement on the matter as elaborated by chairman John Reid:

AFTER recent events involving the match at Tannadice, and yesterday's SFA statement, Celtic have issued the following statement.

Celtic Chairman John Reid said: "Following events at Tannadice, it was Celtic's absolute right to request clarification on a matter of this nature. Indeed, it is widely accepted that this was an incident which deserved some explanation.

"It was also correct that the Scottish Football Association conduct an investigation into events following the resignation of an assistant referee. Clearly, as a result of this investigation it is very unfortunate that dishonesty has been proven. This, of course, is a matter for the SFA to deal with.

"However, we are encouraged by the proposals of the new Chief Executive Stewart Regan, to address a series of issues within the SFA and to allow greater transparency and openness in all future decision making. While we would have liked a review to be more independent in nature, Stewart Regan's objectives are to be applauded.

"We fully understand that there is intense pressure on referees in a high-profile environment. We know too that they carry out a very difficult job.

"We now look forward to the review process being carried out and to the implementation of the appropriate recommendations."

Phew! Somebody give than madman a chill pill.

Make the Perpetrator the Victim

The day after Celtic's defeat to the Establishment club, Richard Wilson, dabbing an onion to his eye, informed a sobbing Herald readership that the most heart-rending story of the decade was "*Willie Collum loneliest man on the pitch after penalty mistake*".

"*Is there any individual more isolated on an Old Firm day, or left more vulnerable to the terrible burden of trying to make sense of the convulsions of the game, than the referee?*

Willie Collum was the sole figure in the midst of all the recriminations at Celtic Park, and he might never have felt so stripped bare of everything but his judgment and even this has to be delivered instantly."

After putting his trowel away Wilson goes on to inform his distraught readers that "*There is a sensitivity at Celtic Park to decisions that go against the team,*", as if all eleven other SPL sides are the epitome of grace and frivolity when the victims of refereeing mistakes. Wilson adds, "*even if the worst that might be said of Scotland's officials is that the standard is not as uniformly high as it should be.*" Well one or two people may think that's really not the worst that can be said at all, no in fact I'm pretty certain about that.

If you haven't got the picture by now, of a trembling Collum set upon by bullying Tims and thrust wailing into the seething cauldron of Celtic Park during a Glasgow derby, then Wilson obviously thought he'd make sure by laying it on ever so thick: "*The effect was to call every one of Collum's decisions in this game into question even before he made them, and this pressure followed him on to the pitch as he led out both teams. A 31-year-old Religious Education teacher, he was in some ways the central figure. Small, thin, pale, he seemed a slight representation of authority.*" In case you are wondering, having never seen Willie Collum before, he is in fact an adult from Lanarkshire, and not a starving, Albanian toddler as depicted by the over-enthusiastic lapdog.

Wilson finished his article by touching upon the nub of the matter at last; the fact that Collum followed the standard practice of match officials during derby games by awarding the most controversial decisions in Rangers favour. Wilson, to his credit, hints that match officials have some form on this matter, but inevitably bottles out of directly venturing into such media heresy, blithely stating that nothing nefarious is going on and that all controversial decisions were just "*bad calls*": "*Collum then had to face up to the realisation that two decisions would be highlighted, that the failure to send off McCulloch and the penalty call would be pored over. And that the mistakes would, in some places, be seen as evidence of something different, a kind of prejudice. They were not, they were bad calls. But there is no more damned figure than a referee on Old Firm day.*"

Wilson, as with every other Scottish journalist refuses to discern any pattern in the routine awarding of such "*bad calls*" to Rangers, nor of any pattern where decisions are given in Rangers favour that wouldn't be awarded to Celtic in a decade of Sundays. Such analysis would of course raise questions, and Scottish sports journalists are loath to raise any questions that could cause discomfort or embarrassment to the sport's Establishment. Critics of modern mainstream journalism, and even journalists themselves, refer to this as the centripetal tendency; the heavy reliance on, and facing towards, the centres of power for facts and opinions.

During the hue and cry following match officials "honest mistakes", the mainstream media sticks to its tried and trusted method of casting the perpetrator as a victim, and the injured party as the villain, as we saw, when Richard Wilson placed Celtic in the role of bogeyman for having the temerity to complain about the antics of Dougie McDonald. Complaining about decisions by match officials can never be justified according to Scottish sports journalists, as any possibility that non-"honest mistakes" occur can never be considered, hence there are no grounds to complain. When "honest mistakes" can be predicted to occur in one team's favour on a regular basis, then this awkward situation is countered by a simple refusal to refrain from acting like the three monkeys of popular legend.

It's not as if we're all screaming for the media to turn round and admit there's been an Establishment conspiracy against Celtic for nigh on a hundred years (shades of My Happy's sidekick). Personally, I would be happy just to hear one solitary Scottish journalist say "You know, there's something worth looking into there, maybe Celtic have a point". This fanciful prospect is merely the minimum that would be expected of a "journalist" under the traditional, out-dated, naïve definition of the word. I guess none of those really exist in Scottish football any longer.

The "Neutral" Character Witnesses

Propaganda is basically about smoke and mirrors – creating an illusion that diverts the onlookers attention from the fundamental issues at the heart of the question, onto issues that are irrelevant or insignificant. This is underpinned by only providing a partial picture of the facts, discarding those that don't fit the desired inference and then reaching the pre-determined conclusion that the propagandist set out to arrive at. This can then be presented as fact based on the relevant evidence, where nothing could be further from the truth. The genius of it, is that there's just enough truth in the distorted version of reality to maintain the illusion of fact, whilst certain relevant information is kept out of the picture.

For example, a propagandist may be argue that it is unfair to a particular team who wear blue jerseys and are really dignified, that the season can't be extended to help them with a particularly congested period of fixtures in the run up to a UEFA Cup final, especially when a certain other Timmy team were allowed "help" when they reached a UEFA Cup final five years previously. Taken at face value, this certainly seems unfair, and undeniably all the information contained in that statement is incontrovertible truth. With all the facts presented it would certainly seem fair to conclude that any extension request should be granted to the poor little victimised Establishment club.

Of course the propagandist, or Jim Traynor as he's otherwise known, has quite deliberately missed out key information to arrive at the desired conclusion. The key lies in the detail regarding the "help" that was so benevolently dispensed by the Scottish football Establishment to that treacherous Timmy team all those years ago. Some key relevant facts that were "dropped" from the picture:

1. The "help" consisted of allowing Celtic to bring **forward** an SPL fixture against Dundee, thereby reducing the preparation time available for this match
2. The "help" did not involve extending the season in any way, shape or form
3. Extending the season would have no impact on Rangers' attempts to win the UEFA Cup, the true intention was to improve their prospects of winning the SPL title

As discussed earlier another missile in the propagandists armoury is the 'Straw Man' smear. This is usually complemented by an 'Iron Man' protagonist who the 'Straw Man' can be unfavourably compared to. Often, several 'Iron Men' are served up to expose the sheer absurdity of the 'Straw Man's' position.

So it was, back in March 2010, following the first Dougie McDonald show (we actually have to number his shambolic pro-Rangers performances), that that bastion of the Laptop Loyal wheeled out a neutral "*English ref*" to comment on the debacle from an objective viewpoint. Except, of course, that who the NOTW turned to, just coincidentally happened to be a rampant Rangers fan who writes a blog on his exploits supporting the Queen's Eleven:

English ref runs the rule over controversial Old firm game

JEFF WINTER CHECKS OUT DOUGIE McDONALD'S PERFORMANCE IN POWDERKEG CLASH

News of the World By Kenny MacDonald, 07/03/2010

RANGERS legend Richard Gough called for English refs to take control of future Old Firm derbies in last week's Sport of the World.

And we always have to listen to what Rangers legends have to say don't we? Not like those mad paranoid Timmy ones who ramble on about 50 years of dodgy refereeing.

So we invited former top whistler Jeff Winter to run the rule over Dougie McDonald's performance at Ibrox after Sky TV supplied him with a DVD of the action.

Not only is he a rabid cream bun, he's a "top" whistler too! Good choice Kenny.

His verdict is that McDonald could come out of the game with his conscience clear - even over the red card for Scott Brown.

Stop the presses! Get that headline ready – "Rangers supporting referee backs fellow referee who sent off Celtic player against Rangers – SHOCK!".

He said: "Overall the referee had a good game. You're not going to get every decision right."

Celtic fans fully agree that referees are not going to get every decision right, but this is merely more of the tiresomely predictable smoke and mirrors game, with the media building up the mad unreasonable Celtic Straw Man, who expects no less than absolute perfection from our Scottish referees. This is simply biased propaganda nonsense. No Celtic fan, player, manager or official has ever "demanded" [(c) The Sun] that referees get every decision correct – we've simply raised concerns around the ostensible **fact** that they continue to make **howling mistakes** that **consistently** go against **Celtic** and favour **Rangers**. But this unpleasant line of enquiry can't be countenanced by our Establishment media, so they have to spin it into a scenario of big bad bully Tims and their crazy unrealistic demands.

"The big decision was the Brown red card and it's pretty simple. If Dougie McDonald thinks Brown has head-butted Lafferty in the chest he's got to show a red card."

Oh right, so that's what FIFA's Laws of the Game say do they, Mr ex-Premiership referee? "A red card shall be administered if the referee **thinks** someone is guilty of violent conduct" – is that what the rule book says? So basically, it doesn't matter what **actually** took place, any decision by the referee is de facto correct? It may sound absurd, in fact there is no "may" about it, but this is the Establishment line – that effectively referees can't make mistakes because they give what they **think** was the correct decision at the time. However there is an exception to this rule, which applies if the referee's decision can be proven to be "incredible" in a Kangaroo Court of the Scottish media.

"When you see it again and again it's six of one and half-a-dozen of the other and in retrospect you'd maybe view it as a nothing incident, take them both aside and show a yellow card each."

OK.... so, having backed the referee's decision through some bizarre "I think, therefore it is" logic, Winter now describes the sending off as a *"nothing incident"*. I may be crazy and paranoid, but does that not seem ever so slightly contradictory to you? Surely Dougie McDonald must then have been wrong to send Brown off on the basis of a *"nothing incident"*? Maybe that's just me though. However, the reason this mealy mouthed weasel backtracking is required, is that for Winter to get the instigator of the whole incident – Lafferty – off the hook, the incident has to be played down, whilst at the same time exaggerating Brown's part in it all to justify his red card, resulting in two conflicting assertions. Nearly all Scottish newspapers helped in this regard by publishing the most incriminating photo possible alongside their coverage of the incident, one that appeared to show Brown headbutting Lafferty in the chest and his poor victim with arms akimbo reeling under the hammer blow. Anyone who hadn't seen from TV footage that there was almost no forward momentum in the head movement, their natural reaction would be to believe that Brown was guilty of violent conduct. The almost universal use of that photo by Scottish newspapers constituting yet another inexplicable coincidence.

A Rangers supporter I spoke to soon after had a real foot in mouth moment when justifying McDonald's decision not to refer the matter to the Review Panel – "it was the media's fault with that photo they all used making it look worse than it was" she said. And therein lies the key problem for the propagandist – the tangled web of lies inevitably leads to contradictory and often absurd juxtapositions of argument i.e. in this case, in his rush to defend the unbiased referee, the Rangers apologist had inadvertently implicated his Establishment media accomplices.

Of course, if Winter was a genuinely objective observer there would be no need for such gymnastics of logic to explain why the Rangers player got off Scot-free (so to speak). The reason would be – to borrow a phrase again – the referee f****d up.

"Lafferty may - not for the first time, I might say - have over-reacted but if the referee sees that forward movement of the head it's violent conduct and not too many people would say that the referee's done anything wrong."

Well I'll give Jeffrey something, at least he acknowledges that Laughable has form in this area, but on the other hand, observe the ever so careful and dainty language. One is left to ponder why the neutral and objective English ex-Premiership referee didn't choose to use a slightly more accurate term like "dive", or, to borrow a phrase from… himself… "*cheating b*****d*". Nope, I'm left scratching my head over that one.

Maybe Scott Brown should have just kicked Lafferty in the head and everyone would have agreed how "ridiculous" McDonald's decision was, and the appeal would have been upheld by now, letting us all get on with eating our mooncheesecake before getting on Pegasus for a wee ride over the rainbow to the land of Oz.

"*The incident confirmed what I have thought about Scottish football in general - that it's handled very strictly. In some ways, the referees are more consistent than we are in England because of that. Everyone knows where they stand.*"

Yes I'm sure the Celtic players know exactly where they stand Jeff, as do quite a few of the Establishment FC players who are rather nifty with their elbows. Just one minor quibble though, I'd be tempted to replace the words "*strictly*" and "*consistent*" with "biasedly" and "biased".

"For quite some time, having been to seven or eight of them in the flesh, I've thought the Glasgow derby is the biggest club game in the world. I've refereed every big derby in England and nothing compares"

Jeff's been at seven or eight Us-V-Them games has he. I wonder who he was supporting? Give me a few guesses.

"I'd also suggest it's the most difficult game to handle. In Scotland everything is concentrated in the central belt and everything focuses on the Old Firm game when it comes around. Throw in the religious aspect in Scotland and it's inevitable that **conspiracy theories** *are going to arise."*

Ah, the old 'conspiracy theories' smear. I wonder who Jeff could be getting at with that comment? Aye, he may be English but like his pal Goram, he's been really quick on the uptake when it comes to such unsavoury aspects of Scottish life.

"In saying all that, every referee in the world wants to handle the big games where there's passion and drama and I'd have loved to do it."

No thanks. We're good for biased pro-Rangers refs up here for the foreseeable future. You could try your luck at getting a column in a Scottish newspaper though. I mean if that semi-literate Hateley can get one then surely you can with a bit of crayola training.

"He [Bougherra] had four fouls on Celtic players after his booking and it didn't appear to me that the referee even spoke to him, either directly or through the Rangers captain although of course he might have done so because we don't know what conversations were going on when the cameras weren't on the referee. Overall I thought Boughherra was fortunate."

So it's the referee's responsibility to seek out and speak to Rangers players, or the Rangers captain, to ensure he doesn't have to send a Rangers player off, is it? That sounds about right.

Both sides had penalty claims waved away - and Winter makes an interesting point regarding TV's influence on coverage. "Kamara looked to me like he was going down in the incident involving him. With Maurice Edu and Andreas Hinkel, there is contact between the players but you can make penalties out of both incidents if you watch them in slow motion. **The referee has to be 100 per cent sure before he can give that kind of decision.**"

Yes, call me mental and slap me in the face with a rubber glove full of jelly, but I always was a big believer that a referee should only give a penalty for infringements he can actually see, and it also helps if a foul has actually taken place. Here we have the crazy doublespeak propaganda juxtaposition problem again, as seven months later the Scottish media would be rushing to defend a referee who gave a penalty to Rangers for a challenge that wasn't even a challenge, never mind a foul, and that he couldn't have seen, whilst here we have one of their apologist stooges rattling on about how a referee has to be 100 percent sure to give a penalty.

"The build-up to the game was difficult for the referee because of Celtic's leaked statements about what had happened in previous games. I thought that was silly. Leaking statements criticising referees three days before an Old Firm game? It's not going to buy you any favours that are going, is it? Maybe someone thought it was a Fergie-style mind game but it just seemed like a pointless exercise."

A wee bit more Celtic bashing from this "neutral" English ex-Premiership referee just for good measure. Again, I would have to quibble slightly with this doublespeak propaganda shite, but how the fuck can you "leak" a "statement"? A statement by it's very nature is something that is announced to whomever it may concern. What was actually "leaked", was a request for clarification around several refereeing errors". Not quite the same thing as *"leaking statements criticising referees"* any fair-minded person would agree. And there was only one request, not several as Winter implies with the use of the plural *"statements.* As it happens, Celtic were not looking for any *"favours"* – the smoke and mirrors twister game still being played effectively here - , what we were looking for, was fair and balanced refereeing, which was seemingly too much to ask for, and Winter is so ironically on the money in his assessment that this was a pointless exercise.

You might have by now, built up a picture as to why Celtic fans and officials are so keen on the notion of "fair-minded" individuals, as such individuals are as rare as rocking horse jobbies within the Scottish media – and also the ex-Premiership referee community it would seem.

Winter says Hampden beaks have shown their strength this season - in their handling of Rangers boss Walter Smith. Winter said: "Walter Smith was banned from the touchline for four games this season for criticising a referee. That shows they can hand out strong punishment.

It also shows just how much previous Sir Dignity has for this *"referees witchhunt"* kind of thing, yet the Sun and the Daily Record et al, haven't published any snarling photos of the Rangers manager alongside headlines like "Walter's fury at refs" or "Walter blasts officials". Another honest mistake surely.

So when the "Dougie, Dougie" controversy erupted, who else for the Daily Record to turn to for an objective view on events than Jeff "Refereeing Guru" Winter. And knock me over with a feather, the neutral *"refereeing guru"* backed Dougie McDonald to the hilt :

Celtic cover-up was down to match officials not having guts to admit mistake, says refereeing guru Jeff Winter
Daily Record 1st Nov 2010 By Gavin Berry

Before we even get into the story we've got propaganda spin diarrhoea oozing out of the page. Note that this is all a *"Celtic"* cover-up, not a *"Dougie McDonald"* cover-up or even an *"SFA"* cover-up. Now, if Jeff Winter is a refereeing *"guru"* then Keith Jackson is a tim. Still, the Record hack has an Iron Man to build…

Now, before I go any further I want to re-set the "conspiracy theory quote" clock to zero.

conspiracy theory count = 0

*Craven has since resigned and McDonald has been warned but Winter says what happened in the aftermath of the match should not be an excuse for **conspiracy theorists** to jump on the bandwagon.*

conspiracy theory count = 1

It just fuels the conspiracy theorists, of whom there are plenty in Scotland.

conspiracy theory count = 2

Who are these "*conspiracy theorists*" you speak of Mr Guru? Are they the type who claim that Aberdeen only ever try in games against them, or that the SPL have got it in for them and fix the post-split fixtures to screw them over, or that the SFA are deliberately bringing forward Review Panel hearings to make sure their players miss key games? Because as far as conspiracy theories go, those are absolute belters.

"*I can see why they've done it because the truth makes the referee look a little bit foolish. He gave the penalty, then thought to himself he shouldn't have. The only thing is it would have made him look a bit silly. Not wrong and not dishonest just a little bit silly.*"

Not as silly as you sound here with your semi-literate propaganda rambling apologist drivel. But it gets better...

"*You can say they've lied **but it's to sell the decision**. It all seems a bit petty.*"

Here we have a "*refereeing guru*", telling us that it's "*petty*" to object to match officials conspiring to deceive the Celtic manager, the match observer, the SFA and the general public, to stop Dougie McDonald looking a bit silly.

Although I'm keenly aware of what Willie Collum does for a living, I can't say the same for Dougie McDonald, but it seems second-hand car salesman may be a possibility. Surely if the referee gets decisions correct in the first place there's no need to "*sell*" decisions. I'm sure most fair-minded people would agree that talk of referee's "*selling*" decisions is something that is inconsistent with fairness and objectivity.

"*But this will do nothing to help the accusations some people jump to with regard to football in Scotland.*"

A near "conspiracy theory" mention miss. Whoever can Mr Guru be referring to? I wonder if these accusations involve naming the Irish sounding linesman, or everybody wanting decisions against them and it's just no fair.

Craven revealed in yesterday's Sunday Mail he had an on-going problem with refs chief Hugh Dallas and his sidekick John Fleming and Winter is suspicious over the linesman's reasons for quitting.

He said: "You've got to ask yourself why the assistant took the stance he did. Is it something personal between him and the SFA? I can't say because I'm not close enough to it, but it seems that way"

That's beauty – "*I can't say because I'm not close enough to it*", but then I'll just go ahead anyway and promote my biased tripe as more believable than the reasons given by the person concerned. This is reminiscent of the guff regularly trotted out by fans from the Dark Side whenever some referee has the temerity (and career suicidal tendency) to award a penalty against them. After whining about the award– that came with 10 seconds to go and Rangers winning 3-0 - for half an hour, they will invariably finish off their rant, devoid of any irony whatsoever, with - "aye but we don't complain, we just get on with it".

It's funny how us Celtic fans are expected to take everything at face value and unquestionably swallow the hollow assurances trotted about by the apologists, yet these same Establishment stonewallers can leap on a conspiracy theory when it suits them quicker than a pigeon on a pavement pizza.

Well, I've asked myself why Steven Craven took the stance he did and I've concluded that it's for the reasons he stated, so do me a favour and cut out the paranoid conspiracy theory shite please.

"*This incident could have happened in any game, the fact it involved Celtic shouldn't fuel the conspiracy theorists.*"

conspiracy theory count = 3

"*It also puts Dougie McDonald in an unenviable position. There will be doubts over his integrity. That shouldn't be the case as he's not done anything wrong - it's just the way they went about getting their stories straight* **to sell it**.*"*

"*Post-match it's agreed what's going in a report because the last thing you want is the referee saying black and the assistant saying white. It's about everyone singing from the same hymn sheet. You don't alter a story but you talk it through so you're all going to be writing the same thing.*"

This defies belief. How much of a meathead buffoon do you need to be to prattle on about how nobody should give an credence to conspiracy theories and then... go on to describe how normal it is for referees to conspire with assistants to "decide" what's going in the report. Again, a revolutionary idea would be to get decisions correct and then be honest about the, but that might be a step too far for Scotland.

"*It's like in a court of law with the police. If one says there were five of them and another says there were 10 of them then people would say 'Hang on, they don't really know what happened here*".

Yeah, a bit like if a referee made a string of errors consistently benefiting the same team and the SFA said "honest mistakes", the media would say "Hang on....", sorry no, scratch that.

"You don't go into darkened rooms and write your report but normally there's nothing sinister, it's just talking about an incident with the players, the crowd or a manager."

Well it's good to know that referees do their conspiring in well-lit rooms.

I could be generous and say, the Daily Record made a serious error of judgement, and simply didn't know this guy's pro-Rangers background in their determined quest for a neutral refereeing "guru" to comment on the latest controversy surrounding Celtic. This is barely credible as it is, but the Daily Record's complete lack of concern for maintaining any semblance of neutrality, and their utter contempt for Celtic fans becomes clear when you consider the very same rag published the story below back in May 2010:

Celtic fury at ex-Premiership ref Jeff Winter's internet slurs on club
Daily Record 8th May 2010 By Neil Cameron

*CELTIC last night demanded an apology from ex-ref **Jeff Winter** after he called **Aiden McGeady a "cheating b******"** and branded **Neil Lennon a hate figure.***

*The former Premiership whistler, **a Rangers fan**, spoke out on his wesbite after attending Tuesday's Old Firm game.*

*Record Sport was inundated with calls from angry Celtic fans about an article on Jeff Winter; the Ref Fights Back in which **he described Celtic Park as "The Glitter Dome"** - a reference to the abuse scandal at Celtic Boys' Club.*

*Regarding McGeady, Winter said: "Lee McCulloch was unwise to launch himself into a challenge having already been booked but **the cheating b****** McGeady** did not help matters by deliberately going to ground without any contact being made."*

*Later in the article Winter added: "So Lennon got his victory and I, like most Rangers fans, would be happy to see him get the job. **He provides an excellent 'hate' figure** and also it would mean he does not join Chesney (Gordon Strachan) at Middlesbrough."*

And the Daily Record later wheels out this clown as a refereeing "guru" to back up Dougie McDonald and tell the Tims to shut up and stop being so paranoid.

Mixu Paatelainen talked about referees being found out if they were biased, yet the media can be so shamelessly pro-Rangers and nobody raises an eyebrow (except "paranoid" Celtic fans of course).

Having established that Jeff Winter is a bitter bluenose, it's interesting to note that another ex-Premiership referee commented on the "Dougie, Dougie" fiasco, yet mysteriously his opinion wasn't plastered all over the pages of the Laptop Loyal in flashing lights, neither was he described as a "guru". The man in question was ex-FIFA referee Graham Poll and when you read what he had to say, you begin to get a picture as to why the Scottish press were a tad less enthusiastic to publicise his opinion on the matter:

Graham Poll said: "It was bizarre. It's player pressure working, which is something we shouldn't see.

"The ref has got a clear-ish view of it and thinks the keeper has taken the centre-forward out and gives a penalty - so far nice and simple. The players know that the keeper has got a touch on the ball but it should still be a foul.

"They pressurise the referee, he feels that pressure and goes to talk to the assistant and the assistant says to him 'the keeper got a touch to the ball' and the ref says 'no penalty, my mistake, I'm sorry guys'.

"If refs make mistakes and admit they've blown the whistle when they shouldn't have done, then you can respect him.

"But for me it was a penalty all day. It's a glaring error."

This is reminiscent of another ex-English referee, whose opinions failed to make into flashing lights in the Scottish press. This one's Irishy sounding name would have flagged up the Laptop Loyal's Defcon responses at an early stage, allowing them to prevent any mention in the Loyal Trinity of the Sun, Daily Record and Evening Time:

And Gallagher - who refereed in England's top flight for 15 years from 1992 to 2007 and was a FIFA-listed official from 1994 to 2002 - insists both Brown and Lafferty were guilty of a similar crime.

He said: "I did not think it was a red card. The referee positioning appears to be behind Lafferty when the incident takes place. The reason why this is not a red card for me is because I feel Lafferty was just as guilty as Brown in all of this.

"The referee should have treated both players the same. I think the official sent Brown off because of a head-butting motion. But the official looked to be behind Brown when it happened.

"I don't think it is a red card at all and I would be gutted if I was a player and I got sent off for that.

Foreign referees can't come quick enough, although I would have some reservations over English ones.

Talking of referee's, a minor point that received no attention in the aftermath of "Dougie, Dougie"

The FIFA Laws of the Game on 'Showing dissent by action or word', page 116, states that "A player who is guilty of dissent by protesting (verbally or non-verbally) against a referee's decision must be cautioned."

Note, **must** be cautioned, not *may* be cautioned, **must** be cautioned.

See the picture below. Immediately prior to rescinding Celtic's penalty against Dundee United, referee Dougie McDonald was surrounded by **six** protesting Dundee United players, one of whom placed a hand on McDonald's arm.

No yellow cards resulted and Jim McBurney the match observer reported: *"Management of players was good, in the 69th minute (rescinded penalty) incident the referee maintained his composure and managed to get his message across to players without any requirement to sanction"*.

So don't believe your lying eyes, believe what we tell you.

The More Things Change

And so it goes on, it was ever thus…

The very weekend after the controversy surrounding Clubfoot and the penalty-that-was-but-never-should-have-been, referee Ian Brines failed to award Inverness a penalty at Ibrox despite a blatant illegal body-check on Richie Foran in the Rangers penalty area. The Scottish media went to sleep, totally ignoring it, or in a few isolated cases, reporting in passing that the Inverness striker *"went down"* in the box. There appears to be an inordinate proportion of vertigo sufferers among visiting teams to Ibrox. That well-known paranoid tim, Inverness manager Terry Butcher ruefully stated in his after match interview "[visitors] *don't get penalties at Ibrox*". Careful now Tel. It defies credibility to imagine the media would have totally ignored such a glaring referee error in Celtic's favour, after all, the media have already subjected us to levels of mass hysteria over a penalty and two goals that were **correctly** given to Celtic this season. God forbid if an honest mistake ever went our way. And make no mistake – Celtic **will** benefit from a **genuine** howler at some point or another, as referees are only human after all. And we can be sure the media will go to town on it, pointing their spindly fingers and screeching that everything has evened itself out. You can be pretty sure too, that this will happen either very early in the season or in April or May if or when Rangers have wrapped up another league title brought to you by The Honest Mistakes.

Welcome to the world of the Scottish football media – propaganda peddled by spineless, amoral toadies and vocational liars. Noam Chomsky is particularly good on the dynamics of this type of corporate fake reality in which the real story is the one thing that is ignored while half-truths taken out of context, deliberate misrepresentations and downright lies throw up a smokescreen around the guilty parties and turn them into the heroes of the hour. And so it is with the Scottish media.

The **real** story, the **blindingly obvious** story, the **inescapable** story, is the different treatment that Celtic and Rangers receive from the same groups - the officials, the media and the authorities, who all favour Rangers, and have done for decades.

But instead the media will talk about how lonely Willie Collum looks.

Instead they'll talk about alleged, unproven and tediously predictable reports of an unpleasant phone call or two

Instead they'll taint the issue through terminology like "conspiracy theory" and "war on whistlers"

Instead they'll ambush Mixu Paateleinen with a leading question and distort his answer into "Mixu Slams Lennon".

Instead they'll harangue Craig Brown to try and get him to call Shaun Maloney a diver

And instead they'll turn a blind eye to the histrionics of the spoilt child Establishment club as they fire off their "strongly-worded" letters to the SFA and fling around accusations at the SPL over the fixture list year after year, and at other clubs, accusing them of only trying in games against them.

In contrast to our paranoia, all of this will be spun by the media as a club fighting back against unfair treatment.

All of it is pathetically predictable.

If the press and the officials were honest and if they were doing their job properly, they would at the **very, very least** recognise that
Celtic do consistently get the worst of refereeing mistakes and that
they don't even themselves out in the end. The recognition of this straightforward fact does not compel anybody to conclude that there is a conspiracy to cheat Celtic (any more than being unable to identify a particular flying object is grounds for believing that there is life on Mars.)

It does provide a moral imperative to investigate the issue though, and any honest man would be troubled by such a consistent variation from the laws of chance. He would be open to an explanation of why such a strange, unexplained phenomenon should persistently manifest itself, and would leave no stone unturned in his earnest and honest desire to root out an anomaly which simply should not exist.

The fact that the media and the rest of the Establishment poodles spring into attack mode whenever Celtic have the cheek to talk out of line – with Neil Lennon returning to the top of their hate list – points to a wagon-circling exercise designed to preserve the anomaly, not to correct it. The logical conclusion is that they have no interest in truth as the truth does not serve their interests.

The fact that many of these newspapers and radio hacks have in the past been forced by legal action, or the threat thereof, to publish apologies to Celtic players and officials to atone for their previous lies, is also reasonable grounds for doubting their integrity. The list is impressive –

Lennon, O'Neill, Sutton, Lawwell, Boruc – not to mention the "astounded of forehead" reaction of the Bologna chairman to their transfer lies about Nakamura, and the lengths they will go to to slander Celtic fans. The "Celtic fans in hammer attack on Burkey" story being a particular classic, concerning as it did – confirmed by Burke's father –, the inadvertent smashing of a restaurant window by Rangers fans (with no hammer in sight) waving at Chris Burke, and not as "accidentally" reported by the Sun "*hate-filled fans wearing Celtic strips shouting abuse and wielding a hammer*". Not only is this scandalous and revealing in itself, but stands in stark contrast to the Scottish media's repeated pandering to the real hooligans who regularly rampage around Europe, but are constantly described as being the victims of heavy-handed policing / Chelsea fans / a big screen failure / a KGB conspiracy etc etc etc by our pathetic press.

The fact that Jim Farry was stoutly defended right up to, and in some cases, even beyond the bitter end, by his colleagues and the press alike, demonstrates that those parties had no intention of assessing honestly the overwhelming case against him which Fergus McCann had clearly and meticulously outlined for those of a more impartial mindset.

There are too many defences of official irregularities which are regularly punctuated with declarations that "Dougie/Hugh/Willie/Craig/Iain is an honest guy..." not to make one suspect that this, rather than incompetence, is the issue which they most fear being caught out on. Methinks that they do protest too much about that.

In any case, at least **one** of Hugh Dallas, Dougie McDonald and Steven Craven **is** telling porkies, of that, there can be no doubt, even though I've heard numerous pundits tell us that "Hugh/Dougie/Steven" is an honest guy...

Hugh Dallas and Stewart Regan have been dragged centre stage, and the issue is now not only the behaviour of McDonald, but whether a greater issue exists regarding the honesty of match officials and the validity of the SFA's whole management structure, especially concerning referees. As Ewan Murray in The Guardian said: "*For the make-up of the committee, to which Regan reported the findings of his investigation into the Dundee events, highlights one of many obvious flaws within the SFA. Its refereeing committee comprises six former referees out of a seven-man panel. This is the equivalent of the players' union presiding over disciplinary matters relating to their own members in the Scottish Premier League*".

Murray also touches upon the issue of the integrity of match officials: "*If such issues are subjective in part, the proof that the SFA is willing to go easy on a referee found guilty of being economical with the truth is cut and dried; there has been a clemency displayed that leaves onlookers to wonder on what other matters officials can collude with each passing game. The relationship between the outside world and Scottish referees, already at an all-time low, will continue to deteriorate.*"

Jim Traynor's message to Celtic a mess of contradictions

I said earlier that a key problem for the Establishment propagandist is the propensity for his hypocrisy and double-standards to lead him down a path of making wildly contradictory statements that can subsequently be held up to ridicule. What the propagandist depends on to a great degree is the short-term memory of the gullible public – the fact that they are highly unlikely to remember the completely contradictory waffle that the journalist spouted several weeks or months previously. It is not difficult for the Celtic supporter to think of multiple examples in the weird and wonderful world of Scottish football journalism. The common perception of football fans is that we are all lumpen proleteriat who are incapable of remembering what we had for dinner yesterday and will believe any old horse manure. Certainly this must be the conclusion drawn for some of the excrement served up in Scottish newspapers dressed up as news or fact.

In reality it hardly seems necessary to state that football fans are spread across many demographics, occupations and social classes, and a brief search of the Internet turns up websites with more far accurate, informed and eloquent comment than could ever be found in the Shitey Trinity of the Sun, Record and Evening Times. Clearly this is what Traynor and co are scared of. Certainly there are great swathes of online knuckle-draggers venting their spleen too, and don't the hacks love to point and laugh, and in the process, pann the Internet as an appropriate medium for expressing valid opinion. Participants offering lucidly written observations based upon verifiable sources (the likes of me and you) are referred to as "cybernuts" by cliché wielding buffoons with their crayolas and stencils. Of course, the journalistic bourgeoisie don't have any qualms about providing the lumpen proles with a soap box via their radio phone-ins and hotlines. Of course that's where the money is.

But to return to the matter of the pitfalls of the propagandist, although there is always the hazard that some smart arse will go back through the archives and hold up your previous totally contradictory proclamations to ridicule [ahem!], it is relatively rare for a lapdog to actually be so dense as to contradict himself *in the same article*. But this is what Jim Traynor achieved in the first week of November 2010, in an attempt to blame Celtic for all the issies

Open up or shut up
Daily Record 1st Nov 2010 By Jim Traynor

This could be a big week for Celtic. Over the next few days the Parkhead club have an opportunity to stand apart from the baying mob and bring some sanity back to the game.

Where is this "*baying mob*" Jim? That wouldn't be you looking to smear Celtic fans again by painting them as a bunch of foaming at the mouth degenerates by any chance? Even for a paper famed for spouting its nakedly jaundiced opinion there is a real irony in Traynor calling for the Celtic to "*open up*" in a case where the they have made a submission to the SFA, been stonewalled on it, only for the media to then totally ignore it – that would be a media who claim to be choc to the brim full of diligent investigative journalists. If anyone needs to open up it's not Celtic. There has been no analysis of Dr Reid's e-dossier that was released to the selected media sources at the end of last season. Why has this been hushed up by the media? Even Mr Spiers has not commented, despite being probed on the matter on the "award winning" radio show he frequents. Didn't know that there were awards for anal verbosity, but there you go.

Why do I get the feeling that if Celtic did issue a statement regarding this incident Jim Traynor would the first e to tell us to shut up? Must be that paranoia again.

Celtic have this chance to lock down a lid on a tawdry affair that has been boiling and bubbling since Dougie McDonald's mistake at Tannadice just more than two weeks ago. Celtic can rise above the clamour and instead of sounding like the voice of the delusional they could be heard as the voice of reason.

Celtic have the chance to "*lock down the lid*" on a "*tawdry affair*" that has been "*boiling and bubbling since*" do they? Two questions spring to mind that seem pertinent here:

A. Who "unlocked" the lid, and who has kept the issue "boiling and bubbling"?

You and your fellow lapdogs in the media Mr Traynor

331

B. Who is responsible for the whole "tawdry affair"?

Dougie McDonald and his cohorts at the SFA

I'm struggling to understand how Celtic can calm this down. They asked a question and were told a lie. Surely the only people who can truly put this to bed are the SFA, or is Traynor simply asking Celtic - the offended against party - to apologise for asking the question and then roll into the corner? The simplest solution is actually for Traynor and his hack pals to stop constantly baiting the Celtic manager for soundbites that they then twist and exaggerate to print headlines like "Livid Lennon" and "Lennon's war on whistlers". But by a magnificent feat of intellectual gymnastics, Jim Traynor is able to lay the blame for all of this fuss at Celtic's door. A fuss that no doubt helped to sell a few extra copies of Mr Traynor's rag, yet he feels qualified to take a pious tone with us on the morality of "inciting" lunatics.

Let's go over this again, before we get lost in the psychedelic world of Jim Traynor's spin - Dougie McDonald **lied** to his boss and then **lied** to Neil Lennon. Lennon had just witnessed McDonald give his team a penaly and then take it away. Of course he was going to question it. It's not his fault the explanation he was given was something McDonald and his assistants made up five minutes earlier. Lennon also has the right to ask questions when, a week later, he sees a referee give a penalty against his club for something he didn't even see. You can bet your mortgage that Sir Dignity over at Ibrox would have had something to say about that if it ever happened to his club. (Sorry, I must've got sucked into Jim Traynor's hallucinogenic world there for a minute or two where such occurrences can be contemplated). Any manager in the SPL worth his salt would do this same, and if he didn't he would be negligent in his duty to act in the best interests of his club. The SFA and Dougie McDonald are wholly responsible for this mess and owe Celtic and Neil Lennon an apology.

By questioning decisions and demanding answers on a regular basis a club as big as Celtic could eventually get into the heads of referees. They might then worry about making calls against that particular team knowing they can be called to account and doubted when all they're guilty of is refereeing honestly, if also a little poorly.

So a club "*as big as Celtic*" could get into referee's heads, but a club the size of Rangers can't? Is Jim Traynor saying Celtic are a bigger club than Rangers? So when the manager of Rangers is having a go at an official with an Irish surname or describing another decision as "incredible" and questioning why aforementioned Irish official is appointed to run another Rangers game five months later, this cannot have any effect on officials? Only Celtic have that mystic power do they?

We need to believe in their honesty because that's the only way we can accept their decisions no matter how strange or ridiculous they might appear. Fans may doubt the talents of officials but never their integrity because if we ever get to the point where we cannot believe in officials the game is finished.

So no matter how obvious the evidence before us, we must cover our ears and avert our gaze so that we must avoid the truth. Seemingly it is not the prospect of the game actually being tainted that disturbs Traynor it's the notion that we might prove it that disturbs him. This is classic make the perpetrator the victim stuff. Traynor's message is basically "Shut up and know your place Timmy".

If Celtic's hierarchy believes referees, or their bosses, are conspiring against them they should come right out and say it. If they really think there are forces acting against them they should step into the open and demand justice.

Again Traynor would at the head of the queue squealing "paranoia" if this ever came to pass. What a loathsome hypocrite this man is.

If Celtic think they are being victimised they have every right to say so and offer up their proof. They should lay out any evidence they have and a full-scale enquiry could get started.

Celtic already have. The club sent evidence to the SFA and have been stonewalled. The ever alert media have gone to sleep in it, but yet again it's supposed to be Celtic's fault.

That's what happens in decent grown-up societies so let's get it all spread out on a big table and deal with it. If the chairman John Reid is convinced there is a conspiracy he should be screaming about it instead of allowing this questionable strategy of writing to the SFA seeking explanations about certain decisions.

With yet more farcical irony Jim Traynor speaks of *"decent grown-up societies"* when he writes for an Establishment publication that would put Pravda to shame with it's homogenic reverence of one institution over all others, and with his "shut up and stop asking questions" diktats. As for the SFA, they operate a system that dictators the world over would be proud of. The only recourse for appeal depends on the person who took the initial punitive action against the plaintiff, agreeing that they were mistaken. Would that be acceptable policy at your work place, or indeed in any throughout the land? And if an individual is found to have breached the regulations that govern the game, he faces a committee of his own friends and cronies. These practices have no place in our country and any organisation that has any pretence to democracy or representing member's interests fairly. Freedom of expression is a right that underpins our society, but the SFA appears to expect that it can opt out, an organisation that looks upon criticism as a taboo and who's answer to consistently inadequate performance among its members is to introduce a raft of measures to protect them from criticism.

Traynor supports this system, yet lectures Celtic fans on the values of *"decent grown-up societes"*.

Incidentally, I'd be interested in learning the difference between a decent "grown-up" society and a decent "juvenile" one, but I guess that's just another of his wee digs at Celtic.

Celtic cannot openly question referees and then wash their hands of any responsibility when an official (Collum) receives phone calls at home from the deranged after an error of judgment in last weekend's Old Firm game. Of course this is not to say Celtic were to blame for those calls but I am saying clubs must be aware their words and actions can and do influence the thought processes of some of their fans.

Another cracker – Celtic can't be held responsible for the actions of one or two lunatics… but really, they can, so they should shut up.

So, to sum up this classic piece from the Traynor school of contradictory doublespeak propaganda nonsense, his message to Celtic is:

Stop skirting around the issue and come straight out and say what it is you've got to say by… er… shutting up and stop asking questions. You can't be held responsible for the actions of one or two mentalists, so just come right out with it, but be careful about what you say because if anyone gets hurt it's you fault. So… em…shut up.

Isn't it funny that despite his convoluted back-tracking attempts to convince us otherwise, Traynor, and the media in general, can hold Celtic responsible for the actions of one or two lunatics – yet time and time again they defend that famous "minority" of Rangers fans with a passion that would outdo Al Pacino's final courtroom scene in *And Justice For All!*

The bottom line is maybe Celtic wouldn't have to write to the SFA if any journalist had the balls or inclination to ask a few of the glaringly obvious questions themselves. Don't panic by the way Jim – don't think anybody will be expecting you to be one of them. Just do us a favour though; stop pussy-footing around and name the article the way you really mean it by dropping the "*Open up*" part.

The Myth of the Man with Nosurname

Today is the 12th of November 2010, and this tome is almost complete, but Jim Traynor is the hack who just keeps on giving when it comes to the most laughable doublespeak shite.

Two days ago, Celtic lost 1-2 to Hearts and the latest "honest mistake" was a blatant penalty that referee Craig Thomson failed to award to Celtic. Whilst not quite being up to "honest mistake" standard, Joe Ledley was sent off for a tackle that you just know Lee McCulloch wouldn't even have been booked for. Neil Lennon was slightly peeved at this turn of events and was not shy in verbalising his emotions at the time. This led to the tiresomely inevitable derision and fake moral posturing from our morally bankrupt Scottish media. You see, Scottish football is almost exclusively populated by clubs managed by timid 'after you m'lud' Hugh Grant types. And Jim Jeffries.

However, once again, Jim Traynor beat off the competition with a masterpiece of breath-taking sycophancy and, what Alan Pattullo might describe as "mistruth", to take the title of Poodle of the Month:

It would be easy, probably too easy, to suggest Neil Lennon study the way Walter Smith conducts himself after matches.

These fans see and hear Rangers' manager get his messages across with a practised, polished ease and wish their man would do the same.

Take the other night. Rather than blame the referee Smith pointed to himself and said he got it wrong by asking too much from the same players.

Don't think for a minute he didn't see some decisions he thought were blatantly against his side because he could rhyme a few off but there was no need. Let someone else make the noise.

Now I hardly need to comment for the reader to collapse to the ground in a paroxysm of mirth at Traynor's fantasy crawly bum lick drivel. This "Rangers don't complain about decisions" myth is akin to congratulating someone on not complaining to a bank which has been paying thousands of pounds a month into their account in error every month for ten years. Yes, absurd isn't it.

However I will point out that I came across one of Traynor's bumptious opinion pieces in the Record a couple of years ago, where he actually had the gall to refer to take a thinly vieled swipe at his peers by referring to "the manager with nosurname". Yes gall hardly covers it, does it? I hear the SFA have plenty of Brasso that Jim could put to good use.

I will not labour the point as Sir Dignity's outbursts.... sorry..."*practised, polished ease*"...are covered adequately elsewhere, but I will present a couple of gems that slipped out from the dignified lips of the Manager with Nosurname after another trip to his second favourite ground, Pittodrie:

Walter Smith hits out at Aberdeen players for only raising their game against Rangers

Daily Record 27th Sep 2010 David McCarthy

Walter Smith last night accused Aberdeen of only ever wanting to beat Rangers.

Note the complete lack of the words "raging / seething / blasted / insisted / amazingly" etc etc The Man with Nosurname's words are to be treated as indisputible fact – rule number 1 in the Lapdog handbook.

Surely Jim Traynor should be calling Sir Dignity to account a-la Chris Sutton, you know like he would in a "decent grown-up" society?

Smith couldn't resist a dig at the Dons. He said: "Aberdeen seem to take great pleasure in saying that the only team they want to beat is Rangers. I'm not like that, I prefer my team to try to beat everybody we play.

"If there is an innocuous foul it is like a crime against humanity up here, for both teams."

For both teams?? So Nosurname is saying that his team is just as guilty of this unseemly trying-too-hard carry on? The Wisdom of Waldo right enough.

In the online version of this Pullitzer winner in the sycophancy category, a chap called Alex, who seemed genuinely neutral to me made the following comment (after the usual 'the wee teams get nothing and Celtic and Rangers get everything, try supporting a wee team and seeing what it's like' blah blah yawn):

"*Walter Smith is a much more mature (and generous) appraiser of football matches*"

Traynor and the Record are just too easy a target but somehow I never tire of mocking their undying devotion to the greatest football manager who ever walked the face of the earth. As I said, this is well covered within these pages so I'll settle for listing a few wee choice headlines and comments.

Oct 2010 "*McGregor's was an innocuous foul. In fact it wasn't even a foul, but that is how they see it and we can't do anything about it. Last season, they (the SFA) quickly organised a disciplinary hearing for Kenny Miller's appeal, so that he would miss the Celtic game.*"

Oct 2010 "*Walter accuses Aberdeen of only wanting to beat Rangers*"

Sep 2010 "*If he's happy with the way Scottish football is at the moment, then he's in the wrong job. Was the Kilmarnock chairman one of the people who agreed to the Setanta deal?*"

May 2010 "*Walter hits Andreas Hinkel with a stinging blast , Who do you think you are?*"

Apr 2010 "*Walter Smith last night promised an official complaint to the SPL after insisting Rangers have been unfairly disadvantaged by fixture anomalies since the controversial league split was introduced 10 years ago*"

Walter - "*Somebody somewhere is making a conscious decision to do this to us*"

Apr 2010 "*Everyone one wants players sent off against us, everyone wants penalties against us, everyone wants everything against us*"

Mar 2010 "*Smith rages at Thomson sending off in Co-op Cup final*"

Dec 2009 "*Smith left seething after Collum sends off Kenny Miller*"

Oct 2009 Walter "*Gonnae just pack it in and stop asking me difficult questions*"

Sep 2009 *Smith says Konko of Seville should have been sent off*"

Sep 2009 "*Furious Smith accuses ref Jonas Eriksson of bottling out of doing his job*"

Sep 2009 " *SFA spokesman said Smith was adopting a threatning and aggressive attitude after Mendes was red carded at Kilmarnock*"

August 2009 "*No it wasn't a sending off it was an opportunity for the referee to send him* [Thomson] *off*"

May 2009 "*Smith blasts 'incredible' Bougherra sending off*"

Apr 2009 "*The SFA have started a new trend in criminality - if you leave the scene of a crime early, you are not guilty.*"

Nov 2008 "*The linesman Murphy was quick to allow a Celtic goal against us at Celtic Park and quick to disallow that one tonight*"

Aug 2008 "*It's an incredible decision for a linesman who is in line with the play. We got a bad one at Tannadice earlier this season, which has been forgotten about, maybe because we don't make that much of a fuss about it*"

May 2008 "*They made it perfectly clear there is no willingness on anybody's part to give us anything. There has been no willingness at all to help Rangers so they're not going to help us now are they*"

Mar 2008 "*Smith sent to stand after a furious bust up with Paatelainen*"

Dec 2007 "*The Aberdeen crown wound Lee McCulloch up and the linesman ran 70 yards to get him sent off, if he wants to be a referee he should be one and not a linesman. We seem to bring the best out in Aberdeen, they only try against us...*"

And that's where I came in.

So Neil Lennon, it turns out you've got a long, long way to go before your record compares with Mr Smith at Rangers, and I don't mean trophies.

Epilogue: The Near Death of a Salesman

You will have gathered by now that I'm quite fond of a wee hypothetical scenario here and there, so how about another one to finish:

You are a successful sales executive at a well-known company (Scotprem). The company is not as prestigious as it used to be and it is clear to everyone that it's on the wane. The company is completely overshadowed by a competitor just down the road (Ingprem), widely regarded as one of the best companies in its field in the world. You have been Scotprem's best performing sales executive several times over the past ten years, winning many lucrative contracts throughout Europe, the highlight being a momentous deal with a company in Seville seven years ago. However for the past two years this title has moved to another sales executive, Wally, amid some strange goings on. Several years ago it was anecdotally known that Wally was under severe financial strain having totally mismanaged his personal finances, and that he was going to have to win some major contracts to prevent himself being declared bankrupt. Wally was in direct competition with you to win the necessary contracts. The Communication and Media Relations (PR) department of the company always vigorously denied these financial problems and accused anyone making such an assertion of paranoia and vindictiveness. They also published numerous highly complimentary articles about their number 1 sales executive in the monthly company newsletter. Despite this everyone else in the company knew these financial problems certainly did exist, as the information to ascertain this was readily available to anyone with an interest, far less a trained journalist. The only doubt was to the extent of the problem.

That was until, after a particularly poor day at the office through in Edinburgh, Wally came close to having a nervous breakdown by starting to rant and rave about the bank taking control of his finances after being asked a simple question by a member of the PR staff about the day's events. The PR department was now left in the awkward position of being no longer able to flatly deny the obvious, but at the same time having to continue perpetrating the image of their favourite son as a successful and dignified sales executive. They barely managed to maintain this façade via a stream of positive memos about his multi-millionaire friends who were, they assured everyone, ready to step in to provide financial support, ignoring such details as lack of necessary financial resources, or possible criminal charges.

In contrast – you noticed that the company, and the PR dept in particular, seemed to be undermining your every move, questioning your motives and accusing you of irrational outbursts at the most reasonable requests for information or support in your daily duties. Some months before Wally's outburst, he was involved in a disciplinary hearing alleging he had assaulted a colleague. It appeared to all within the company to be an open-and-shut case, with CCTV footage of the incident available as evidence. However, then a very strange thing happened – in his defence, Wally described the allegation as "ridiculous" and no sooner had he uttered these words, but PR staff were tearing around the office using the same terminology and issuing indignant memos to the effect that an "incredible" injustice had been perpetrated against Wally. The charges were subsequently dropped, much to the bewilderment of everyone outside the PR department and Wally's immediate circle of friends, with little apparent difference between the first group and the second.

Around the same time, you were cited to appear before the Human Resources manager on the basis of information supplied by the PR department – which you knew to be full of Wally's friends and cohorts – to face disciplinary charges in relation to two minor transgressions, one of which was actually dealt with at the time by a senior manager. Colleagues within the company were surprised that a matter that was already closed off by another manager had been re-opened by Human Resources under lobby of the PR department. The net effect of this was to make your defence of the new charge (the one not already dealt with by a senior manager) untenable. You were subsequently suspended from work for a period of a week, in which time Wally gained valuable ground in the chase to win important contracts. Although there were pockets of sympathy within the company for your plight, when you attempted to persuade anyone of a link in motive between the PR dept, Wally, and the pressure brought to bear on the Human Resources, you were faced with open hostility and slights against your mental health. It transpired also, that the head of Human Resources is a member of Wally's family and that the majority of the PR department are also his direct relatives, but this cuts no ice with anyone within the company. Everyone now openly regards you as paranoid.

But worse was to follow – only a few weeks before Wally's breakdown, you had begun to notice a definite pattern of mistakes by the office administrators that continually hampered you in your work – important files being misplaced, failure to record messages from key clients, falsely accusing you of transgressing company policies and other such occurrences on a weekly basis. This was bad enough, but you also managed to find out – despite the PR department's strenuous attempts to censor the information – that some of these lost files were turning up on Wally's desk, the missed phone calls from key clients were being passed to Wally's office and Wally himself was regularly transgressing company policy with impunity. This continued for a period of a year, with your own performance deteriorating in direct correlation with these administrative "mistakes" that were encumbering you in your work. Wally was winning more and more contracts and by late summer had a complete monopoly on highly lucrative European contracts.

The steady increase in administrative mistakes and bad publicity had coincided directly with the urgency of Wally's financial problems, which by now the PR department had simply decided to stop mentioning. It was anecdotally known that had Wally not secured those European contracts he would amost certainly have gone bankrupt, although the PR department strenuously denied this. With your prospects for fair redress dwindling by the day, you decided it was time to take the initiative yourself and pursue the matter with the new head of Human Resources (the previous one having left under a cloud but having been sorted out with a nice little consultancy role within the PR department through a family friend). So you sent him a letter requesting a meeting, outlining in some detail, your concerns, referring to a lengthy list of administrative mistakes which had beset you over the previous year and seeking some clarification and assurance on the matter.

However this request was leaked to the PR department – filled with Wally's friends and allies – who reacted with fury and who immediately went on the offensive in an attempt to assassinate your character. Their response was to send out a memo to the entire company acknowledging that some mistakes had been made and the administrative department had indeed fallen below the standards expected, but that these errors in no way impinged on one individual to the disadvantage of any another and had been distributed according to a pattern of random chance. Not only that, but they then went on to blame **you** for this poor level of performance on the basis that your expectation levels – i.e. one free from repeated catastrophic error to your detriment – was totally unrealistic and constituted an intolerable stress burden on the poor unfairly maligned administrative team – one that no human being should be subjected to. They also presented as fact, accounts of several members of the administrative team and their families receiving abuse in the street, this despite strong rebuttal of the story from some of those supposedly on the receiving end. You were blamed squarely for the actions of the lunatics carrying out these acts (if indeed they existed) despite there being no evidence that any of these persons was linked to you.

The PR department then presented a paper from a retired administrator based in Englan as a character witness, strongly supporting the actions of the administrative team. You remembered this person vividly because when you met him earlier in the year he called you a "cheating bastard" and described your home as "the Glitter Dome" – but of course, the PR department censored any mention of his links with Wally or his hostile attitude towards you. The final string to this character assassination bow, was to wheel out several other sales executives who were obviously jealous of your level of success to recount stories of all sorts of imagined injustices they'd suffered, far outweighing anything you have had to endure. They go so far, in fact, as to state that the adminstrative team have actually been giving **you** undue support to the detriment of others, an incredible assertion that nevertheless is considered to be conventional wisdom within the company.

But the piece de resistance was when they wheeled out Wally himself to magnanimously defend the administrative team for their sterling work in the face of unjustifiable demands and pressure. Yes Wally – the man who has been poaching your client list as a direct result of these "honest mistakes", was somehow portrayed as a sensible voice with no vested interests, the man who would never stoop to such levels of criticism, despite having had much more than you to say in condemnation of not only the administrative team, but Human Resources themselves in recent years. In a famous and sustained outburst two years ago, Wally accused the sales department of conspiring against him to fix the sales team rota to his disadvantage, despite the changes to the rota originating as a direct result of bowing to his demand for time off at short notice to prepare for a big French account that he subsequently made a mess of. Wally has continued to moan and bleat about this at regular intervals to the present day.

But despite all of this, his friends in the PR department managed to maintain an unblemished image of personified dignity and success, whereas your reputation now resembled a car wreck of paranoia and rage. Needless to say, the official response from Human Resources was merely a watered down, more polite version of the PR department's smear campaign. This left you at an impasse with seemingly no further options available to confront and deal with your unfair treatment at the hands of Wally and his friends in Human Resources and the PR department.

With increasing desperation you applied for a job at Ingprem, the company down the road, that world leader in your field. But whilst they recognised your potential there were insurmountable legal issues preventing them from hiring you, not to mention resistance within due to the self-interest of their existing sales team. They also indicated that they would have to hire Wally too as a package deal – without really explaining why – but having witnessed his temperamental behaviour at a number of sales conferences across the country, particularly one in Manchester two years ago, decided against it. Although you were not involved in any of these episodes you had been tarnished by association in the eyes of the Ingprem directors being a fellow employee of Scotprem. This has not been helped by Wally's friends in the PR department firefighting these personal crises by attempting forcefully to persuade everyone that this behaviour was a rare aberration, despite it happening repeatedly over many years. They also blamed some delegates from London for starting trouble, and the police of over-reacting to the ensuing kefuffle. They also deflected attention from Wally by insisting that this is something you are equally guilty of, a claim that could not have been further from the truth – having received several official commendations for your exemplary performance at these conferences. The PR department were very vocal in proclaiming that if Wally should be punished, why should you not be punished too.

This slur infuriated you but your protestations made no impression with colleagues. Your fellow sales executives resented your success and so were unwilling to offer any support. The furthest they would go was to criticise both of you equally, which more often that not meant criticising Wally for his unacceptable behaviour and then scrambling around to manufacture a similar charge to present against you. In fact, the more you attempted to highlight the harassment you were encountering, the more resentful they seemed to get – "You should put your own house in order first… you should be good enough to overcome it" they would say, blissfully unaware of the contradiction in telling you there was no harassment, but at the same time saying that you should be good enough to overcome the very harassment that did not exist. They were also fond of casting up a contract you won in Paisley nearly three years before, accusing you of impropriety in that deal, much to your bemusement, as if, even if such a claim were true it somehow cancelled out all of the naked agendas and skullduggery you've had to put up with since.

Once Wally had secured the sales executive of the year title and his monopoly on the European contracts at the end of the financial year, you thought perhaps things might die down a bit. There had been no talk of Wally's financial difficulties for a long time, in fact the PR department announced in June that his house was no longer up for sale which seemed odd to everyone else, as although the for-sale sign had been removed from his garden, the advertisements were still running in the newspapers and estate agent windows. Still, on the surface, things seemed to be much better, and Wally was even able to afford a couple of new suits to help keep up appearances in his appointments with clients, although one was rumoured to be rented and the other was second-hand and well past its best condition.

But only two months into the new financial year it was clear the agenda and harassment was as strong as ever, in fact if anything, it was escalating, and Human Resources and the PR department were barely even attempting to conceal their hostility towards you by this stage. This had also made you deeply unpopular with the other sales executives. In October, you won the company a contract in Dundee, only to have it taken back off you by Human Resources. In the end, you managed to obtain another one from the same customer but the writing was on the wall. The very next week another important client file went missing only for you to find that it had somehow managed to turn up on Wally's desk at a fortuitous time, allowing him to secure a lucrative order from the customer. It turned out a young secretary – Jilly Gollum – had mistakenly left the file in Wally's office after being handed it by one of Wally's pals, Kirsty Clubfoot. You were deeply sceptical of Gollum's story and you already knew what a reprehensible chancer Clubfoot was, but it was hardly worth mentioning as you were only too aware of the inevitable hostile response you would receive, but still you spoke up.

This time, though, not only were you derided as parnoid, the PR department then levelled accusations that you had flown into a rage, phoned Ms Gollum and threatened to assault her. This was a ridiculous slur, and you strongly suspected that it was a set-up courtesy of a few of Wally's friends in the PR department. After all, they had been exposed when one of them had carried out a similar act earlier in the year, posing as you in a company podcast and spouting a load of wild accusations and theories which were then used to justify slaughtering you reputation throughout the company. Of course the host of that podcast was a good friend of Wally and was only too happy to play along, although he denied this association and made a big show of claiming to be more friendly with another company in Edinburgh much to the amusement of most within Scotprem.

With the situation reaching a critical point, you turned to your Uncle Cesar, the most successful sales executive in the history of ScotPrem for advice. He said that this favouritism and harassment had been going on for 50 years, from Wally's grandfather down to his grandson today, and that the only way to beat him was to be twice as strong. Grateful and heartened though you were for this advice, it didn't provide any practical solutions and by now you were at your lowest point. You were only slightly behind Wally in terms of sales targets for the financial year but it was clear that Human Resources and the PR department were absolutely determined to put every possible obstacle in your way and things were only going to get worse. The future was looking bleak.

Then one day the auditor turned up.

A rogue member of the PR department had published a memo many months prior to this unannounced visit, speculating that an audit was on the cards due to some of Wally's more questionable practices. However the rest of his PR colleagues were quick to play down this notion; after all the auditors were from the same stock as them and a full audit wasn't due for several years.

So it was a shock to nearly everyone in the company when Mrs Windsor from Head Office turned up at the door asking to look at the books. Mrs Windsor's requests were of the kind that could not be turned down. Human Resources and the PR department were immediately plunged into a frenzy of impotent attempts at cover-up and obfuscation. "Mrs Windsor isn't expecting other debtors to meet their full obligations" they shrieked, "Wally is a company institution, you can't do this!" they wailed. But of course, Mrs Windsor *could* do this, and she had every intention of doing so.

After a couple of hours it became clear things were not going well. Mrs Windsor had requested the assistance of Mr Judge and Mr Plod in her inquiries. Human Resources and the PR department were getting frantic, so much so that they came to *you* for help. All of these two-faced PR executives, their faces bloated on succulent lamb and red wine, who had vilified and bullied you for over ten years were now coming to *you* for help.

"The company can't survive without Wally, you'll need to help" they pleaded.

"Think of that joint contract you have with the brewery, that'll hit the skids if Wally goes down" they cried desperately.

"I don't think Mr Windsor will take much notice of a paranoiac nutcase I'm afraid" you ironically responded, knowing full well that it would be entirely possible for you to re-negotiate the contract on more favourable terms, or even secure a different buyer altogether.

Karl Ding and Jack Keithson, two senior PR executives, were now openly weeping. John Derekston was so distresses he couldn't even finish his seventh pie. Tim Jaynor was wittering on about how a company in Airdrie from fine upstanding stock had gone through a similar problem and came back stronger than ever, their chairman even rising to president of Human Resources. These were hollow words however, and everyone knew it. The demise of Wally was on a whole new scale, and for a sales executive who's unique selling point was bombast and superiority, the humiliation of bankruptcy and jail would be all but impossible to recover from.

And this is what was happening before our very eyes – Wally was going to jail.

Yick Cheung, Gordon Waffle, Kew Heevins… they all watched in stunned silence as Wally was led out of the building, Mr Judge and Mr Plod at either side and Mrs Windsor leading the way. Wally was heard pleading "but I *am* the company… You and me are the same Mrs Windsor, I'm one of your own, you should be protecting me! " he wailed as he was escorted out.

As you peered out of the office window at the pitiful sight of this man being usherd into a police car, once Lord of all he surveyed, now a broken shell – Lil Beckie, a PR executive from Paisley suddenly confronted you. His tear-stained tie presented a different image to the one he had vigorously promoted for many years, a staunch Paisley man, defender of the wee guy against Wally and Timothy, the big bad bullies. His face was a deep shade of crimson and his eyes bulged in apoplexy as he bawled at you – "I don't know what *you're* smiling at Timothy!! Without Wally, *you'll* be down the toilet with the rest of us!!".

Casting your eye over a list of companies who would have big European contracts up for grabs in the coming months, you simply sat back in your chair, kicked back and said "Oh, I'll be fine, Lil…"

"Timothy will be just fine…."

The Lickspittle Galleries

CELTIC SIGN A BLANK CZECH

He's 62 and hasn't got a work permit

Dr Jo might not have had a work permit but he did have a European Championship Title with Czechoslovakia under his belt. Typical understated and unbiased headline from the Daily Record as Celtic unveil new manager **July 1998**

Celtic fans have been waiting for months for a new manager. They queued up outside Parkhead yesterday expecting a big name like Gullitt or Vogts. Instead they got...

DR WHO

The Daily Record would have appointed Bertie Vogts ahead of Dr Jo. Hugh Keevins would have spent double the money Celtic spent on Lubo to sign John Spencer. Where would us fan luddites be without the benefit of such wisdom from these highly paid experts, or fuds? **July 1998**

DICTATOR

One of these men was branded 'a devious, arrogant, uncompromising dictator' by a judge yesterday. The other one is Saddam Hussein!

David 'Moonbeams' Murray borrows money left right and centre, strips sellable assets such as catering and media rights and brings his club to the brink of bankruptcy.

He is lauded in the media as philanthropic visionary and is regularly the object of the kind of sycophantic platitudes that would have embarrassed Princess Di. Succulent lamb - say no more.

Fergus 'The Bunnet' McCann brings his club back from the brink of bankruptcy, builds the biggest stadium in Britain (at the time), quadruples season book sales and finances the first league title win in 10 years.

He is branded a bully and a penny-pincher, an outsider with no understanding of Scottish football (If that was the case he'd have been perfectly suited as a football writer for the Sun, Record, Express et al). He was regularly subject to the kind of headlines illustrated above and his Bhoys Against Bigotry campaign was derided by a Scottish media who, with no hint of self awareness or embarrassment, would then attempt to lecture the rest of us on the subject.

Hands up who thinks the media treatment of Fergus and Murray was fair and balanced?
Daily Record February 1998

Fergus: I saved us a fortune

By GORDON SIMPSON

PENNY-PINCHER Fergus McCann has revealed how he saved Celtic a cool £700,000 by holding Roma to ransom over Enrico Annoni.

The Parkhead chief finally landed the 30-year-old Italian tough guy last night for a bargain basement £250,000.

The cut-price deal was struck after weeks of wrangling with the Serie A giants, who had threatened to pull the plug on Annoni's switch to Scotland.

Even Celtic boss Tommy Burns feared the move might collapse as McCann fought to reduce Roma's cash demands.

PENNY PINCHER ... McCann saved cash

The Daily Ranger Friday 21st February

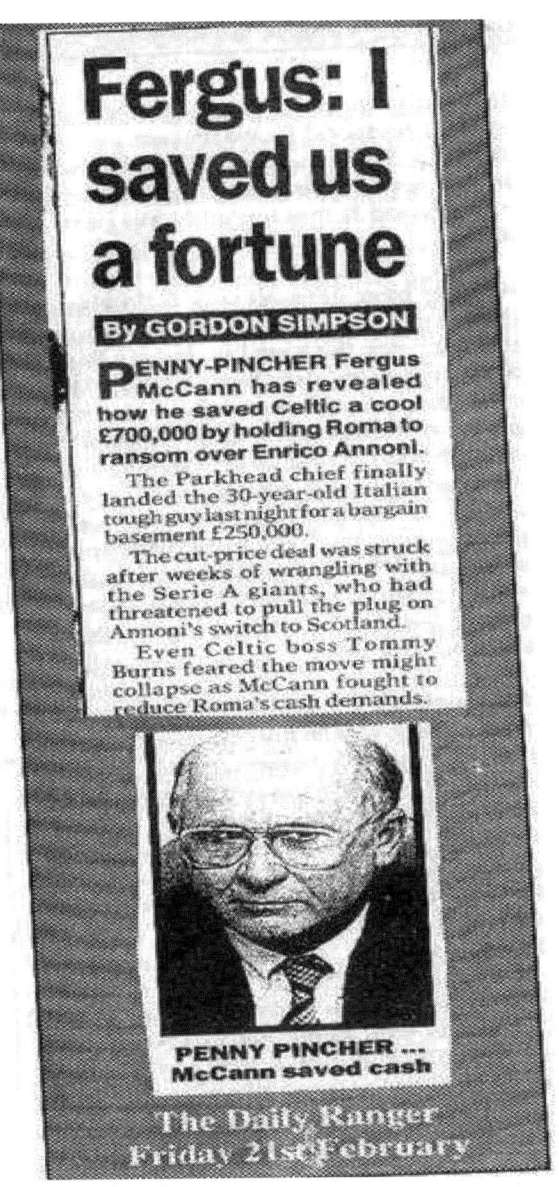

The Daily Ranger labels a man who put £9million of his own money into Celtic a "penny-pincher". Who would've thought that a mere 10 years later, it would be Glasgow Rangers turn to be "held to ransom" by the mighty Kilmarnock FC over their refusal to accept empty ginger bottles as a fee for Steven Naismith. Not sure the Daily Ranger covered that story in the same way though... **February 1998**

> **Man U faced Liverpool, Madrid, then Newcastle and now play Arsenal. Next week it's Madrid again. They don't moan about their big games**
>
> Gers ace de Boer takes swipe at Celtic chiefs
>
> WISH IT WAS US: Alex McLeish and Ronald de Boer would love a Euro semi

Daily Record headline after Celtic complained about having to play Rangers at Ibrox just over 48 hours after returning from a UEFA Cup semi final in Portugal.

To be fair to the Daily Record they were equally scathing of Rangers when they complained about fixture scheduling in 2008. Anyway.... **April 2008**

FARCE

Just what the hell were you playing at Celtic?

The Daily Record getting tore in again re the 2003 fixture fixing. Jim No-neck Traynor urged Celtic to "Shut up and get on with it". We were told that the highest priority had to be to ensure that at all costs no Celtic-Huns game could ever be a title decider. This was on orders from the Glesga Polis. The polis did make a provision for one exemption though - If either team have an Algerian centre half who would otherwise be suspended if the non-title decider rule was strictly enforced the rule may be relaxed so as not to impinge on Rangers chances of winning the league. Oh, and when there's a ladies fun run on as well, that's another excuse, even though the Glesga Polis can handle 60,000 at Celtic Park in the Champions League and another 60,000 at Hampden for a U2 concert on the same night. These ladies fun runners are bad ass though. **April 2008**

POPE ON A DOPE
Boruc T-shirt fury

The Scottish Sun foams at the mouth at the sight of the Pope's face on a T-shirt. Better check my watch and see what century it is. **April 2008**

Neil Lennon: An apology

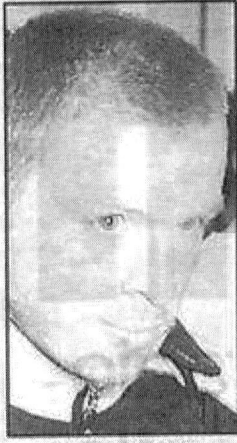

THE Daily Record, in its edition of December 20, 2002, published a series of articles concerning events which took place on the evening of December 17, 2002, when members of the Celtic Football Club had a night out in Newcastle-upon-Tyne.

We regret that this article alleged that it was highly likely Neil Lennon had pursued and robbed a Daily Record photographer of £12,000 worth of equipment.

We accept that this allegation was without foundation and we apologise sincerely and unreservedly to Mr Lennon for the distress and anxiety caused to him.

The Daily Record has agreed to pay Mr Lennon damages and his legal costs.

NEIL LENNON

The Daily Ranger choke on their own bile as they manage to force out an apology under the threat of legal action. We're sorry, it just sort of accidentally slipped out into print through copy editor, sub-editor, sports editor, editor etc etc. **August 2004**

Cartoon in the Scottish Sun just after Neil Lennon receives potentially life threatening injuries at the hands of bigoted lowlife the evening of Rangers 4-2 win over Celtic in August 2008 (God knows what they'd have done if Rangers had lost). The Sun lives down to its gutter reputation by revelling in both the Rangers victory and the serious assault on a Celtic FC employee. All that's missing is a "weearrrappeepul" headline
September 2008

354

CHAMPIONS LEAGUE CRUNCH

ROMANIACS

Burberry-clad Cockney geezers and a night of madness in the town from hell

DAVID McCARTHY

The Daily Record rallies to the defence of it's own. David McCarthy provides his "verdict" as if he's some sort of statesmanlike lawlord rather than a two bob lying hack. McCarthy's verdict? "It was aw Cockney geezers in burberry guv". Anyway, ra loyal claimed they were provoked by a tri-colour so it's no their fault. Note also that this all took place in the "town from hell". I suppose that means they deserved to have their stewards battered for not having a town fit to be pished and puked on. I'm sure it *was* the town from hell for the duration of the Queen's XI's visit. When are they going to give up with this "It was all English casuals" shite? **November 2009**

Printed in Great Britain
by Amazon.co.uk, Ltd.,
Marston Gate.